Mark
and the
Symbolism of Captain America,
1985–1995

Mark Gruenwald and the Star Spangled Symbolism of Captain America, 1985–1995

Jason Olsen

McFarland & Company, Inc., Publishers

Jefferson, North Carolina

This book has undergone peer review.

LIBRARY OF CONGRESS CATALOGUING-IN-PUBLICATION DATA

Names: Olsen, Jason, 1974– author.
Title: Mark Gruenwald and the star spangled symbolism
   of Captain America, 1985-1995 / Jason Olsen.
Description: Jefferson, North Carolina : McFarland & Company, Inc.,
   Publishers, 2021 | Includes bibliographical references and index.
Identifiers: LCCN 2021014584 | ISBN 9781476681504 (paperback :
   acid free paper) ∞
   ISBN 9781476642611 (ebook)
Subjects: LCSH: Captain America (Fictitious character) | Gruenwald, Mark—
   Criticism and interpretation. | Comic books, strips, etc.—United States—
   History and criticism. | Literature and society—United States—History—
   20th century. | National characteristics, American, in literature. | BISAC:
   LITERARY CRITICISM / Comics & Graphic Novels
Classification: LCC PN6728.C35 O57 2021 | DDC 741.5/973—dc23
LC record available at https://lccn.loc.gov/2021014584

BRITISH LIBRARY CATALOGUING DATA ARE AVAILABLE

ISBN (print) 978-1-4766-8150-4
ISBN (ebook) 978-1-4766-4261-1

Front cover images © 2021 Shutterstock

Printed in the United States of America

*McFarland & Company, Inc., Publishers
   Box 611, Jefferson, North Carolina 28640
   www.mcfarlandpub.com*

Acknowledgments

The comics referenced in this book were accessed through Marvel Unlimited online (and cited with the pages numbers from Marvel Unlimited) with the exception of *The Thing* #35, *Spider-Woman* #33, and the letter pages of *Captain America* #398, #428, #429, #439, and #442, which were not available through Marvel Unlimited. In each relevant case, I cited the page numbers from the original print editions.

I would like to thank the following people for helping make this book happen: Chapel Taylor-Olsen for her endless support during the creation of this book, our children Eliza and Tate, Shane Bench and Ken Kotce for research guidance, and Layla Milholen and everybody I worked with at McFarland. I would also like to thank Greg Dart at Utah State University Eastern for invaluable professional support.

I also extend thanks to my mother, Tina-Marie Olsen, for never allowing me to run short of comics to read when I was kid.

My grandmother, Patricia Johnston, passed away as I was working on this project and my late grandfather, Thomas Johnston, and I read many of these comics together and I thought often of them both often as I worked on this book.

Table of Contents

Preface

Mark Gruenwald's run as writer of Marvel Comics' *Captain America* during the 1980s and 1990s is unquestionably epic. That distinction of "epic" can refer to content, though, admittedly, the long-term cultural impact of Gruenwald's stories from this era is smaller than those taking place concurrently on other comics, including some Marvel titles such as *Uncanny X-Men*. No, this use of "epic" comes from length—his 137-issue run, spanning a full decade—is a monumental amount of stability for a comic and character that had simply never enjoyed such a thing before. Other comics and characters certainly had experienced this type of longevity from a single writer—Chris Claremont wrote *Uncanny X-Men* from 1975 to 1991—but not Cap. Gruenwald himself acknowledges this in a 1988 interview with Joe Field when he explains that his three years on the comic at the time matched the longest term for a writer in the history of Captain America's solo title. Gruenwald theorizes in this interview that this lack of continuity led the character to have "ups and downs" because of "constantly having change in handling by different writers" ("Mark Gruenwald Interviewed by Joe Field").

Gruenwald, unlike some writers who would start on a pre-established title, is unwilling to disregard the history—as sporadic in quality and consistency as it was—of the character and instead forges ahead with the template and framework that was established, including that which was started immediately prior by previous writer Michael Carlin. In fact, Gruenwald's first issue (#307) deals with the immediate aftermath of Carlin's prior story by placing Cap (and I will refer to the character in this familiar way, alternatingly with "Captain America" throughout this book, while using "Steve Rogers" when discussing the character when he is out of uniform or when the conversation is about Rogers specifically rather than Cap or to clarify when describing situations in which there is more than one Captain America) on a plane flight back from England where he has interacted with Captain Britain. Gruenwald initiates no massive reboot. His previous role as

1

editor for this title prior to writing the comic certainly influences his expertise, but he could have still revamped things dramatically. Things change
over the course of his decade as writer, but he feels no need to incorporate
massive change all at once. The run on the comic is very much about the
process and not about initiating change for its own sake.

Basic rules matter to Gruenwald and he is not interested in disregard-
ing the past, but he also has a specific idea of what "continuity" means. In
his editor's comments on the letters page of *Invincible Iron Man* #217, he
explains that he is not interested in a continuity that sacrifices art:

> [Continuity is not] a slavish single-minded devotion to trivial details found in
> ancient storylines and a strange compulsion to resurrect and glorify said details
> at the expense of other story values. That, my friends, is indeed a problem that
> certain comics writers have been afflicted with, but that isn't "continuity." That's
> an obsessive love for trivia [qtd. in "Mark Gruenwald on 'Continuity'"].

He is criticizing those who confuse completion with art. Instead, in the
same column, he writes, "What is most important is that a writer stay true
to the spirit and basic legend of the character." This is important because
every pre-established character, perhaps especially Cap in the Marvel comics universe, has a "basic legend" that must be honored. The writer needs
to maintain and stay true to that, but not at the expense of watering down
the character or, most significantly, compromising the character just to
check off boxes of verified continuity. Gruenwald continues stories and
keeps characters consistent, but he resists the compulsion to let trivia dic-
tate storytelling.

He maintains the basics of the comic and the character, but he also
creates something new. Over the course of his tenure, he changes and
modifies many things without ever compromising the character. This
137-issue run is worth studying in detail because of several key reasons.
First, the aforementioned continuity of having one writer over a long
period gives the reader a unique opportunity (for *Captain America* readers, at least) to see an essential character under one creator. While perhaps this run did not set up the specific template for Captain America's
Marvel Cinematic Universe (MCU) adventures, it did provide a contemporary refocusing of the character that ultimately led toward the film version (and Gruenwald's version of Captain America is certainly represented
in the MCU interpretation).

As Gruenwald develops his take on the character in these issues, Steve
Rogers' identity is more closely aligned to the Avengers and adventuring in
general with less pretense of a "normal life" that is seen in other characters
(and was interpreted in *Captain America* in the first half of the 1980s). Gruenwald shows that Steve Rogers is Captain America and Captain America is

a full-time job. Again, referencing Gruenwald's first few issues, Steve Rogers and his personal interactions with others get more panel time than Cap in uniform, but this serves as a way of transitioning to stories in which Cap and Rogers overlap (without much need for a secret identity). This is a way of organically shifting toward the portrayal Gruenwald is most interested in providing—Steve Rogers is not an escape from Captain America (or vice versa) because the mission never ends.

In two of Gruenwald's first few issues, Captain America's sidekick at the time, Nomad, is given the heavy lifting of masked heroics. Why would a creator take over a comic and immediately minimize the hero's central adventures in favor of a sidekick character he eventually intends to write out as a full-time character? It is because Gruenwald is no typical writer—he saw a longer-term plan of building up recurring supporting characters and giving Cap himself more significant challenges than a standard "recurring villain of the month" motif. Maybe he planned to write Nomad out of the comic from the beginning, but he also knew that writing in such a way that lead to organic change to pave the way for a pointed return would be more interesting than just having the character leave without setting it up.

The second reason a serious study of Gruenwald's run is essential is that these issues can be used to discuss the writing techniques and tendencies of a writer who deserves to be in the conversation of the premiere comic writers of his generation. A serious academic study of his work is as warranted as it is for the most revered writers of his generation. Gruenwald's era has perhaps lacked the cultural cache that is deserved. For example, aside from the character of Crossbones in the MCU (and he is tangential in the MCU at best and certainly not depicted in any way that evokes the character from these comics), one of the most direct references to Gruenwald's original work on this comic is a gag outside of the literal movies. Kevin Feige, announcing the titles for the films in Marvel's "Phase Three" in October 2014, first announced Captain America's third film by presenting a graphic that read *Captain America: Serpent Society* ("Full Marvel Phase 3 Announcement"). The Serpent Society is a key group of villains that feature prominently throughout Gruenwald's long run and will be discussed in detail in this book, predominantly in Chapter Seven. By the end, Feige laughs off the *Serpent Society* subtitle as inferior and unveils the film as *Captain America: Civil War*, promising a film based on a storyline that took place long after Gruenwald's time on the comic. A serious discussion of Gruenwald's work is, in light of such dismissals, necessary.

Third, a single sustained run by a writer will help us see how comic content, especially in terms of storytelling and influence from the exterior world, evolves and changes from 1985 to 1995, a period of amazing upheaval in both the world at large, and the artform and industry of comic books. Even more significantly, this analysis will be through the lens of Captain America, a highly influential character in the Marvel comics universe. By the mid-nineties, the industry was in clear decline (both in regard to sales and creative perception) and the creative solution was an endless wave of long-form stories and crossovers that promised too often to "change everything," and could be seen as efforts more designed to create headlines than to create work of artistic value. The industry was suffering because of this. The '90s valued vigilante characters and violence in a way that made a character like Captain America look antiquated. The social and political evolution of this ten-year-period will be discussed as well. Looking at how Gruenwald dealt with the volatility of this era will help us understand it overall, especially considering how both culture and comic crossovers enter into Cap's universe and some of those "edgier" elements affect Cap's world. Perhaps the comic is not typically political in an overt way (and Steve Rogers' unwillingness to choose political sides is certainly a reason for that), but there are many underlying political elements that give us great insight into the era.

This book will provide necessary study of a character, a comics writer, and an era by looking at various aspects of Gruenwald's run. These three elements are intertwined throughout this book. This book is structured into three parts: "Patriotic Symbolism," "Villainous Opposition," and "Death and Distractions." The first section includes a chapter on Gruenwald's use of symbolism (Chapter One); patriotism in different guises (Chapters Two and Three); and the generational tension inherently at play in these specific comics and how it reflects political and patriotic differences (Chapter Four). The second section begins with a chapter about Red Skull and the looming presence of World War II even in the Cold War 1980s and post–Cold War 1990s (Chapter Five), continues with a discussion of Gruenwald's deliberate intentions to create ideologically driven villains and what that says about his interpretation of the Captain America character (Chapter Six), and concludes with an analysis of how the depiction of the Serpent Society is a complicated critique of American Labor Unions (Chapter Seven). Finally, the third part discusses the vigilante nature of heroes and villains in comparison to Cap's sense of justice (Chapter Eight); how the comic falls into the trappings of the '80s "War on Drugs" era—and where it pushes back, specifically in regard to the "Streets of Poison" storyline that runs through issues #372–378 (Chapter Nine); and how Captain America and Mark Gruenwald approach death in the "Fighting Chance" storyline (Chapter Ten). This is an important investigation into a crucial period of American comics and culture. This book is organized so that each section will provide the reader with a better overall understanding of the era and the context, building upon each preceding chapter until we know the importance of the era, both to comics and culture.

My research for this book, obviously, starts with the primary source material—*Captain America*, Vol. 1, issues 307–422, 424–443 (as well as editorials and notes Gruenwald and other editors wrote in letter pages of this title and other related titles). I have also delved into the available interviews with Gruenwald, and whatever available scholarship and popular articles that exist. I also use research from more academic perspectives to help form the type of scholarship I wish to create with this book.

Gruenwald himself died in August of 1996, after a heart attack at 43, leaving a legacy remarkable despite his early passing. Obviously, that legacy should have been greater, but the artifacts that remain are something to value. After reading this book, I hope the reader has a greater appreciation of his work and how it helped truly shape a defining character and both the era in which these comics were written and beyond.

Introduction

Gruenwald's Captain America

Mark Gruenwald's death in 1996 left a hole in an industry already in the midst of major change. He was serving as Marvel's senior executive editor at the time of his death and his professional presence would be greatly missed within Marvel Comics and the industry as a whole. Beyond his professional role, he was an "all-around morale booster" behind the scenes, a lifelong comics fan with a passion for the art form and an innate ability to entertain and inspire those around him (Reed). He was a Midwesterner (born in Oshkosh, Wisconsin) and that can be seen in his comics, both in intimate literal ways (Cap's girlfriend Bernice Rosenthal moves to Madison to attend law school) and larger ways (Steve Rogers' decision to not work exclusively in New York and instead use it as a home base while fighting threats across the country, including in America's heartland). Gruenwald's impact on comics is in no way limited to his work on *Captain America*; he edited a number of comics (including *Iron Man* #160–232), created *The Official Handbook of the Marvel Universe* (a character-by-character guide to Marvel Comics mythology), contributed as a writer and occasional penciler on a variety of comics, and wrote and created *Squadron Supreme*, a twelve-part series that ran from September 1985 to August 1986 (overlapping roughly his first year as writer of *Captain America*). On *Squadron Supreme*, Gruenwald provides an influential darker take on the superhero genre by presenting a group of heroes who must deal with more real-life circumstances (such as public distrust and governmental conflict) than would be typical in a superhero comic at the time. Alan Moore and Dave Gibbon's *Watchmen* twelve-part series, the first issue appearing in September 1986, coincidentally one month after the conclusion of *Squadron Supreme*, had an even darker take on comic heroism and became an academically and culturally significant work, but while *Watchmen* created a universe in which the heroes (with the notable exception of Doctor Manhattan, among others) were people of normal abilities—some well-intended, and some ill-intended—the *Squadron Supreme* universe is less gritty and more traditionally derived in the vein of a superhero comic. It is a more mature take on a superhero reality, but still maintains the vibrancy and mythology traditional of the superhero comic at the time. On *Captain American*, a much more traditional superhero comic, Gruenwald incorporates some of those themes that so fascinated him in *Squadron Supreme* without sacrificing the key decency of the titular character.

If *Watchmen* and *Squadron Supreme* were pushing the boundaries of comic depictions of heroism at the time, their inclusion into academic discussion is clear. Both works are explicitly innovative (with *Watchman* gaining the most long-term accolades for its merit and influence) in part because of their daring willingness to deconstruct comic norms. What about Gruenwald's work on *Captain America*? His run is not necessarily deconstructing norms. While Gruenwald's work on the title certainly expanded and changed the fictional world as it was established prior to his run, it does not facilitate a full-on reinvention of genre. When analyzing a body of work such as Gruenwald's on *Captain America*, it is fair to ask basic questions of its consequence and influence. What makes a piece of writing more than just itself? At what point should we stop regarding a work as a mere text and start thinking of it as literature? Obviously, the answer is complicated since it was not until the later 20th century that the critical public started to recognize the artistic value of comics[1] (though, more specifically perhaps, this recognition has remained primarily focused upon the long-form graphic novel). Even with the eventual credibility for certain aspects of the genre, the traditional superhero genre, the one focused upon with Gruenwald and *Captain America*, is often less acknowledged.

Obviously, "Academics takes comics very seriously" (Eagan), and there is much more attention paid to comics now than in previous decades; Gruenwald's *Captain America* (and similar traditional superhero titles) are often less discussed, in part because other, more sophisticated titles are critically praised (justifiably) for their mature handling of difficult topics on a routine basis, as opposed to occasional forays into mature topics.[2] When other superhero comic books are singled out for critical praise, it is generally when those titles have moved toward maturity and sophistication. Gruenwald is less inclined toward these moves toward maturity, in part because his audiences are potentially less sophisticated than those Art Spiegelman, writer and artist of *Maus*, and Moore & Gibbons are courting. Gruenwald's work on *Captain America* is essential to an understanding of the comics of this era because of its handling of a deceptively challenging character, its understated (though effective) moral teaching, and the manner in which it helps define one of the most important comic characters of any era (and how unafraid it is to portray that character's complications in regard to his unassailable but perhaps too rigid morality).

Benefits of Formula

While recent comic scholarship has made and proven the argument of comic's academic merit, a traditional superhero comic such as *Captain America,* uninterested in overt realism and innovation, still feels, on a surface level, to fall short of literary inclusion. In that regard, we can discuss the value of the formulaic nature of Gruenwald's *Captain America.* Both in spite of and because of its reliance on formula, the comic is able to make a significant artistic impact. In this context, the term "formula" is not necessarily negative. In *Comic Book Nation,* Bradford Wright acknowledges the definition of "formula" summarized by John G. Cawelti: "ways in which specific cultural themes and stereotypes become embodied in more universal story archetypes" (xv). Wright further explains, "formulas that appeal to audiences tend to proliferate and endure, while those that do not, do neither" (xv). *Captain America* is a comic that is exploring the much tread territory of the morally-driven hero who is opposed by villains who can be easily described by an ideology or ability.[3] For several months in 1989 (during "The Bloodstone Saga" storyline), 1990 ("Streets of Poison"), 1991 ("The Superia Stratagem"), and 1992 ("Man and Wolf"), *Captain America* was published twice monthly, so the comic clearly proliferated specifically under Gruenwald's care, and the mere fact Gruenwald was able to write the comic for ten years speaks to both its and his endurance. The longevity of the character since Gruenwald's run (and its much-increased profile in the 21st century) cements that fact even further.

Gruenwald takes advantage of his own longevity to create a version of Captain America that, while staying true to the earlier versions of the character, is able to branch off into new directions that push toward new possibilities without deviating from the pre-established template. Gruenwald does respect both the good soldier of the character's earliest incarnations and the more disillusioned rendition from the 1970s, but he also paves new ground. Examples of narrative innovations in this comic include getting Cap into more frequent adventures throughout the country (and not just New York City) and allowing Rogers to reassess his relationship with the government.

Race and Realization

While race relations are not a touchstone issue for Gruenwald on this comic, a particular example of how race is handled shows us his willingness to grow upon preexisting themes, even if it happens by accident. Gruenwald writes Cap as having an African American partner but does so in a way that both reflects and resists earlier efforts made by prior writers in regard to the characterization of the Falcon, Cap's first African American partner (and the first African American Marvel superhero). When Stan Lee first introduces Sam Wilson/The Falcon in *Captain America* #117, Wilson is seemingly a normal man (who is an avid bird enthusiast) that Cap is able to groom into a worthy partner. Considering the Falcon is positioned as the hero of Harlem, Wilson's race is highly relevant in the comics,[4] but it is not until *Captain American* #186 in 1975 that writer Steve Englehart rewrites Wilson's origin in a racially problematic way. In Englehart's storyline, instead of Wilson being seen exclusively as an upstanding social worker of his community with an implied pristine past, Englehart reveals that Wilson was, in fact, a criminal named "Snap" Wilson that the Red Skull (via the Cosmic Cube) manipulated into being Cap's partner for the Skull's own nefarious purposes. With this gesture, Falcon went from being an idealized representation of African American heroism to a cliché. In flashback, he was revealed as a street-level criminal working with the "local mob" who had a propensity toward flamboyant pimp-like suits (6). "Snap" serves as a racially insensitive reworking of a character that needed no revision.

Much later in 1987, Gruenwald replaces Steve Rogers with John Walker, a white man who becomes a more violent version of Captain America. A government appointee, Walker is paired with an old military friend named Lemar Hoskins. Hoskins is African American. Hoskins (first known as "Bucky" and eventually "Battlestar") serves as a voice for pointing out problems with the government missions he and Walker are sent on. In issue #343, when John Walker's Captain America and Battlestar are ordered by the government to retrieve a mutant, Hoskins is sympathetic and uncomfortable with the mission, while Walker is willing to do whatever he is asked to do. To contrast, Hoskins thinks, "Poor guy's scared spitless. Barely out of his teens, I'd reckon!" (3), while Walker, within the same panel, tells the person they are pursuing (known as "Quill"), "Sorry, pal, but when you failed to register yourself as a mutant, you forfeited your right to be left alone!" Hoskins reminds us of the humanity lost in the character of Captain America when Walker takes over. Sam Wilson's Falcon had a different role when he was Steve Rogers' partner. An audience never doubts Rogers' integrity, so Wilson does not need to serve as a moral voice. Instead, he begins as an example of Rogers' open-mindedness, and becomes a character with his own needs and wants. Hoskins is a deviation from this template because he serves as a moral voice for the audience, but he does not have Falcon's agency.

Falcon is much more interested in social change than is Hoskins. While Englehart retcons[5] Wilson into a criminal in issue #186, Hoskins already is a criminal when he becomes Bucky. An early appearance in issue #327 depicts Hoskins (and two other allies) directly engaging in hate crimes against a foreign student housing building at John Walker's behest, establishing both Walker and Hoskins as criminals. Falcon's rewritten biography does not allow for redemption because he is merely a man manipulated by the Red Skull. Gruenwald makes up for lack of potential redemption by allowing Hoskins to learn about the type of positive social impact he can have on society as he progresses in his role.

Hoskins is initially named "Bucky" as a callback to Rogers' World War II partner (and a clear trolling of Rogers by the government that named him), but upon meeting an older African American man (depicted in issue #341), he realizes the problematic nature of the name. This man (a guard at the Vault, a prison for super-powered criminals) expresses his appreciation of Hoskins being "a high profile black super hero" but wonders, "what kind of name is Bucky?" Hoskin responds (naively) that it is also the name of Cap's original partner, but the man reminds Hoskins that the original Bucky was a "young white kid who died forty years ago" and that it is not a "fitting name for a black man who's the same age as Cap and has the same power as Cap, and is bigger to boot!" The man additionally points out that "'Buck' is an offensive term for a black man" in parts of the country and that the name was given to Hoskins by the government "to keep you in your place!" (11). Gruenwald uses the guard, a man clearly Hoskins' senior, to address problematic racial aspects of the character's name. This name change helps facilitate a character trait that depicts Hoskins as being a more socially aware and thoughtful individual who is capable of potential growth.

The impetus for this change, however, was not completely character-based (or wholly magnanimous). The change of name from Bucky to Battlestar was triggered by fan letter responses expressing concerns about the name. Reader LaMont Ridgell's letter in #340 expresses outrage about creating an offensive "Black Bucky." Editor Ralph Macchio responds to the letter by assuring Ridgell (and all readers) that they had no idea the name and character would be offensive. Macchio explains that Gruenwald "turned a ghastly shade of purple when someone first informed him that in some parts of the country 'buck' is a derogatory term for a black man" (24), the language echoed in the words the Vault guard will share with Hoskins in #341. Macchio further explains that Gruenwald was unfamiliar with the racial connotations of the phrase and would never have brought it to print had he known otherwise. Gruenwald realized the character's name was problematic and he fixed it, creating an ultimately more compelling character (because Hoskins himself becomes more aware of his identity as Gruenwald becomes more aware of the mistakes caused by his own naiveté). Marvel Comics would assuredly improve in terms of racial sensitivity as time progressed, but the positive instincts Gruenwald possesses (and how he responds to a culturally insensitive mistake) paves the way to greater inclusivity. It also reflects Gruenwald's nature toward moving forward (as opposed to the Englehart retcon of Falcon's origin, which was a clear movement backward).

Politics of Immediacy

Gruenwald's Captain America is very much a product of its era, artistically and politically (even if its politics are not aggressively presented). This is an important element of its value as literature rather than a simple ephemeral text. Philosopher Jean-Paul Sartre proposes that "committed literature" must address the political climate of the time, lest the writer ignore those issues and therefore support the status quo (Flynn). Sartre is saying that relevance (including long-term relevance) is contingent upon political timeliness. While Gruenwald's work is not as political as, say, Watchmen, it is still completely aware of the political climate of its era. As established, it is also addressing an audience different than that desired and targeted by Moore and Gibbons. While the audiences of the two comics would have significant overlap, the mature themes of Watchmen would have excluded some of the younger readers of the more kid-friendly Captain America. If the critical perception of Watchmen is that it is not "a superhero comic, it's about normal people being superheroes," (Godin) then we can argue Captain America is a superhero comic about a person with an estimable set of morals and values who is balancing the dangers of society with a deeply driven desire to do right. Captain America, throughout Gruenwald's time on the title, is unabashedly a superhero comic that is occasionally campy and also aware of the cultural and political landscape in which it is created. The comic succeeds because it knows exactly what it is.

While other comics of the era were drastically changing their formula or getting darker, this title does not do that. Even when the formula is changed (and the aforementioned John Walker becomes Captain America), the centering of the comic does not change. During Gruenwald's run, this comic is always about Steve Rogers and who he is, what he represents, and why he does what he does. Even in issues in which Rogers does not appear and Walker serves as Cap, the shadow of Rogers is strong. When we think of *Watchmen* depicting superheroes in a real-world setting, we see them as real because Moore is able to depict them as flawed and relatable. We do not see Captain America as flawed (though Rogers himself would counter that idea). We cannot see Cap as "real" because he is representing an ideal a reader might think is too lofty to achieve. Perhaps the mistake is that readers often feel that they can only see deeply flawed characters as relatable, and it is easy to dismiss Steve Rogers' decency as boring (or unrealistic). What Gruenwald does in these pages is present a Rogers that sees *himself* as being, if not flawed, not always living up the ideal he has set up for himself. While it does not happen often, Gruenwald is willing to give Cap existential moments of self-doubt. The reader might not default to seeing him as flawed, but Rogers does allow himself to worry about his potential flaws. The character flaws that Rogers sees in himself are his inflexibility and his inability (or unwillingness) to separate himself from his position as Captain America.

Gruenwald gives us a Cap that faces dark moments and his inability to know how to handle such moments makes a reader afraid (because adversity that even Captain America cannot handle is something that the rest of the world could never deal with). Cap deals with paralysis and death in 1995's "Fighting Chance" storyline (in issues #425–436 and to be discussed in detail in Chapter Ten) and its aftermath, but there is another quieter internal crisis Gruenwald forces Cap to fight—self-doubt and depression.

A Hero's Loneliness

In issue #371, Cap longs for a normal life: "For years my American Dream has been to fight to give other people the chance to realize whatever their American Dreams might be. I guess I've lost track of how this commitment to others has left me with so little time for myself" (18). He is a character defined by selflessness to his own detriment. He is lonely but only eventually can come to the realization of his own loneliness. This internal monologue comes after Rachel Leighton (Diamondback), Cap's main romantic interest during Gruenwald's run, has asked him to go on a date. Cap instinctively declines, seemingly by reflex: *he is Captain America; he cannot go on a date.* He has lost track of his own humanity and interests because of his dedication to a cause. He is not a perfect human being— he is a person who has self-sacrificed to the point of not even being aware of what the man behind the mask would find enjoyable. He is so committed to his superhero persona that the idea of social outing with a reforming supervillain feels improper. As far as the date with Leighton (and they are out of uniform on the date, so it is their civilian identities that partake in the social outing), he relents. They have an enjoyable time together, though their relationship after this date is always stifled by Rogers' unwillingness to commit to a relationship; Leighton's criminality feels more like an excuse than a reason (considering Cap's other relationships end badly). He is a character who sees his role as hero as absolute and, while he is willing to take Diamondback on as a partner for adventures, he cannot allow himself to be compromised as a hero by committing too much of himself to a relationship. In this regard, Cap often makes the conscious choice toward loneliness. It is as if his moral code requires this level of loneliness to maintain his insanely high standards of heroism.

Due to those high standards he puts on himself, Gruenwald's Cap is also often a victim of disappointment over how others behave when he feels they have not lived up to his moral expectations. One of those times where Cap cannot keep these feelings internalized is in *Captain America* #401, where we find Steve Rogers as a tired and nearly broken man. He and the rest of the Avengers are recovering from the effects of "Operation Galactic Storm," a closed crossover story that involves *Captain America* and the other Avengers titles.[6] Issue #401 serves as an epilogue to this crossover event (which encompasses nineteen parts across a number of Avengers-related titles) and begins with Captain America standing in shadows, asking the Avengers to vote as to whether or not he should step down as head of the Avengers (2). Penciler Rik Levins draws him dark, his eyes completely covered in shadow, helping the reader understand the darkness and difficulty of this moment. Cap appears alone on this first page. We assume he is speaking to others because of context, but we do not see them. This creates the illusion of an isolated and alone Cap.

The truth is anything but. What follows is a two-page image of Avengers responding in the negative to Cap's request (3). The first page to next two pages is a movement from shadow to light. Cap's shadowy face is replaced by a menagerie of colorful characters. Including Cap, eighteen characters appear in this Avengers boardroom, ranging from gods (Thor, Hercules, and Gilgamesh) to cosmic heroes (Quasar, Starfox, Captain Marvel) to everything in between. The colors (by Scheele/Going) are bright and dynamic (especially in contrast to the previous page)—reds, purples, and greens dance dynamically across the page. This is important because even as the book is leading us through an introspective and difficult moment, Gruenwald and his artists push back, balancing between Cap's depression and the influence of his friends. This image reinforces that there is great brightness in Cap's life, but he cannot always see it himself. Even though the color livens up from the first page to the next for the reader, Cap himself still sees things in dark and clouded tones.

Issue #401 is worth discussing because it is one of the issues in which Cap feels his lowest during Gruenwald's run. Ultimately, he is propelled out of this darkness by friends who are reciprocating the type of personal care he has given so freely throughout his life. On page 6, after being told by Peggy Carter that Diamondback has disappeared, Cap drops from a standing position to being seated, red gloved hands over his downward turned head, musing, "I go away and the whole world falls apart." This comment is not accompanied (as so many similar comments are) by an exclamation point or a thought bubble indicating that Cap is trying to figure out the problem. Cap is not thinking about this manically—nor is it something that Cap feels can even be reasoned away. This is a hero who feels like the limits to who he can protect and how often he can protect them are being pushed so far, there is little left he can do. Even Peggy Carter, his longtime confidant, is surprised by his reaction (her thoughts shown simply as an exclamation point in a chain thought bubble). This is not the Cap she has known for so long.

Over his decade as writer, Gruenwald is unafraid to raise the stakes, not necessarily with an endless array of villains (though that happens), but with increased internal problems. Cap's bout with depression reaches a peak when he arrives to address the assembled Avengers for a discussion on ethics (an invitation he extends to the body of membership as seen earlier in the issue). When he arrives, he finds but three Avengers in attendance (out of the 17 who appeared earlier in the issue). Those three (Hawkeye, Black Widow, and Scarlet Witch) try to make excuses for the others, but Cap is clearly hurt by the low turnout. Levins provides a striking image of Cap after he walks into the conference room and approaches the podium. It is of only the right side of Cap's face, downtrodden and sad, accentuated by a splash of red that underlines the hard, emotional feelings going through his mind. After he realizes the only attending Avengers are these three, he begins to speak, but changes his mind, turning away from the podium, saying only, "This is pointless. Sorry I wasted all your time" (10). In this sequence, Cap is once again in shadow, and the literal audience to his plaintive and defeated words is surprised (Hawkeye blurts out "whoa!" when Cap turns away from the podium). After Cap leaves, Thor[7] dramatically enters late to comedic effect, but the impact of Cap's influence and actions on the rest of the remaining Avengers is clear to the reader even if it is not clear to him personally. He tells the three heroes who attended (on time) that they did not need this discussion as much as others and those three heroes (again, Black Widow, Hawkeye, and Scarlet Witch) are three exemplary examples of Cap's influence. All three are reformed villains and all three first served as Avengers under his leadership and guidance. It is a reminder of the type of influence he can have on others, but Cap himself is in too dark a place to actually see it.

"Cheerin' up depressed living legends"

The issue hits its strongest emotional moments when Cap meets with Tony Stark. Hawkeye (Clint Barton) is encouraged by the Black Widow (Natasha Romanov) to try to "dispel the gloom" by taking him out to get him talking. Hawkeye doubts his ability to do this successfully—"cheerin' up depressed living legends ain't one of my specialties" (9)—but he tries. He refuses to allow Cap to decline his offer. Hawkeye literally jumps on Cap's bed and threatens to continue doing so until Cap gets out of bed. This eventually forces Cap to acquiesce to the invitation. Cap's malaise feels like depression in this issue (Hawkeye even acknowledges that he is "depressed") but it is not sustained enough over the course of several issues to be viewed as chronic. Still, Gruenwald is adding depth to a character that an outside eye might dismiss as being too thinly developed by making him human, in ways both gratifying and challenging.

As Hawkeye and Cap (more accurately, Barton and Rogers) arrive out of costume into a seedy bar far away from the Avengers Mansion, they sit surrounded by smoke and vaguely familiar pop culture figures—including, among many others, The Addams Family, Groucho Marx, Elvis Presley, and Humphrey Bogart. Playing pool with Bogart are John Steed and Emma Peel (of the 1960s British television series *The Avengers*, a clear play on Cap's Avengers, something Cap is forcing himself to be singularly focused upon in this issue). While Neal Adams uses a similar strategy for the cover to 1978's *Superman vs. Muhammad Ali*, Adams' cover is showing the massive widespread appeal of the pairing of Superman and Ali, and Levins' familiar faces are a fun diversion while Barton and Rogers have a serious discussion about the state of Rogers' life. Adams uses the device to make his scene more epic; Levins uses it to show how unimportant Barton and Rogers are out of costume. Importantly, these famous faces are not present to watch Hawkeye and Captain America; they are ignoring Clint Barton and Steve Rogers. Rogers' unwavering focus on his own problems and Barton's focus on the needs of his friend and mentor are illustrating an obvious inability for either to see the obvious in spite of its proximity.

Eventually, Tony Stark (out of his Iron Man armor) enters the bar, surprising both Rogers and Barton. Stark asks Barton to give him and Rogers some time alone and Barton acquiesces, albeit reluctantly; Barton's priority is Roger's mental health and he worries about leaving

Rogers to sit alone with a person who has proven to be a significant cause of tension in Rogers' life. This conversation between Stark and Rogers is something Gruenwald has been building for years over multiple titles. In issue #340, Rogers (in the guise of The Captain) is attempting to apprehend Stark for his, as the narrator explains, "personal crusade, attacking individuals who wore high tech body armor like Stark wore as Iron Man!" (3). During this period (called the "Armor Wars"), Stark is routinely violating the law in order to stop this unauthorized use of his technology. Rogers, dedicated to the law beyond all else, feels obligated to apprehend him. They fight twice and Iron Man stifles Cap's efforts to apprehend him both times. In #340, the narration further emphasizes the seemingly irreparable rift between the two: "both men know that a bond has been broken that may never be whole again" (3).

In issue #341, where the second of these fights is depicted, Iron Man attempts to explain his position (rationally explaining his fear as to what would happen if his technology fell into the wrong hands), but Cap is unmoved. Cap, while penciler Kieron Dwyer depicts Cap grabbing Iron Man's legs and slowing him down, tells Iron Man, "what you did was way out of line" (7). Stark wants to justify his actions with logic, but Cap cannot see logic when laws are broken. Stark feels he needs to end this conversation because he cannot reasonably discuss his actions with Cap, so he hits Cap with a temporarily debilitating "high density beam" that incapacitates Cap long enough for Stark to flee (8). Before Stark flees, he tells Cap, "I promise you this Steve, when I have finished what I have to do, I'll look you up and we'll have a long talk about ethics" (9). The issue depicting these battles (and the "Armor Wars" saga) is published in 1988 and they finally have that long-promised discussion in *Captain America* #401, released in June 1992.[8] This is obviously something that has been lingering between the two for years and, interestingly, when Gruenwald finally decides to let the conversation take place, he does so in an issue without traditional superhero action sequences. This is too important a conversation to risk it being overshadowed by spectacle.

When the conversation begins, Stark revisits the "Armor Wars" storyline and the recently completed "Operation Galactic Storm" storyline (in which Stark leads a group of Avengers to execute the Kree Supreme Intelligence, a move Rogers stands strongly against on moral grounds). While Stark argues, "conventional standards of morality are inapplicable in times of war," Rogers counters by saying the Kree Supreme Intelligence "should have been put on trial like the war criminals after WWII" (18). Due to the strength of their personal beliefs (and their respective stubbornness), their ideological differences simply are not going to be overcome with the mere passage of time. Gruenwald is too good a writer (and knows these characters far too well) to simplify things. Stark has ostensibly come to apologize, but before he does so, they need to talk ethics (as Stark promised earlier). Stark (drawn in the same shadows that Levins and the art team used so effectively on the first page to present a sad and isolated Captain America) says,

> We [the Avengers who wanted to kill the Kree Supreme Intelligence] may not think or act like you—but we still respect you and appreciate what you do and the way you do it. You're an idealist in a world that is far from ideal. I don't know how you can do it, Steve ... how you can keep all the ugliness from getting to you ... hardening you.... I can't. I'm not as perfect as you.... Forgive me [20].

Gruenwald presents a Stark who is resolute in both his ideological beliefs and his respect for the man he ideologically disagrees with. It is a powerful moment to see Tony Stark, a recovering alcoholic, enter a bar to meet with his estranged old friend to ask for forgiveness (but not to admit wrongdoing). It faithful to Stark's character and, most importantly, it is faithful to the character of Cap, to elicit this kind of contrition from a friend. Rogers accepts this apology, acknowledging first that he is himself hardly perfect, citing specifically his inability to properly forgive others. He apologizes too, saying, "I'm really sorry our ideological differences bent our friendship out of shape" (21). Neither man is willing to acknowledge flaws in their personal ideologies and the reader would not expect them to do so—but they find common ground in order to reconcile. That common ground comes from a well-established friendship and Stark's admiration for Cap's ethics.

Contemporary Comics Culture

Cap himself does not stay locked in his own anguish for long before he realizes the importance of Captain America to both the citizens of the country and the world at large. Accordingly, Gruenwald and his artistic team understand the importance of the actual outside world to this comic and are unwilling to let this title exist within a vacuum. Great literature should be aware of both its time in general and other significant artworks of its time. In issue #350, Gruenwald and penciller Kieron Dwyer pay quick tribute to *Watchmen* by depicting Steve Rogers buying a newspaper from a newsstand (8). As Rogers buys the paper, Dwyer draws a young African American man sitting next to the newsstand reading a comic book, similar to an image shown and revisited several times in *Watchmen* series. In Moore and Gibbon's *Watchmen*, the character is reading the fictional *Tales of the Black Freighter.* According to Mark Wolf in his essay "World Building in *Watchmen*,"

> Gibbons figured that [in a fictional world populated] with real superheroes, audiences would not want to read comic books about them, and so pirate comics are the most popular comics genre, with *Tales of the Black Freighter* as the comic-within-a-comic commenting on and mirroring *Watchmen*'s themes, its images often textured with dot-matrix halftones reminiscent of early pulp comics.

In *Watchmen*, the content of *Tales of the Black Freighter* is depicted to, as Wolf states, comment and provide parallel to the main themes. In *Captain America* #350, the comic within the comic is *Captain America* #350. While the visual of the character sitting and reading a comic is a quick nod toward *Watchmen*, Gruenwald and Dwyer also establish a key difference between the two universes. If Moore and Gibbon's universe does not find escapist value in superhero adventures, the universe of *Captain America* most certainly does. In Gruenwald's world, Cap is both reality and fantasy. He is a real person who could potentially save a baby and an apple pie from being struck by a runaway vehicle (as literally occurs in #350 right after Rogers buys the newspaper), and his adventures could further serve as both informative and escapist. They can be both morally instructive and entertaining. Cap acknowledges this as a reason why the Avengers allow Marvel to publish versions of their adventures (as seen in *Captain America* #310) and why Cap supports the comics industry enough to actually draw for them for a short time (getting the job after an interview in #311).

When Steve Rogers interviews to draw for Marvel Comics, it is implied that he has a preternatural ability to draw Captain America. Readers know why Rogers understands Captain America's body and physicality so innately even if the Marvel staff is not as aware (though the person who interviews him does acknowledge Rogers' resemblance to what Captain America must look like). Often, when the writer of a superhero comic wants to delve deeper into the personality of a hero to give the reader greater insight into what it is about a given character that makes them behave as they do, the writer will delve into the personality of the person under the mask. With this method, the mask comes off and we learn more about the "real" person, not the alter ego. Certainly, in earlier iterations of this comic, there was an effort to delve into Steve Rogers the person. Even before Gruenwald, exploring the person behind the mask was not as significant a presence for Cap as it would be for, say, Spider-Man. He still was given a real job (in the 1970s as a policeman and later as an artist) and a down-to-earth girlfriend, a glassblower—later lawyer—named Bernie Rosenthal.[9]

None of these efforts were particularly successful in giving us insight into Rogers, but Gruenwald realized something that became essential throughout his 137 issues. If Steve Rogers ever was a "regular Joe" at some point in his life, that part of him likely died years earlier and what remained of that persona was ultimately frozen completely out of him. Steve Rogers is not Peter Parker or Tony Stark—he is not a person who has different priorities outside of the uniform. He is not Bruce Wayne, living his "true" life in high profile while secretly ridding his city of crime at night. He is not Clark Kent, an alien taking on the guise of a forgettable human in order to fit in and protect. Steve Rogers and Captain America are one and the same—a person trying to do good and not particularly concerned with a secret identity. Under Gruenwald, he does indeed have a secret identity, but he does not prioritize it as much as do other crimefighters (though under previous writers, including Steve Englehart, his secret identity is highly protected).

Though the Marvel Cinematic Universe (MCU) has largely discarded the import of "secret identities" in the comics from this era, the concept was still standard.[10] While characters such as Stark and Bruce Wayne go to great lengths to hide their identities, Captain America does not commit to the same level of secrecy. There is no real distance between the two parts of his identity. He does not explicitly tell everyone (in the way Tony Stark does in the aforementioned MCU films), but it is not uncommon for Cap to reveal his unmasked face to strangers, in part because he is not a public figure (like Stark or Wayne) nor he is particularly concerned that villains will learn his identity and hurt his loved ones (as Peter Parker, for example, worries) because he does not have many of those types of people outside the Avengers (especially after Gruenwald minimizes Bernie Rosenthal's role) and those he is close to, including the Avengers and Diamondback, can take care of themselves.

In this regard, *Captain America* is doing something profoundly different from most other superhero comics of the time while still being aware of what is happening during this era of comics and culture. It also means that Rogers does not really escape the character. He is always Captain America, unable to simply play different roles. This inability to switch between these worlds does, at times, take a large emotional toll upon him, but he is too guarded for the reader to always know.

Challenges of Captain America's Ethical Code

Often, however, Gruenwald thoughtfully depicts Cap's ethics as so rigid as to be problematic. While he is aware that not everyone shares his ethical standards, Cap's rigidity can still complicate interactions with others. In issue #424, Sidewinder (the leader of the Serpent Society, the criminal organization that once employed Diamondback) comes to Cap asking for money to pay for his sick daughter's surgery and therefore letting Cap prevent him from committing future crimes. Sidewinder explains that the experimental procedure will cost "at least a quarter of a million dollars" (8) and Cap explains that he cannot afford that amount on his own and would not feel comfortable taking such a sum from the Avengers fund. Cap asks Diamondback, Sidewinder's former ally, to verify that Sidewinder has a daughter and she refuses to do so ("Are … you asking me to betray his confidence?" she asks on page 9), thus establishing her loyalty to those who have aided her in the past (even when they are clearly criminal and she is attempting to leave that period of her life behind). She (like Cap) is following an honor code.

Cap respects and recognizes this and, while he asks her for information, he does not press her in a way that makes her particularly uncomfortable. When Diamondback again explains that she does not want to betray Sidewinder's trust, Cap states, "I just bring them to justice, Rachel. The courts put the guilty away" (10). In the panel in which Cap says this, artist Phil Gosier draws Cap in the forefront and Diamondback in the background, seemingly responding to Cap's words with her facial reaction. While it is subtle, her reaction is subdued, and her pursed lips and sideways glance speak of frustration. She loves Cap for his integrity, but it is obvious that this integrity can come with a price.

Predictably, Sidewinder commits a crime (after all, he told Cap he would do so). After he has returned home to count his bounty, Diamondback arrives to check on him. She does so without directly telling Cap, informing him instead that she is leaving to "follow up on something of [her] own" (11). While she does not directly explain where she is going, Cap would likely infer (especially when paired with her hasty exit) that it would be in regard to something of which he would disapprove. She is not direct about her intentions because of his inevitable moral objections, but her loyalty for Sidewinder, her one-time ally, dictates her personal moral obligation even over Cap, her current ally and love interest. Cap's respect for her loyalty to Sidewinder prevents him from pushing her farther.

Sidewinder asks her to assist with the procurement of more money and she declines, telling him that she is not involved in that life anymore. Sidewinder can interpret her presence to mean that she is supportive of him and, possibly, the decisions he is making, but she herself refuses to be involved in the act. He tries to persuade her by explaining that he is only stealing from low-level criminals, but she tells him that "stealing's stealing" (13) and again refuses. While Cap himself would see merely visiting

Sidewinder as an implicit endorsement of illegal actions, she is caught between Cap's world and Sidewinder's. She is starting to believe Cap's moral stances (and she thus is unwilling to help Sidewinder by committing crimes), but she is not nearly as rigid as is Cap. She ultimately agrees to accept his "beeper" that will notify her if he ends up in any trouble (13), a compromise that allows her to help her former ally/mentor without assisting (or even endorsing) his illegal behavior.

When she does hear from Sidewinder, she fears for his safety and asks Cap to assist. They both arrive on the scene and help him (Diamondback assists an injured Sidewinder while Cap takes out the criminals). Cap does not let Sidewinder keep the money he is stealing (Cap describes the money as "state's evidence" on page 19) but instead assures him that he can financially assist with Sidewinder's daughter's surgery, later telling Diamondback that he could go to one of his "well-off friends" (20). Cap then reassures Sidewinder by telling him that if he cooperates, he could be acquitted, to which Sidewinder responds that an acquittal will not happen if Cap testifies in court against him. To this, Cap simply states, "We'll see" (20), as non-committal as a response could be. To summarize the key moments of the story, Sidewinder asks Cap to financially help with his sick daughter's medical costs or Sidewinder will be forced to engage in crimes. Cap declines to help. Sidewinder then commits crimes. Cap gets involved and enables Sidewinder's capture and arrest. After his arrest (and only then), he tells Sidewinder that he could indeed assist the daughter's procedure. While insinuating Sidewinder could go free if he is cooperative with the courts, Cap refuses to commit to the idea of not testifying against him.

In certain contexts, Cap's moralistically driven decisions could be seen as insufferable. He is inflexible and there is ultimately no room for moral discussion. As is discussed throughout this book, Cap's morality influences people throughout his sphere, including allies and enemies. But when it comes to being morally influenced by others, as Saltzstein and Takagi explain in their study on moral development, "one has to understand *what* is being acquired before proposing how it is acquired" (21). What these friends, acquaintances, and antagonists are learning from Cap is not as easy to quantify as one might think—it is not simply a matter of the following mentality: *Captain America is good, so working alongside him makes me want to be a better person.* It is helpful to look at Cap through the lens of Kohlberg's Stages of Moral Development to get greater insight into Cap's behavior and decision making. These stages reflect moral growth over time but, while one does not necessarily descend back into previous stages, it is also reasonable to exist within related stages (Sanders).

The stages begin with Stage One (obedience), which would be most common in young children and reflects a blind adherence to the rules. It also values potential punishment as a main deterrent to improper behavior. This one is too simplistic for Cap because, while he follows the laws, obviously he is willing to say when something is not functioning in the way it should. When he personally does do something that violates the law (typically a minor violation in support of a larger cause), he owns up to it and accepts that punishment, so the punishment does not typically serve as a deterrent. Stage Two (self-interest) is about what is best for the individual committing the act. Clearly, this is entirely self-serving and does not fit any reading or depiction of Steve Rogers. Stage Three is about social roles and conformity. Again, fitting in is not a priority for Steve Rogers or his heroic ego. Stage Four is closer to the interpretation of the character—it is about law and order but is much less simplistic than Stage One's simple obedience (and fear of consequence). Stage Four is likely where Cap sits on this scale because this stage values laws as an essential element of an efficient society. If an individual violates the law, regardless of reason, they should be stopped, lest that negative act (and the influence of that act) break the cultural norms. In Stage Five, the individuality of people is valued (and different people should be evaluated differently).

Cap is entrenched in Stage Four. He sympathizes with Sidewinder's daughter's plight and he would like to help (and eventually does), but his morality will simply not let him treat Sidewinder differently than another villain committing a crime for a different reason (hence invalidating the possibility of him occupying Stage Five). He will not even commit to the possibility of not testifying against Sidewinder in court. Iron Man, for example, frequently enters Stage Five. This is why Captain America and Iron Man have so many conflicts, including over what Cap sees as Tony Stark's vigilante behavior in the "Iron Wars" storyline. Stage Six is a step beyond even this, built around universal ethics and the concept that laws are less important than the abstractions that guide people's behavior, a much too obtuse philosophy for Cap to adopt. Cap values the literal laws and the potential of the country's founding documents to be guided by these abstractions. These stages are built around reason and an emphasis on an individual's capacity to reason through the various stages (with greater enlightenment guiding one through each of the stages of life).

It is argued that reason alone cannot lead toward ideal moral behavior—moral psychologist Augusto Blasi "has long regarded the self as the missing motivational link in Kohlberg's theory, arguing that it is a need for self-consistency that provide the sense of 'personal necessity,' or obligation, required for a person to act in accordance with his or her moral beliefs" (Arnold 371). The moral influence and modeling are important, but it is up to the individual to fully assimilate the influence or it will have minimal long-term impact. Cap models but does not necessarily follow up that modeling with individual guidance. Cap is more apt to act and then expect his allies assisting him on a given mission to keep up. What Cap does provide is enough influence to inspire the individual to motivate that "personal necessity" that could help cement moral commitment in the "student." Based on this reading of Kohlberg's stages, Cap does not transcend toward the highest levels of enlightenment because of his dedication to his humane (and mostly unflinching) sense of justice.

Captain America and the "Trolley Problem"

Cap's modeling of morality is a key aspect of Gruenwald's work, but part of Gruenwald's strength in presenting that morality is that it is occasionally more difficult to forecast than one might think. There is unexpectedly complexity at work. For instance, what would Captain America do with the "trolley problem?" The modern version of this dilemma was introduced by Phillipa Foot who proposed a scenario of a trolley veering out of control and inevitably hitting (and killing) five people (Hacker-Wright). In this scenario, the trolley operator could change the course of the trolley, but there is a single person on the other side, so changing the course will still kill, but only a single person. What is a superhero (especially *this* superhero) to do with such a scenario? It can be proposed that Cap would not change the course of the trolley away from the five likely victims because he could not acknowledge that he could fail or that there would even be a choice that would involve sacrificing any life whatsoever. He would lunge in front of the trolley to defend the five people, holding up his shield to protect them at any cost. In a Marvel comic, this would be enough to stop the vehicle, but in the "trolley problem" and its world of absolutes, it would not be possible and Cap would die alongside the others he is trying to save.

Would other characters do the same? Assuredly Falcon would follow Cap's model, as would Cap's short-term partner D–Man, because both partners have adopted Cap's modeled behavior. What about Nomad, another of his one-time partners, one who is heroic but more emotional and self-serving? Gruenwald's depiction of Nomad goes from characterizing him as a naïve and eager partner to later as a darker figure willing to take chances to do good (and he ends up more of a vigilante). Perhaps he changes the course of the trolley and kills one rather than five. Maybe Diamondback, the former criminal just learning what it means to be heroic, would change course too. Black Widow, a clearly heroic figure but a hardened pragmatist, would assuredly do so.

While this example is from the world outside of Gruenwald's, the MCU films *Infinity War* and *Endgame* give us a specific answer for how Doctor Strange (a character mentioned several times in Gruenwald's run on *Captain America*, but who never actually appears) would respond to the trolley problem. In *Infinity War*, Strange uses the Time Stone to witness 14,000,605 possible futures of the conflict between the Avengers and Thanos. Tony Stark asks him how many of those scenarios see the heroes "win" and Strange replies, "one." Strange later does something completely out of character, especially considering conversations earlier in the film in which he explains that he will never, in any circumstance, give up the Time Stone. As Thanos is pummeling Stark in battle, Strange unexpectedly gives the Stone to Thanos, much to Stark's surprise. When Stark asks why, Strange simply says, "There was no other way." Using the Time Stone (as well as the other collected Infinity Stones), Thanos later wipes out half of life in the universe (including Doctor Strange himself).

In *Endgame*, Stark, Captain America, and the remaining heroes undertake a plan that allows them to collect the Infinity Stones from other locations in time and ultimately retrieve the previously lost lives wiped out by Thanos' earlier action (including Doctor Strange). During the final battle with Thanos, when Thanos is about to wipe out all life on Earth, Stark and Strange share a knowing look. Strange then lifts his index finger as if to say this is the one scenario out of the fourteen million in which the heroes win. Stark knows this means victory for the heroes but the loss of his own life. He sacrifices himself, kills Thanos, and ends all of Thanos' efforts to wipe out all life in the universe.

Using the above "trolley problem" example, Doctor Strange is the trolley operator. On one track is all life in the universe. On the other track is Tony Stark. Strange moves the trolley and takes out Stark to save the universe. It is possible that he saw, in those 14,000,605 scenarios, a number of other heroes in the similar situation of trying to sacrifice themselves and failing (perhaps the Iron Man armor extended Stark's ability to handle the power of the Infinity Stones and maybe, for example, Cap would have been destroyed by the power of the Stone before he could have snapped Thanos away). While perhaps the Stark/Rogers dynamic is less contentious during Gruenwald's run than during the *Civil War* comic event in 2007,[11] Gruenwald's *Captain America* still has many moments of tension between the two, leading toward that quiet moment of intimacy between the two friends (and frequent moral antagonists) in #401. Would Cap (Gruenwald's version or any other) have sacrificed Tony Stark or any other single person to stop Thanos (not including, of course, himself)?[12] The answer is clearly never. Whether this is out of heroic obsession or inherent decency is a question that Gruenwald, at least, leaves to the reader.

Decency, Morality, and Firing the Canon

Sometimes in Gruenwald's world, people are simply decent, even when every signal is telling the reader they should not be. When Diamondback (calling herself Rachel) finally talks Captain America (who reveals himself only as "Steve") into going on a date with her in the aforementioned issue #371, her friends Black Mamba and the Asp, two criminal members of the Serpent Society, trail Rachel and Steve throughout the night, resolving several incidents that, had he noticed them, would have caused Steve to immediately jump into action as Captain America. Thanks to the efforts of Black Mamba and the Asp (and later Anaconda as well), Cap does not have to suit up (and in fact does not know of any danger at all) and the two have an uneventful first date.

Over his decade on the comic, Gruenwald shapes big moments and small moments (and many moments in-between). He creates a narrative voice in these pages that can deftly dance between tones and dangers. This voice also creates an innately likable attitude for the comic overall. Great literature can be defined by the emotional feeling someone gets as they read a book and not just a detached analytical response. Holden Caulfield in Salinger's *Catcher in the Rye* tells us, "What really knocks me out is a book that, when you're all done reading it, you wish the author that wrote it was a terrific friend of yours and you could call him up on the phone whenever you felt like it" (22).[13] That well represents Gruenwald's work—his characters (even some of the villains) exude a decency that informs the ethos that defines the comic.

Poet Beckian Fritz Goldberg explains that "reading is a dialogue that involves both the mind and the body in a pleasurable seeking, and it is not separate from breathing, sleeping, eating, or taking out fresh sheets from the dryer" (177). Looking for pleasure in reading is innate and should not be vilified. If reading an issue of Mark Gruenwald's *Captain America* brings joy, then it is a successful work. But Goldberg goes on to say that literature can be challenging and upsetting as well as pleasurable: "we may be shocked or repulsed, but if we don't recognize the hand of longing here and the mystery of what the body means, we are not reading the right book" (177). Gruenwald's issues are filled with moments both triumphant (Cap finally besting John Walker in #350) and tragic (Scourge's massacre of supervillains in #319 and Hiram Ridley's story about his mother in #443). Gruenwald's *Captain America* comics tell stories that are redemptive but honest. For example, we struggle alongside Diamondback in her efforts to do good in a world in which she has done so much bad. There is a genuine struggle for her to be the kind of person she feels like she could be. These comics have moments like Tony Stark reaching out to old friend Steve Rogers and seeking a way to smooth the tension that only exists between two people as determined and unmovable in their values and views as are they.

When asked about his feelings about the literary canon in an interview with Scott Esposito, novelist and critic Tim Parks responded, "The canon is finished. Anyone who believes that one can construct a canon from the tidal wave of narrative produced today is guilty of wishful thinking." Perhaps that is the best answer to the idea of what makes for worthy literature in the contemporary world—society is at a point (and in 1985 when Gruenwald started on *Captain America* this trek is only beginning) where the oversaturation of text (and so much of it worthy by varying standards) makes it impossible for objective ideal selections of literary value. While Parks is discussing the end of the canon, he does little to cry for it: "But, perhaps, the canon was always a fairly heavy-handed tool and little more than a convenience. The only thing is to follow one's nose and listen carefully to the way others talk about books, learn whose opinion takes you to interesting places." If Gruenwald's world has anything at all, it has engaging characters going to interesting places.

Preternatural Preparedness

Cap finds himself in the Citadel of Justice on the Kree capital of Hala in issue #400. This is an issue that takes place during the aforementioned "Operation Galactic Storm" and this particular issue focuses on a stranded Cap stuck in enemy territory after Iron Man and the Avengers left him behind to protect their mission (and Tony Stark apologizes for this decision in #401, discussed above). The issue, unlike the others discussed in this chapter, is filled with action and shorter on the character-building interactions that define the previously discussed #371 and #401. Gruenwald's ability to showcase the character during action sequences such as those present in #400 is a key aspect to his successful writing on the comic.

Gruenwald dramatically sets up the challenge that Cap is facing in the issue. Iron Man (racked with guilt over his decision to leave Cap behind) is telling Clint Barton (here in the guise of Giant-Man rather than Hawkeye) that Cap is going to survive and escape, but his internal monologue betrays his concerns: "Can Cap survive everything the Kree may throw at him? Will the blood of one of the greatest heroes the human race's ever brought forth be on my conscience…?" (5). Gruenwald is building up Cap's challenge (putting it in dramatic terms) and Iron Man's moral dilemma about his choice (setting up for the emotional moment in the subsequent issue). On Hala, Cap survives an explosion and ends up in a large and seemingly empty room. Suddenly, he is attacked by Cobra. And then Batroc. Flag-Smasher and Viper arrive on the scene, and finally Red Skull and Crossbones do the same. Knowing he is "billions of miles from Earth" (as Cap says on page 19), Cap tries to figure out the legitimacy of the six archvillains (in many ways, the six defining villains of the Gruenwald era, and assuredly six villains that are covered in detail throughout this book), even as he fights to the death against them. Their appearance on this world is illogical, even if the villains themselves try to make it logical by creating a story as to how they arrived on Hala.[14]

Even in this strange and improbable battle, Cap's approach is as consistent as it would be for something far more straight-forward. Cap never fights purely on instinct; Gruenwald's use of chain thought bubbles gives readers insight into the planning always taking place in his head. In this particular situation, it turns out that Cap's suspicions are justified and these are not, in fact, Cap's real flesh and blood adversaries, but rather facsimiles created into physical form by the Kree Supreme Intelligence in order to kill Cap and subsequently absorb him into the Supreme Intelligence. The facsimiles are created entirely from Cap's subconscious, down to details about what Cap knows and cares about (including their fighting styles and attitudes). Cap does not know this, of course, when he is first fighting them, but he is figuring everybody and everything out. It is unfair to say that Gruenwald is at his best at writing Cap when he puts him in the midst of a fight, showing Cap's skill and reasoning to survive and succeed, because he is also quite adept at quieter moments as those depicted above, but Gruenwald makes these action sequences matter, even one like this that can be argued to matter very little (the villains are only imitations, after all).

These sequences are not a glorification of violence. Too often, fight scenes in other writers' hands feel like excess or filler, but Gruenwald gives these moments weight and gravity (and he never lets action sequences feel like obligatory inclusions). They are opportunities to show Cap's resourcefulness and cleverness. And Gruenwald does this, not just by writing fight scenes that rely on splash pages by talented pencillers—he does it by giving every fight gravity. This is a fight that has high stakes (if he dies, he will be assimilated into the Kree Supreme Intelligence) but Cap himself is not really sure it does (he mentally goes through a variety of possibilities of what these enemies actually are as he fights them). Still, he uses both his wits and fighting ability in the one-on-six fight, ultimately surviving because of, not his wits or fighting ability, but his remarkable observational skills.

Continuity of Character

The Kree create the six archenemies solely out of Cap's memories, and those memories are so complete that Cap can be fooled by them, but they are also so complete they capture all aspects that Cap has observed over frequent encounters with these enemies, especially (as discussed in Chapter Seven) Batroc's sense of honor. When Cap is held down by each limb and about to be defeated by the Red Skull's poisoned smoke, Batroc lets go and gives Cap a sporting chance. Cap takes full advantage of this opportunity and quickly dismisses the other five enemies. Cap asks Batroc to remove his mask so he can know for sure if these enemies are real. Batroc agrees but asks (quite rationally) that, since Cap has never seen his unmasked face, what could removing his mask possibly reveal? Cap encourages him to do so anyway. When Batroc removes the mask, the once-concealed area is simply blank. Cap does not know what Batroc's face looks like and this Batroc is created by Cap's memories, so Batroc does not have a full face. Many heroes win battles thanks to their wits and not just skill and brawn, but Cap takes that motif to a different level. He is a consummate student and leader, always learning, always surviving.

For Gruenwald, Captain America is not a pacifist, but neither is he a soldier in desperate need of a war. The wars find him, and he finds a way to end them that, typically, values life over ultimate victory. For instance, Gruenwald depicts Cap as being anti-gun, something that is contradicted by earlier versions of the character. For Phillip L. Cunningham, who discusses Captain America's divergent views on guns and violence in the essay "Stevie's Got a Gun," Gruenwald's approach is "troubling" because it "virtually ignores Capitan America's origins and *raison d'etre*" (178).[15] While Gruenwald's adherence to continuity is rightfully applauded, he was uninterested in continuity merely for its own sake.[16] What is most important for Gruenwald (and what makes him potentially troubling to some readers or critics) is that he is willing to disregard certain elements of the character's history (such as Cap using guns) in order to shape the hero that Gruenwald wants him to be. Even if there are holes in continuity for this trait, it helps create a clear consistency for the style of combat he favors.

Gruenwald's *Captain America* is an essential piece of comics literature because it knows when to acknowledge the character's past and when to rewrite it. Not only is this run a crucial piece of understanding 1980s and 1990s culture, Gruenwald's efforts to both respond to the era and define it through his psychological and moral interpretation of the character make it a relevant text today, one that is not merely worthwhile because of its influence or historical value, but also for the merit of Gruenwald's stories themselves.

PART I

PATRIOTISM
AND SYMBOLISM

In 1969's *Easy Rider*, one of the most visible counter-culture films of its era, Peter Fonda's character Wyatt is referred to as "Captain America." In *Comic Book Nation*, Bradford Wright looks at this as an example of counter-culture recognition of comics while acknowledging that Fonda (who co-wrote the film) could also be appropriating the name ironically for his cocaine-distributing motorcycle-riding character (230). The symbolic weight of "Captain America" is significant enough to carry the full interpretation. Cap is straitlaced, but even at the time of *Easy Rider*, there was the ability to co-opt the character into something edgier. Cap is mostly uninvolved in the Vietnam War during this era, a decision that Shawn Gillian, writing about Cap in the Vietnam Era, calls "puzzling" (105). He concludes that the explanation is that Lee's take on the character in *Captain America* in the late 1960s was "a surprisingly integrative study of a character suffering from an array of symptoms that can best be described as a psychological disorder, in Cap's case Post-Traumatic Stress Disorder (PTSD)" (105–106). Using Captain America symbolically for counter-cultural media makes sense in this context—in a messed up world, Cap is as messed up as the world is. He, too, is avoiding the trauma waiting in Vietnam.

The next four chapters will delve into different aspects of Captain America's symbolism by looking in extensive detail at how Captain America serves as a patriotic symbol depending on who is in the costume and how they are representing the role. This symbolism can be interpreted differently by those of different generations and Cap's transcendence into different generational profiles greatly affects his role as symbol.

ONE

Star Spangled Symbolism

The United States is a nation overflowing with symbols. There are animals, statues, and fictional characters that symbolize America. These patriotic symbols[1] typically are not organically generated to represent the concepts they grow to represent and are instead created (and appointed) specifically in order to symbolize. Captain America is no exception to this. The character was created by Joe Simon and Jack Kirby for Timely Comics (a company that was a precursor to Marvel) and debuted in 1940 with the first issue featuring a cover of Cap literally on the brink of punching Hitler. These early comics were both patriotic and popular. Cap was even featured in a film reel series in the 1940s, an obvious sign of mainstream success. When the war ended, interest waned. While eventually an aborted attempt was made to reestablish the character in the 1950s, the proper comic reboot of Captain America would not occur in earnest until *Avengers* #4 in 1964 (Bellotto).

By the 1980s and 1990s, the character was fully integrated into the larger Marvel universe, but he was clearly a lower-tier comic character in terms of general popularity as compared to Spider-Man or the X-Men, for example. What does one gain by specifically studying the symbolism of this star-spangled superhero? Gruenwald uses this character and title as a starting point for discussions of modern American life, in regard to things both good and bad about the contemporary age. While he creates a character for Steve Rogers, Rogers himself recognizes that Captain America, unlike any other Marvel superhero, is a symbol of the capacity of good inherent within the American system and is not just a crime fighter. Rogers knows that not everything America does is good, but he understands the good things America and Americans are capable of creating, and he stands as a symbolic representation of exactly that. Gruenwald understands this too and structures the character accordingly.

Philosopher Noam Chomsky tells us, "We shouldn't be looking for heroes. We should be looking for good ideas," but what if the hero we find is a character built out of ideas as much as action? Captain America is a comic hero who is deeply invested in his own symbolically ideological value and is greatly concerned with people who would improperly assess what he represents. He embraces his symbolism, his assumed ideology, and the ideals he attempts to represent—he just wants to make sure the world gets all the details of his symbolism right. Cap knows symbols are significant to the nation, but they are also fleeting. Ernst Lehner, discussing historical American symbolism, describes a number of early American symbols that once "served their purpose for a time [and] have long since been forgotten" (7). A misrepresentation of what Cap represents (or a public shift to thinking that Cap and his purpose are antiquated) would leave him outdated and both Gruenwald and Cap himself want to avoid that sentiment.

Historical Framing

In 1985, the United States was still in the midst of the Cold War. The world was two years removed from President Reagan's "Mr. Gorbachev, tear down this wall" declaration and, when the first issue of Mark Gruenwald's tenure as writer on *Captain America* appeared in July, four months remained before the November 1985 Geneva Convention (in which Reagan and Mikhail Gorbachev first sat down to discuss possible paths toward peace). Gorbachev was newly the Prime Minister and the 1984 Los Angeles Olympics, so defined by the Soviet boycott, were still recent. International tensions ran high.

Only two years had passed since what historian Doug Rossinow calls "the greatest peril of nuclear war since the Cuban Missile Crisis of 1962" in the form of President Reagan's increased obsession within the Caribbean and specifically Grenada. Rossinow writes, "The result was a worldwide fear and tension of a kind that Americans aged twenty and younger had never before witnessed" (101). Also, in 1983, ABC debuted *The Day After*, a made-for-TV movie depicting a Soviet nuclear attack on the American heartland.[2] The possibility of nuclear war was not seen as inevitable, but it was viewed as possible and that possibility had a clear social and political effect. According to Deron Overpeck, writing about *The Day After*:

> Two days after the broadcast, President Reagan himself spoke on the film, which he described as "well-handled." But, he added, "it didn't say anything we didn't already know, that is that nuclear war would be horrible, which is why we're doing what we're doing—so there won't be one." Reagan also added that he believed that his administration's policies represented the extent that could be done to prevent a nuclear war. After leaving office, Reagan wrote in his

memoirs that *The Day After* "left me greatly depressed" and resolved "to do all we can to have a deterrent and see that there is never a nuclear war" [282].

Reagan's words about the film's personal effect on him were not public until well after the height of the tension though, at the time of the film's release, Reagan's administration did little to change their already aggressive course. According to Overpeck, "the film had no immediately noticeable impact on Reagan's foreign policy" (282). It certainly had an effect on the American public (and, privately, Reagan himself).

This is the backdrop in front of which Gruenwald begins writing this comic. He wrote and served as editor for several notable comics during his time at Marvel (including *Captain America* prior to serving as writer), but considering only one of those comics he worked on features a title character who wears a red, white, and blue suit with a giant "A" displayed on their mask, it is wholly fitting to discuss the American and international political landscape when discussing this specific title. When he is crafted by a capable and understanding writer, Captain America is a character for whom American history and current events are innately tied together. Understanding the pulse of the country during this time period when Gruenwald is creating *Captain America* is important because anyone who writes Cap effectively (and rejects turning him into a hollow patriotic symbol) must connect him to the cultural zeitgeist and history of the moment and portray him as responding to that moment in an honest and organic way.

Gruenwald certainly does this. Regardless of the specific era, there are aspects of Cap that remain consistent, including his adherence to the First Amendment: "Gruenwald continues to make most of Cap's cultural conflict related to his status as a symbol and his concerns about free speech" (Stevens 161). Cap values freedoms—both of life and of rhetoric. He knows that he has to maintain a consistency to his ideology, particularly because of the symbolism connected with him. He maintains that dedication to promoting freedom, but he also is functioning within a modern world. He is not unaware of evolving American culture. How can a character properly symbolize America unless that character is representing not just the country that was but also the country it is evolving to become?

By the time Gruenwald's tenure ends in 1995, the world has changed in profound ways. The Cold War has ended and the Berlin Wall has fallen. In the ten years in-between, three American Presidents have been in office.[3] The Gulf War, Operation Desert Storm, is fought and Cap fights in the similarly named though otherwise unrelated "Operation Galactic Storm" in 1992 (which crosses over in issues #398–401, with an epilogue in #401), the Rodney King beating occurs, as does the 1993 World Trade Center bombing. NAFTA is signed into law. The world is changing and technology is bringing people closer together. Obviously, the world Cap was introduced to in 1941 was wildly different than the world he was reintroduced to in 1964. Likewise, 1985 and 1995 are very different Americas.

Cultural Touchstones

All serialized literature has some awareness of its time, even if the creative forces behind a given work do not prioritize that objective. Sometimes, this is limited to cultural references (which certainly work their way into these issues) or major historical and cultural touchstones. Some writers are compromised from fear of ultimately being perceived as *dated* and try to avoid these types of cultural touchstones. Gruenwald's work shows a lack of concern for this inevitability of "datedness," and he writes for the moment in which he and his readers are living. For example, in *Captain America* #327 (entitled "Clashing Symbols" and released in 1987), Steve Rogers visits Bernie Rosenthal in Madison, Wisconsin, where we see a poster depicting the cover of Elvis Costello's 1981 album *Trust*. Later in the same issue, Cap attends a charity concert where many familiar faces are mentioned and/or seen (such as Willie Nelson, Bruce Springsteen, Madonna, and Run D.M.C., among others). While in the Joss Weedon directed 2011 film *Marvel's Avengers*, Captain America's lack of pop culture knowledge is played as a punchline (Cap proudly announces "I understood that reference" when Nick Fury utters a cultural reference he comprehends), here Cap is not clueless (though he gives Bernie Rosenthal credit for his knowledge): "Wow, it's like the who's who in pop music back here. Thanks to Bernie broadening my musical tastes while we were an item, I actually recognize most of these musicians. Is that Tina Turner?" (14).

Cap is not presented as being wildly savvy about pop culture, but he is not clueless at all. In fact, it can be read that he is charmingly star-struck by musician Tina Turner. The scene is now a time capsule to mid-'80s pop culture, but in its time, it granted the Captain America character with valuable popular culture capital. These references are not used to make Cap seem out of touch, nor do they paint him to be implausibly current on popular culture. Not only does Gruenwald not worry about a given character in an issue making a reference to a popular musical act or pop culture figure, he seems to take great delight in it. This is valuable as we dig through these issues because Gruenwald immerses Cap in his time, including having him respond to current crises that are outside of Cap's normal rogues' gallery of foreign foes (including a multipart story where Cap tackles the drug war).

"Man out of time" No Longer

Cap's origin story in the 1960s (when the Avengers find him frozen in ice and subsequently thaw him out) is tied to the "man out of time" trope. But by the mid-'80s, that trope no longer applies—he has acclimated to the culture of the world, though the priorities he was taught from his coming of age still apply. When Gruenwald takes over the comic, Cap's decades-long war with the Red Skull has ended. Seven issues before Gruenwald's debut as writer, Captain America defeats the Red Skull and carries away his dead body in issue #300. In that issue, written by J.M. DeMatteis (plot) and Michael Ellis (story), everything points toward finality. The cover promises a fight "to the death." The issue itself is entitled "Das Ende." The issue delivers on this promise when Red Skull dies in Cap's arms (both men old and poisoned) after their fight but not before pleading with Cap to deliver a killing blow so that, in Skull's mind, he would at least have the decency of dying in combat. Cap refuses and Skull dies without that perceived dignity. As aged Cap carries the Skull's dead body away from the scene of their battle (and penciller Paul Neary draws the dead Red Skull grotesque with mouth agape), Cap speaks to his fallen archenemy:

> How do you not see, Skull? We are not two gods in a cosmic dance, just two tired old men! You did your best to bring me down to your level, and, God help me, you came close! But in the end, you failed and died a pathetic death. But you're not taking me with you. I'm going to find a way to beat the poison. I'm going to live! [17].

The issue is conclusive. The Red Skull is dead and Captain America will begin a new chapter. Not only has the Skull died, he has died in a way that is "pathetic" and without dignity. To Cap, that is fitting. Importantly, it is also decisive. Carrying Red Skull's dead body away in the last two panels, Cap describes the Red Skull as "the past." He follows that up by adding, "And, it's time—at long last—to bury the past ... for good" (22). Instead of a letters page, "American Graffiti," the typical space for reader letters, contains no letters at all, instead simply a picture of Cap and Skull in battle from the issue with "THE END OF AN ERA!" prominently featured above (23).

Gruenwald is able to move the character and title into a new direction after this because, in many ways, the burden of the past is lifted. He moves the character into the rest of the '80s and into the '90s with new ideologically driven villains (including a more modern take on the Red Skull when he makes his inevitable return in issue #350) that take the place of some of those aforementioned foreign menaces, and a new agency for Captain America to be part of his current era. He is less a man out of time in these issues than a man of a different generation and life experience adeptly adapting to the technology and norms of the day. This is not an effort to fit in. Considering his uniform and ideology, Captain America hardly "fits in" anywhere. Additionally, his dedication and adherence to his personal moral code are viewed by virtually everyone as extraordinary.

Mockingbird (Bobbi Morse), an Avenger and Hawkeye's (Clint Barton) wife at the time, sums up the way Gruenwald wants the world at large to view Cap when, in issue #308, she thinks, "In the few months I've been an Avenger, I've seen a lot of superheroes, but Cap is it, as far as I'm concerned" (5), after he has easily bypassed the Avengers security system in an effort to test it out. Following the leads of previous writers, Gruenwald works toward giving Captain America an unmistakable aura of greatness, observed not only by the public, but also other adventurers. Throughout these issues, every effort is made to ensure that Cap always seems special.

Technology and "Social Networking"

In *Captain America* #312, Steve Rogers unexpectedly receives a million dollar check as backpay from the United States government (6). When presented with this windfall, he decides to use it to broaden his ability to help Americans. He uses technology to create a phone network and computer system (with the assistance of a team of computer whizzes called the "Stars and Stripes") to enable Americans all over the country to contact him with problems the local authorities cannot handle (7). This would not have been as feasible a plot point in the '60s or '70s and, though the emphasis on "telecommunications" feels dated now, this was a concerted effort to get an increased tech-savviness into the comics to show the lengths to which Cap is willing to go to increase his capacity to help (and, additionally, increase his ability to fulfill his symbolic role as protector to all Americans). It is also further evidence of the extraordinary effort Cap puts into his job—this is not simply a uniform he puts on at night to fight crime. It is an all-day, every-day commitment, perhaps more so than any comparable superhero (considering others often retreat into a human identity and perhaps the normalcy that accompanies said identity).

Not only is he motivated to connect with every citizen who could possibly need him, but he also strives to connect with his fellow heroes as well. An analysis into connections between Marvel characters (envisioning them as a social network) by Ricardo Alberich, Joe Miro-Julia, and Francesc Rosselló shows that Cap is the character with the most connections to other characters, meaning he has more meaningful ties to other Marvel characters than any other Marvel character (Stevens 3). Cap feels most comfortable (and is the best heroic version of himself) when he is the center of things. Korkid Akepanidtaworn, in an article entitled "Social Network Analysis of Marvel Universe Characters," discusses how the data from the above Marvel social media allowed him to observe that Captain America is second on the list of characters who cross over with other characters (behind only Spider-Man). He is connected and finds ways to stay connected. Forays into modern themes and technologies still stay true to Cap as a character because, unlike mercenaries who would do such a thing for profit, he sees these missions as means of fulfilling the overall objective of his duties.

In addition to the example of modern telecommunication technology, musical and popular culture references scattered about these issues fully immerse the series in its historical moment and add contemporary relevance to the issues (though Gruenwald's interest in the rock group The Talking Heads will perhaps give future readers an overstated view of their cultural footprint). These examples of technology and popular culture, it is important to add, are never used to make Cap himself look like a relic or in any way out of touch with the times. In fact, Cap is timeless and adaptable (at least until the last eighteen issues of Gruenwald's run that depict a dying Cap having more difficulty in this regard), and these are never seen as obstacles.

Cap as Symbol

The historical shift of advancing technology and changing popular culture elements over the course of Gruenwald's run is worth considering with Captain America because of the unique status of this character as a symbol. Gruenwald is attempting to shape and refine a character who sees himself as a symbol as much as a person. Indeed, it is not simply the public-at-large or Cap's enemies that see him as a symbol—Cap himself acknowledges the same. Steve Rogers' humanity is tied inextricably to his role as a symbol. While perhaps an argument could be made for Superman and Wonder Woman also being symbolic in this regard, no Marvel hero is as synonymous with symbolism, and, significantly, no comic book hero is *more aware* of the significance of their symbolism than Captain America, especially under Gruenwald. In fact, one of Gruenwald's defining tropes on this title is his interest in figuring out where the symbol and man separate and where they ultimately meet. Cap himself embraces this question throughout the run, especially when changing his uniform after giving up the Captain America position due to government interference in his mission (a storyline that will be discussed in detail in Chapter Two and elsewhere). He stops being Captain America, but he finds another uniform, gets another shield, and continues his good fight, despite his color scheme changing temporarily from red, white, and blue to black, red, and white.

The idea of Captain America as symbol is not just dependent upon Steve Rogers' own perception of his worth but is also reflected in the way his enemies view him. To these villains, a confrontation with and potential victory over Captain America represents something symbolically significant. Cap is generally not just some random obstacle to stop their crimes; he is not a hero blocking a villain's objective. *He is the objective.* Flag-Smasher, a villain who is anti-nationalist and believes in the overthrow of all governments, regardless of the ideology of that government, in order to create a perfect and fully connected society, is one of Cap's most symbol-driven adversaries. In his first appearance in #312, Flag-Smasher explains, "I will bring [the world] the message of peace through world unity—even if I have to destroy every symbol of separatism on Earth!" (13). When he hears of a Captain America public appearance, he sees it as "a perfect opportunity to challenge the fool—and crush him and the ideals his stands for!" (11). For Flag-Smasher, the man behind the Captain America uniform is irrelevant.[4] For Flag-Smasher, what matters about Captain America is the symbolism and ideology Cap represents. Superia, a villain who believes that men are inferior and women should take over the world, also discusses Cap in these symbolic ways. In a conversation with Rachel Leighton (also known by her superhero/supervillain alias Diamondback), a reformed (at the time of this conversation in issue #433) criminal who has started a relationship with Cap, Superia tells her: "He sees himself as a symbol more than a man. As such, he will not let his symbolism be compromised by too close an association with contaminating elements—like you!" (15). This works in a couple of ways—first, Superia is playing mind games with Diamondback over Diamondback's insecurities about how her past crimes and indiscretions will never let her be worthy of a genuine romantic relationship with Cap. Superia is genuine about her perceptions of Cap as symbol. The idea of Cap as "symbol more than a man" is something that Cap's villains often understand better than his allies (because these villains, too, are typically more symbol than people, at least under Gruenwald's creative lead).

Captain America has constant interior monologues throughout the series in which he personally attempts to assess his own humanity in the face of the symbolism he so clearly recognizes within his persona. He is also unafraid to note his awareness of his own symbolism—and his ownership of the importance of that symbolism to himself and his country—to others. After first hearing Super-Patriot John Walker speak ill of Captain America at a patriotic rally in issue #323, Steve Rogers follows him and subsequently confronts him about his intentions while Walker is having dinner at an upscale restaurant. During this verbal confrontation, both men are out of their symbolic uniforms though Steve Rogers wears a red and blue tie, managing to still one-up his rival in terms of symbolism. Even without the red, white, and blue uniform, Rogers is attempting to directly take the symbolic advantage in this confrontation by wearing the tie. Rogers explains to Walker that "being a symbol of liberty and justice is something you have to earn" (18). He follows that up by telling Walker, "If you want to be a symbol of America, you'd darn well better be worthy of it" (19). He is building up his own value by emphasizing what he has personally earned the right to wear and do, and also disparaging Super-Patriot who, in Cap's mind, is an empty uniform and, potentially, a criminal staging attacks to increase his own reputation (which is ultimately proven to be true). The rivalry between these characters, though it does become physical, is very much a war of symbolic intentions.

The adherence to symbolism in the character of Captain America and his eponymous comic can be easily misinterpreted by those who either do not read the comics clearly or, of course, at all. He can be easily dismissed as a propaganda tool, a fact that is assuredly true in his origins, but something the character objectively outgrows. After all, the flag-inspired outfit and patriotic moniker can immediately repel an audience who assumes that Captain America is a character who serves as a right-wing tool. Peter Drier and Dick Flacks explain in their essay "Patriotism and Progressivism" (speaking mostly of a perception in effect since the 1960s): "It has become conventional wisdom that conservatives wave the American flag while leftists burn it. Patriotic Americans display the flag on their homes; progressives turn it upside down to show contempt" (39). American conservative politicians have long attempted to use patriotism to counter what they have determined is a lack of dedication by their political opponents to the nation's symbolic ideals. Ronald Reagan, the first of the three presidents who served during Gruenwald's run, said, "Republicans believe every day is the Fourth of July, but the Democrats believe every day is April 15." This is reiterating a well-established talking point (and equally well-established belief in certain political circles) that Republicans care about freedoms and liberties while Democrats just want to frivolously spend tax dollars.

From this perspective, patriotism is a strategy; the person most willing to display their patriotism through visible symbolism or rhetoric is the one who is most dedicated to their country. In other words, the loudest and most aggressive flag waving will reveal the clear "winner" amongst those attempting to show how much they love their country. Right-wing American politicians, especially since the 1960s, have attempted to politically *own* patriotism to demean the sincerity of the opposing party. This has become a more proliferated problem in the decades since Gruenwald's passing with the rise of meme culture and the internet, where "the American flag is frequently used to polarize and present the left as unpatriotic" (Grygiel). The internet is saturated with political images (and text) created for the purpose of being easily shared amongst politically like-minded social media users. One example of such a meme features a background of multiple flowing American flags against a bright blue sky with the statement "Are you an American or a Democrat" in bold, all uppercase letters. These types of memes often saturate certain corners of the internet with little indication of origins but a clear sense of purpose. The message of such a meme is obvious—the Republican party is patriotic and the Democratic party is anti–American. While *Captain America* rarely wades into truly partisan waters, Gruenwald certainly is willing to dip his toes inside.

Captain America's Politics

If a patriotic person is one who displays an American flag in front of their house, what is the unfathomable level of patriotism required to wear the flag in the form of a skintight battle uniform?[5] If public perception of patriotism leads us to believe that patriotic symbolism is analogous with the political right, then someone approaching a Captain America comic from this mentality would obviously assume that he would be a symbolic representation of this idea of American right-wing partisan political patriotism. During the 1980s, there was a movement in right-wing American politics to use "anti-elitist language of the past" to "promote their moral and nationalist agenda" (Bennett 399). The simplicity of a garishly-attired patriotic figure is something that could be easily co-opted into a symbol of that movement. Gruenwald knows this so he has to push Cap himself against the mentality. There is still a risk. The potential audience repelled by the thought of an unabashedly patriotic hero constantly espousing pro–America rhetoric will not read the comic, and the audience that would look for that type of character in these pages would potentially be disappointed, especially in the case of the aforementioned Super-Patriot who is presented as a more politically conservative patriotic superhero and is subsequently depicted as a villain, especially as he first debuts.[6] Walker's political leanings are clearly cemented during his first missions as Captain America (and he is also slowly becoming more heroic at those points, though it takes a while). At the very least, the symbolism of the Captain America character to less astute readers would tie him to a patriotism that not only embraces the United States in general but is linked more specifically to the American government.

Cap's politics have been a point of conversation for a long time, both for readers and, occasionally, within the stories themselves. For example, in *Captain America* #327, Paul, a law school colleague of Bernie Rosenthal's, broaches the topic of Cap's political leanings. He first posits the question as to whether or not Cap voted for Reagan. He then theorizes: "I believe that he did. I see Captain A as a staunch Republican-type with a militant conservative streaks down his back about a mile wide" (10). The comic itself does not take the theory very seriously. Paul is saying this as Steve Rogers arrives at their residence to meet Rosenthal. In the image from the comic, penciller Paul Neary draws Paul's speech bubble above Rogers' head as he enters the room, allowing Rogers to literally and symbolically ignore his words. Rosenthal then cuts off Paul dismissively: "Oh, enough with your nightly claptrap, Paul."

In his earliest return in the 1950s, Cap was written with this overly conservative approach. Before the Stan Lee 1960s reboot of the character, Cap and Bucky were depicted as anti-communist and this approach did not resonate with readers. Even after the '60s return of the character, he was still written as a more traditional character. As Richard J. Stevens observes in his book *Captain America, Masculinity, and Violence: The Evolution of a Nation Icon*, upon his rescue by the Avengers (in comics written in the early-to-mid 1960s), Cap is outwardly more conservative, advising the Avengers to pray for an injured Wasp in one adventure and otherwise "espousing his 1940s values freely" (85–6), something that was not resonating with members of the young comic audiences of the 1960s.

Stan Lee, therefore, does not stay content with this characterization, instead depicting a Captain America that looks inward to find his place in an increasingly volatile world. One of the key elements that led to a change in Cap's attitude and perspective came from reader responses that expressed interest in depicting Captain America as a liberal crusader rather than an adversary for communist and racist stereotypes. When Lee and Kirby started to include flashback 1940s stories in *Tales of Suspense*, a comic that preceded *Captain America* as a showcase for Cap's solo adventures, fans were critical (Steven 88). These letters proved to be ultimately influential in the philosophical journey the character would take.

Lee and Kirby began to make Cap more vocal in expressing liberalism in his dialogue and speeches. In *Captain America* #103 from July of 1968, the Red Skull discusses the "Master Race," and Rogers is quick to counter: "There is no Master Race—and you know it." He continues, "We're all human beings—all equal before our creator." Skull counters by shouting, "Equality! You fool—equality is a myth!" Rogers responds, "It's tyranny which is the myth—and bigotry—which is an abomination before the eyes of mankind!" (20–21). This dialogue exchange occurs in the midst of a fistfight between the two men, their words presenting their respective ideologies while their fists emphasize the spoken points. Rogers' statement of "and you know it" to Red Skull is an interesting inclusion. It is Rogers' way of calling out what he views as an insincerity to Skull's ideology. There is ultimately no point in these stories in which the readers doubt the dedication of Red Skull's adherence to Nazi bigotry and hate, but Rogers mocks him here.

Ultimately, Lee would pair Cap with The Falcon, an African American partner, and Cap frequently works with Falcon in the predominantly African American streets of Harlem (without depicting Cap as being uncomfortable in these environs). Cap's evolving conscience becomes a key part of the character that is heavily observed in the 1970s and beyond (into Gruenwald's time as writer). Ultimately, the frequent reader letters and calls for Cap to evolve "resulted in a transformed liberal crusader who participated in what would become a pattern of 'relevant comics' in the 1970s" (Stevens 100). While this type of political relevance is not as present by the mid–1980s, Gruenwald still carries on these character traits and conveys the innate thoughtfulness and constant deliberation present within the character.

"Like the Statue of Liberty…"

Captain America is very aware of the symbolic nature of his uniform, title, and role, but refuses to let others define who he is based on that. The comics themselves also refuse to depict him as a one-dimensional symbol of jingoism. The narrator in *Captain America* #323 (a previously referenced pivotal issue in which Steve Rogers first meets John Walker, the man who would eventually take over the role of Captain America), emphasizing the importance of comparing Rogers to Walker, describes Steve Rogers as Captain America as follows: "Like the Statue of Liberty, this man is a symbol of freedom and the American Dream. But this symbol is a living breathing man. His name is Captain America" (4). The key elements of this description are threefold. First, the significance of his symbolism is compared directly to that of the Statue of Liberty, a symbol with origins far removed from aggressive patriotism. Second, the specifics of Captain America's symbolism are identified as being about freedom and the American Dream. Finally, there is a clear irony between the concept of Captain America as a "living breathing man" and the reality of a fictional character as the audience reads him (and he is most certainly not a "living breathing man").

The plan for the statue began amongst a band of French thinkers including Édouard René de Laboulaye in 1865. Laboulaye was a passionate supporter of American liberty and "recognized the bond of a common love for liberty that existed between the people of France and the United States" (Gilder 10). The project was consummated by French admirers of American possibilities.

The Statue of Liberty is a convenient yet still intriguing place to anchor the concept of Cap's symbolism. At the statue's dedication in 1886, President Grover Cleveland remarked first on what the statue was not: "Unlike those statues 'representative of a fierce and warlike god, filled with wrath and vengeance ... we contemplate [in this statue] our own peaceful deity keeping watch before the open gates of America'" (qtd. in Khan 179). In addition to its power and scope, there is a serenity to the statue.

It is also a statue that is symbolically speaking directly to former slaves, the nation's most vulnerable—and, indeed, the world's most vulnerable—in order to give them hope. While the narrative of welcoming immigrants is a valid perspective on the statue's purpose, the statue itself was created post–Civil War to provide a beacon of hope for freed slaves and the statue serving as a beacon to immigrants was a later phenomenon (Brockell). At its development and construction, the statue celebrated "100 years of independence and the Union victory in the Civil War. Its message of freedom for all citizens, particularly former slaves [was] reinforced by the broken shackles that lie at Lady Liberty's feet" (Greene 22). As Bertrand Dard writes about Liberty, "Yet the core symbolism of Liberty survives intact.... Liberty is the premier monumental icon of modern times" (Dillon and Kotler 71). In those "modern times," the statue was revitalized. Between 1982 and 1986, the Statue of Liberty underwent a process of renovation: "A team of French and American architects, engineers, and conservators came together to determine what was needed to ensure the Statue's preservation into the next century" ("Restoring the Statue"). Therefore, at the onset of Gruenwald's time on the comic, Liberty was in the midst of being literally strengthened (which assuredly also strengthened the power of its symbolism). Using the Statue of Liberty in the mid–1980s is a powerful symbol because this preservation was clear in the public's mind and the Statue of Liberty's literal strength was at its peak.

Emma Lazarus' poem "The New Colossus" is engraved upon the base of the statue and its words, though added later, have become synonymous with the statue's meaning over time (in fact, defining the twentieth-century-and-beyond interpretation of the statue):

> Not like the brazen giant of Greek fame,
> With conquering limbs astride from land to land;
> Here at our sea-washed, sunset gates shall stand
> A mighty woman with a torch, whose flame
> Is the imprisoned lightning, and her name
> Mother of Exiles. From her beacon-hand

Glows world-wide welcome; her mild eyes command
The air-bridged harbor that twin cities frame.
"Keep, ancient lands, your storied pomp!" cries she
With silent lips. "Give me your tired, your poor,
Your huddled masses yearning to breathe free,
The wretched refuse of your teeming shore.
Send these, the homeless, tempest-tost to me,
I lift my lamp beside the golden door!" (qtd. in "The New Colossus")

Lazarus was a supporter of socialist policies who wrote those lines "as an effort to project an inclusive and egalitarian definition of the American dream" (Drier and Flacks 40). The statue was dedicated in 1886; Lazarus' poem was added in 1903.[7] This correlation between a statue that symbolizes unity with France and an embrace of immigrants, and a World War II soldier who fought in France for global liberation is important.

The statue is a symbol of patriotism that may emanate from New York City but shines much farther. It is speaking to all Americans, regardless of their place in society. It is also a symbol to the world at large of American decency and its willingness to protect. For Gruenwald, it is important to depict Captain America as a similar beacon—one that protects and supports Americans, but also serves as an idealization of liberty to those outside the nation.

"This man is a symbol of freedom and the American Dream"

The second key to that above description of Cap is the specification of what Captain America actually stands for: "freedom and the American Dream." The definition of both of these concepts are wrestled with throughout Gruenwald's run (and toward the end of the run, Cap certainly faces disillusion in regard to how well he has served to symbolize these qualities), but it is significant that this symbolism is not representative of American military might or even some concept of American exceptionalism, defined as "the notion that the United States is not only qualitatively different from other states but it is morally superior" (Forsythe and McMahon 16). Instead, it is freedom.

For Cap, freedom is a concept that dictates everything else he does. For example, Cap is unwilling to use guns.[8] His reason is related directly to seeing the use of guns as a violation of freedoms. In issue #321, Cap is forced to use an enemy's gun in order to stop a terrorist from further firing into the crowd (23). In issue #322, Cap thinks, "You'll notice everybody around here uses guns except me. I believe that guns are for killing, and killing is the ultimate violation of individual rights—the ultimate denial of freedom. I never carry a gun. I have never taken another person's life" (5). Cap does not believe in the murder of others for a very specific reason and that reason is not directly addressing morality—instead, Cap is against murder because it is the "ultimate denial" of freedom.

There are multiple interpretations of freedom that help elucidate Cap's perspective. Philosopher Michel Foucault "says goodbye to the modern/romantic notion of freedom as liberation from power through truth about our authentic selves" (Virisova 68). For Cap, like Foucault, absence of bondage is not what defines freedom. Freedom is not a "liberation from power," but a new and greater form of power. Foucault describes "free subjects" as "individual or collective subjects who are faced with a field of possibilities in which several ways of behaving, several reactions and diverse comportments, may be realized" (qtd. in Golob 676). Freedom is action, reaction, and behaviors. It is also about finding myriad ways of exploring those actions and reactions. Life is the ultimate freedom. Gruenwald's Cap strives obsessively to not take the freedom of life from anyone else. As philosopher George W. Morgan writes, "Freedom belongs to the person and can be known only by an approach that respects the person" (323). Freedom, for Cap, is not an individualist philosophy but a philosophy that understands the need for everyone's freedom, including but not limited to one's own. Cap's sense of freedom is communal, not individualistic.

The other aspect of his symbolism, according to the above quote, is that Captain America is representing the "American Dream." This is a concept riddled with vagueness and, often, political motivation thanks to the troubling conceit of the aforementioned American Exceptionalism (and the racism and sexism potentially inherent within that). The pursuit of the American Dream is also, perhaps, a tool to keep the impoverished content by providing the possibility (though not the promise) that the have-nots will someday join the haves. Lawrence Samuel, in his book *The American Dream: A Cultural History*, explains that the most "significant" thing about the American Dream is that it does not exist in any specific and detailed form (1). It has no traits that are consistent in every individual's perception of it. Therefore, people can make it whatever they need it to be, though, perhaps, it ends up fueling inadequacy as much as motivation.

Despite its fluidity, the American Dream is still something most Americans see as central to their personal narratives, though Americans also see it as threatened—a 2019 RealClearPolitics poll found that only 27 percent of Americans saw the American Dream as "alive and well" for "them personally," while the rest of those surveyed found it either threatened or already dead. When the question was asked in regard to younger generations, only 21 percent saw it as alive and well for those younger individuals. Despite these low numbers, 69 percent of Americans saw the American Dream as still obtainable "if they work hard" ("RealClear Opinion Research"). Americans are cynical about the American Dream as something that future generations will likely not reach but optimistic about the potential for it to be achieved overall. It is a contradiction, but a contradiction built on faith.

As Samuel continues: "No idea or mythology—not even religion, I believe—has as much influence on our individual and collective lives" as does the American Dream (2). The pull of the American Dream is something affecting Americans and their ambitions in ways they likely do not understand. Considering the overarching significance of the concept (and its natural fit with the character of Captain America), it is no surprise that Gruenwald incorporates it into the comic as much as he does. Taking Samuel's lead of thinking of mythology, other Marvel comics deal with classics and mythology to engage in their mythmaking—some of Cap's fellow Avengers include Thor (of Norse Mythology) and Hercules (of Greek Mythology). Following this influence of classical themes, the idea of myth creation through the American Dream to educate a superhero character is a logical fit. According to Hollywood executive and screenwriter Christopher Vogler, "A myth is a story that tells of a holy intrusion. And that holiness is charged with the idealized qualities of the sacred world." In the pages of Gruenwald's *Captain America*, that "holiness" is a pure form of the American Dream (with an awareness that the American Dream is still something that can be corrupted for political gain).

In these pages, this "holiness" is not explicitly Christian. While Cap has been depicted in various stories and media as Christian—upon seeing Thor and Loki in 2012 *Marvel's Avengers* film, Chris Evans as Captain America tells Black Widow, "There's only one God, ma'am, and I'm pretty sure he doesn't dress like that"—but Gruenwald's Cap is not as overt. There are moments of spiritual reflection, especially as he is facing his seemingly inevitable death in the "Fighting Chance" storyline and its epilogue (issues #425–443), and his preferred expression of surprise is "God and Country!" but his faith is a minor element at best in Gruenwald's hands. In fact, in issue #383, Cap meets John Henry (and more about this issue will be discussed below) while Cap is in pursuit of a strange costumed figure. John Henry tells him to "climb to the top 'o creation" and Cap immediately thinks of Moses, eventually asking Henry, "Is.... God at the top of these mountains?" John Henry's answer reveals the religious leanings of Gruenwald's work: "No, suh. The land is everywhere" (14). God is not at the end of a specific journey. The land *is* the journey. The American landscape, and not Christianity,[9] is the fabric of faith in the reality of these books. The mythology is built on the American Dream to the point that Captain America is specifically identified as a symbol for that Dream. The American landscape (and Cap's interpretation of the American Dream possible within that landscape) is the spirituality of these comics.

Gruenwald is not interested in any simplistic expression of the Dream that reflects a desire for basic money or power. Cap, considering the way he and the guise of Captain America are viewed, recognizes the American Dream as the main point of what he symbolizes. In issue #322, Cap thinks,

> I'm just one man. One man who's dedicated his life to the ideals of freedom, justice, and equality. Some folks misunderstand me. They think I represent the American government, its political system, or its official policies. I don't. I represent the American Dream—the notion that human beings should have the opportunity to their lives and attain their noblest aspirations [3].

To Cap, the American Dream is relatively modest. It's about "opportunity" and "nobility." It is not about money (at least not directly), nor is it about living in a big house on a hill overlooking everyone else. It is in no way about American Exceptionalism. He is a symbol, not of potential of wealth or power, but of the need for opportunity and decency.

Legendary America

This idea of Captain America as a vessel of symbolic mythmaking is featured often and in significant ways. Issue #383 from 1991 (celebrating Captain America's Fiftieth Anniversary as a character) features a surreal story in which Captain America stumbles upon an elderly costumed figure who goads Cap into chasing him into a different dimension—one with an inaccurate (something Cap himself acknowledges) American landscape that is populated with figures of American mythology. As Cap journeys through this landscape looking for the costumed man (who identifies as Father Time), he meets mythical figures beginning with one based on a real person (Johnny Appleseed) and then several who are completely fictional (culminating with Uncle Sam).

In their eventual meeting, Uncle Sam explains that Cap and all of these other American figures from myth (Appleseed, Pecos Bill, the aforementioned John Henry, Paul Bunyan, and Uncle Sam) have a significant shared ethos: "we take hold of the American public's imagination, embody a specific heroic archetype, and assume mythic stature" (19). This places Cap in the same status of myth as these archetypes.[10] In the same conversation, Uncle Sam reveals the identity of the strange place where Cap has found himself. He explains, "This here's Legendary America, the place where the American Dream is a reality, where heroes live forever, and heroes become legends" (19). Uncle Sam sees the place as a positive; Cap is less willing to do so.

Father Time attempts to persuade Cap to stay through rhetoric first and then violence, but Cap refuses. Cap sees Legendary America as a retirement home, and he makes it clear he is not ready for retirement. Ultimately, the legitimacy of the place itself is questioned, as is everything that occurs there. When Cap leaves Legendary America, he arrives in his real world and he finds fellow Avenger Hawkeye is the one dressed in Father Time's costume. Accordingly, Cap is not sure if any of the experience actually happened. Whether Legendary America is a real experience or is simply a strange dream is left unrevealed, but if it *is* a figment created entirely in Cap's imagination, then it clearly establishes that Cap sees himself as a mythical figure and an embodiment of the American Dream (which he frequently makes clear), but is not yet willing to forgo his physical presence, humanity, and usefulness to fully embrace that role of myth. If Cap does indeed see himself as a figure of mythical importance, it means he himself acknowledges that his long-term notoriety is going to be tied to his symbol, not his humanity. Cap is aware that future generations might not realize he was a real person at all. By consciously leaving Legendary America, Cap makes it clear that he is not fully ready for the fate of being a myth, though he understands its inevitability.

To take it further (and to return to a discussion of Christianity), a Holy Trinity can further explain the character's relationship with his mythos and duty. To borrow Christian language, the title and mythos of Captain America is the Father"; Steve Rogers, the human (thus potentially fallible) person who fills that mythical costume, is the "Son"; and the Holy Ghost is the "American Dream," a spiritual concept that can mean something different to so many people. While Rogers, the man, is desperate to promote his conception of the American Dream, the presence of the "Father" here makes it difficult. The presence of "Captain America" as a mythical concept dictates his actions even when Steve Rogers, the man, just wants to do tangible good in the world.

"But this symbol is a living breathing man"

The third part of relevance in the narrator's quote from issue #323 about Captain America as a symbol is that he is a "living, breathing man." In the world of the comics, this is obviously factual and crucial. He is a symbol, certainly, but he is not a museum piece or legend found in the pages of a book (as are those figures he encounters in Legendary America)—he is an active costumed adventurer who attempts to benefit the lives of real people through his heroics. In this universe, literal threats appear constantly, and Cap and other heroes are always there to stop them. This act of "living [and] breathing" makes him something other than an artifact—he is a tangible and essential piece of life in the Marvel Comics Universe. Earth-616, the name designated for the primary Marvel Comics timeline (and the Earth of these adventures), is not our Earth. He serves as a role model to many people, a friend and ally to others, and a flesh and blood human being.

To the reader, however, he is not a "living, breathing man." He is already a character found in the pages of a book (to the reader, he's already achieved the myth status promised in Legendary America). The relationship a reader has with Captain America is different than the relationship that occurs between Cap and the people he saves and otherwise interacts with within these pages. Readers are asked to see the character as living flesh and blood but, obviously, he is not flesh and blood. In his world, Cap has to emphasize his symbolism because that is something his status as a "living, breathing" person can work to undermine. For the benefit of our world, Gruenwald has to reinforce Cap as a decision-making character because his symbolism is where readers would default to seeing him as a character.

Patriotism: New vs. Old

While Steve Rogers is the primary Captain America during Gruenwald's run, John Walker also holds the moniker for a significant number of issues. While Walker's aggressive (though seemingly sincere) brand of patriotism will be examined in more detail in Chapter Three (and elsewhere), it is important, while considering the symbolism inherent within this title, to note that Rogers and Walker are both obsessively focused on their personal symbolism. Before Walker is tapped by the U.S. government to become the new Captain America in issue #332, he dubs himself the Super-Patriot and attempts to usurp Captain America as the nation's heroic symbol.

In issue #327, prior to giving a speech at a Farm-Aid type event (as mentioned above), Walker (in uniform as Super-Patriot) is asked why he wears a mask. Super-Patriot responds that the mask protects his anonymity, not as a means of protecting those close to him (as is often the reason superheroes would give), but to protect his *symbolism*. Walker says, "with my face showing, I'm an individual. Masked, I'm a symbol of the patriotic spirit that unites all of the individuals in this, the greatest country on God's earth" (12). Steve Rogers would see this as a reasonable response. While Rogers has friends and loved ones, he does not have a family to protect in the way that others do, including Walker.[11] Rogers is not as obsessive about protecting his alias (he unmasks on several occasions, though he does not often compromise his civilian identity), and Walker's explanation helps inform that, for both of these characters, concealing identity has more to do with symbolism than practicality.

When pressed about the presence of Captain America as an already established national symbol in #327, Walker dismisses Rogers as an "old has-been" and says, "he's hardly fit to be a symbol of the [sic] social security!" (12). His self-congratulatory language and his derisive insults of Rogers are all symbol-related (and ageist, recognizing generational shifts discussed in Chapter Four). As in our world, symbolism is inescapable in this fictional world, both in regard to Captain America and his rivals. Everyone embraces what they symbolize and lets that define them. But this symbolism cannot emerge solely from internal perception. As Michel Foucault writes in *The Order of Things*, "The relation of representation to itself, and the relations of order it becomes possible to determine apart from all quantitative forms of measurement, now pass through conditions exterior to the actuality of representation itself" (237). The thing (or person) being represented gains value from outside perceptions. The interior and exterior are equally essential. Captain America needs the exterior world to help cement that symbolism.

Humanity Within Symbolism

This emphasis on symbolism should function to deemphasize his humanity, but this is not what occurs within these pages. Generally, a writer reveals the humanity of a superhero character by highlighting the person behind the costume. For example, a reader cares about Spider-Man primarily because the reader cares about Peter Parker, the awkward yet appealing kid trying to balance the two worlds in which he occupies. Gruenwald does a unique thing in these pages, however—while the writers prior to him on *Captain America* did try to humanize him by giving Steve Rogers a job in advertising and a non-superpowered girlfriend (Bernie Rosenthal), Gruenwald slowly pulls Steve Rogers out of faking a place in the real world. The reality of Steve Rogers is that he is, in no way, a normal person. Instead, that relationship with Rosenthal dissolves because of his too-frequent absences (and her personal ambitions to change the world), Rogers moves out of his apartment, leaves the advertising business, and occupies his time by starting that aforementioned hotline where people all over the country can reach him with their Cap-worthy problems. Instead of having a romantic partner who is more comfortable in the civilian world, Cap's main love interest during Gruenwald's run is a fellow costumed adventurer. Diamondback (Rachel Leighton), a member of the villainous Serpent Society, who works to convince Cap that she can be reformed from her criminal past.[12] Basically, what Gruenwald does is dull the division between Rogers and Captain America.

In a particularly meta move, Rogers' artistic job after leaving advertising is as a comic artist—on *Captain America*. This gives even the real-life alter ego a job that still depends upon Captain America. There is no separation between Rogers and Captain America, not in the way we are accustomed to thinking of alter-egos in comics. A reader would see, for example, Bruce Wayne as the "real" person and Batman as the identity he adopts to protect the city, and many have argued that Superman is the "real" person in that situation and Clark Kent is the false identity Superman creates in order to easily navigate the human world. Quentin Tarantino's Bill (played by David Carradine) explains this perspective on Superman in *Kill Bill, Vol. 2*:

> I find the whole mythology surrounding superheroes fascinating. Take my favorite superhero, Superman. Not a great comic book, not particularly well-drawn ... but the mythology. The mythology is not great, it's unique.... Now, a staple of the superhero mythology is, there's the superhero and there's the alter-ego. Batman is actually Bruce Wayne, Spider-Man is actually Peter Parker. When that character wakes up in the morning, he's Peter Parker. He has to put on a costume to become Spider-Man. And it is in that characteristic Superman stands alone. Superman didn't become Superman. Superman was born Superman. When Superman wakes up in the morning, he's Superman. His alter ego is Clark Kent. His outfit, with the big red "S," that's the blanket he was wrapped in as a baby when the Kents found him. Those are his clothes. What Kent wears—the glasses, the business suit—that's the costume. That's the costume Superman wears to blend in with us.

Captain America is unique. There's no real difference, ultimately, between Steve Rogers and Captain America. When Bruce Wayne dons the cowl of Batman, he sees the world differently in part because of the way the world sees him. But for Steve Rogers, Captain America is simply who he is. Unlike Superman, Steve Rogers is who he is too. "Steve Rogers" is not an effort to blend into society. It is just an equal part of who he is.

Gruenwald knew this better than any writer that preceded him. Steve Rogers is not a man who needs to find footing in the real world. Gruenwald, being a writer so unflinchingly dedicated to maintaining an organic connection to the comics that preceded issue #307, is conscious and faithful to arcs and character beats in place before his arrival, though not to a narrative fault (Gruenwald writes out Nomad, Cap's partner, in his first year as writer, but not before giving him a couple of issues where he is the primary protagonist, thus explaining why he decides to leave his role as sidekick). Gruenwald rushes nothing and achieves his goals in ways that feel natural and earned (and never plodding). He does not simply write out Bernie Rosenthal in an issue or two (though her departure is arguably premeditated). He lets the life of Captain America that Steve Rogers has chosen to prioritize get in the way of the relationship. Eventually, Cap moves into the Avengers Mansion and spends most of his free time in training. Gruenwald's Rogers prioritizes Captain America because that is who Rogers most clearly is.

Ultimately, saying that Steve Rogers is Captain America and Captain America is Steve Rogers is too simple. Much will be discussed in Chapter Two about the story arc that sees Steve Rogers voluntarily give up the role of Captain America, but even that event does not stop him from continuing his role as a protector. As per the arrangement made when he walks away from being Captain America, the government does not allow him to wear any red, white, and blue suit or use the name "Captain America." Rogers agrees. He dons a black uniform that is very similar to the original and, instead of calling himself "Captain America," he goes simply by the moniker of "The Captain." Rogers is not simply Captain America (or vice-versa). Rogers is instead a hero whose passion for the role of hero for the people he has sworn to protect transcends mere titles and uniforms. The symbolism is rampant, obviously, in the Captain America uniforms and moniker. But for Steve Rogers, the symbolism emanates from within. Again, repeating Rogers' words to Super-Patriot: "being a symbol of liberty and justice is something you have to earn." For Rogers, this symbolism is not something that happens by simply putting on a suit—it is what is radiating from the person inside. Because of this, he can make even the Captain's black suit resonate with symbolism.

Captain America is a symbol, certainly, but that symbolism is more than just a representation of people and the American Dream. There's a textual symbolism based on the character and his relationship with the fictional world he occupies. For readers, he symbolizes a type of character that resonates because of a deliberateness of moral motive. He symbolizes a persona that others can trust and believe in. He does not embody what is possible for even the most well-intentioned human because the feats that Gruenwald chronicles in his decade at the helm of this series are not reproducible in our real world. He does, however, symbolize something of the potential of the human spirit, even if not the body (again, thinking of the Holy Trinity as it can apply to Rogers' relationship with the role of Captain America). For Mark Gruenwald, what Captain America symbolizes most, beyond those things emblazoned upon his costume and shield, is the inherent good that is possible by simply recognizing the value of being alive.

Two

Captain Un-America-ed
Steve Rogers and Positive Patriotism

The cover of *Captain America* #332 is not interested in subtleties. This pivotal issue, in which Steve Rogers hands the literal uniform and shield (and the symbolism that goes along with them) to the United States government and declines their rigid offer to remain in service as Captain America, is a fascinating look at what drives Steve Rogers as Captain America, especially when paired with the insight of the ongoing Cold War, the events that follow for Steve Rogers in the comic (including the adoption of a new costumed identity), and a comparison to a previous *Captain America* storyline from 1974 by Steve Englehart in which Rogers makes a similar decision (but for significantly different reasons). In addition to character motivations in both storylines, the most significant differences lie in the eras in which the stories are created. Life and politics in the Reagan era unquestionably create a different canvas for Gruenwald to shape his Captain America stories than did Nixon's 1970s for Englehart, and connecting Captain America's motivations to the Reagan era is an essential part of understanding Gruenwald's work on this comic.

Michael Zeck's cover of #332 depicts Captain America, head down, hands open and empty, standing in front of a massive reimagined version of the American flag. Cap's head is low and his posture is slumping. The reader can see most of the "A" on his cowl, but not all of it, and his eyes are virtually blocked. His posture tells much of the story and, for a character who never wavers on proper posture, the slumped shoulders indicate a broken man. He is positioned differently than the reader would be accustomed to finding him. He is looking down at his hands, empty, and holding his shield. Each hand is turned toward the other, as if his hands are looking for something but finding nothing. The flag behind him features tattered stripes that tear behind him and then remain tattered on the floor. The red stripes are the ones in tatters and, as they continue down his body, they transform into blood, oozing around Cap, slightly pooling around his feet. The blood imagery of the cover indicates nothing literal in the issue but further establishes the inherent dread within. The title on the cover contains not only the title of the comic in its standard (at the time) font and size, but also, in the same font and size, the words "NO MORE!" to further emphasize the dark and foreboding tone. This is an issue promising something decisive and narrative-altering. Indeed, it fulfills that promise.

If readers are still not *completely* sure about how they are supposed to be feeling here, the box in the upper left-hand corner that contains the price, issue number, etc., and the typical picture of the hero (or heroes) for a given title provides another clue. In this case, the image of a smiling Captain America actively bounding toward the reader[1] has been replaced with a portrait of Abraham Lincoln, colorized but otherwise identical to his portrait on a five-dollar bill. Unlike the image on the bill, however, in this cover image, Lincoln is shedding a single tear. Clearly, the sense of dread and sadness of the main cover image of a downtrodden Captain America is reinforced everywhere else of note on the cover too. Again, none of this is particularly subtle, but the storyline that is progressing in this issue is not propelled by subtlety—instead, it is an exploration of what drives Steve Rogers and, as his government is pushing against him, what shapes his view of patriotism as one who supports his country but can still question that country's government without becoming so disillusioned that he cannot act in a way that benefits society.

The main crisis within this issue happens in three locales: a seedy hotel (all a suddenly financially compromised Steve Rogers can afford), Rogers' mind as he debates the decision, and in a hearing room in Washington D.C., where literally elevated government officials look down upon Captain America and threaten him with regulations and highly restrictive contracts. While there's a secondary plot that involves Super-Patriot stopping a terrorist on the Washington Monument (and that will be discussed in Chapter Three), the most crucial moving pieces of the issue involve the decision Rogers must make. That decision—whether to remain Captain America and allow the government to maintain a stricter set of regulations (and coordination of his missions) or give up the shield and uniform to be free of government oversight (while possibly being labeled as a vigilante by the government)—is one that not only dictates the direction of *Captain America* over the eighteen issues that follow before the status quo is returned but also gives us significant insight into the type of patriotism that Gruenwald is promoting. Steve Rogers' brand of Cold War patriotism is the stuff of symbol and, as a symbol, he would rather walk away from the Captain America uniform than let the symbol he has worked so hard to embody become sullied by undesirable actions he is forced to take. In time, he ultimately learns that the symbolic damage done to the reputation of the title of Captain America can indeed be undone (and he takes his rightful place as Captain America after John Walker is forced out), but he himself cannot bear to be the one personally sullying that reputation (as he fears going on government-sanctioned missions would do).

Steve Rogers Without Captain America

When using the word "symbol" here, it is important to think of it as an internalized motif for Rogers. He knows that this government committee that has so callously forced him into this decision will find a replacement Captain America and Rogers will have no control over who that person will be or how they will function. He knows that handing over the shield will lead toward another person in this role and that person could potentially harm this symbolism. In fact, in issue #332, when going through the problems with stepping away from the title of Captain America, he states that "worst of all, I'd have to deal with the fact that someone else was in my uniform, using my shield and name" (16). In the image that accompanies the text, penciller Tom Morgan draws a scene with Steve Rogers (with an amazed look on his face accentuated by a burst of pink emanating from his head) standing in the background watching as another Cap—specifically here an African American man—lunges across the forefront, wearing the Captain America uniform with shield in hand. Gruenwald's Steve Rogers is never bothered by race and the hypothetical replacement's race is likely a tool of convenience, designed to not too closely parallel the look of Rogers as Cap (or give away the next issue's reveal of John Walker's appointment as the replacement Cap). The most important aspect of the moment is that Rogers sees a replacement as the "worst" part of his potential surrender of the Captain America role.

Ultimately in the storyline, Rogers is less bothered by the reality of another person in the uniform than he likely expected, mostly ignoring Walker's Captain America at first. Eventually, the two cross paths and he cannot ignore him any longer, but that is not the case at first. The nation is large enough—and has enough problems—for them to exist separately, at least for a while. While Rogers is aware that someone else is Captain America, he is mostly nonplussed. In *Captain America* #336, the first post–Cap appearance of Rogers, Gruenwald and penciller Morgan depict him in a bar with a television playing the news in the background with the newscaster's text informing the reader of John Walker Captain America's most recent mission (2–4). Gruenwald gives the reader no sign of what Rogers is thinking. He is able to accept his transitioning role from Captain America to a differently named and garbed crimefighter with relative ease. It does not take long for Steve Rogers to know that what matters about Captain America is within him personally, not the suit and shield, though the suit and shield make conveying that sentiment to others easier.

President Reagan and the Iran-Contra Affair

Rogers sees himself as symbol both in and out of the uniform and having to undertake government-sanctioned missions himself would, in his mind, sully the symbolism that he himself emanates (regardless of the uniform's design). Again, Rogers feels the damage done to Captain America's reputation could be overcome; damage done to his own moral compass could not. So he is willing to risk the symbolic damage done to the Captain America title by another person, as opposed to choosing to end his personal mission of protecting the country. From a practical perspective, he would also be less able to operate under his own volition; thus, he would have less direct impact on the American people if forced to work for a government that has not maintained his trust.

While the Iran-Contra affair is not discussed in specific terms in *Captain America*, when issue #332 issue was published in the summer of 1987, Oliver North was testifying in front of a joint session of Congress on his role in the affair, a scandal that was casting a "negative pall over the Reagan administration" (Rosenberg). President Reagan publicly denied any wrongdoing in the Iran-Contra situation and defended the deals made by the U.S. Government on moral grounds. The American public was decidedly skeptical of his responses: "Polls showed that only 14 percent of Americans believed the president when he said he had not traded arms for hostages" ("The Iran Contra Affair"). There was nationwide distrust of the American government and this was the political landscape that existed while Gruenwald was writing about Steve Rogers' decision. Even though Reagan himself is ultimately revealed not to be involved in the decision to oust Rogers in the comics (though the implication as of issue #332 is that he might be), this reality of the public's perception of the Reagan administration's perceived corruption was clearly in Gruenwald's mind as he constructed the storyline.

It is in Rogers' head too—while, indeed, Reagan is not involved in the master plan to strip Rogers of the uniform and shield, Rogers imagines Reagan is indeed behind the machinations in a dream shown in #339 (4–6). In the dream sequence, Rogers sees himself in the Captain America uniform fighting a giant man wearing "an immaculate three-piece suit" while being watched by the Commission (the group that forced him out as Captain America). The narration notes that the fight is taking place in the government chamber where he resigned being Captain America, calling it "the scene of his greatest loss." The giant (drawn and inked by Kieron Dwyer and Tony Dezuniga to have eyes that are mostly black and undefined, creating further menace) is supernaturally infused, stripping Rogers first of his shield and later his uniform.[2] When Cap sees his black and white "Captain" uniform, he attempts to put it on but is attacked by the giant who shoots literal "red tape" from his fingers. Rogers claws at the giant's face to first find Ronald Reagan and then, after additional clawing, Rogers' own face. This dream sequence reveals Rogers' fears of bureaucratic cover-ups and conspiracies, thus subconsciously allowing himself to blame Reagan before giving himself the blame by seeing himself as the ultimate villain.[3]

Several issues later, Rogers engages in a fight with the President when Reagan is depicted as an innocent pawn in Viper's plan to turn all Americans into mindless snakes in issue #344. The creative team's willingness to depict even a controlled and manipulated Reagan in a negative light is shown through the cover's designation of the snake version of Reagan as "the deadliest snake of all," a statement much bolder and more politically pointed at Reagan than anything conveyed within the issue itself. Rogers never fully believes that Reagan is behind his troubles with the Commission (and he is proven correct), but he both subconsciously feels it could be true (as conveyed by the dream sequence in #339) and is willing to engage in physical conflict with the devolved and savage snake-version of the president when left with no other choice.

Rogers' Decision Making

This period of Gruenwald's run is very much defined by the choices Rogers must make. The decision to decline the government's offer to continue under the Captain America mantle while operating under greater governmental control is not the only decision Rogers makes during this point in Gruenwald's tenure. There are two other decisions that occur prior to that one and, to a reader accustomed to Cap's very clear moral code, the ultimate decisions he makes in each case are predictable, but the amount of internal deliberation is not. In #321, while overseas, Cap uses a terrorist's gun to stop another terrorist from firing into the crowd of hostages. In doing so, he kills the gunman and saves the hostages (albeit with a massive moral crisis over his actions).

In #323, after he and S.H.I.E.L.D. (known at the time as "Supreme Headquarters, International Espionage, Law-enforcement Division,"[4] Marvel's main espionage/peacekeeping organization) have fully stopped the terrorist organization known as U.L.T.I.M.A.T.U.M.[5] in those previous issues, he is debriefed by S.H.I.E.L.D. on his situation. Cap is shown a newspaper with a headline that reads, "Captain America Guns Down Terrorist" and is told further that, unlike the S.H.I.E.L.D. agents, he is not sanctioned to participate in these types of international incidents (and was observed by witnesses as doing so). Therefore, this incident is not just a potential blemish that forces the public to reconsider how Cap operates; it could also become an international incident where Captain America would stand trial for manslaughter. S.H.I.E.L.D.'s Jasper Sitwell presents a deal in which Cap would formally join S.H.I.E.L.D. and, by "fudging the dates," be officially recognized as an agent prior to the event, thus being removed from culpability as a result of S.H.I.E.L.D.'s globally granted flexibility (8). The suggestion is perhaps unethical, but it would solve a serious potential problem.

Cap eventually says no, but this is not a decision quickly reached. This contemplation is surprising considering the consistent moral unambiguity with which he sees the world (and a reader would assume this would be challenged by Sitwell's morally questionable suggestion of "fudging the numbers"). He internally debates the matter, recognizing the potential benefit of joining S.H.I.E.L.D., but it is ultimately his concern with having to leave the Avengers and give up his hotline that allows him to talk himself out of it (these are also factors that he considers when he contemplates stepping down as Cap nine issues later). His decision is not directly related to the moral challenges of S.H.I.E.L.D.'s offer but is instead dictated by heroic practicality. He is operating in a world of emerging challenges and is unwilling to risk leaving Americans unprotected. While a noble explanation, the time it takes to reach this conclusion is uncharacteristic. A reader would think he would quickly say no because the alternative would be dishonest. In addition, if he joined S.H.I.E.L.D. under these conditions, Rogers' commitment to his own symbolism would be violated because he would be working for an organization more covert and more willing to bend the rules than the Avengers.

Similarly, a few issues later, Cap is investigating how the Super-Patriot and his allies have received their remarkable strength. He finds an organization that uses a risky and inorganic method to give individuals extraordinary strength. In issue #328, Cap is captured and placed into one of the augmenting machines from which Super-Patriot, Cap's occasional partner D–Man, and others have received their extraordinary strength. Cap is left indefinitely in this machine so that he would grow so unnaturally large that eventually his muscles would explode. He escapes before that fate befalls him (thanks to a timely rescue from D–Man), and he gains some increased strength. The strength enhancement he has been granted from the augmentation machine is revealed to be temporary unless the process is continued.

Cap does ponder whether or not he should continue the treatment to increase his power, thus being able to keep us with the super-strong types he had been running into (specifically Super-Patriot). He admits that his "first impulse is to go for it," but ultimately decides, "if nothing's broke, why fix it?" (21). In issue #329, Cap discovers the remarkable risk of the process and the unethical treatment of the subjects that failed the Augmentation process. Perhaps his decision would not have been difficult if these realities were immediately known to him, but as it is, the reader is only given a dilemma and what feels like a half-hearted "why fix it?" Certainly, Cap could consciously choose artificially augmenting his body despite the ethical and health concerns inherent within the treatment. He undertook the treatment that allowed him to become Captain America in the first place, but the character's moral compass generally overrides any ambiguities.[6]

Considering this augmentation question along with his hesitation on the S.H.I.E.L.D. situation earlier, we can conclude Cap's dedication to his patriotic cause does allow him to see merit that could override opposition to these ultimately minor ethical issues (though he certainly would not hesitate to confront an ally who makes what Cap views as a morally questionable decision). Even though he ultimately decides against the augmentation treatment, in issue #329, he asks himself, "Did I make a wise choice?" (4). This uncharacteristic second-guessing sets the stage for the larger decision of stepping away from Captain America that is depicted just a few issues later.[7] Gruenwald presents a less certain Cap, a man morally centered but still confused by a changing world. The challenges around him are greater than ever and, in order to further his personal goals, some considerations that would, at one time, have been quickly dismissed are given more thought. To further emphasize Cap's ethical debates, he associates himself with the Shroud and the Nightshift,[8] a team of known criminals, to stop the monsters living underneath the streets of Los Angeles (caused by the failures of the augmentation procedure). Though he internally debates the ethics of working with these criminals, he continues to do so anyway (#330), aware of a greater good. Narratively, all of these ethical dilemmas lead to Steve Rogers' highest stakes decision and his ultimate resignation from the position.

1980s American Patriotism

These conundrums are present for more than just the sake of ethical debate. America in 1987 is, again, a world in which government scandals are blasting on television screens with minimal consequence for those involved.[9] The previously established methods for handling difficult situations are becoming less effective, both for people in the real world and the comic book version of the real world. In issue #332, the Commission deciding whether to keep him on as Captain America explains to Cap that, after an investigation into Cap's actions (and history), they have decided that Cap will, going forward, "resume [his] official position as America's super soldier and have all of [his] activities coordinated and assigned by this office" (9).

After hearing this demand, Cap makes a request of his own. He asks for the opportunity to choose whether or not he wants to operate under such jurisdiction and the committee, despite being surprised that Cap sees it as a choice (and assuming he would simply acquiesce to their requests), grants him 24 hours to decide. The chair of the committee (who is eventually revealed to be working for the Red Skull, the individual secretly manipulating the nefarious scheme into reality) makes clear that the country "needs a popular high-profile mascot and operative" and that, he, Steve Rogers, is personally replaceable: "have no doubt that we will find someone else to be Captain America!" (10). Rogers then spends the duration of the issue seeking advice and guidance on what he should do. This is a Steve Rogers torn between patriotic duty and governmental distrust. This is an important distinction because it qualifies Rogers' ability to distinguish patriotism as an apolitical phenomenon. Patriotism does not eliminate a distrust of governmental structures.

This is the highly charged political 1980s in which patriotism was very much a political tool. In discussing the Republican ideals of patriotism in an article entitled "The Language of Patriotism," Heather Cox Richardson explains that Democrats lost the patriotism argument to Republicans "amidst the counter culture upheaval of the 1960s" and completely lost the battle during the Reagan years (5). She explains that in the 1960s, "patriotism centered around the image of a maverick individual soldier fighting Communism. Now it's built around service, community, and family loyalty" (5). Rogers is very much embracing the older school perception of patriotism by being a man alone (eventually with only his closest allies) protecting the country. He rejects the government-sponsored role (and the limitations concordant with it) in order to be that maverick soldier. While Richardson is writing in 2018, it is relevant to discuss that this shift was happening firmly in the 1980s and Rogers is careful not to play partisan politics because Gruenwald does not want the book to feel partisan (and Steve Rogers also does not want to show partisanship). Despite what feels like left-leaning moments from Gruenwald at times, he depicts a Captain America who would remain loyal to the ideals of the nation, not its political parties. Cap is in no way leaning toward one party over the over. He shows occasional adherence to certain philosophies more connected to one party than another, certainly, but he is never partisan.[10]

In fact, there are times during this storyline where Rogers is unwilling to implicate the President, even though there is every reason to assume that the Commission (a presidential committee) has been ordered to act by the President (though, as previously mentioned, it turns out that the plan is secretly orchestrated by the Red Skull and the President is not involved). Cap sounds naïve when, in issue #336, in conversation with Bernie Rosenthal, his friend and former fiancée, he says, "the commission was hand-picked by President Reagan, one of the most popular presidents in history. The President must be aware of what happened. It must be okay with him!" (8). There is not any bitterness about Reagan in this comment; he is simply accepting the decision of the President (and assuming its validity because of the importance of the office and his popularity). Rosenthal then takes on the cynicism of a reader (and writer) aware of concerns about Reagan's mental faculties and his administration's trustworthiness in 1987: "I wouldn't make assumptions about what the president knows, Steve" (8).

In 1987, *The New Republic* published an article entitled, "Is Reagan Senile?" but while that article was interpreted as being about "Reagan's seemingly calculated forgetfulness" as opposed to actual senility (Hart), it clearly illustrates concerns with Reagan's declining mental state. Rosenthal's retort encompasses skepticism about the President's mental state and, possibly, the corrupt people around him, though she does so gently. She is aware of Steve's hesitancies toward inflammatory words and actions, especially toward the elected officials of the United States government. Additionally, Gruenwald may accordingly be wary of alienating any audience members because of too blatant partisanship. In the end, Captain America is not a political figure (at least in Steve Rogers' interpretation), so showing partisanship in Cap would be a failure in properly depicting the character.

Rogers' patriotism is left unbroken when he steps down; there is no illusion that he will give up his heroics. In fact, in that same flashback in issue #336 when he is talking to Rosenthal, he says, "being a hero is in my blood. I've tried to give it up before, and I just can't. I guess I'm going to have to be the best hero I can be without being Captain America" (7). When he states that he "tried to give it up before," he is referring to a past period of disillusionment that led him to step away from crime-fighting. In this situation, there is no real sense of the same type of disillusion that leads him to give up the uniform and title in the 1970s. Gruenwald is careful to handle things quite differently in this storyline. Despite the things he has lost, there is never a moment where Rogers gives up, either on himself or his country. If there is disillusionment here, it is with the government and its desire to interfere in his activities (which manifests itself more in the form of frustration). It is not a disillusionment with the country overall or with its people. It is also not about the potential futility of heroism (which defines the 1970s storyline but is a thought by which 1987 Steve Rogers would not abide).

Watergate and Resignations

In the letters page of issue #371, reader Jeffery DesRosiers suggests that the 1970s storyline by Steve Englehart in which Steve Rogers stops being Cap for a short time is the *"same story"* (italics from the original letter) as the 1980s storyline in which Rogers temporarily steps down as Cap. Editor Ralph Macchio responds in the same letter column, "we happen to think there's a world of difference between Cap deciding to not be Cap because of personal disillusionment (the '70s) and Cap deciding to not be Cap because government representatives stipulate the conditions under which he can be Cap" (24). Gruenwald's Steve Rogers is motivated by what he views as distrustful governmental bureaucracy and excessive red tape; Englehart's Steve Rogers is motivated by personal disillusionment over what he sees as a corrupt American government. Gruenwald's Steve Rogers is not personally disillusioned in any way—if he was, the idea of him immediately continuing his life as a masked adventurer would be absurd.

As Macchio continues, "That's why [1980s Rogers] lost no time soul searching and got right down to the business at hand doing what he does best." In Rogers' mind, his mission (whether in the official uniform and title or not) is too important to disregard. The 1980s is also a significantly different time than the 1970s. In 1974, when Englehart wrote his Steve Rogers resignation storyline, government trust was in significant decline amongst the American people. According to Gallup data, a survey of Americans in April 1974 indicated that 36 percent (compared to 54 percent just two years earlier) expressed trust in the American government most or all of the time ("Public Trust in Government"). Englehart's story is a Watergate response.[11] Though Watergate is not mentioned often in the storyline, it is occasionally named and is always strongly implied.[12] In *Captain America* #175, Cap unmasks Number One, the secret leader of the Secret Empire, and then watches Number One commit suicide by shooting himself in the head (19). This villain's identity, while ostensibly hidden from the reader, is ultimately obvious in the context of the era: "anyone reading the comic in 1974 knew that the leader of the Secret Empire was Richard Nixon.... Englehart made the President of the United States the leader of a terrorist organization and then had Nixon commit suicide" (Sacks 130).

The objective narrator of the issue describes Number One as possessing a "naked lust for domination" (3) and, after he is unmasked (Cap sees his identity, even if the reader does not), Number One (Nixon) explains that "high political office didn't satisfy [him because his] power was still too constrained by legalities" (19).

This storyline is inspired by general American disillusionment. Nixon was seen as a villain in American reality and a supervillain in the comics. Englehart is aware of the nation's pulse and feels obligated to reflect that sentiment in the comic book that depicts the nation's most identifiable patriotic superhero. However, in the summer of 1987, that same data indicates that 47 percent (compared to 1974's 36 percent) answered that they express trust in the American government ("Public Trust in Government, 1958–2019"), even though the public overwhelmingly thought Reagan was lying about the Iran-Contra Affair. The public was more optimistic about the government at large, even if individual situations elicited more cynical responses. Steve Rogers' decision to immediately continue to fight crime after his 1987 decision is dictated by the pulse of the American people who were not completely disillusioned themselves. They might not have trusted the president and they were certainly skeptical, but they were not completely distrusting of the American government, at least not as much as the nation was thirteen years earlier.

In the 1970s storyline, Englehart's Cap no longer saw himself as an effective symbol for the nation. In issue #183, Rogers (in the role of Nomad, the identity he adopts in the storyline after leaving the Captain America position) thinks to himself, "the days where you were a symbol to anyone are long gone. You're your own man now—responsible only for yourself!" (7). That sense of personal responsibility is still intact for the 1980s Captain America, but he does not lose track of his personal symbolism. Rogers in the 1980s is unwilling to stop being "a symbol to anyone." For Gruenwald, Rogers is not disillusioned with the American Dream; Rogers is unwilling to work within a bureaucracy that he cannot trust because his personal mission is not going to be that bureaucracy's priority.

If these still seem like the same reason (as that aforementioned letter writer concluded), the details give us a greater insight. In Steve Englehart's storyline in issue #176, Steve Rogers expresses his reasons for walking away from the role of Captain America to Thor: "I've seen America rocked with scandal—seen it manipulated by demagogues with sweet, empty words—seen all the things I hated when I saw those [World War II] newsreels" (8). In conversation with Iron Man, he further explains that he knew his efforts were appreciated over time, but the value people held for Captain America started to wane: "I guess it just lost its meaning for those people" (10). He is blaming his personal disillusionment (and his lessening belief in the power of patriotism) on an American public who have, in his mind, been less loyal to him. Iron Man does not disagree with Cap's conclusion, but he tries to keep him focused on the positive: "But it doesn't have to lose meaning for you!" Cap is blaming his feelings of disillusionment on the public (and government leaders), but Iron Man is redirecting Cap toward the main source of his disillusionment—Cap himself. The narrative impetus for these feelings is the reveal of Nixon as Number One an issue earlier, but Englehart makes it clear that this disillusionment was developing over time. He finally announces his decision to an assembly of allies—his partner Falcon, various Avengers (including Iron Man and Thor), and love interests past (Peggy Carter) and present (Sharon Carter).[13] This decision is personal and the announcement is private and intimate.

In Gruenwald's issue #332, however, several things are different. First, instead of announcing his final decision to his friends, he does so to a government agency. This takes the personal sense of disillusionment out of the equation by emphasizing government procedure. His language to the committee emphasizes this emotional distance: "my commitment to the ideals of this country is greater than my commitment to a 40-year old document" (24). This is not a discussion of values and beliefs; it is about red tape, paperwork, and bureaucracy. Cap is distinguishing between his duty to his beliefs in patriotism and his duty to government. The 1974 story makes no distinctions. Secondly, in 1987, he does not blame the American people for his disillusionment (as he does in 1974), nor does he implicate the evils of the American government as harshly.

In his final comments to the Commission in issue #332 as he resigns from the position, he explains, "I cannot represent the American Government; the president does that. I must represent the American people" (24). He sees the American people, not as contributing to his struggle, but potential victims within that struggle. In Englehart's story in issue #176, Cap is equating the American government directly with Nazis. When Cap says he has "seen all the things [he] hated when [he] saw those newsreels" (8), he is referring to the films that convinced him of Nazi evils: "I knew the Nazis were rotten, from the minute I set my eyes on them [in the newsreels]… they were suppressing … then murdering the people of Europe" (3). In no veiled terms, Englehart's Cap is saying that the American government in 1974 reminds him of Nazi Germany. Englehart connects Nixon to terrorism and the American government at large to Nazism. Gruenwald's Cap is less inflammatory in his language, acknowledging (but not vilifying) the potential role of the president. Further, he emphasizes that it is his duty to the "people" that drives him. Accordingly, he keeps fighting, just on different terms.

Brother Nature

After Steve Rogers gives up the title of Captain America, the series focuses on the government's search for a replacement Captain America and then two issues that depict the new Cap adjusting to the position and training for it (and these issues will be discussed in Chapter Three). Steve Rogers eventually returns to the comic after a brief hiatus in *Captain America* #336, entitled "Natural Calling." The title plays on the word "natural" because Steve Rogers challenges an eco-villain named "Brother Nature," but the issue itself focuses on Steve Rogers' inclination toward heroism, whether he is in the Captain America suit or he is sporting an unkempt beard in the pacific northwest after months of traveling. He uses this time after his resignation both to consider his next move and to reconnect with his country. As he will tell Falcon in issue #337, he's been traveling the country after not being Captain America in order to get "in touch with the people" (12). His objective at all times is people-oriented rather than simply goal-oriented. His patriotism is driven by ideology, sure, but if it is said to be results-oriented, those results are in terms of people either saved or influenced toward good. It is simplistic but genuine. Despite changing his appearance and traveling to Washington state, he does not keep a low-profile.

As a hero, considering the easily identifiable nature of his uniform, he is clearly not someone concerned with a low-profile. That is the case even when he is not in uniform. In issue #336, while in a tavern filled with lumberjacks, Rogers watches a television report tell a story about how Brother Nature is hampering the timber industry. The locals get angry and begin to leave the bar en masse to storm the ranger station to express their discontent, presumably with violence. Rogers, who is not known by these people, steps up quickly to intervene: "Whoa!" he says, standing in front of the door, holding up his hands to stop the potential riot: "you shouldn't take the law into your own hands!" (5). He cannot blend into a crowd. His ideology does not allow for passive tendencies. He later faces off against Brother Nature and, despite Brother Nature's destructive behavior, he sees himself in this new rival. He thinks (though he does not speak this aloud), "This man's situation parallels mine in certain respects. We've both devoted ourselves to higher ideals" (22). He then wonders if he should follow a "guerrilla" path (23) similar to Brother Nature.

Ultimately, the proper path of heroism is revealed, and that path is not paved with "guerrilla" tactics. In the issue's final two panels, Brother Nature, head in hands, body bent forward in grief, realizes the errors of his ways: "I blew it! I did the very thing I was trying to prevent!" (23). Rogers tells him, "That's the danger of crossing the line and becoming a renegade." As Rogers delivers this lecture, penciler Tom Morgan draws Rogers with fists clenched and looking a bit off in the distance to his left, seemingly away from Brother Nature who, based on positioning in earlier panels, would logically be to his right. Rogers is now feeling a purpose and understanding, and he no longer is concerned with Brother Nature. Brother Nature is an obstacle who helps position Rogers in the direction he needs to go. Rogers gained what was needed from the interaction and now he has moved forward. He internalizes his thoughts after completing his lecture to Brother Nature: "If I were to wage war against the Commission for the right to be Captain America, I too may have to go so far that I would hurt the ideal I serve" (23). Tellingly, there is no past tense on the word "serve." Rogers never contemplates retirement—he is just trying to ascertain how he is going to still serve his "ideal" while still looking at his new Captain America-less reality.

"Back down to business"

In issue #337, he refers specifically to getting "back down to business" (13). He adds to that statement, "I'm ready. Now." There is no additional time or self-reflection necessary. He is a hero who, after reuniting with his former partners Falcon, Nomad, and D–Man, now has both a team and a purpose. He decides to take up a new costumed identity and travel the country to protect the people. Interestingly, in issue #336, that is exactly what he was doing even before he makes this declaration, costume be damned (he even identifies himself as "The Captain" to Brother Nature, establishing the new moniker he uses until regaining the Captain America name in issue #350). While he does not see himself as formally being an adventurer again at that point, that is exactly what he is doing when confronting Brother Nature. Steve Rogers' patriotic duty is so engrained, he cannot turn it off. He is as heroic out of the costume as he is in it, and the blurring of these two identities shows readers what connects Steve Rogers to Captain America (or whatever other identity he adopts)—his sense of patriotic purpose.

When he returns to more formal crime-fighting, he chooses to take on a new identity. There is precedent for Steve Roger's decision to do so. In issue #180, during the 1974 Englehart storyline, Rogers adopts the name "Nomad" and refers to himself as "The Man Without a Country" (and he drops said moniker and reassumes the role in issue #177 after the Red Skull kills a replacement Cap and Rogers realizes only he can handle the responsibility and risks of the job in issue #183). Upon hearing Rogers' proclamation to take a non–Captain America identity in #337, the new Nomad, his former partner Jack Monroe, immediately offers the identity back. Rogers declines and explains, "I'm not a nomad, a man without a country. I have a country—America. And I intend to keep on serving my country and its people, no matter what obstacles politicians throw in my way" (13). In 1987, Rogers can see the problematic politicians as being separate from the country itself and the American people. In 1974, he could not. In Gruenwald's hands, his patriotism is, perhaps, if not cynical exactly, realistically idealistic. His idealism prevents his cynicism from dominating his beliefs. He knows the system is not perfect but he does not let the flaws of that system embitter him to the country overall. That is why he is so quick to take up a new crimefighting identity. The Captain America spirit is something embodied within Steve Rogers, not without.

Captain America vs. Captain America

Eventually (in issue #350), in a battle of The Captain vs. Captain America, Rogers and John Walker (the replacement Captain America) square off in unarmed battle. Rogers definitively learns that the government interference into Captain America and the role of the position is a plan orchestrated by the Red Skull.[14] When Rogers defeats Walker in hand to hand combat, Rogers immediately thinks, "I've reclaimed a part of myself!" (36). Since fighting Walker to a frustrating standstill in issue #327 (and then seeing him serve most disgracefully as Captain America), Rogers has seen Walker as a dark counterpoint to both him personally and his patriotic ideology. He cannot savor the victory for long because the Red Skull (in a cloned body of Steve Rogers) enters the fray, but it is significant that he indeed savors it for a moment. To say that he has "reclaimed a part" of himself emphasizes how much he feels he had previously lost of himself. Fighting Walker to a draw in issue #327 is difficult for Rogers to take emotionally—he instinctively knows that he can best anyone in hand-to-hand combat, and finding that Walker is more than his equal affects his sense of self and, considering how his sense of self is tied so closely to his patriotism, it also affects his perceived ability to fulfill his mission, thus his worthiness of being the nation's leading patriotic symbol. This victory is as important symbolically and emotionally to Rogers as it is important literally.

In issue #350, thanks to a timely assist from Walker, the Skull is defeated and flees after his face is transformed into the hideous visage[15] of a Red Skull so that he no longer possesses, as the Red Skull states earlier, Rogers' "Aryan" attributes (36). Rogers and Walker then meet in front of the Commission, which is now missing the traitorous member who was working for (and subsequently murdered by) the Red Skull, in order to discover the Commission's final decision as to which of the two will permanently serve as Captain America. The Commission decides that Walker must step down because of his inappropriately violent and erratic behavior in the uniform and hand the title, suit, and shield to Rogers. Rogers, who surprises the committee in issue #332 by declining to serve as Captain America with bureaucratic strings, surprises them again in #350 by declining to serve even without said strings: "I do not want [the title and its accompanying materials] back. I have learned that I can serve my ideals—the ideals of this great country—even without the uniform" (39). Over the 18 issues of this storyline, Rogers learns that Captain America is what is within him and not what he wears. The patriotic sense of self exists whether the star-spangled uniform is on or off.

While the committee is surprised, the reader likely is not. Frankly, it would seem that this would be a conclusion he would have been able to reach prior, but the circumstances of the ordeal make it clearer to him personally. Rogers is a character who seems to act often on impulse, but his frequent chain thought bubbles reveal to the reader that he is someone who rarely acts without a full understanding of a situation. He is a deliberator— in combat, he is simply able to do so quickly, but in decision-making outside of combat, it takes him much longer. He then walks away from the Commission, with both the head of the Commission and John Walker so surprised, their reactions are limited to dramatic punctuation marks (a question mark for Walker and an exclamation point for the Commission chair). After Rogers leaves, striding out of the room, Walker stops him and tells him that he ought to take the mantle back, telling him that he is obviously the definitive Captain America:

> Who's kidding who? You may not have come up with the name or stitched the uniform together, but you create the role of Captain America—his code of conduct, his reputation, his legend! I've had it up to here with people who expect me to be exactly like you. I'm not. I'll never be. I have my own way of serving this nation that I love. And it's not the way of Captain America! They're taking this uniform away from me anyway. I have no idea what they'll do with me after that. Come on, take the darn thing back—[40].

Walker, a character of violent impulse, makes a conscious decision that allows Rogers to comfortably reaffirm his role, recognizing their philosophical differences and acknowledging that, based on his "code of conduct," Rogers is the only person who could truly fulfill the role.

The final page of #350, then, is Rogers agreeing with Walker and donning the suit once again, triumphantly. The narration explains, underneath a full-page image of a smiling and relaxed Cap (above a gold banner dedicating the issue and arguably entire storyline to Simon and Kirby, Cap's original creators), "he's back. He did it his way. And it feels right" (41). Part of this idea of Rogers doing it "his way" is that he only agrees to take back the identity when Walker suggests it, not the committee. This entire affair (though it was indeed orchestrated by the Red Skull) was built on Rogers' unwillingness to get constricted by bureaucracy. For him to have agreed to retake the position in the same exact spot he yielded it would be futile, as if the circle could infinitely repeat. Instead, it is Walker's plea that convinces Rogers to return to the role. His distaste for governmental red tape would prevent him from doing so without Walker's urging. Walker and Rogers are, obviously, no allies, but the idea of being encouraged by even a flawed fellow adventurer (and not a bureaucrat) is enough to help Rogers make the decision he so desperately wants to make.

Flag-Smasher's Anti-Patriotism

If Rogers evolves as a character over the course of this storyline, it is in his awareness of his own capacity to understand his worth as a patriotic symbol. It is not his patriotism itself that changes. In fact, Cap's patriotism is fully formed by Gruenwald before he regains the position of Captain America in #350. For example, in issue #322, Cap engages in an ideological discussion with Flag-Smasher, an ideologically driven villain. Flag-Smasher is an anti-nationalist with a modus operandi of destroying national boundaries to bring the people of the world closer together. After a battle, Cap saves Flag-Smasher from likely death in the frozen tundra, despite great risk to Cap himself.

Upon regaining consciousness, Flag-Smasher tells Cap, "If you expect these heroic gestures of yours will in any way make me more sympathetic to your insipid patriotic cause, think again." Cap responds, "That's not why I'm doing this, Flag. I'm doing this out of my love for humanity, my reverence for life—concepts beyond your notion of patriotism" (17). Flag-Smasher is staunchly anti-patriotic, thus Flag-Smasher's "notion of patriotism" is that it is a destructive force keeping people from being together. For Flag-Smasher, national pride and national boundaries create irreparable distances between peoples of different countries and belief systems. Cap's patriotism does not preclude a love of country but does make a "love for humanity" a central part of its treatise whereas Flag-Smasher would feel like he is doing more to reflect a "love for humanity" by fighting to unite the global community. Flag-Smasher sees patriotism as purely competitive, colonizing, and compartmentalizing (which perhaps has more to do with nationalism than patriotism, though Flag-Smasher himself treats both ideologies equally). To Flag-Smasher, patriotism only exists to divide, and he thus sees Cap as a divisive figure. Cap's perception of patriotism (at least his personal patriotism) is inclusive, even to others, including both those who are not American or disagree with him (or both). For him, patriotism is not about feeling superior to those from other countries and places, but instead sharing the resources and opportunities of the United States with others. Cap's "love for humanity" is not separated by borders, but it is a guiding aspect of his personal patriotism.

As he continues to discuss his patriotism with Flag-Smasher, he refuses to deny that he is a patriot, but he clarifies the type of patriot he is: "I'm not a knee-jerk patriot. I don't believe in my country right or wrong. I support America in its concept, its essence, its ideal. Its political system, its foreign and domestic policies, its vast book of laws—I am not America's official advocate of any of that" (18). The belief in "America in its concept ... its ideal" is very different than blindly supporting America in any current state. As discussed earlier, this is America in the 1980s—a place where the public believes its leaders are dishonest but is still willing to believe that the government can function. If specific leaders are seen as flawed, the citizens can be the element that redeems the failure of government. In the 1974 Englehart-penned storyline, Cap feels betrayed by the public; here, the public is the country's saving grace. This devotion to the people is what, ultimately, he uses to justify stepping down as Cap in #332.

"Freedom, justice, equality, opportunity"

Cap finishes the speech to Flag-Smasher with a summary of his position: "What I represent are the principles that America's politics, laws, and policies are based upon ... freedom, justice, equality, opportunity" (18). Cap will not allow himself to be a pawn for the government (or any political party), and the values he espouses are, to his mind, transcendent of politics (at least they should be). The "principles" he lists here are, however, completely intertwined with contemporary politics.

One thing that is interesting about the four terms that he lists here is how they weave in-between the perceptions of the two major American political parties (who, Cap may argue, are composed of many "knee jerk patriots"). Conservative writer George F. Will writes, "Conservatives tend to favor freedom, and consequently are inclined to be somewhat sanguine about inequalities of outcomes." Obviously, this idea of conservatives "favor[ing] freedom" is an editorial opinion presented by a prominent conservative voice, but it is worthwhile to see a self-awareness of where two of Captain America's self-appointed objectives fail to interconnect in conservative politics. But for Cap, these two concepts—freedom and equality—do coexist.

This is using an example far removed from Gruenwald's timeline, but seeing how the two parties view the concepts now gives us insight on the hypothesis into these four concepts as being politically charged terms that can be valued (and differently interpreted) by both parties. In both National Party Platforms from 2016, there are instances of these specific terms within each party's official document and this provides a contemporary opportunity to see how these parties value the concepts Cap emphasizes in his speech to Flag-Smasher and how those concepts have evolved over time. In the *1988 Democratic National Party Platform*, the word "Freedom" is mentioned four times, "Justice" is mentioned three times, "Equality" is not mentioned (though "equal" appears nine times), and "Opportunity" 28 times. For the *1988 Republican National Party Platform*, "Freedom" appears 54 times, "Justice" appears six times, "Equality" once (and "equal" an additional 15 times), and "Opportunity" 36 times. Obviously, these are terms that had relevance to political discourse at the time, but they help us understand where the discourse would evolve over time.

By comparing these terms in the 1988 platforms to more contemporary platforms, we can see how Cap's philosophy not only reflects political discourse, but how that discourse evolves.[16] The political discussion in the 1980s shows a clear Republican rhetorical leaning toward "Freedom" and "Opportunity," while still using Cap's rhetoric a bit more on "Justice" and "Equality." Over time, that evolves somewhat. In the 45-page *2016 Democratic Party Platform*, the word "Freedom" is mentioned 11 times, "Justice" is mentioned 28 times (paired with "Criminal," "Environmental," and "Climate," among others, with no references to the Supreme Court), "Equality" is mentioned four times (though there are eight additional references to "inequality" for a total of twelve references to the term), and "Opportunity" is mentioned 16 times. The *Republican Platform 2016* contains 54 pages of positions (excluding acknowledgments for the platform committee). It mentions "Freedom" 45 times, "Justice" appears 22 times (seven of these paired with "Criminal," five times in reference to Supreme Court Justices, and four times in reference to the Department of Justice), "Equality" appears twice (and "inequality" never appears), and "Opportunity" appears 19 times. Of the roughly 27,000 words in the *Democratic Platform*, .0004 percent are "Freedom," .001 percent are "Justice," .0004 percent are "Equality" and "Inequality" (combined here because they are referring to alternating sides of the same basic concept), and .0006 percent are "Opportunity." Of the roughly 36,000 words in *The Republican Platform*, .00125 percent are "Freedom," .0006 percent are "Justice," .00006 percent are "Equality," and .0005 percent are "Opportunity."

Breaking this down further, Republicans take greatest ownership of "Freedom" (as Will summarizes above) and Democrats mention "Justice" most frequently. Democrats also mention "Freedom" (though not as often as Republicans) and "Equality"/"Inequality" (and Republicans are far less likely to reference "Equality," also as Will summarized). Finally, both parties are equally inclined toward "Opportunity," and this is the least politically weighted word in Cap's specific list. Cap's words embody a patriotism that is not partisan, nor is it aggressive. It is the inclusive and positive manifesto that embodies Gruenwald's take on the character.

Philosopher Noam Chomsky says, "Every effort is made by power and doctrinal systems to stir up the more dangerous and destructive forms of 'patriotism'; every effort is made by people committed to peace and justice to organize and encourage the beneficial kinds" (qtd. in "Noam Chomsky"). Chomsky is recognizing the degrees of patriotism and, indeed, acknowledging that there are "beneficial kinds" of patriotism that exist in counter to the "dangerous" patriotism that power structures work so hard to create. That is the heart of Steve Rogers' dilemma when the government forces him to decide whether to remain in the role of Captain America and do so on their terms. The conflict is of the contradictory forms of patriotism that Chomsky fears. Captain America fears it too—he is not interested in stirring up conflict. Gruenwald tones down villains that represent "evil" foreign adversaries that would have been more common with previous writers and instead creates villains defined by ideology other than nationalism (and a study of these villains appears in Chapter Six). Patriotism is espoused in this comic; nationalism is not celebrated.

Final Years of the Cold War

The pallor of the late Cold War resonates in the first half of Gruenwald's run and that shadow of the Cold War had been felt on the America Public for decades. American opinions of the Soviet Union were, predictably, negative in the 1950s and 1960s. In 1954, 91.1 percent of Americans expressed unfavorable views of the Soviet Union. In the 1970s, American opinions changed. By 1974, 35.6 percent of Americans felt unfavorably (with 45.3 percent expressing "mixed" feelings, up from 8.5 percent who expressed "mixed" in 1954 [Smith]). In 1974, Americans were concerned with the domestic situation of distrust in their own government, and the Cold War felt external. When Ronald Reagan was elected president in 1980, Americans once again developed a distrust in Soviet Russia. Between February 1979 and June 1980 (during Reagan's campaign for president and a time period in which the Soviets invaded Afghanistan, the Iranian hostage situation occurred, and the U.S. boycotted the 1980 Summer Olympics),

American perceptions of Russian jumped from 48.9 percent unfavorable to 73 percent unfavorable.

By the time Gruenwald takes over this comic, the United States and the Soviet Union are closer to resolving the Cold War, but American public opinion was still anxious. In 1988, 60 percent of Americans saw the Soviet Union as a "serious" or "very serious" threat. However, by early 1990, the percentage of Americans who saw the Soviet Union as a "serious" or "very serious" threat was down to 26 percent and 7 percent, respectively. Therefore, Americans could once again look domestically and away from international struggles (without the political domestic crises that defined the 1970s). Accordingly, Captain America is focused, not on the problems of a foreign government, but very much on the problems of his own. By the end of the 1980s, the Cold War is waning and tensions are softening, but there is still a need for vigilance, and Captain America is embodying that while protecting America (and its heartland) with skill, kindness, and positive symbolism.

When Steve Rogers declines to be Captain America in #332, he is not turning his back on the responsibilities of the title and he is not rejecting his country. Ultimately, his decision to stop being Captain America is a remarkably patriotic act, perhaps the most patriotic act he undertakes during Gruenwald's run. He sees an unfairness in the system, detects that a good thing (his role as Captain America) could be exploited, and he says, "No More." Captain America's patriotism is not the flag-waving stuff of manipulative political rallies. Cap's patriotism is about knowing when America needs Steve Rogers more than it needs Captain America, and then finding a way to reconnect the two and, most importantly to Cap, doing it in a way that maintains the integrity and value of the personal patriotism that he cherishes.

THREE

Patriot and Super-Patriot
John Walker and Negative Patriotism

When John Walker, the character who would ultimately replace Steve Rogers as Captain America (albeit temporarily) in *Captain America #333*, debuts in issue #323, he is in the guise of the Super-Patriot, an opportunistic con-man who riles up crowds with aggressive patriotic rhetoric. By the time Rogers gives up the title and shield and Walker is asked by the government to take his place, Gruenwald has given us a more sympathetic character, at least to a point. We know that his seemingly insincere patriotic act is likely earnest, and he is willing to abandon his morally questionable manager (and potential financial gain) in order to fulfill a greater calling. By issue #350, he is a character who has suffered and lost greatly. He is also willing to concede to Steve Rogers that Rogers is the superior Captain America, and he is forced to step aside from the role of Captain America after losing a fight to Rogers and being removed from the position by the Commission.

After stepping away from the role of Captain America, Walker allows the government to fake his death in order to be reborn as the U.S.Agent,[1] a new costumed hero with an opportunity to begin a new journey. His journey from Super-Patriot to Captain America to U.S.Agent, from an arrogant and insincere charlatan to a hero that Steve Rogers can reasonably and sincerely thank for help in issue #401[2] is an arc that reflects the potential for individual growth and, while Walker's patriotism is something that, even in his earliest appearance, could give the readers hope for his redemption, the type of patriotism espoused by John Walker is not the same as that preached and practiced by Steve Rogers. Walker's patriotism, much like Walker himself, is aggressive and violent, built on cynicism and confrontation. He indeed matures from his days as Super-Patriot, but his view of the world, while perhaps becoming more nuanced, evolves in a relatively limited way. Rogers' approach to patriotism is about people and

76

inclusion; Walker's leans more toward exclusion and an elevated view of the state.

"Captain America More Like Rambo"

Creating a Captain America who commits acts of violence liberally and is morally compromised because of his rage is a key part of what Gruenwald envisioned when he created the John Walker character. The impetus for the character, according to Gruenwald, came about because of public interest in a Captain America with a darker edge. In a 1988 interview with Joe Field ("Mark Gruenwald Interviewed by Joe Field"), Gruenwald explains, "I've been getting a lot of letters that said, 'you should do Captain America more like Rambo.' And personally, I don't feel in my reading of the character that there's any way Steve Rogers could become like that. So I said, if they want Captain America like Rambo, I'll give them it, but it can't be Steve Rogers." He was intrigued enough by the public interest in a "Rambo"-like figure (a vengeful, shoot-first, ask questions eventually type character) to try it (and he also admits that stagnant sales on the title affected his decision to incorporate the change).

In the same interview, Gruenwald also shows his dedication to creating ideological villains to counter Cap's patriotic idealism:

> I realized that because Captain America [Steve Rogers] was the good guy, it seemed to be saying patriotism had to be good because patriotism was Captain America and he was the good guy. So I wanted to show the dark side of patriotism, so I invented the character Super-Patriot [John Walker] to show that.

While more is discussed of these other ideologically driven villains in Chapter Six, this awareness of patriotism's "dark side" greatly educates our readings of Walker. As Molloy points out in an essay questioning the place of patriotism in contemporary society, the challenge of understanding patriotism is that there is a difficulty even in pinning down what exactly it is: "Simply defining it as love of country deprives the word of its weight." Even as both Super-Patriot and Captain America, Walker never truly defines his patriotism and simply carries his with him (especially as Super-Patriot) as a badge of honor. He feels that his patriotism is better than anybody else's. In her book *Give Me Liberty: A Handbook for American Revolutionaries*, Naomi Wolf argues that patriotism has been "dumbed down," in part because "the left let the right 'brand' patriotism… 'Patriotism' became identified with blind loyalty and a sense that America is innately better than the rest of the world" (24). Even if that was the case in the 1980s, it was effective: "Lipset and Schneider (1987) provided a comprehensive review of poll data demonstrating that—compared with the late 1970s—in [1980s] mid-decade satisfaction with the nation was high and resentment toward taxes was diminishing" (Racjeki et al. 402). Patriotism is treated as a positive emotion in these pages through Steve Rogers, but Walker is an attempt to show a darker side.

Rogers is a heroic representation of idealistic patriotism and the American Dream, while Walker's representation of the American Dream is far more cynical. This is not an accident. In the same interview with Joe Field, Gruenwald explains Super-Patriot is "the American Dream as most people think of it. Which is come to America, make a lot of money at the expense of others and do whatever it takes to get ahead ... that is not Steve Rogers' idea." Accordingly, when Walker debuts in these pages, there seems to be little nuance or complexity to his character. He is an opportunist and a conman. We see him give speeches that encourage cheers from crowds, but he is not necessarily shown living his life in a way that shows a true adherence to the values he espouses (he speaks of the working class at his rallies, but then rides in limousines and dines at fine restaurants). He is also shown consulting with his manager about almost everything, showing his personal lack of confidence (and need to be given orders). However, the most important decision Walker makes (to accept the government's offer to become Captain America) occurs quickly and without consultation with his manager.

Walker as Super-Patriot

When Gruenwald first introduces the reader to John Walker, before he follows Rogers as Captain America, it is in the guise of Super-Patriot. Super-Patriot is, publicly, a heroic figure; he clearly exists in these pages to create a shadowy counterpart to the patriotic drive of Captain America himself. That public persona is driven by a sense of self-righteousness and aggressive patriotism that makes the reader less inclined toward his ostensibly sympathetic message. This all makes Steve Rogers uncomfortable (and would have repulsed Flag-Smasher, a character defined by his anti-nationalist and anti-patriotism philosophies completely). One challenge for readers concerning Super-Patriot in his earliest appearances in issues #323 and #327 is not knowing what is a genuine ideology and what is fabricated in order to boost his personal brand. Since we know that he eventually accepts the position of Captain America in issue #332 without any hesitation (or need for consultation), a reader can lean toward the belief that Super-Patriot's patriotic ideology is sincere, even if his behavior in these early appearances is abhorrent.

The first substantial speech we hear from Super-Patriot is in issue #323 at a rally in New York that Steve Rogers (out of uniform) happens to attend. Most of Super-Patriot's initial comments revolve around insulting Captain America, something that affects Rogers (Rogers admits that the insults about his age and techniques hurt him personally in his internal monologue on page 13). Insults and personal attacks do not constitute an ideology. Super-Patriot does get closer to an ideology when he speaks of himself as a "weapon—for freedom and peace!" before launching into a staged fight (though Rogers and the audience do not realize that the fight is staged) with three supposed Captain America supporters. His ideology is that patriotism is violence. Cap would never see himself as a "weapon" and, if others saw him this way, he would be disgusted. Super-Patriot evokes the thought casually. Super-Patriot throws two of the "Buckies"—the "Bold Urban Commandos"—into one another and calls it a "lesson in citizenship" (14–16). While the great majority of Super-Patriot's speech is filled with personal attacks on Captain America, the ideology we get from the speech is focused on patriotism and civics through violence. When Rogers later confronts Walker (both out of uniform), Rogers accuses him of using patriotism as an act. Walker gets defensive: "You're wrong, pal! I love my country" (18). His convictions seem sincere—it is the aggressiveness of his beliefs (and the lack of morality displayed within them) that are problematic. Cap cannot comprehend a violent patriotism like that espoused by Super-Patriot as something sincere.

While Super-Patriot's sincerity and ideology can be debated, the discussion of whether or not his portrayal is that of a villain in these early appearances is much clearer. He is. At the beginning of issue #327, we see him offer congratulation to his allies after they have vandalized and set fire to an international student house on the University of Wisconsin campus, and he tells them that he wishes he could join them. This is a stunt that involves writing out the words "Forreners [sic] go home" in gasoline on the lawn in front of the house and lighting it on fire (4). Super-Patriot is party to a clear racially motivated hate crime. Even if it was a hate crime designed to villainize Cap, it seems obvious that Walker's allies believe in the message.[3]

When Cap arrives at the scene of the hate crime to investigate, he realizes that Super-Patriot's allies were dressed similarly to him in order to disparage his reputation. It works, and he is accused of participating in the act by the victims (and applauded by white protesters outside the scene who agree with the idea of "send[ing] these traitors packing" [9–10]). The stunt (like others pulled off by Super-Patriot and his team) is part of a plan designed to make Cap look like a "reactionary Bigot" (11). Super-Patriot agrees with the message of these stunts—one of the "Buckies" (whom we would later know better as Lemar "Bucky"/"Battle Star" Hoskins) tells one of the others that "roughin' up a bunch of un–American slimeballs sure does [his] patriotic heart good" (3). That he says this to one of his allies makes it likely that this is expressing a sincere thought and, if one of the Buckies is feeling this way (especially one who will later take the mantle of a patriotic superhero himself), it seems clear that Gruenwald wants us to see this as Super-Patriot's belief as well. So Super-Patriot is attempting to discredit Captain America by blaming him for a series of hate crimes that he himself agrees with in ideology and principle.

Cap then travels from Madison to Milwaukee to attend Americaid, a Farm-Aid-type event[4] at which Super-Patriot is speaking. Onstage, Super-Patriot speaks of American excellence, emphasizing that America invented rock and roll (13). He then speaks on behalf of "farmers [and] the factory workers" and expresses regret for their struggles. This is rhetoric that does not constitute an ideology and mostly feels political. He makes no claims as to how he would support farm and factory workers—he simply states that he regrets their plight. When Captain America and Super-Patriot finally square off in battle, Super-Patriot unleashes the same insults that he has most often used against Cap in speeches—he calls Cap "grampaw" (as well as "grandpaw" and "gramps") multiple times and makes insinuations about Cap's advancing age (16–21).

He also establishes himself as an isolationist. Super-Patriot attacks a retreating Cap and Cap decries his ambushes as "sneak attacks." In response, Super-Patriot states, "Oh? How about the bombing of Libya?" (17). This issue was released in March 1987 and President Reagan ordered airstrikes on Libya in response to an attack on a West Berlin dance club a year earlier in April 1986. The American bombing of Libya was roundly criticized at the time with the United Nations General Assembly voting to condemn the attack. However, the *New York Times* reported at the time that 77 percent of Americans approved of the bombing (Clymer). Super-Patriot, surprisingly, is in the minority of the American public. Since he is depicted as a pretty clear conservative in subsequent appearances, this might seem surprising (and it is possible that Walker would assume that Cap would be a government lackey so he is bringing it up mostly to get into Cap's head), but it also establishes an isolationist perspective—Super-Patriot is uncomfortable with international interventions of any type and genuinely wants to focus on domestic issues. We can assume Cap feels interventions are necessary to protect lives (and Cap believes in this concept on a galactic level), but he typically acts through actions and not just words and, obviously, this is the only perspective expressed on the Libyan bombing (so, essentially, Super-Patriot creates Cap's perspective through his opposition to the bombing). Super-Patriot serves as a foil for Cap, one that represents a shadowy version of his own ideals, a technique used often in Captain America comics.[5]

Patriotism and Nationalism

The distinction between patriotism and nationalism is a key place to discuss the gap between Steve Rogers and John Walker, though the terms are intertwined in such a way that makes a clear delineation difficult. When discussing the two concepts in an article entitled "Is There Really a Difference Between Patriotism and Nationalism?" Jared A. Goldstein defines patriotism as "citizens' love and loyalty to their country," though Goldstein admits that it is difficult to ascertain how that diverges from Nationalism because the terms can be observed to overlap. Psychologist David Crittendon adds this to the definition of the concept of patriotism: "love for one's country with a commitment or readiness to sacrifice for that nation" (1). Nationalism, in contrast, is often associated with "an unhealthy national self-concept, and an arrogant perception of superiority or desire to dominate others, particularly minority groups" (Crittendon 1). Further, while modern nationalism can be observed as harmless, Classical Nationalism "claims that a primary duty of each member is to abide by one's recognizably ethno-national culture in all cultural matters," therefore prioritizing the cultural aspects of the nation as a priority ("Nationalism"). Further, "moderate nationalism" is less demanding than classical nationalism and sometimes goes under the name of "patriotism" ("Nationalism").

President Donald Trump's 2018 embrace of nationalism[6] brought further scrutiny to the concept, including Conservative commentators and writers dulling the distinction between the terms. For instance, F.H. Buckley, in an essay adapted from remarks at a National Conservatism Conference, differentiates American Nationalism from other forms, calling it "benign because (1) it is a liberal nationalism; (2) it is a multicultural nationalism; (3) it is a fraternal nationalism" (16). Trump later elaborated that his immediate presidential predecessors were globalist rather than nationalist: "our leaders have been more worried about the world than they have about the United States and they leave us in this mess" (qtd. in Goldstein).

Clearly, there are complications in these definitions, but Steve Rogers' patriotism embraces not just country, but the global community as well. With Rogers, patriotism is positive and Gruenwald works diligently to avoid his patriotism veering into a nationalism that potentially disparages others. Walker would favor Buckley and Trump's definitions of nationalism because he prioritizes American "greatness" over a commitment to a global community.

John Walker as Villain

Even in the Captain America identity—and even when Walker is slowly on a path of redemption (though he never truly realizes the potential of selfless heroism that Rogers models), Walker is ostensibly the villain. He is a villain showing readers not just the corrupting power of aggressive nationalism, but also showing how an opportunist could use the perception of patriotism to manipulate the public to his desires. It is easy to point to his earliest appearances to see this most clearly illustrated. In *Captain America* #327, Walker is a shrewd con-man, using his heroic persona as a means to fame and wealth (showing the clear connection to Gruenwald's cynicism about the American Dream being about fame and money that is expressed in the aforementioned interview). When he meets up with his allies who have just joyously committed acts of ethnically charged vandalism, they invite him to participate in future hate crimes. He says that, despite his willingness to do so, he would need to consult with his agent and, essentially, discuss how that type of action would play with focus groups (5). He is obsessed with personal branding and image. When he becomes Captain America, he changes from the charismatic patriotic symbol he is as Super-Patriot— Bernie Rosenthal acknowledges his charisma upon seeing him speak in issue #327 (13)—to a more physical and visceral figure, one who seems less an inspirational motivator of people (as he certainly is in his choreographed and scripted appearances in front of festival crowds and television cameras in these earliest appearances) and more an aggressive brute (and the government allows very minimal public appearances to allow him to refine his image).

While his earliest appearances (specifically in #323 and #327) establish him as a villain (and we cannot truly trust the sincerity of his patriotism in those appearances, though it is indeed shown to be sincere over his subsequent appearances), issue #332 is a bit more complicated. Walker is still a showman more than a hero, but Gruenwald does depict him performing a clear act of dangerous heroism. As discussed in Chapter Two, #332's main storyline depicts Steve Rogers' decision to step down as Captain America. The other major plot of the issue shows John Walker (in his Super-Patriot persona) thwart the plans of a would-be terrorist bomber atop the Washington Monument. Before this issue, Walker is not a character readers have had an opportunity to know. In issue #323, Walker/Super-Patriot has 33 panels in which he has dialogue and nine panels of chain thought bubbles to indicate internal processes. In issue #327, Walker is given 27 panels in which he speaks but only one panel of internal thoughts. To create a comparison, in issue #323, Steve Rogers/Captain America is given 30 panels in which he has dialogue and 39 in which he is given thought chain bubbles to convey internal thoughts. In issue #323, Walker talks more than Rogers but has a third of his internal thoughts. Walker is a character whom the reader does not truly grasp because of the mystery of what he is thinking. Gruenwald does not let the reader fully understand who he is, likely because creating mystery with the character gives more intrigue into fully understanding who he is once he becomes the primary (alongside Rogers in his "The Captain" persona) protagonist of the comic.

Considering Walker is asked to become the new Captain America in issue #333, the content of #332 is pivotal for understanding the shaping of this character. At this point, Gruenwald not only knows Walker is going to become Captain America, but it is also telegraphed to the reader that such a succession into the position is going to occur. For that reason, Gruenwald needs to give readers a reason not simply to stop disliking Walker (which does not seem to be his objective) but to truly be invested in him, likable or not. The process through which Walker stops (and kills) the terrorist here is functioning as both an audition in front of the governmental agency in charge of appointing Rogers' replacement (and they use this particular event as the rationalization for choosing him) and an audition for the reader. The A-story in the issue is about the resignation of Steve Rogers, so it is not difficult for a reader to leap to the conclusion that this unlikable patriotic rival is going to be fulfilling the Captain America role. Gruenwald, therefore, begins the attempt of making the character somewhat more sympathetic (while adding layers to his violent tendencies in order to explore the clearly intended path of seeing what an aggressive and murderous Captain America would look like).[7]

Walker's Audition

Issue #332 begins with a figure parachuting toward the top of the Washington Monument. The man is heavily armed with a bandolier of bullets and additional bullets around his waist. Bullets aside, he has the look of a counterculture liberal from the '60s and '70s with his long hair and mustache, but when he reaches the top of the monument and lets his parachute hang from the top, a giant message is revealed and it is obvious that the weapons and bandolier are a more accurate way to read this character's intentions than his hairstyle. The message on the parachute, written in sloppy red paint (looking like dripping blood in places) is "MAKE WAR SOME MORE—WARHEAD" (3). Warhead (as he subsequently calls himself in the next panel) climbs to the very top of the monument, affixes a chair to the top, and sits down, prepared for his next move.

The first step of his operation is obviously to attract attention (hence the parachute sign). This succeeds, drawing a police response and immediate large crowds. Gruenwald then ups the dramatic tension by revealing a "thermonuclear device" that Warhead has brought to the top of the monument (4). In some ways, this could be seen as a textbook set up for a Captain America adversary, but Steve Rogers' antagonists during this era (and earlier) are generally in garish costumes and often with a gregariously explained ideology. While Warhead has a nickname and explains some of his ideology (and it is mostly self-explanatory), he is depicted as more of a real-world threat than, say, a leaping French kickboxer in a purple jumpsuit.[8] There is a plausible visceral quality to Warhead's threat.

The attention goes well beyond the literal crowd in Washington, D.C., and ultimately reaches John Walker and Ethan Thurm in a hotel room in Atlanta. A news bulletin announces the situation at the Monument. Thurm sees this as an ideal moment for Super-Patriot to debut in action in order to get more publicity. Thurm crows, "the monument is soooo symbolic" (11), establishing that the plan for building notoriety for Super-Patriot is to further build patriotic capital. Walker is reluctant, preoccupied with a Super-Patriot rally scheduled for that evening. Thurm convinces Walker to get on a flight with him for D.C. because "this one stunt is worth twenty rallies!" (10).

Walker's reluctance is built around comfort. For a character so defined by arrogance, Walker is someone who, at this point, needs familiarity to be truly comfortable in a situation. The idea of a dangerous bit of heroics is intimidating to Walker, though he does little more than outwardly question the choice, unwilling to risk his insecurities going public. Walker needs a script (and, later, government-directed orders) to maintain his comfort level. At his rallies, he has exactly that. Thurm, in part because he is not the one taking a risk, is unconcerned with maintaining the status quo. We see the detachment to danger and reality for Thurm simply in his choice of the word "stunt" in order to describe the act of stopping a heavily armed terrorist. Thurm sees Super-Patriot as an entertainer and not a hero, but he needs to play "hero" in order to raise his "entertainer" profile. He is so focused on the entertainment and marketing possibilities, he cannot see actual danger. Walker cannot confide in Thurm because Thurm cannot comprehend this apprehension in any way. For Thurm, it is all entertainment (and, subsequently, profit). Walker's Super-Patriot persona would laugh away danger. Out of the costume, Walker is more pragmatic.

Walker is not fully prepared for a mission of this level of danger and difficulty, emotionally or practically. Gruenwald shows him filled with unease and self-doubt throughout his preparations to stop Warhead and the attempt to do so itself. However, he is never depicted as a coward. He proceeds, but does so with reasonable caution (though, of course, the reader knows Steve Rogers would bound ahead and formulate a plan without hesitation). When Walker and Thurm arrive at the scene with Walker in his Super-Patriot uniform, Walker expresses reservations: "I'm not so sure about this, Thurm. I may be brave, but I'm not stupid" (15). Gruenwald is in the early stages of giving this one-dimensional character some depth; Walker is pragmatic and reasonable in this situation. He expresses further viable concerns about the wisdom of an amateur hero accosting a terrorist who possesses a nuclear bomb at the top of the Washington Monument. He does not have a plan, and he is, accordingly, uneasy about how to approach the situation. Thurm literally interrupts Walker to deliver some empty encouraging words: "Think positive ... this'll make you a national hero!" (14). These words have no impact; Walker knows that stopping a terrorist with a nuclear weapon is not accomplished through mere positivity. Thurm is so results-oriented that he cannot be bothered to comprehend the danger of the act itself.

The next panel then shows Walker addressing a police officer. Walker offers to help, but the officer declines. Walker tries to change the officer's mind by showing off his strength (he breaks a large wooden sign), but the officer tells him to move along. Walker then returns to Thurm and explains the authorities do not want his help so they should leave (15). This shows the reader that leaving is what Walker would rather be doing anyway. Again, he is not a coward, but he is a pragmatist. A few pages later, Walker is still there, preparing to act. He thinks, "I ought to have my head examined, letting Ethan talk me into this ... if I want to make a bigger name for myself than Captain America, I gotta use deeds, not words..." (17). So, we see a hesitant John Walker balk at the idea of getting involved and but still letting Sturm talk him into it again, despite his instincts. Walker is a character who, at this stage of his development, needs a mentor or, more specifically, needs orders. He is most comfortable receiving orders.

That does not mean that his ego is not involved in the decision-making; it most certainly is. Walker is not a character who simply takes orders from anyone—those orders have to fit into a larger plan and Thurm knows that the easiest path to convincing Walker to do something is to play to his ego. The ultimate motivation he receives is hubris—only a grand act will eclipse the success of his rival. He is not motivated by patriotism or moral righteousness to stop Warhead. He is motivated by the positive publicity it will generate. This is not to say that Walker is not patriotic. He clearly is.

But Thurm does not tell him, "Do this for your country." Based on Walker's paraphrase, the reader knows that Thurm told him that this act would help him "make a bigger name ... than Captain America." He is motivated by the promise of glory.

As Walker ascends the monument, his internal monologue informs the reader of his lack of confidence by repeated instances of him calming himself and talking himself through the ordeal. Intriguingly, Warhead is also shown as lacking in confidence and experience. He is able to touch down successfully on top of the monument, of course, and this is no small feat, but as he settles in to begin the next phase of his plan, he allows his rations to be blown off his ledge. Gruenwald could have made this character menacing and villainous without bothering to add any character traits or qualities, but by filling Warhead with self-doubt (which is seen as he is landing on top of the monument) and incompetence, he is setting up Warhead and Super-Patriot as parallel inexperienced figures. This is a valuable parallel because Gruenwald wants to emphasize the neophyte aspect of this mission and to have both hero and villain in uncharted territory emphasizes that newness. By giving Super-Patriot an enemy who is also in a bit over his head, it gives a great plausibility to Super-Patriot's eventual victory considering it is indeed Super-Patriot's first real mission and we cannot assume he would be victorious against just anyone.

This is opposed, for example, to pairing him off against a more seasoned and skilled enemy like Flag-Smasher who, even when faced with a much more experienced Walker in issue #348, defeats Walker anyway. Ultimately, Super-Patriot's performance in this battle reveals several important factors. One, his initial trepidation is relatable and, considering his bombast and insensitivity in earlier appearances, this goes a long way toward creating a character that readers can respect while still be appropriately repelled by (Gruenwald is certainly not interested in the reader becoming overly invested in Walker emotionally, especially not at this stage). Two, his casual use of violence in the confrontation is a major character point. He might be legitimately patriotic, but his patriotism is often overwhelmed by violent and aggressive acts.

If Steve Rogers is a Captain America who defeats enemies often through defense, John Walker promises an offensive-minded Cap. Steve Rogers would have never simply killed Warhead (or any other enemy) to end the threat (unless the situation was clearly risking multiple lives, but even then, he would do everything he could to avoid it). Perhaps Walker's technique in the fight (to simply throw his adversary through the air) is driven by his insecurities, but he does it, and his violence becomes normalized internally (and stays there). He also expresses no remorse whatsoever (a contrast to Rogers' extended period of regret and self-doubt following his killing of an U.L.T.I.M.A.T.U.M. soldier in issue #321). Walker enjoys "success" via the violent act (and this continues as he becomes Captain America, as seen in the fatal beating of Professor Power that his partner Hoskins justifies as a result of properly following orders) and this leads to more violent acts: "Aggressive behavior that is rewarded tends to be repeated, and that which is punished tends to be inhibited" (Moyers). Throwing Warhead off the monument is a violent act that is rewarded (this battle with Warhead is the exact impetus that leads the government committee to offer him the role of Captain America). When he starts to personally question his violent acts, Walker does "inhibit" those acts, at least to a degree, but his patriotism and loyalty to country are overmatched by his anger. His self-regulating attempts at inhibiting himself are failures.

The Replacement

In the following issue (#333), the government agency that accepted Steve Rogers' resignation must choose his replacement (the issue is entitled "The Replacement," thus emphasizing the impossibility of any person to truly become Captain America without being seen merely as a replacement to Rogers). The issue begins with Walker (in his Super-Patriot uniform) interviewed on a television program and, based on the interactions we see in earlier issues where he is clearly performing in hopes of glory and fortune, we doubt his sincerity. He tells the reporter, "I do what I do, not for glory, but because it's the right thing to do. Any less would be to squander my God-given talents" (6). First, this idea of acting because of his moral righteousness and not because of glory rings hollow. Is it possible that Walker was humbled by his heroics at the Washington Monument and subsequently motivated to act out of a sense of moral imperative going forward? Of course. But this is the same character who, in issue #323, responds to his agent, upon being advised that they stop their limo and assist an old lady being mugged: "If it won't make the headlines, the Super-Patriot isn't interested." (9). As both a character and moral leader, Steve Rogers is mostly a finished product. While Rogers might be open to change, there is not much, ultimately, that he ought to change.

As a character who needs change (and capable of such change), Walker is an intriguing figure. He is deeply flawed, but if his flaws are erased through an evolved moral sense, perhaps a reader's investment is worthwhile. As the TV interview continues, we are struck by Walker's embellishments of the truth. When the reporter asks in #333 how he managed to maintain such calm in the face of danger, Walker responds, "I spent a lot of time training myself to the peak of my abilities. I know just what my body is

capable of. I calculated the risk as best I could, and decided it was worth it"
(7). Considering the reader is in his head through frequent chain thought
bubbles as he arrives on the scene and as he scales the Washington Monument, we know this to be a fabrication. He also uses this interview to criticize Steve Rogers as Captain America for being a relic unwilling to go as
far to help people as did Walker, pointing out "you didn't see him up there,
did you?" (7) which, unbeknownst to Walker or virtually anyone else, was
because Rogers was resigning as Captain America at the time. Rogers very
well would have handled the situation himself; he was just busy.

As Walker and Thurm are celebrating the effectiveness of his interview, they are interrupted by FBI agents who wish for Walker to speak with
a presidential advisor. While Thurm immediately dismisses the request by
wondering why he has not been asked to speak to the President (because of
Super-Patriot's importance and sudden celebrity), Walker obliges: "When
my government wants to talk, I'll listen. That's the kind of American I am"
(8). Walker accepts the invitation but does so with both arrogance and
showiness—he needs others to grasp the depth of his patriotism. Walker
presents his nationalism as patriotism. This is problematic because it can
seem insincere (in light of other insincerities) and it is aggressive in its
self-righteousness. Every comment he makes about patriotism and America feels like it is not just a celebration of his personal values, but a commentary about how insufficient he views everyone else's level of patriotism.
This moment is a prime example.

His statement of the "kind of American" he is reeks of arrogance, but
he also means it. His patriotism, ultimately, is not insincere—he is willing
to change everything he and Thurm had planned with the Super-Patriot
persona in order to take the job of Captain America, seemingly because
of duty to country (though certainly glory plays a role in his decision)—
but his idea of patriotism as a contest is a cynical way of depicting how
Gruenwald sees the Reagan Republicans using patriotism in the 1980s. Historian Howard Zinn writes that "if patriotism is supporting your government's policies without question, then we are on our way to a totalitarian
state" (223), thus explaining the dangers of nationalism that disguises itself
as something more pristine. A national contest of patriotic one-upmanship
is a blueprint for failure.

After he becomes Captain America, Walker descends into murder
and violence, all in support of his government (occasionally at the expense
of enemies with which he is ideologically inclined to agree). Walker cannot fathom his government would mislead him, and while a reader can
look at this behavior as foolish or naïve, a key aspect (and Gruenwald certainly implies this in Walker's subsequent behaviors) is that this behavior is
depicted as setting a dangerous precedent. Zinn continues his discussion of

patriotism by saying, "defining patriotism as obedience to government— as an uncritical acceptance of any war the leaders of a government decide must be fought—has been disastrous for the American people" (225). Gruenwald accordingly sees Walker's behavior as a disaster because of both his violence and the disrespect his actions show to the position of Captain America. Walker is both blindly obedient and out of control. Walker's patriotism is aligned with obedience and that is a problem.

Walker's Political Leanings

Walker's political leanings are more consistently present in his mind than they are for Rogers, though Walker does consciously attempt (though not outwardly) to come to terms with those values when they coincide too closely with a criminal (or criminal organization) he has been assigned to apprehend. He identifies with 1980s Republican political positions (at least on social issues), but he is still willing to oppose ideologically like-minded domestic terror groups when he is ordered to do so. At the beginning of his missions, he is always the soldier following orders (though his rage will typically challenge or sabotage said mission before its completion). The first mission to which he is assigned is to stop a domestic terrorist organization known as the Watchdogs. In a mission debriefing Walker receives in #335, he is told that the Watchdogs "are against pornography, sex education, abortion, the teaching of evolution—anything they believe to be immoral" (10). While Walker follows through with the mission (and is outwardly agreeable to the mission), his internal monologues, while scant in this issue (certainly compared to the frequent internal thoughts Gruenwald writes for Rogers), show us his misgivings because of both his personal values and relationships. He is sympathetic to the Watchdog's ideology, but he is first a soldier, so following orders trumps ideology.[9]

Primarily, his concerns arise because the Watchdogs' positions on these issues mirror his own. Upon receiving the list of the Watchdogs' values, Walker thinks, "hmm.... I'm against those things too" (10). During this moment of contemplation, Walker is drawn by Tom Morgan in this panel in uniform with his face exposed, his red gloved hand resting pensively on his chin while he ponders his personal belief system and how it resembles that of the Watchdogs. We are not getting a moment of self-doubt, it seems, that threatens Walker's beliefs (he is not suddenly questioning everything he holds to be true), but he acknowledges the parallels between him and this terrorist group. At no point does he outwardly consider that, if he and the Watchdogs share these perspectives, perhaps his personal philosophies could become harmful to others.

Instead, it warrants only internal acknowledgment (and a "hmmm"). Also interestingly, the lettering in Walker's thoughts helps tell the full story. He thinks, "I'm against those things too," and in the lettering by Jack Morelli (and inks by Dave Hunt), the word "I'm" is in boldface, emphasizing Walker's personal struggle, but this struggle is not enough to compromise his acceptance of the mission or his personal beliefs. He internally hits that "I'm" to contemplate his role. While he could be rationalizing that it is okay he agrees with the motivating morality of this terrorist organization (since he opposes their terrorist methods), he is likely emphasizing his personal values in order to consciously separate them from his mission. Yes, he has similar values, but the Watchdogs' methods of emphasizing those values differ. In John Walker's previous appearances, there is nary a mention of these politically conservative beliefs, though the implication of a conservative philosophy is perhaps insinuated in these earlier issues through his southern white rural upbringing, something that is perhaps dangerously veering toward stereotyping.[10] Most importantly, this mission requires him to remove himself philosophically and emotionally. Walker's fatal flaw as Captain America will ultimately be that he cannot remove himself emotionally from missions, despite the fact that he begins each mission as consciously detached as possible.

In addition, he is told that this mission will take him to his hometown in Georgia where he is to go undercover to infiltrate the Watchdogs. At that point, he is worried about having to potentially "turn in somebody [he] know[s]" (11). The reader is lead to believe that he is troubled by his loyalty to his personal beliefs (which may make him sympathetic to the organization he is assigned to take down), but in truth, he is more concerned with loyalty to the people he will potentially have to apprehend (even though their involvement with a domestic terrorist organization would warrant arrest). He never really questions his own beliefs (aside from acknowledging that he and the Watchdogs have overlapping beliefs). He verbalizes none of these concerns to his superiors, a notable fact because it shows his willingness to suppress his political and moral values (and his loyalty to his community) for his larger mission (though, again, the repression of his concerns and feelings leads to his uncontrollable bouts of rage later).

After Lemar Hoskins (eventually known as Battle Star, but here codenamed Bucky[11]), his African American partner, expresses concerns over potentially being lynched, Walker defends the people of his hometown by explaining that "they're good people, just a bit provincial in some ways" (13) thus undermining his partner's very valid concerns based only on his personal naiveté and the shared politics (and personal history) he possesses with those from his hometown. Those concerns are valid because the Watchdogs do eventually capture and string up Hoskins in a noose before (off-panel) he is able to escape on his own. Walker defends the citizens of his hometown at the expense of his friend and partner. In addition, it is difficult to hear his insistence that they are "good people" in our current era and not connect it to President Donald Trump's 2017 infamous claim that there were "very fine people on both sides" when Trump was referring to a conflict between white nationalists and protesters after riots and confrontations in Charlottesville, Virginia ("Full Text: Trump's Comments on White Supremacists, 'Alt-Left' in Charlottesville"). Gruenwald's ability to depict Walker's rationalizations in order to avoid unwanted conflict with people with whom he sympathizes have been proven to be timeless.

Steve Rogers as Captain America is, in many ways, a political blank slate. Most of his thoughts and actions are politically ambiguous enough to make both a Republican or a Democrat feel confident in arguing that he is among their ranks. Gruenwald is careful to keep Rogers as a symbol that transcends the political. Walker is not drawn from the same pen. He makes Walker's political leanings clear to the reader at the onset of his time as Captain America, going so far in this storyline under discussion to align his beliefs with those of a terrorist organization. This allows Gruenwald to do two major things with Walker in terms of reader perceptions: Walker is potentially a political ideologue who favors a belief system that can lead to the use of extreme measures when apprehending criminals, but he is also a nationalist figure who is willing to fight aggressively for his country. His nationalism progresses from being toxic early on (driven by aggression and power) to something more akin to patriotism—self-sacrificing and less self-interested.

At the point depicted when he is embarking on a mission against the Watchdogs in issue #335, his patriotism is tied to following orders. For Walker, this is a high order of patriotism. When Walker is introduced, he resents Rogers and sees him as an obstacle to his own personal goals. As he observes Rogers over time (both from a distance when learning techniques from videos of Rogers in action and more intimately when they meet face-to-face), he ultimately realizes Rogers' unique and innate decency (as well as remarkable fighting skills) and grows to admire him.[12] Thanks to those factors, as well as because of Rogers' unadulterated, admirable, and non-aggressive patriotism, Walker is eventually able to reexamine his own philosophies, examining the nationalism he imagines to be patriotism.

Because of those explicit references to Walker's politics, it is impossible not to look at Walker's patriotism without considering his politics. While Walker is forced to apprehend the Watchdogs because of his orders, he never seems to refute their beliefs, and he actively defends them as people. Obviously, his relationship with the Watchdogs becomes more adversarial as it proceeds, though he seems relatively unfazed by the attempted murder of his partner. Perhaps this is because he is overwhelmed by the personal nature of the mission. He is internally endorsing the Watchdogs' politics, just not the method. There is the implication that, in Walker's mind, the message is pure but the messenger has been corrupted by outside influences, but Gruenwald wants the reader to ponder whether Walker can truly have it both ways by separating the messenger and the message.

Both the messengers and messages of the early American right-wing movement (dating back to the origins of the country) were toxic: "They [early participants in the American Right] were leaders and members of the party of fear.... As moralists of the Right, they were idealists whose vision of utopia was in the past ... 'America' is a dream from the past periled; it needs protectors to preserve its promise for future generations" (Bennett 3). This feels very in line with the Watchdogs' mission. By fixating on the message and believing in the idealism of the message, Walker is also able to fall into this perspective of America as a "dream from the past periled," and Gruenwald appears to use that to make the reader, in a moment like this, sympathize with his earnestness, but also be concerned with his future behavior because of the American history of the ideology he is supporting.

Conflicting Vows

The ideologies in this issue cling to formal ceremonies, and Walker is asked to engage in those procedures. In issue #335, Walker takes two formal pledges within this single issue (complete with repeated words stated while his hand rests upon a Bible), and he acknowledges to himself that doing so makes him feel like a "hypocrite" (18). The first is immediately after a training session and is conducted by the U.S. Government. The second is at the swearing-in ceremony for the Watchdogs (where Walker is working undercover). Considering Gruenwald is so deliberate about including both scenes (and allowing them to contrast), it is worthwhile to look at the text used in both swearing-in ceremonies in detail. First, the pledge recited by Walker when he is being sworn in as Captain America reads as follows:

> I solemnly swear to obey the laws of the nation ... to uphold the constitution ... and to defend liberty, justice, and the American way.... I shall carry out the directives of the commission ... to the best of my ability ... in or out of uniform ... in perpetuity ... so help me God! [5]

Here is the text of the Watchdogs' pledge used during Walker's initiation into the group:

I solemnly vow to walk the virtuous path … to safeguard society from the forces that would corrupt it … and to destroy the enemies of decency … of morality, and of the values upon which our country was founded [18].

These two texts are similar in tone and length. They both begin with solemnity (and the specific word of "solemn," establishing a parallel gravity). Both emphasize protection (the Watchdogs "safeguard" and the government "defend[s]") and the values that drive each entity (the government specifies "liberty, justice, and the American way," while the Watchdogs celebrate "decency" and "morality"). The length of these two vows is almost identical (the government's text has 42 words, and the Watchdogs' text has 36). These similarities encourage the reader to focus on the parallels and therefore sympathize with Walker's personal dilemma of feeling like a hypocrite. However, the similarities are clearly in place as well, correlating the rituals of the American government with those of a terrorist organization. To Walker, it is somewhat awkward that the two are similar in so many ways, but a reader might find the similarities to indicate a closer proximation between the government and a terrorist organization.

Both vows are admirable in their basic elements but problematic in others. If Walker was an experienced spy, perhaps he would have none of these feelings of being a "hypocrite," but he is not (and has no training in that capacity as far as the reader is informed). Beyond that lack of proper preparation, however, the major source of Walker's conflict is that he believes in both pledges. When a person takes two pledges, one out of duty and honor and the other only to fit into a group for an undercover mission, it seems obvious that the first pledge would feel sincere and the second would not. There would be no sense of conflict. Walker believes in both messages (at least to some degree), so conflict exists. A major difference between the two is clearly the Watchdogs' vow of aggression (to "destroy" enemies), and the government vow asks for explicit loyalty in a way that the Watchdogs do not (for the government, Walker vows to "carry out the directives of the commission"). The Watchdogs' vow also emphasizes a right-wing reimagining of the country's history, tying back to the idea of America being a "dream from the past periled," and the government's vow says nothing of history. It can be implied that Walker is conflicted because he is indeed sympathetic to the Watchdogs' basic driving purpose.

Walker ponders this conflict (between national duty and personal principles) while he is being inducted into the Watchdogs. The rest of the group is reciting its oaths emphasizing its values, and Walker thinks how "weird" it is that he "believe[s] in the things their oath is about" (17). He later expresses internal frustration over being "forced to oppose guys whose stand [he's] in basic agreement with" (20). The second comment comes after the Watchdogs are attempting to lynch Hoskins, thus hammering home, through this internal conflict, Walker's status as an ideologue. At the time of the attempted hate crime murder of Hoskins, Walker cannot know confidently Hoskins will survive (it is their first mission and he has no reason to be confident in his partner's ability to escape) and leaves Hoskins in order to protect his cover with the Watchdogs. This turns out to be the right decision, but it is notable that Walker's fierce temper is not ignited by the hate crime against his partner and friend. In fact, even after they begin their attempted lynching of Hoskins, Walker is still considering his "basic agreement" with their "moral stand" (20). He is obviously distraught about the lynching, but he does not waver from the "basic agreement" he feels with their philosophies. Walker separates the villainous tactics of the Watchdogs from their ideology with which Walker sympathizes.

The Good Soldier

In #333, when Walker meets with Valerie Cooper, a government agent who was previously involved in Rogers' removal as Captain America, Gruenwald shows that John Walker's exterior displays of patriotism are related to his innate trust in government. Cooper begins her meeting by telling Walker that she needs to know everything about him in order to possibly make him a remarkable offer and, while he is concerned that this is merely a way for the government to learn about Super-Patriot in order to keep further tabs (and Ethan Thurm, his agent, would have strongly advised against doing so), he goes along with it because, as he thinks, "I refuse to believe a high-ranking official of the good ol' U.S.A. would be party to such trickery" (9), and he proceeds to tell her his biography. This is an internal thought depicted in a chain thought bubble, so there is no doubt to question its sincerity (Gruenwald is a firm believer in the chain thought bubble's ability to give us the truth that even a duplicitous character may be thinking).

His trust of government strikes a reader as naïve, especially in light of Steve Rogers' situation with the Commission, the same committee that is trying to hire Walker, but it was not uncommon for Republicans at the time to maintain this trust in government (and his reactions to the Watchdogs' philosophy shows that he falls in line with these beliefs, though not in the extremist fashion as the Watchdogs themselves). In June 1987 (soon before this issue was published), 59 percent of Republicans said they trusted the government always or most of the time ("Public Trust in Government"). One can argue that the number is inflated because there was a Republican President at the time (only 38 percent of Democrats expressed a consistent trust in government in the same poll), but the more recent lack of trust in government influences the way one views these historical numbers. In March 2019, the number of Republicans who said they trusted the government always or most of the time was 21 percent and that was also during a Republican presidential administration. Clearly, time has changed public perceptions of trust, but Walker's trust is not unreasonable for a Southern Republican from a military/farming family in the mid–1980s.

Walker's background and personal ideology are not lost on the United States government. Walker is assigned the position of Captain America in part because of the government's belief that he will be easier to control than his predecessor. After Walker and his partner Hoskins have completed a training session in issue #335, two government officials (a military general and a man in a suit) share a conversation in which the General expresses concern over Walker's willingness to follow orders (in contrast to Rogers). The man in the suit replies, "Oh, we have ourselves a good soldier this time, General. I know it!" (5). Eventually, Walker's failings as Captain America come about because of his inability to control himself in pressure situations (thus causing harm and disgrace to the title of Captain America), but the initial government instinct is that he will be easier to control precisely because he is a "good soldier" and, therefore, will be more apt to follow orders is indeed true. Walker sees himself in this light and prides himself on it.

Also in issue #335, Walker is speculating on why the original Captain America left the position: Rogers "really shirked his duties to the country by refusing to go along with the commission's plan to coordinate his official activities" (7). To Walker, the idea of the Commission dictating Captain America's duties is common sense. His words reveal no alarm over the Commission's plan to exert control over the position. While Rogers was concerned enough about that governmental control to leave the job behind, Walker sees such obedience as a given. He continues to speculate: "Still can't figure out what motivated him to toss in the towel. Ego, I guess … couldn't handle taking orders" (7). To Walker, taking orders from your superiors *is* patriotism. Refusing to take orders (or, even worse, being incapable of taking orders as Walker speculates) is a sign of profound weakness. While the Commission sees Rogers' behavior as an act of insubordination, Walker thinks of his predecessor as a bad soldier, one that is putting his own needs ahead of his duties. Walker, especially early in his tenure, sees the Captain America position as that of a soldier and, in his interpretation of the rule of a soldier, the ideal soldier is one who follows direction. He sees himself as the ideal soldier because of his personal confidence in his abilities and his understanding of the role.

Because he does not act on his ideological sympathies with the Watchdogs (and does not ultimately align with them), his willingness to follow orders is reinforced. It is a moment where his dedication to his government outweighs his personal political leanings (but his personal political leanings do not seem to be as affected by the fact that the group he somewhat sympathizes with is attempting to lynch his African American friend as they much as they likely should be). Gruenwald gives us a vision of an imposing team of adversaries for a more consistently noble Captain America—John Walker, with both his natural and augmented skills, allied with the Watchdogs, would be a difficult if not impossible team to stop. It does not happen (and, in fact, Walker subdues the Watchdogs to end the mission) because of his pivotal desire to be a "good soldier" above all else. His ideology as an idealist "whose vision of utopia was in the past" (as expressed above by David Bennett in his book *The Party of Fear: The American Far Right from Nativism to the Militia Movement*) is shaped by his trust in governmental structure. He believes in the past because that was when the American government and people were at their strongest (echoed in more contemporary times by Donald Trump's "Make America Great Again" rallying cry).

"At any cost..."

Growth for Walker comes as he begins to question whether or not he is doing right, despite the fact that his orders are being fulfilled. In issue #338, he and Hoskins are assigned a mission in which they are to "neutralize" Professor Power[13] and to do so, as Hoskins reminds Walker, "at any cost, and by any means necessary" (23). Walker does indeed pay "any cost," unnecessarily pummeling Power to death with his steroid-powered punches. Penciller Kieron Dwyer emphasizes this violence with red-tinged close-ups of Walker's fist at different proximities from Power's head, Walker's fist covered in splattered blood. We see Walker's eyes in three consecutive descending panels to reveal his state of mind—in the first, as his rage is building, his eyes are dark, seemingly black; in the second panel, in the full throes of his fury, his eyes are a demonic red; finally, as he realizes what he has done, we see his eyes in close-up one last time in this sequence and they are back to his natural blue and seemingly full of regret (23). After Hoskins has attempted to comfort him by assuring him that they have followed the protocol of the mission (and Power's death at Walker's hand is an acceptable result), Walker refuses to believe he had handled it correctly: "I...blew it." Hoskins tries to reassure him by saying the "boys in Washington" are "gonna love us," but Walker is still unwilling to look past his own actions: "What I did ... is not what I should have done. I'm not the government's official executioner. I'm supposed to fight the good fight, and fight it right" (23). Walker is evolving into someone who is uncertain about the moral correctness of his own actions, but he is not fully evolving into someone who can do anything about it. Steve Rogers is never depicted as someone who needs to morally evolve, and this is a moment where Walker is beginning to see the moral challenges Captain America must face (and how much Rogers excelled in this regard).

He does let himself rationalize his violent actions by agreeing that those actions were within protocol (though he is still internally upset about the actions). Walker is evolving, but he cannot control his rage. The social cognitive theory of self-regulation posits that an individual's "moral agency is manifested in the power to behave, or refrain from behaving, inhumanely" (Shen, et al.). Walker's moral agency acts too late too often, and he still commits violent inhumane acts and must deal with the emotional consequence of regret. He exhibits immoral violent behavior (which is Walker's default), but he develops enough of a moral consciousness to question that behavior, but typically only after it has occurred. In an article entitled "How Social Support Affects Moral Disengagement: The Role of Anger and Hostility," Shen, Sun, and Xin tell us that "Anger and hostility may be considered as risk factors contributing to high levels of moral disengagement," and, while Walker's inability to contain his hostility is a key character trait, his relationship to moral disengagement is ultimately more complicated than simply lacking it. He has a moral center, but his opportunism (most significantly in his early appearances), and his rage (most clearly during his time as Captain America), outweigh whatever personal good he wants to accomplish. The fact he regrets these actions does indeed give the reader hope for his eventual redemption, but his regret does not undo what has been done (and, in fact, simply provides the act with more gravity because even he who commits the act is filled with eventual regret).

Walker, like Rogers, does not lack for confidence. Rogers is always confident he will win a fight or get through a difficult situation. When he first meets Walker in #323, Rogers does not hesitate to believe he would best him in combat (though in issue #327, when they fight to a standstill, that proves to be a more difficult task than he had thought). While Rogers' arrogance is generally more appealing (and coming from a place of reasonable awareness of his abilities), Walker's is less endearing and, possibly, can be viewed as a defense technique to overcome insecurities. For example, when he is reviewing tape of Steve Rogers in action to learn how best to perform as Captain America in issue #334, he thinks to himself, "No matter how good he was, I'm going to be better!" (2). Walker considers how he became Captain America (after Rogers' resignation) and concludes (again, in his own thoughts), "I am the best man for the job." Studying Rogers in action begins to soften Walker's arrogance and subsequent dismissal of Rogers' aptitude. This is important because the influence of Rogers on people (even through video research sessions in this particular scene) encourages them to change (as we see in countless interactions during Gruenwald's run, most notably with his partner and love interest Diamondback). Rogers sees his role as a way to influence both the people and world around him, and Walker sees his role as to promote the needs of the state and defend its interests.

Rogers sees the position as a protector of the nation, certainly, but also as an ambassador of the country to those around the globe. We never see Walker's Captain America in that way because he is forced to fight the government's domestic missions (though his patriotic mentality does not lend us to see Walker as an ideal international ambassador). The contrast of their approaches leads toward thinking about how more global-looking ideologies fit into the role of Captain America (and what a rejection of that philosophy says about Walker). The personal worldview of the person in the Captain America uniform is important for how that person will fulfill the role and, if that person thinks favorably of a cosmopolitan philosophy, Captain America will function differently than if performed by someone who does not follow said philosophy.

Political cosmopolitanism can be interpreted as a "centralized world state, [while] some favor a federal system with a comprehensive global body of limited coercive power, some would prefer international political institutions that are limited in scope" (Kleingeld and Brown). This is not a philosophy that either Captain America would particularly favor (Rogers and Walker both value America as a nation and entity), but Walker's dedication to governmental structure makes him less willing to coalesce behind the philosophy. A less extreme interpretation of Cosmopolitanism can argue, "Nations, for instance, properly exist for the benefit of persons, not the other way around. Broadly speaking, then, cosmopolitanism gives some degree of priority to the interests of humanity over those of nations, and the stronger the priority, the stronger the cosmopolitanism" (Audi 372). This takes us more to Rogers' perspective. We can argue that Walker's patriotism is a sort of aggressive response to the worldview of cosmopolitanism. Rogers' patriotism, as discussed in Chapter Two, is global and willing to see cosmopolitanism as a feasible path. Walker's patriotism is closer to nationalism. Rogers was raised in Brooklyn, a city far more diverse than Walker's Custer's Grove, Georgia, likely further influencing their individual worldviews.[14]

Potential of Patriotism

Walker's patriotism is structured and fully aligned with the belief that the United States is the ideal incarnation of a state. Rogers believes in the potential of Americans; Walker believes in the potential of America as an entity (and not necessarily as a collective of people). Nineteenth-century German poet Christoph Martin Wieland claimed that patriotism is "love of the present constitution of the commonwealth" (qtd. in Kleingeld 34), something that, perhaps, would seem more in line with Rogers' optimism than Walker's structured patriotic loyalty, but it can be argued that neither man is truly dedicated to the "present constitution." Rogers resigns as Captain America because of his inability to trust the governmental structure that is requiring his complicity. Walker trusts that structure (even allowing the government to fake his death and give him a new identity) and is closer to possessing appreciation for the present structure of the government as opposed to what it once was (or could be).

Rogers has more trust in what the country *can* become, and Walker has more trust in what it *used to be*. In Gruenwald's time on the comic, we are decades from Donald Trump's calls to "Make America Great Again," but we see the fabric of why that slogan could resonate with certain portions of the populace as demonstrated with Walker. Walker also values youth and progress, as long as it progresses things in a way that maintains his personal ideals (and gets back to what he values). Walker's constant dismissals of Rogers as being old and out of touch show that he feels Rogers is too old to be a proper contemporary symbol. Wieldland elaborates that "Patriotism is the natural product of the contentment of the people ... based on the justice of the laws and the reliability of their enforcement" (qtd. in Kleingeld 34).

If Walker feels that patriotism is based on how safe and content is the populace, and he subsequently decides that indeed the populace is appropriately safe, he is deluding himself. Though he is naïve early (proven in part by his insistence that the racist residents of his hometown are good people), after he has served as Captain America and the realities of the corruption of the world become clear, he becomes more disillusioned. For Gruenwald, this is progress. One has to be aware of the dangers around them to mature as a person. Both Captain Americas realize further that one person in a red, white, and blue uniform cannot protect all Americans, regardless of the strength, integrity, or skill of that person. Therefore, Wieldland's view of patriotism is unattainable in Gruenwald's reality, though Walker's Captain America might be more inclined to believe in the possibility.

Eventually, Walker realizes the faults and potential corruption of the government. As U.S. Agent, he still works within that system rather than disowning it. He also grows enough as a character to realize that Rogers is a better fit for the role of Captain America than is he. In *Kant and Cosmopolitanism: The Philosophical Ideal of World Citizenship*, Kleinig writes, If "one's patriotism involves a complex engagement with one's country, confronting the murky past or even present will not generally undermine a patriotic commitment." (39). Indeed, it does not corrupt Walker's resolve in serving his country. It hardens him and the wide-eyed young man looking to impress the government is not the man that occupies the U.S.Agent costume (and, in this persona, he ends up both fulfilling obligation and duty to country while maturing into a hero who is more capable of controlling his rage). Ultimately, Walker learns more from Steve Rogers than simply watching Rogers' combat expertise with a shield. When Walker first learns of Rogers' resignation in issue #333, he is shocked, wondering, "Why would anyone who says he loves his country do a thing like that?" (10).

By issue #350, Walker can go to the Commission that gave him the shield in the first place and accept their decision to force him out too. He learns that patriotism is not blind trust: "One may stay resolutely patriotic at the same time as one acknowledges the failures and crimes of the past" (Kleingeld 39). When the character first appears, Walker is convinced that the present is not ideal and a positive future needs to take the cue of that past. That changes. Gruenwald creates a John Walker who genuinely loves his country (albeit with a love that is naïve and lacking in complexity) and is manipulated by others as a result of that simplistic patriotism. Once his patriotism is exploited and he realizes where it has led him, Walker does not give up his love of country. Instead, he invests further, taking on a new identity and becoming a different hero, one still willing to serve and trust his country, but doing so with the experience of one who was misled as a result of his trust.

FOUR

Generation Cap

Generational Interactions
in Gruenwald's Captain America

Generationally speaking, the Gruenwald era on *Captain America* has a lot going on. Cap, technically, is a senior citizen. Born in 1920,[1] he would be in his 60s and 70s during the time of these issues. Despite this, he has the body of a preposterously fit man in his 20s or 30s. This is an important dynamic in these comics—he is an older man (with values and beliefs reinforced in an earlier age) who has to pass himself off (especially when he is playing the part of Steve Rogers to those who do not know he is Captain America) as a younger man in a dramatically different time from when he was originally coming of age. That is a key tension constantly in play in the comics dating from Stan Lee's reintroduction of the character to Gruenwald's interpretation and beyond. It is also only the start—there is also the tension of this temporally misplaced man being written by a Baby Boomer (a generation responding against the parental guidance of the G.I. Generation and Silent Generation that preceded them). Add to that the fact that this character is being created for the entertainment (and, arguably, moral education) of an entirely different group—Generation X (and, in the later stages of Gruenwald's run, Millennials).

Obviously, the audience for these comics would not be limited to just Generation X (or any one generation at all). While later Boomers certainly could be seen as part of the audience and, considering Cap's identity, perhaps even older readers relating to his background, the style and approach of these comics (the language and violence content) are tame compared to writers appealing to more mature audiences. Alan Moore's work[2] comes to mind as a contemporary example of this type of maturity, and the stories themselves lack the narrative complexity of Chris Claremont's work on *Uncanny X-Men*.[3] These factors establish *Captain America* as being geared toward a younger audience. In addition, the advertisements in these issues are mostly promoting toys, cartoons, and candies, thus further establishing that younger readers were, if not the primary audience, the most targeted audience. By analyzing the individual wants and needs of those in these varied generations and how Gruenwald responds to the unique circumstance of each generation, we can see how he took this tension and made it into a vital representation of generational connection and conflict. Perhaps this tension is not so evident that younger readers would be aware of the conflict, but serious readings certainly reveal this perspective. These comics can provide a clear understanding of what, despite their differences, these generations can do for each other.

Aging in Comic Books

Aging in comics is rarely depicted as linear—Spider-Man/Peter Parker can be 15 in 1962 and only be in his 20s in the 1990s, so ages (and generations) are never easy to delineate. *Captain America* (and most comics) function within a floating timeline, a concept in which characters not portrayed by actors who are subjected to the inevitable laws of aging (including animated and drawn characters) do not age.[4] Rex Stout, who created the detective character Nero Wolf, discussed the concept of a floating timeline:

> Those stories have ignored time for thirty-nine years. Any reader who can't or won't do the same should skip them. I didn't age the characters because I didn't want to. That would have made it cumbersome and would seem to have centered attention on the characters rather than the stories [qtd. in M. Taylor].

This mentality is present in these comics as well though, obviously, this method is in no way unique to Gruenwald or any individual comics writer. It was just the silently agreed-upon method once these comics stories continued.

The challenge this presents for a discussion of comic book characters and their generational profiles is obvious—the Steve Rogers in a Stan Lee-penned comic in the 1960s is the same age as he is in a Mark Gruenwald comic in the 1990s. So the generational profiles discussed therein are based on estimates of character ages as they appear in a given comic and not based on the character's previous longevity. Steve Rogers and Sam Wilson first meet in 1969's issue #116 and are partners for the better part of the next decade. After some time of not working together, they reunite in 1987's issue #337. Although over 20 years of real-time have passed, they are seemingly the same ages they would have been in 1969. Importantly, though, those times together are in no way erased. They still share those experiences. If Gruenwald in 1987 was to refer to some previous mission originally written in the 1970s and have it recapped in flashback, we can assume that the details of the adventure would remain the same even though the setting and landscape would potentially be updated.

This discussion, then, is based on relationships and experiences, and makes no effort to be exact. The only moments in which specific ages can be determined are when the comic provides them in the context of the issue (though if a character is identified as being a certain age in one issue, that in no way guarantees that character's age in a later issue).

Captain America's Generational Profile

Captain America's complicated generational profile is a logical place to begin this discussion because he is encompassing different generations within his single person. Steve Rogers' birth generation, the G.I. Generation, was defined by an "unprecedented level of commitment to American society in the war effort and beyond," but that commitment declined as they became senior citizens (Sweet-Cushman, et al.). Cap, of course, does not follow the fellow members of his generation into old age because of his accidental suspended animation, so perhaps this helps explain his deviation from this generational pattern (though his thorough dedication to his cause is certainly unique and not explained by any generational traits). Obviously, Cap's level of commitment to the American people does not waver, but his willingness to support the American government does.[5] This shows him as a man split between his moral commitment of loyalty to government and country, and the power of the individual emphasized by Baby Boomers.

The Baby Boom generation is one of which he is not technically part but, considering his time as an adult in this era, is a generation with which he clearly identifies in key ways. Traits that define aging Baby Boomers that Cap shares (and these are traits identified in Boomer's older years, after Gruenwald's time on the comic, though they are still relevant because they were established over time) include rational and well-considered decision making and discipline (Abramson). This generation (in the 1970s and early 1980s especially) was also deemed the "Me Generation" by Tom Wolfe for its self-obsession and lack of attachment to institutions (Patrick). While the latter traits do not seem like a particularly logical fit for Cap (and would not have to be, following the idea that he encompasses and rejects traits from multiple generational profiles), it can be argued that it would take a narcissistic personality to accept the responsibility of his mission and he does indeed show a willingness to join, leave, and rejoin the Avengers with some frequency.

Cap may show the standard Narcissistic Personality Disorder (NPD) belief that an individual "is special and can only be understood by or associate with special people or institutions" ("Narcissistic Personality Disorder") and, as defined by the Mayo Clinic, he has difficulty with basic emotions, an unwillingness to deal with others who fall short of his own expectations, and he secretly feels insecure ("Narcissistic Personality Disorder," Mayo Clinic). These last few traits come especially to the surface in #401, an issue focusing upon Cap's self-doubt (and that issue is discussed in the Introduction). Ultimately, if it can be said Cap does show narcissistic tendencies, they fit more in the spectrum of "Healthy Adult Narcissism," considering that he certainly does not lack empathy and he maintains a sense of creativity, characteristics representative of Healthy Adult Narcissism as laid out by Nina Brown (7). Obviously, not all Boomers are narcissists, but he is again displaying aspects of multiple groups while fitting neatly into none.

This creates a unique dichotomy. The straight-arrow part of his personality is a product of what was instilled in the G.I. Generation in childhood:

> During their childhood, G.I.'s have been fussed over by protective parents determined to raise up kids as good as the Lost Generation [that preceded this generation] had been bad. Youth clubs, vitamins, safe playgrounds, pasteurized milk, child labor laws, even Prohibition: these were all efforts to keep kids away from the danger and decadence of the prior generation [Strauss and Howe 158].

Captain America clearly embodies this ideal—he does not drink[6] or smoke, and he outwardly emphasizes optimism and the power of cooperation. In his abstention from drugs and alcohol, he is also showing signs of never fully maturing past that G.I. Generation childhood, which is perhaps illustrated even further by his simple and rigid moral code. Rogers' unwillingness to drink because it would not properly project the kind of moral properness he wishes to convey to youth is so well-known to the public at large that, in issue #425, a second Super-Patriot (later revealed to be to Steve Rogers' former neighbor Mike Ferrell) attempts to discredit Captain America by donning the Captain America uniform, walking into a bar, and drinking.

Ferrell, in the Cap uniform, sits at the bar and orders a "drink," adding "make it a stiff one," to which the bartender admits he did not know Cap drank alcohol. Ferrell responds curtly, "you do now" (9). When the bartender explains that Cap's presence in this seedy bar is hurting his potential business because the real Cap has come into conflict with many of the patrons, Ferrell lifts up a bottle and declares drinks are on him. Rogers has so carefully cultivated a certain type of reputation, even a legal and permissible act (ordering a drink at a bar) followed by a generous deed (buying drinks for others) could come across as inflammatory. Ferrell's attention to detail in attempting to discredit the notoriously morally upstanding and non-drinking Captain America is notable—instead of ordering any specific drink (which most other people at a bar would do), he is purposefully vague. He creates the false character of a Captain America who does not know specifics (which would likely be true for Steve Rogers in such a situation) in an attempt to accurately mimic him.

In addition to his belief in morally abstaining from alcohol, drugs, and cigarettes (things from which the parents of those in the G.I. Generation may have tried to shield their children but certainly failed in most cases, at least in the long run), he also adheres strongly to the power of teamwork (a crucial G.I. Generation trait, and one not as traditionally shared by Baby Boomers in the 1980s).[7] His loyalty to the Avengers (both in concept and execution) is unflinching and, despite *Captain America* being a solo title, he actually participates in relatively few adventures completely on his own, aided by either other Avengers, like Hawkeye in issues #316–317 or Black Widow in issues #372–377 among many examples, or his own personal partners such as Falcon, Diamondback, Demolition Man, and Nomad (all featured in too many issues in this run for it to be helpful to list their appearances). He is a team-player, whether that is proven by his time leading (or simply as a member of) the Avengers, or frequently collaborating with other heroes in his own pages. Most of these adventures in which Cap is working without an ally happen at two specific points in Gruenwald's run—at the beginning of it (where Gruenwald is more interested in fleshing out both Cap's villains and Cap's basic characteristics) and after #350 once Steve Rogers has once again taken over the role of Captain America. In both cases, he takes on allies to help his cause in time (calling in D–Man, Nomad, and Falcon to assist him which he takes on the guise of The Captain starting in issue #336 and #337, and teaming up with Diamondback frequently after she assists him in "The Bloodstone Hunt" starting in #357). He is most comfortable as a member of a team and, specifically, as leader of said team.

Those in the G.I. Generation (also known as the "Greatest Generation") are those born between 1900 and 1924 ("American Generation Fast Facts").[8] The shadow of the G.I. Generation looms large culturally. Historian and G.I. Generation member William Manchester recalls, "we were a special generation. We *were* America. You get used to that" (qtd. in Strauss and Howe 158). This is true in both our reality and the reality of these comics. The difference, of course, is that, in the comics, Captain America himself *is* America in the way Manchester recalls his own perceptions. He represents this generation's greatness. The contributions of his generation—and significantly of Captain America himself—defined the era and dictated the direction the world would take for a century and, based on generational raising, it did not happen by accident. Steve Rogers himself takes on that responsibility by very much embracing the symbolism of his role and uniform to position himself as America (in the way Manchester alludes).

The G.I. Generation was well prepared by their parents and was given an example to react against from the Lost Generation, the generation that precedes the G.I. Generation, seen as those born between 1883 and 1900 (Longley). Cap himself specifically echoes this sentiment in #421: "Each generation has the chance to go beyond the accomplishment, good or bad, of the previous one" (18). And, thanks to the longevity granted by the Super-Soldier treatment he undertook as a young man and the suspended animation that would lead him to live vital years in an era that was not his birthright, he has a unique ability to experience the active response of one generation that is not his own to a generation that is his own while feeling potential attachment (and detachment) to both.

Obviously, it is important to be cautious of generalizing, even as we engage in an activity so requiring of generalization as discussing the traits of a generation. While we see the childhoods of those in the G.I. Generation as defined by parents trying to avoid the mistakes of the Lost Generation, young Steve Rogers did not have the idyllic childhood that such a generalization would assume. In issue #421, Cap explains, "My father was an alcoholic, a wife beater, a quitter" (18). This educates the title and the character in multiple ways. It avoids letting us look at Cap's generation (or his childhood) as a perfect one. He is unique in his circumstances, even if he shares vital traits with those of his birth generation. It also may be a potentially relatable trait for those of younger generations of readers who have (statistically-speaking) experienced less idyllic childhoods (based on the statistical likelihood of divorce rates) than what may have been the generational standard for the G.I. Generation. Susan Thomas-Gregory says that the unifying question that a person can ask someone from Gen-X (in the same manner as an older Baby Boomer could easily recall where they were when John F. Kennedy was shot, for example) is "When did your parents get divorced?" While Cap is very much an individual with unique experiences and is a person adjusting to an era in which people going through life at the same age as he seems to be aware of a younger generation, he still most closely embodies the G.I. Generation, especially since Gruenwald essentially lets him show signs of aging as his run on the title continues.

Early in the run, Cap fits in with the Boomers that surround him (more independent, more prone to associate with other Boomers), but as the title eases into the '90s, he has a harder time. He frequently becomes frustrated with young people he encounters. In issue #422, Cap is outside and passes a group of young people listening loudly to contemporary music (the song is the very nineties hip-hop song "Whoomp! [There It Is]" by Tag Team). In an interior monologue, he expresses how he wants to ask them to turn it down, but he ultimately does not do so because he is too busy (5).[9] It seems unlikely that Cap earlier in this run would have been much bothered by the music (and he seems to enjoy watching and listening in to conversations between younger people in those earlier Gruenwald issues).

In #419, he also notes "a vicious streak" in women he encounters "these days" (10), revealing him as out of touch with women (which is a trait that Diamondback is often frustrated with during her interactions and romantic aspirations with Cap). This also shows that Cap is perhaps poorly navigating the world of women around him, something a person of outdated views would potentially demonstrate. One of the women he specifies as he considers this "vicious streak" thought is the anarchist terrorist Viper, for whom "mean streak" seems insufficient, but overall it is still an unfair generalization.[10] So, while he tends toward the "get off my lawn" mentality in these final issues of Gruenwald's, he still reaches out to younger generations in specific cases (as will be discussed in key examples below), as he maintains connections with the generation most closely attributed to him by birth. So even this aging Cap (and his aging is most clearly illustrated by his declining physical abilities and his lessening capacity to hide his temper and frustration[11]) is not unwilling to reach out to and work with people in younger generations.

Cap's World War II "Reverie"

Cap is not the type of World War II vet that looks back on what he did with a sense of nostalgia as if the accomplishments once achieved can never be surpassed. In issue #307, he is on a flight back from London's Heathrow Airport (dressed in full uniform) when he sits beside a man who waxes on nostalgically about his personal experience during World War II. The man speaks proudly of his accomplishments and personal physical strength at the time. "The Luftwaffe never stood a chance…" he says (3). As the man says this, he does not look at Cap, who is sitting next to him—instead, he looks off ahead a bit, and the small printing of the letters (by letterer Diana Albers) makes his words feel far away, as if to indicate that these thoughts are mostly for his own benefit.

The man clearly is not saying these things to impress Captain America; he is saying these things because they are of value to him personally. They are taking him back to a time in which he truly mattered. The man, drawn by penciler Paul Neary as bald and overweight, is clearly reminiscing about what he sees as his finest days and accomplishments. Cap knows full well that World War II is in no way the only time in his life in which he mattered (though the other man might be inclined toward that sentiment). While Cap is not interested in lingering on the past, he too reminiscences at this moment, just not verbally as does the man beside him. Cap first, in a thought bubble, expresses his wish that his "seatmate will ease up a bit" (2). He is not rude—the thought is internal, and the "seatmate" seems very content with his own memories.

Cap is jetting from one adventure to what he knows will be another adventure soon. He needs to sleep. Cap closes his eyes and imagines his World War II days. It is a reverie, too, just like the passenger beside him— Gruenwald even uses the word "reverie" in the text—but it is short and pleasant and personal. He does not linger over Bucky's death (his partner who, as far as continuity was concerned in 1985, lost his life in World War II); that is a reality long since accepted. Instead, he thinks of his time fighting alongside The Invaders (his World War II team of heroic adventurers), drifts off to sleep, and the recollection retakes its proper place in the reserve of Cap's memories. It does not need to be at the forefront; he just has it available for recall whenever it is needed. This is showing that Cap is both of his generation (willing to linger back on the events that defined his generation) and apart from it (able to let go). It is also worth noting that Cap's hibernation keeps Cap's recollections of the war closer to his consciousness. For the World War II vet next to him on the plane, the war was decades ago. For Cap, it is more recent. Cap is frozen before the war ends and is revived twenty years later with everything still vivid.[12]

G.I. Generation Allies

A minor character and friend of Cap's worth discussing in regard to the G.I. Generation is Rogers' old friend Arnie Roth. Roth is his oldest living friend and, while they are of the same generation by birth and hold the same basic ideals, they have had different overall experiences and, of course, have very different bodies and physical capacities. After Cap moves out of the Avengers Mansion, he takes up a new headquarters. In issue #428, he recruits personal friends and allies (rather than Avengers) to help him when his health is diminishing. The bottom of the headquarters is a costume shop—a front—and Cap asks Roth, who has been living in Florida, to help him by running the costume shop. Roth, a member of this generation defined by dedication and loyalty, indeed comes back to New York for his old friend's sake.

Gruenwald's final issues are defined by Captain America's decaying body slowly killing him. In issue #428, Cap reveals to his oldest friend that he is dying, and Roth reciprocates the confession with one of his own: "I've got bone cancer. That's why I came back to help you. If I have less than a year to live, I wanted to do something useful" (21). Then they embrace silently—two dying men of the World War II generation—a generation on the brink of dying out—looking for their last chance to continue to do good. For both men, the objective is "to do something useful." This is the philosophy that has driven Steve Rogers since before taking on the mantle of Captain America and it clearly has driven Roth as well. This gesture of doing something good for humanity is what has propelled the choices and decisions they have made.

This portrayal of Roth is clearly flattering. So too are his depictions of other characters in the G.I. Generation (a place we can put Nick Fury, who makes a few appearances, but is limited in these pages). Peggy Carter, an associate of Cap's from wartime, is employed by Cap at Avengers headquarters and is in charge of updating Cap on missions and transmissions. She, like Roth as described above, is equally eager to help, but her role is limited, likely by gender (a problem that comes up in these issues on occasion). She is depicted as relentlessly loyal and a hard worker (she works much longer hours than Cap asks her to). Cap treats her respectfully and she reciprocates that respect. Gruenwald portrays these characters as respectful (though Nick Fury is less inclined in this fashion), dedicated to service, and loyal.

A character from this generation who does not embody these positive traits is the Red Skull, but this villain from Cap's World War II days would be evil regardless of generational designation. What is important to note here, however, is that Gruenwald's version of Red Skull is perhaps more Gordon Gekko from Oliver Stone's 1987 film *Wall Street* than the Nazi manipulator/madman readers encounter in earlier versions.[13] His consciousness has been inserted into a clone of Steve Rogers so he has Rogers' body (though his face is grotesquely turned red and skull-like). He wears a suit and takes up an office in Washington D.C. to look over the country he wants to destroy. He presents himself as a businessman, albeit one who is looking to thrust the world into chaos in order to take it over.[14] This Red Skull takes the Nazi lineage that made him such a logical foil to Cap in the 1940s, and Gruenwald adds the elements of greedy, evil, politically well-connected American businessmen to make him a logical foil for Cap in the 1980s and 1990s. Skull's timeless evil allows him to transcend generational profiles and fit into (and exploit) whatever era he happens to occupy. He is still a madman, but this acquired business acumen allows him to fit into the 1980s landscape.

Cap as Baby Boomer

Even though Cap does not embody traits of the G.I. Generation exclusively and is sympathetic to Baby Boomer characteristics, he is very different from the Boomer characters, good and bad, that surround him (although, of course, Captain America has very few peers when it comes to his personal righteousness and dedication regardless). The Baby Boomer characters in these comics are often impulsive and driven by passion. Cap is not; he is calculating and careful. In issue #323, when John Walker[15] (in his Super-Patriot persona) is disparaging Steve Rogers, he attacks his age, calling him "old, slow, and out of touch" (12). While the storyline reason for these remarks ties back to Cap's uncharacteristic use of a gun in a previous issue, it is an important reminder that the world sees Cap differently from how he often sees himself. He does not linger on his age (save for those aforementioned times in which his body is betraying him, and he is becoming prone to paralysis, but that is less about age than viability). While Steve Rogers can pass for a Baby Boomer, John Walker's age-ist insults remind us that Steve Rogers as Captain America cannot do so. Accordingly, his age and experience are traits by which he is consistently judged.

Nomad

Cap is not the only character featured in this title with a complicated generational profile. Steve Rogers was of enlistment age in the 1940s, but his suspended animation and subsequent reanimation make his age doubly difficult to define. According to the "Nomad (Jack Monroe)" entry on the Marvel.com character database, Nomad was born in 1941 but was eventually also placed in suspended animation. Monroe self-identifies as 23 in a job interview in issue #307 (7), so he does identify age-wise with the Baby Boomer generation, though his initial upbringing would put him as a member of the Silent Generation, a generation called "The Lucky Few" by Elwood Carlson because of both the generation's fortune of having fewer bloody conflicts occur during their coming of age than in the World Wars fought by the G.I. Generation and Lost Generation before them and also the relative economic prosperity of their era (again, especially in comparison to the generations that preceded them). Like Cap, Nomad is of two generations, and the complexity of the character's generational profile makes him a compelling figure to analyze.

Knowing these complexities exist, the depiction of Nomad's

relationship with Captain America can give us insight into multiple generational dynamics; Nomad idolizes Cap and feels unable to fully live up to the legacy Captain America has established. He is also depicted as lazy (it is implied in #307 that he spends a large chunk of his time on Cap's couch), impulsive, and erratic. He desperately wants Cap's approval—Nomad thinks in #325, "Disobeying Cap may make him lose all respect for me, and deep down, I want his approval more than anybody's" (21) as Cap has involved himself in a conflict between Nomad and a mobster villain known as the Slug. His birth generation was seen as cooperative and respectful: "Raised in a paternalistic environment, the silent generation was taught to respect authority. Conformity and conservatism are prized. They tend to be good team players" (Kane). Based on observations dating back to the early 1950s, people of this generation as less inclined toward revolution and hardworking and loyal (Crowley and Florin 37). Nomad's desire for approval from his preceding generation is characteristic of the Silent Generation but, as discussed, there is a generational conflict within him that makes things more complicated.

His Silent Generation respect is outweighed by his personal animosities. Immediately after he internally admits his need to impress Cap, he thinks, "But I'll be flogged before I help that slimy slug" (21), he says, acknowledging that stopping the Slug outweighs his adherence to both Captain America personally and Cap's philosophies. Nomad is impetuous and prone to emotionally-driven decisions that overwhelm his own ability to perform. He clearly overreaches because of his personal drive and confidence. This embodies the Baby Boomer need to fulfill personal gratification and illustrates the overall driven nature of the generation, and his actions reveal a need to rebel against Cap (and, in a fashion, rebel against Cap's generation), despite part of Nomad strongly resisting the urge.

This is an example of the Baby Boomer drive to "implicit[ly] rebuke" the G.I. Generation's "Wonder Bread Culture" (Strauss and Howe 222). In issue #309, Nomad says to Cap: "You tend to take charge of every situation you're in. As a result, a partner of yours might never really learn to be self-reliant ... take the initiative" (23). Nomad is torn—he wants Cap's respect and admiration, but there is still the Boomer that has manifested itself in him and, subsequently, strives for individual accomplishments. He is driven to prove his own worth. After Nomad declines to continue on as Cap's partner, he goes forth as a solo adventurer. When they reunite for the first time in several issues in #325, Cap notices a difference in behavior after Nomad's been out of his tutelage for a while: "Something about Jack has changed. There is a bit of a harder edge to him than when he was my eager to please partner" (16). Under Cap's guidance, he was more able to tap into his natural Silent Generation tendencies of respect and dedication. Without Cap, he is undisciplined and often vindictive. That "harder edge" naturally manifests itself as Nomad lives his life as a twenty-something in the mid–1980s and becomes more aligned with and sympathetic to the Baby Boomer mentality.

While Cap and Nomad are both reflective of some Baby Boomer tendencies, the clearest Baby Boomer at work in these pages is writer Mark Gruenwald himself. This study is not going to look at Gruenwald's personal life to establish the Boomer influence of this comic, but instead at his efforts as a writer, and what his creative choices say about his generation, his generation's priorities, and his generation's relationship with other generations.

John Walker as Baby Boomer Villain

The previously mentioned John Walker (Super-Patriot and eventually Rogers' temporary replacement) is a representative Boomer, and not a particularly positive one. He grew up in the rural south and was a child when his brother was killed in the Vietnam War. Walker then decides to follow in his brother's footsteps in order to also serve his country and, after undergoing a strength-enhancing procedure that leaves him freakishly powerful, opts against a career in professional wrestling (where most of the people who undertake the procedure end up) and decides instead to become a heroic figure. Whatever the impetus of his decision to be a masked patriotic symbol, paying tribute to his brother is hardly on his mind as we meet him in the guise of the Super-Patriot. While the patriotism is likely sincere (though that is cemented later—in his first appearances, his patriotic sincerity is very unclear), his nationalism is a much more brutal form than the reader is used to with Cap's patriotism. He is disrespectfully ageist toward Cap, money-hungry, and dishonest. He is opportunistic, associates with underhanded people, and is desperate for celebrity. He is also, arguably, a critical commentary on Baby Boomers.

Bruce Gibney, author of *A Generation of Sociopaths*, argues what the title of the book states—that Boomers (specifically those who are white and middle class) are disproportionately sociopathic in nature. In an interview with Carolyn Gregoire, Gibney states that Boomers are "rebellious and messy, both in the literal sense and in their approach to their own affairs." He further explains that these Boomers tend to assume things will work out (especially for them), so there is little reason to exert effort (Gregoire). Walker is not inclined to actually seek out real battle situations early on in his time as Super-Patriot.

Baby Boomer Allies

Despite Gruenwald's own membership in the generation, Walker's depiction is a glaring indictment. Other characters are harder to define, generationally, but one can likely put Diamondback, Falcon (Sam Wilson, Cap's partner in this comic during large portions of the 1970s), and Demolition Man (Dennis Dunphy, also known as D–Man) in the Baby Boomer camp, and these are all more flattering depictions than that of John Walker. Their ages are not specified, but Diamondback and D–Man appear fairly early in Gruenwald's run and are both in their 20s or slightly older (Diamondback is likely on the younger end of that spectrum, and Falcon is on the older end though, as discussed above, these are educated guesses).

Diamondback overcomes a youth of poor choices and criminal experience while close to Cap. Her attraction to him is purely physical at first, but she is eventually drawn in by his decency, something missing in her own life (considering her prior associations with the Serpent Society and, earlier, her criminal brother and Crossbones). She is a character making selfish choices before being guided toward the good thanks to her interaction with Cap. In issue #433, she chooses to affiliate with the villain Superia in order to cure the illness that is paralyzing Cap, so even when she does revisit the criminal life, her intentions are more selfless than they once were. Gruenwald is commenting on the potential for change based on learning from respected elders (such as is the case with Cap).[16]

D–Man is a strength-augmented professional wrestler who associates with Cap, and Falcon is Cap's long-time partner (though he serves in that role less often during Gruenwald's term). Both offer complimentary views of Baby Boomers—reflecting Boomer traits, D–Man is passionate and spirited (Strauss and Howe 98) and willing to see the good in people, even those who criticize him (exemplified by the hostility he gets from Nomad). D–Man is honest and leads with a sense of righteousness to the cause. He also is a decent person prior to the influence of Cap, though his earlier friendship with superhero The Thing in the pages of *The Thing* perhaps is influential too. Falcon reflects a rebellious spirit. When offering advice to Cap in #337, he suggests, "It's like the '60s, Steve. You've got to protest! Stand up to the establishment when they commit an injustice!" (10). While Gibney asserts that Boomers did not pass those laws that secured the Voting Rights Act and Civil Rights Acts (it was those of the G.I. Generation and Silent Generation that did so) and in fact "played no part in those foundational victories" (Gregorie), Gruenwald uses Falcon's activism and experience to refute Gibney's claims. These depictions are valuable because they show us that Gruenwald's view of his own generation is not wholly negative, and there is obviously hope for decency, but the self-obsession and greed of the Boomers do not escape his judgment.

Generation X Allies and Leanings

Gruenwald's words were not written just for himself or the Baby Boomer generation, of course. Those of a younger age during this decade are a key part of the demographic audience for most Marvel comics and *Captain America* is no different. Studies have seen a rise in the average age of comic readers over the course of the last several decades until 2019, but those numbers were predominantly teens and younger in the 1980s (Rogers). This is assuredly due, in part, to young comic readers remaining interested as they age. It is anecdotal but useful to take Joe Field—owner of Concord, California, comic shop Flying Colors Comics—and his observations: In 1988, "the average age of [our] customers was about 18" (qtd. in Rogers). While specific demographic data is not available, to say that a Gen X audience was a significant part of who Gruenwald was attempting to reach is not an illogical leap.

In issue #307 in 1985, Gruenwald's first as writer on the comic, there are nine full pages of ads and/or public service announcements—a third of them promote other comics, another third advertise candies and cookies, and the remaining three are comprised of a PSA for reporting sexual abuse, an ad for bicycles, and an ad for a young astronauts club (featuring Captain America himself). Gruenwald's final issue (#443 in 1995) shows some potential age increase but stays within the age-frame (and therefore targeting Millennials): of the ten full page (or two-page spread) ads, two are for family-targeted films, two are for video games, two are for clothing (athletic shoes and jeans), three are food/drink products (a kid's cereal, a snack food, and a soda), and one is for comic subscriptions. One of the two movie ads is for *The Baby-Sitters Club*, which would certainly target an audience of younger Gen X/older Millennial girls. This shows that the audience for these comics was changing even if the age of that audience remained fairly consistent.

This certainly helps us maintain Gen X (and, also, Millennials by 1995) as the key target demographic. Therefore, Generation X, with a loose boundary of birth years between 1965 and 1980 (and while there is no real consensus, those born in the 1970s and soon before are usually considered), is the group identified as the main audience for this run. This is not a perfect encapsulation, as assuredly older audiences would have been more compelled to this title than perhaps to titles with younger protagonists (thanks to its older and arguably old-fashioned protagonist), and some people born in the early to mid-eighties would have been readers by 1995. Considering Gruenwald started this run in 1985, that would put Gen X readers between the ages of 5 and 20 when it starts, and would subsequently follow through most of the childhood for the later Gen Xers (and the increasing age of comic reader over time indicates that many younger readers stayed as comic readers).

Gen Xers were living in a world in which adulthood was valued more than childhood: "American's new consciousness celebrated childhood as an ideal, but it neglected childhood as an actual living experience" (Strauss and Howe 195). This is not to say that Gen Xers did not enjoy childhood, but their childhoods were perhaps, in general terms, more self-guided than previous generations. The Baby Boomers aging deeper into adulthood were larger and more present in society as a group entity and Gen Xers were identified as "slackers"[17] and generally overlooked. That sense of being overlooked evolved into self-reliance. That is not the case with Gen X characters in these pages. In Gruenwald's *Captain America*, the Gen X characters are treated with more consistent respect—they are depicted as less slacker and, in one case at least, more hacker.

Ram Riddley

The best representation of a Gen Xer in the first half of this run is Hiram (Ram) Riddley, a teenager we first meet in issue #313. Cap meets Ram because of unusual computer activity infiltrating the Captain America Hotline (a project Cap undertakes in order to more easily reach the public at large to offer assistance). Ram is a New Jersey teenager (and he appears to be an only child because Gruenwald never shows any siblings around) who is a "hacker" (clarified in the text as a "computer enthusiast" for the mid–1980s reader) communicating with other enthusiasts who want to help Cap solidify his hotline. Suspecting nefarious intentions, Cap immediately starts in on Ram with a lecture about the dangers of Ram's interference, but when Ram's intentions are proven as genuine (and Ram's hero-worship of Cap himself is shown as wholesome), Cap invites him to help his network.

Ram's mother, Holly, later explains to Cap (in issue #321) that she and her husband are divorced and Ram needs outlets (8). Ram's story is textbook Gen X and likely quite relatable to the predominantly young male comic audience of the 1980s. Those in Ram's generation "survived a hurried childhood of divorce, latchkeys, open classrooms, devil-child movies, and a shift from G to R ratings" (Strauss and Howe 137). These points argue on behalf of the de-emphasis on childhood during Gen X coming of age because of both Boomer independence and self-interest. That does not mean that Gen Xers *want* childhood to end early—in fact, Ram clings to it as long as he can. It just means that these "hurried" childhoods encouraged some members of this generation to continue their own pursuit of childhood long after it had ended.

Ram's mother's presence (as well as Cap's influence both when he is physically present in Ram's life and when he is a living symbol from afar) helps minimize the external challenges young Ram faces, but he certainly has endured his parents' divorce and, one can infer, isolation and loneliness. He does have outlets and a hero though, thanks to Captain America. The reader is left with the possibility that life for Ram would be much more difficult—and less purposeful—without Captain America. This is a key to Gruenwald's depiction of Gen X—life is better when Captain America is part of it.

But as the '80s become the '90s, the realities for Gen X become harder. Ram has a very minimal presence during Gruenwald's run, but makes a surprising appearance in issue #443, Gruenwald's last. In the issue, a dying Steve Rogers has been told he has 24 hours to live, and the issue depicts the things he does and the conversations with others he conducts over the course of that final day. He thinks of Ram, so pivotal in helping Cap succeed with the Hotline in its earliest days, and pays him a visit. The young and enthusiastic Ram, eager to please Cap in his earlier appearances, is gone. The teenager looking for a father figure has, instead, been hardened by the realities of an unfair world. Cap arrives at Ram's house to see him sitting on his porch. Upon first seeing him, Cap thinks, "His demeanor ... so sullen. I can almost feel it" (17). Cap is aware of the change of Ram's personality, but still thinks of the boy as the energetic kid he once knew and proceeds accordingly. Cap begins to thank him for his years of service, but Ram angrily cuts him off: "You have nothing to thank me for—I have nothing to thank you for!"

After Cap (quite taken aback) asks him to explain his reactions, Ram tells Cap that his mother was on her way to church when someone forced his way into her car, made her drive away, and then shot her, leaving her comatose. Ram then asks, "What's wrong with this freaking world, Cap?" Cap knows that nothing he can say will reassure Ram, but he tries anyway: "Sometimes, Ram, there are no heroes around" (18). These comments are in no way reassuring (as Ram tells him), but Cap feels obligated to say something, even if nothing he could say would be sufficient. Typically, Cap is able to say the "right" reassuring thing in such a circumstance. Here, he cannot.

While Ram does not know it, Cap is facing his own mortality and is trying to imagine the world he will leave behind him. He knows logically that, after his death, the rest of the Avengers, among many others, will continue his heroic legacy, but we see those aforementioned Boomer narcissistic tendencies as he worries that the world without him will be a world without heroes. Again, storyline-wise, Cap is reaching his perceived demise and is in a difficult place physically and emotionally, but there is more going on than just a dying hero who is not successfully connecting with another person. Cap is truly feeling overwhelmed by the evil and conflict in the world and, while his physical state is preventing him from stopping those evils as easily as he once did, he is emotionally less capable as well. He also is suddenly having trouble connecting with younger people because he has less comprehension of their wants and needs.

Gen X Criticisms

In an article from *The Public Interest*, a long-time conservative policy journal from the late 90s (prior to the 9/11 terror attacks), Diana Shaub suggests that Gen Xers are living in a time of "faded patriotism" without a unifying conflict like those that so affected prior generations (23). This generation was seen as uninterested in politics, though not necessarily uninterested in civic action (Strauss and Howe 137). In his book *Generation X Goes to College: An Eye-Opening Account of Postmodern America*, Peter Sacks (a pseudonym) discusses his experiences teaching at a community college in the '90s: Sacks "was shocked to discover that students liked to talk to one another more than listen to him, came to class late and left early, read newspapers in class, and were frequently rude" (Swift).

Time would add pragmatism to the list of traits associated with this generation, but at the time of Gruenwald's work, it was more typical to see the people of this generation as lazy, alienated (and alienating), as well as cold and self-sufficient. These general criticisms of Gen-X are not unlike those levied against all generations by their elders, but Cap shows a patience that not all in his place would display. Gruenwald's depiction of Ram in those early issues does not directly label him as "lazy," but an observer within the comics universe could see the younger Ram as a teenager who spends hours every day on his computer and make the conclusion that he is indeed "lazy" and otherwise unmotivated in life. These do not seem to be Gruenwald's conclusions about Ram (who is depicted prior to his appearance in #443 as energetic and engaged), but they could be made and subsequently argued. The Ram that confronts Cap in issue #443 about his mother's horrific incident is understandably less optimistic and is assuredly a young man on the brink of a cold and self-sufficient adulthood. It is a representation of the transition from a difficult but still mostly sheltered childhood into a difficult adulthood.

Cap as Generational Father Figure

A key factor that exists in the *Captain America* universe that does not exist in the real world of the reader is, of course, Captain America himself. We can see that some younger characters in this comic are patriotic and motivated despite the social pull of their generation away from patriotism (at least in the real world outside of the comics) because of the presence of a patriotic and moralistic hero who is not a government prop and, essentially, serves as a surrogate father-figure to a generation in clear need (even to those who have never literally interacted with him). To these admirers, he is present for them even if they are not acquainted with him personally (and this is especially true in their childhoods). Cap's philosophy is that he is the hero for all America, and he travels the country fighting crime to enact said philosophy. He is, in this way, every American's hero (unlike, for instance, Batman and Gotham City's relationship, or Spider-Man and the Fantastic Four and New York City).

Free Spirit and Jack Flag are aspiring heroes in their late teens who help a physically compromised Captain America with his missions toward the end of Gruenwald's run. Both are Gen Xers who have idolized Captain America but, unlike Ram, did not become as disillusioned with him (in part because they did not, as it can be argued Ram did, expect Cap to solve all their problems and then blame him when he could not). While Ram and his mother had direct personal experiences with Cap, Free Spirit and Jack Flag did not—they were solely able to admire him from afar (though Jack Flag's work on the Cap hotline would have created some greater feeling of intimacy).

Free Spirit and Jack Flag

Free Spirit debuts in issue #431, entitled "The Next Generation" (to underscore Gruenwald's intention of generational emphasis). She starts as Cathy Webster, an intellectual college student from "somewhere in the Midwest," (5) who is recruited by a disguised Superia[18] and subsequently undergoes a process involving subliminal messages that will, according to Superia, "enhance [her] physical and mental proficiency" (5). Webster is reluctant because she views the process as a "short cut" that will undermine "determination and hard work" (5), but upon being bullied by her college classmates and reminded of her personal athletic shortcomings, she changes her mind. Webster's idealizing of "determination and hard work" feels very connected to Cap's celebration of the concepts more than anything that would be emphasized broadly within her generation.

Unbeknownst to Webster, the process also instills an anti-men message in her mind. She dons a colorful uniform and the "Free Spirit" moniker and crashes a campus frat party. She suddenly hears the message "Hate men! Hunt men! Hurt me!" resonating in her head. Realizing these words that are influencing her actions are not coming from her own consciousness, she runs away in guilt (19) and subsequently pushes back Superia's programming (22), thanks in part to the values that have been already instilled into her by Captain America.

The second young protégé Cap unexpectedly adopts during this time is Jack Flag (Jack Harrison). He debuts three issues later in #434 "taking on a disguise Cap'n A would be proud of" (13) that, like Free Spirit's, incorporates the American flag motif (with Jack Flag integrating his hair into the "disguise" with horizontal blue, white, and red dyed stripes starting from the front). His story begins when he is a young member of Cap's Computer Network (The "Stars and Stripes"—the same group of which Ram was such a pivotal member). He and his brother subsequently begin a "Citizen's Patrol Group" (12) to protect their community, but his brother eventually falls victim to a criminal attack that leaves him paralyzed. Further, his parents buy a home in a retirement community that they are forced to sell after some underhanded actions orchestrated by Cap's longtime adversaries, The Serpent Society. After trying to involve the authorities but finding them to be on the Serpent Society's payroll, Jack decides to investigate them himself and, in order to do so, trains heavily and employs technology created by his brother (13). While Free Spirit stumbles into the superhero life, Jack Flag has been emulating Cap since childhood with, one would assume, superhero aspirations of his own.

Positive Generation X Traits

Both Free Spirit and Jack Flag are brought into the crime-fighting world through the influence of Cap villains, and both are already admirers of Captain America (Webster/Free Spirit has a poster of Cap in front of a waving American flag in her dorm room and Harrison/Jack Flag is, as mentioned above, part of Stars and Stripes). While this shared admiration of Cap is potentially a coincidence, it does create a pattern, albeit one with a small sample size. Of the young people (early 20s and younger) that we see represented in these pages, the ones who already have an admiration of Cap are uniformly heroic (Ram has tragedy in his personal life later, but he is clearly working heroically for Cap earlier on), and those who don't (Baron Zemo's brainwashed stolen children [#432–435] and a number of unnamed young petty criminals, for example) are problems. And because the three most significant characters of Gen X depicted in these issues all idolize Cap, perhaps Gruenwald is saying something larger about inherent Gen X decency (or at least a decency that can be harnessed with the proper influence).

Despite the negative perceptions earlier generations held toward Gen Xers at this time, these characters are absolutely admirable and sympathetic (even when Ram is yelling at Cap for not doing enough, the reader is wholly sympathetic to his pain). These characters complement some Gen X traits that have emerged as this generation progresses currently, in the real world, toward and past middle age—in contemporary 21st-century life, adult Gen Xers are less likely to be seen as leaders (nor are they as interested in being perceived as leaders) than Baby Boomers or Millennials (Bresman and Rao). Free Spirit and Jack Flag are both very content with trainee status under Cap and a partner arrangement when they are working together. They show no inclination to leave Cap's side to prove themselves and chart their own course (as does Nomad).

Additionally, these characters envision and refine their own styles and costumes in ways that represent both themselves and the era: "As the 1990s ... progressed, young adults have asserted more control over their own image" (Strauss and Howe 234), but they are both tied to Cap for their image. This stands in contrast to D–Man, the Boomer sidekick who wears a costume that is simply a combination of Daredevil's and Wolverine's old costumes (and Nomad, who modifies Rogers' own Nomad uniform over time but keeps it pretty similar in its basic essence). D–Man is using influence from heroes he admires too, but he is uninterested in modifying it for his own style. He creates something functional.

On the contrary, Free Spirit and Jack Flag create uniforms with distinct energy and personality. The uniforms are influenced by Cap's, but the two are certainly taking individualistic creative control. Free Spirit's 1995 uniform is similar to Cap's with blue tights and high red boots and long red gloves. But she individualizes it with a face mask and belt that is far longer than necessary, flowing long behind her as she runs. Both Free Spirit and Jack Flag emphasize their hair, not hiding it as does Cap. In Jack Flag's case, his long hair is dyed red, white, and blue (in stripes) and, while his uniform is form-fitting, a long bandana conceals his face. Gen Xers are independent and cynical in the real world, but in the world of *Captain America*, Free Spirit and Jack Flag have an icon who can pull them out of the emotional morass that would otherwise define their generation.

These characters exist as a sort of idealized version of Gen X (in the way that some of the Boomer characters are a more cynical representation of Gruenwald's own generation). They live in a world where much of the popular culture and political structure exists as does our own, but the fact that Captain America is a living, breathing icon changes the overall dynamic of their world. In #435, Free Spirit calls Cap one of her "life-long idols—right up there with Mother Teresa and Michael Stipe" (15), thus emphasizing decency and creativity amongst the traits she values. These characters are young adults who have lived with Cap as a clear role model and have not grown to see Cap as having failed them (as Ram perceives). Because of his failing health, Cap perhaps has more patience with potential apprentices than he would in normal circumstances, but he clearly admires their work ethic and natural moral compass.

Early Millennial Encounters

In issues #432–435, Cap and Diamondback infiltrate the villainous Baron Zemo's fortress and find that Zemo has stolen a number of children and "adopted" them as his own (and forced loyalty and hatred of Captain America onto them). While the ages of these kids are unclear, we can assume they are mostly Millennials considering the time of the issue's publication (1994), Cap is driven to free them but is unsure how to approach these children. He is not someone aware of the social norms of children, nor is he particularly well-versed on the needs of this newer, younger generation. Gen X is hard enough for him to understand, but at least many members of that generation (as well as some Millennials) have had positive exposure to Captain America, his heroics, and his philosophies. Zemo's "children" are brainwashed into hating Captain America, but the Gen Xers Gruenwald has introduced are supportive of him and his cause.

In issue #432, Zemo himself denies the "brainwashing" accusation, stating instead that they are "raised with strong family values" (a key Republican talking point of the era).[19] Zemo further elaborates his definition of "strong family values": "Love and honor your parents and hate those who would take them from you" (2). This issue begins with an introduction that calls the story "a tale of Generation PG-13," a generational label that in no way stuck widely and represents the challenges of labeling. Gruenwald is attempting to construct a generational story, but the tools did not yet exist to truly identify the generation in question.

Another brief example of a likely Millennial is Gavin, a young man who appears in #438. He is a member of the Stars and Stripes,[20] thus establishing (considering Gavin seems to be in his early teens putting him as a very early Millennial) that the influence of Cap through that association with Stars and Stripes is strong in the mid–'90s. In this issue, he is a prisoner of Cap's Globalist Anti-Patriotic enemy Flag-Smasher (and U.L.T.I.M.A.T.U.M., the terrorist organization he leads), one of Cap's more aggressive and violent antagonists. Gavin is bold and brave. Despite being surrounded by a roomful of armed terrorists, Gavin declares to Flag-Smasher (penciller Dave Hoover depicting Gavin with his fist raised high in the air), "You ain't going to get away with your crazy terrorist routines" (6). Later in the issue, Flag-Smasher holds Gavin hostage with a gun pointed toward his head when Cap confronts him.

Gavin, despite his dire circumstance, stomps Flag-Smasher on the foot to distract him long enough for Cap to get a clean shot at Flag-Smasher (19). Gavin is younger than Free Spirit and Jack Flag (and perhaps the same age as some of the older Zemo children), but Cap's influence is still strong. Exposure to Cap's positivity matters, perhaps, more than generational specifics. The implication is that, once Cap has an opportunity to educate more people of the younger generation, the more positive their lives will be as a result.

Gruenwald balances a number of complicated individual parts over the course of these 137 issues (as would be the case for anyone successfully writing a cohesive narrative over so long a period), but his desire to speak to many listeners using so many voices is an important aspect of his work on this comic. One of the true strengths he possesses as a writer is an ambition to include so many perspectives in a single story (or, in some cases, a single character). As in the actual world, the universe depicted within these pages has a difficult time accommodating so many different generational perspectives but, under Gruenwald's creative eye, those generational conflicts (and harmony, when it does occur) give us an understanding of the types of relationships that can make things move more smoothly.

PART II

VILLAINOUS OPPOSITION

Captain America's rogue's gallery is so dominated by a single villain that it is often difficult to see it as a gallery. That villain is, of course, the Red Skull. When Gruenwald takes over this comic in 1985, the Red Skull has been definitively defeated and killed. In issue #300, Cap carries Red Skull's corpse away from their final battle, noting how final this confrontation truly is. This being a comic book series (and knowing the inescapable saga between Cap and his arch-enemy), it is obvious even as Cap holds Red Skull's dead body in his arms that Skull will return eventually (and he does, in shadows for a few issues before fully remerging in issue #350 as the conductor of virtually everything that had been challenging Cap prior).

Considering the manner in which Gruenwald has framed Captain America as a positive symbol of patriotism, it follows that he would paint Cap's adversaries with the same brush of symbolic representation. The Red Skull, a fascist would-be world conqueror, remains those things, but he dons the attire of a 1980s businessman to assimilate himself into the country he is trying to destroy. The Red Skull represents the fascist enemies of Cap's past and Cap's inability to escape those conflicts even as he moves on past them in his own life. The Red Skull is a manifestation of evil and cruelty and those traits help magnify the positive ones held by Cap himself.

In addition to Red Skull, Gruenwald introduces and reintroduces several other villains and villainous organizations, each of which represents something diverse that further allows him to depict Captain America in the way he intends—as a patriotic symbol of hope and positivity.

FIVE

The War That Won't Go Away

Captain America, the Red Skull, and World War II

As has been mentioned, Mark Gruenwald was the writer of the *Captain America* comic series from issue #307 in 1985 to issue #443 in 1995. That is mostly true. For one of the issues from that period, *Captain America* #423, Gruenwald is not the writer. Instead, Roy Thomas takes over for Gruenwald in a "guest writer" capacity.[1] This issue is in no way connected narratively to the issues that either precede it or follow it and, unlike the intricately woven stories favored by Gruenwald, it serves as a free-standing adventure. Even more jarring than having a free-standing story appear in the midst of a larger narrative is seeing that story disregard the chronological flow that has been established in order to tell an unrelated story set in the distant past.

The even more telling thing, however, about this single issue with which Gruenwald is ostensibly uninvolved is the subject matter. The story takes place, not in 1993 when it was published, but in 1941 and it deals with Captain America and his World War II partner Bucky Barnes as they foil the attempts of Namor, the Sub-Mariner, who wishes to thwart American boats. Namor's plan ultimately involves the kidnapping of President Franklin Roosevelt in exchange for a promise from the Americans to "never again sail into the polar sea" (7). As stated earlier, the story is inconsequential in terms of overarching storylines, but it is unusual and ultimately notable for another reason. With the exception of a brief flashback in #307 and a few reflections scattered about,[2] Gruenwald does very little to make World War II any type of focal point for the comic. In fact, when a reader comes across #423 and reads a dedicated World War II story, it feels out of place. The same can be said of *Captain America Annual* #10

125

from 1991. *Annual* #10 is part of a larger story crossing over in several other annuals (once a year issues outside of a given title's normal sequential storytelling), and it also contains an extended World War II flashback, this time of Cap's origin. Like issue #423, these stories in the annual are also not written by Gruenwald (Dan Chichester is the writer of both the crossover story and the origin story in *Captain America Annual* #10).[3]

As a character, Captain America is battle-born. The character was created as and succeeds as a propaganda tool as the United States enters the Second World War, and the identity of the character will always be directly tied to that conflict. Captain America (and Bucky) are so tied to that specific conflict that efforts in the 1950s to reposition Cap as an anti–Communist crusader were met with failure. As Bradford Wright in *Comic Book Nation* writes,

> In [World War II], Captain America and Bucky had defended the American home front against Nazi and Japanese spies and saboteurs. Now they reprised that role against Communist agents, striking at "the betrayers" who hid behind the privileges of a free society to subvert American institutions. The series offered no further discussion of Cold War issues beyond the message that Communists were evil, overweight, and poor dressers [123].

Wright goes on to say that the effort "totally failed," tanking in sales. This version of Cap (and other anti–Communist comics) "essentially reproduced the old superhero formulas, but these no longer proved successful" (Wright 123). While anti-communist Cap was not the only failed attempt to use techniques that worked with Nazi villains with Communists, Cap's deep connections with World War II (and battling Nazis) was an even bigger obstacle to overcome. Even well after his 1960s revival, Cap often found himself in conflict with Red Skull and his seemingly endless parade of Sleeper robots.[4]

Perceptions of Historical Wars

For Gruenwald, World War II was the past and the 1980s and 1990s were not eras that required endless reminders or retellings of that particular war. In fact, if there was a conflict from the past with which readers were most consciously aware in Gruenwald's *Captain America* era (and media of the 1980s to the mid–1990s in general), it was the war in Vietnam. War oriented pop culture of the era was focused on the more recently fought (and more politically disputed) war in Vietnam. Marvel published a comic called *The 'Nam* for 84 issues from 1986 to 1993, and popular cinema was flooded with Vietnam era films, especially in the middle to the latter half of the 1980s (including Oliver Stone's *Platoon*, Stanley Kubrick's *Full Metal Jacket*, John Irving's *Hamburger Hill*, and Barry Levinson's *Good Morning, Vietnam*). *China Beach*, a television show set during the Vietnam War, ran on ABC from 1988 to 1991. Whereas World War II sentiment in the 1980s would have been celebratory of success, the media focus on Vietnam is introspective, both of national failures and emotional sacrifices. In this era, the complexities of Vietnam served as a more compelling narrative frame than World War II's basic heroism—how could one casually glorify the successes of a World War II hero without discrediting the soldiers who went through hell in Vietnam?[5]

To Gruenwald, the answer was to deemphasize Cap's World War II origins in order to focus upon the changing world of the mid-'80s to mid-'90s. The word "deemphasize" in no way is synonymous in this context with "erase." Gruenwald does not change Cap's origin or pretend World War II did not happen. Instead, he does not allow Cap or any of the other characters to fixate upon it, instead letting the comic feel contemporary and untethered to World War II. Cap is neither stuck fighting World War II nor is the war overly romanticized. It is merely one adventure in the life of a hero who has had so many. Gruenwald did not want *Captain America* to be bogged down by the past so he put the characters, even Cap and the Red Skull, into different mindsets and situations.

For Gruenwald, the answer to avoiding getting bogged down in too much dated World War II baggage was to transfer the World War II conflict to a new stage. John Moser, in his essay "Madmen, Morons, and Monocles," writes, "If it can be said that Hitler and his followers made a single lasting contribution to Western Civilization, it is that they have provided American popular culture with a set of appropriately despicable villains" (34). Red Skull (serving as the ultimate Nazi villain) conveys an evil that no single time period can contain. Therefore, even outside the realm of World War II, he is a villain most evil and menacing. Even if their war battles are well in the past and the two enemies do little to dwell upon the war, they are very much combatants placed in their contemporary age.

Captain America and Red Skull— Post-World War II

Gruenwald does not let Cap dwell on that past—Gruenwald's Cap has come to terms with the losses accumulated during the war (especially Bucky's death) and is trying to be a person comfortable in his adopted era. In Gruenwald's hands, the Red Skull has also moved on from the wars of the past as well. The battles between these two adversaries during Grunwald's run are not the hand-to-hand battles that defined their conflicts in previous eras. Instead, the Red Skull becomes an even greater Machiavellian enemy and manipulator, directly engaging with Cap very rarely and instead serving as a primarily shadowy nemesis.[6] The World War II days of clear conflict are in the past. Instead, the Red Skull adopts the veneer of a 1980s businessman who torments Cap through intricate machinations that depend less on muscle and destruction and more on savvy and manipulation (though both Skull and his henchman Crossbones still have plenty of muscle). Prior to Red Skull's return to action in issue #350 (officially—he is hinted at and his name appears a few issues earlier), he is a concept for Cap, an ideology that Cap defeated.

With Skull defeated in #300, Cap's ideology, while not shifting exactly, can be conveyed differently. As Richard Stevens writes in *Captain America, Masculinity, and Violence: The Evolution of a National Icon,*

> Despite his continuing to hold the liberal views he gained from his 1960s and 1970s adventures, his expression of his political views in the 1980s was much more measured and cautious. The character prone to lecture the Red Skull in the 1960s and to moralize out loud with the Falcon in the 1970s seemed rather mute in the 1980s [152].

As Stevens explains, Gruenwald's Cap is less urgent about his politics than perhaps Cap of earlier eras, and he is not the liberal advocate that fights aside Falcon, but he is certainly not a conservative figure. There is a balance. Arguably that balance exists because the Red Skull, early in Gruenwald's run, does not exist. The Red Skull's return is an indictment against change. If the Red Skull is back, then Cap cannot exist in the manner in which he had been existing. The reality of the Red Skull's return would force Cap to revert to who he was when they engaged in sustained conflict.

Captain America's Denial

After besting the Red Skull once and for all (so he thinks) in issue #300, Cap feels free of the ideological fights that defined his dynamic with the Red Skull, and he moves through life without continuing to fight the Second World War.[7] When the Skull specifically returns, this time occupying a cloned body of Steve Rogers, Cap's reaction is not disappointment or regret—it is denial. He is unwilling to admit that Red Skull could still be alive because that admission would invalidate the progress he has managed to make in moving on from their seemingly endless battles of the past.

In issue #326, well before the Red Skull's actual return, Cap is forced to visit Skull-House[8] and he is faced with a visage of the Red Skull and, in trying to figure out the explanation behind it, the "only possibility" he eliminates "is that the Skull is back from the dead" (6). He is unwilling to admit it could happen well before it becomes a real possibility. He remains rigid in that mindset, even when the evidence becomes much clearer over time. When the Red Skull appears once again in the flesh in issue #350, it still takes Captain America twenty issues to admit that his adversary is indeed his true and original archenemy. This is a long time for Cap to reach this conclusion—a span of well over a calendar year of comics between when the reader knows Skull is back and when Rogers admits it.[9] Considering so many of the stories that take place between issue #350 and #370 directly involve the Red Skull as an adversary (with Cap generally pitted against the Skull's minions), it is a remarkably slow realization. Cap simply cannot admit that this is the true Red Skull because, in doing so, he would be admitting truths he does not want to admit—he would be forced to come to terms with the return of an evil he definitively defeated (and the era that is represented by that evil).

In issue #350, after fighting a man with Steve Rogers' face and body (and after he has watched that man's face become literally transformed into the Red Skull when the villain accidentally ingests his own poison), he still cannot believe it to be the actual Red Skull. To the reader, this fact is obvious. The Red Skull refers to Cap immediately as his "old enemy" (36), speaks of his own "past life" and how he is no longer "an easily identified foreign agitator" (37). The Red Skull is making his identity as clear to Rogers as possible (again, also by living in Rogers' cloned body, a feat that no other enemy of Captain America's would likely be scientifically brilliant, diabolical, and vindictive enough to accomplish).

Still, Rogers will not admit this truth, even as clear as it is to the reader. All Rogers can say in response to John Walker's query as to whether or not the man is the Red Skull is a very non-non-committal, "I'm almost beginning to think so" (38). But even that "almost" is too much and it is soon pushed back, and he later more firmly denies the Red Skull's return. In issue #368, he refers to his adversary as "the guy who claims to be the Skull" (17). In issue #370, he thinks, "I met a guy several months back claiming to be the be the be the original Red Skull—but I've refused to believe it!" (15). This last statement indicates an awareness of his own naiveté. To say "I've refused" instead of "I refuse" makes the statement less forceful, as if he is admitting the process of his own denial (rather than emphasizing the denial itself). Ultimately, this makes sense because, by the end of this same issue, he is forced to realize the inevitable and does indeed admit the truth.

Why is he so unwilling for so long? When he first encounters the Red Skull again in issue #350, he notes the Skull's eyes (the feature that will assure him of the Skull's true identity in #370): "But there's something in those eyes--!" (36). He gets a glimpse of one of the Red Skull's most ominous traits (something that emerges even when he is wearing the face of a hero), but Cap's process of denial is only beginning, so he is not yet in a place to process the truth. He is unwilling to admit the Red Skull's successful resurrection because, for one, it will invalidate the battle to the death the two had in issue #300, and that battle was one that, in Cap's mind, truly ended an era in his life. It will invalidate Cap's act of carrying away the dead Red Skull as a literal end to their conflict. Cap had achieved closure. Red Skull's return eradicates that closure.

The Red Skull's death serves also as a symbolic ending to Cap's World War II responsibilities. In #307, Cap briefly reminisces about his World War II time with the Invaders, but otherwise Gruenwald does little to document Cap's consideration of either the war or the Red Skull himself until the Skull's actual reappearance. Cap does not seem to linger on Skull's defeat and death. Also, Cap's World War II memory in #307 is less about the war and more about friends and comradery. Cap does not need the Red Skull or the memories associated with the Skull. Cap won—those events are ancient history in the life of a man who is moving forward. If he admits the Red Skull exists, he will be admitting the Second World War will never stop being fought, and that the things he has dedicated his life to stop cannot, at least in this one key capacity, be stopped. For Cap, a world in which the Red Skull died in their final battle at Skull-House is the only reality where his responsibilities in World War II have ended. Otherwise, that loose end that has followed him not just since the war, but also since his entrance into the contemporary world, will continue to exist. If he admits that the Red Skull is alive, he is admitting that the "most evil man [he'd] ever met," as he says in #326, was alive (3) and, with him, that evil that had been eradicated would return.

During this period of the Red Skull's absence, Cap's villains seem less wholly evil than the Nazi holdovers Cap fought in previous eras. Cap fights a number of adversaries that are political (Flag-Smasher), seemingly morally motivated (Scourge of the Underworld), or financially motivated (like the Serpent Society). Viper can be argued to be politically motivated, but her politics are mostly chaos-based. Villains, certainly, and capable of terrible death and destruction, but the title of "evil" feels like something more exclusive (and something that Sidewinder, for instance, the financially motivated leader of the Serpent Society, despite his frequent misdeeds, falls short of, favoring financial gain and supervillain security to world domination).[10] If the Red Skull is indeed still alive, it means that there is evil in the world not even Captain America can stop. Gruenwald's Cap is unwilling to believe he has to resume a war he has already won multiple times.

Red Skull's Eyes

When Cap is finally able to admit that the adversary who has caused him problems between issues #350 and #370 is, in fact, the original Red Skull, he is looking into the eyes of his enemy and seeing the hatred and vitriol presented within. Cap enters Skull-House as the Red Skull is dying because the Red Skull wants to see his greatest enemy one last time (and Crossbones quickly makes sure the request is fulfilled). In #370, Red Skull tells Cap, weakly, but with building strength, "I was ready to die again … wanted you there to witness it … like last time." (22). While Cap himself has long attempted to distance himself from the literal circumstances of Skull's death in #300, the Red Skull still obsesses on it.

Penciller Ron Lim's image in this panel is a compelling one—it is a close-up of the Skull's right eye, bloodshot and narrowing. In the center of the Red Skull's pupil is the image of Captain America, as if Cap and the Skull are impossible to separate at this point (which is true in terms of Skull's psyche and personal obsession). As the reader realizes the anger exhibited in this image of the Red Skull's narrowed eye, the Skull continues his speech (with the speech bubble for the following sentences being drawn in a clean and standard way [as opposed to the previously used wobbly speech bubble lines to indicate Skull's declining state]). This is the Red Skull overcoming the frailty that leads him (and all others in the room) to believe that his death is inevitable.[11] Red Skull continues, "But now, seeing your wretched face … has stoked the furnace of my hatred, given me reason to go on!" (22). The Red Skull is brought back to life, appropriately for a villain of his ilk and ideology, by his own personal hatred.

The next panel shows Cap himself, wide-eyed, realizing that this once-dying man is, in fact, his greatest enemy. Regardless of how long he keeps himself in denial, Cap now has no choice but to recognize the truth. Red Skull then lets Cap leave, saying that he is too weak to fight, but someday they assuredly will. This is a truth that Cap himself can no longer deny (despite the denial that has defined his feelings toward Red Skull's existence prior to this encounter). Cap silently walks away; his partner Diamondback accompanies him. On their way off the premises, Diamondback cannot understand why Cap walked away as he did. She suggests they should "bust [Red Skull], while he's weak and can't resist" (23). To Diamondback, Red Skull is any other adversary—someone who can be taken into custody or otherwise stopped in the same fashion as other villains. Cap knows that the Skull is a different tier of villain.

When Cap does not respond to her suggestions to "bust" Red Skull, she starts to rationalize why Cap chooses to walk away instead of apprehending his greatest enemy, ultimately growing frustrated and unhappy with her own theories. She is saying what she thinks Cap wants to hear,[12] but she is wholly incapable of understanding his thought processes at this moment. She directly asks him about his silence. Finally, Cap explains what he saw in the Red Skull's eyes: "unfathomably empty, devoid of all compassion ... all humanity. No one else has eyes like that ... no one!" (23). Cap chooses not to arrest him or otherwise stop the Red Skull's allies (The Skeleton Crew) because, in part, of shock. He has now seen the evidence of something he has long denied within himself; when admitting the Skull's return, Cap describes himself as having "lived in a fool's paradise" before his admission (23). By recognizing that the Red Skull is alive, Cap loses a part of the emotional freedom he had been able to carry for so long. It is key to note that, twenty issues earlier (as is discussed above), Cap is taken aback by the Red Skull's eyes, but is unwilling to believe the truth of Skull's resurrection until this moment. Besides, the eyes Cap sees in #370 are more haunting (the Skull's evil eyes in #350 are in a cloned face of Steve Rogers—something that would perhaps mask that evil somewhat). Cap sees something deeper and darker in the eyes of the Red Skull because Skull is at his most desperate (on what the Skull himself assumes is his deathbed). Those eyes take us full circle between these appearances (first meeting Red Skull again in #350 and then Cap's admission that his return is indeed legitimate). It is those eyes that let Captain America know the truth that, for so long, he has been avoiding.

"The Haunting of Skull-House"

Gruenwald does indeed exclude Red Skull from Cap's rogues' gallery in the first four years of his tenure as writer, with one exception to the Red Skull's absence and that is the aforementioned issue #326 ("The Haunting of Skull-House"). While the outcome of this story ultimately solidifies in Cap's mind that the Skull is most assuredly dead (and the Red Skull himself does not appear in the issue, though a mentally induced facsimile does appear), the issue features Captain America reliving his final battle with the Skull, thus referencing Red Skull directly, something that Gruenwald is extraordinarily careful to avoid during much of this portion of his run.

This February 1987 issue occurs within the first two years of Gruenwald's tenure and one of his main objectives in these first two years of his run is to emphasize new adversaries. This compels him to avoid using overly featured villains, even one as integral as Red Skull. Gruenwald is pacing himself and his use of villains, building things up over time, though the return of the Skull is inevitable as soon as he dies in issue #300. In #326, we learn that Cap has had his hotline volunteers watch after Skull-House with the understanding they would contact Cap to report the slightest changes. When that slightest change does occur, Cap receives word of it and, alone, investigates the house. As he does so, he is confronted by his past.

After he walks in, he sees a giant portrait of the Red Skull in his unmasked form and immediately launches into a remembrance of his World War II experiences and how the existence of the Red Skull compelled the United States government to create their own representative soldier, thus insinuating that Cap knows that his existence is, at least in part, because of the Red Skull's ruthless effectiveness in his own role (3–4). This contemplation is without judgment or disgust—Cap is just recollecting facts. This idea of the Red Skull and Captain America being intertwined in their origins is something Cap would have compartmentalized and rationalized much earlier in his life. Gruenwald very rarely allows Cap to travel back into these memories, but that it is not because Cap is unable to deal with them. Cap is very relaxed as he travels through Skull-House, prepared for surprises, certainly, but not emotionally compromised by anything.

In truth, this is ground rarely tread by Gruenwald because Cap has little time for remembrances. The war is over. It does not need to be revisited. Cap simply acknowledges the existence of his shared history with Red Skull and moves forward. He encounters a facsimile of the Red Skull claiming to be a ghost and then is attacked by several villains who recently died in battle with Cap (including the U.L.T.I.M.A.T.U.M. agent Cap kills with a gun in #321). It is later revealed that these villains (and, later, the presumed dead Bucky Barnes, Sharon Carter, and Steve Rogers' parents) are the product of a hallucinogenic drug covertly given to Cap by Doctor Faustus, an old foe who is a master of mental manipulation. While the drug forces Cap to confront deaths that have recently happened (like that of the U.L.T.I.M.A.T.U.M. agent), it also forces him to confront the memories of the Red Skull and World War II, including the specifics of his "final" fight with Red Skull and, eventually, the death of Bucky Barnes. Cap does not default to such a recollection in normal circumstances, but this encounter with Faustus shows that such recollections can be forced.

The Death of Bucky Barnes

Bucky Barnes eventually is brought back to life in the Marvel timeline by Ed Brubaker in the 2000s,[13] but he was a rare comic character to stay dead for decades. In fact, comic historian Peter Sanderson says that back during the era in which Gruenwald was writing these comics, "one of the absolute rules at Marvel was, the two characters who were absolutely permanently dead—and there was no way they'd *ever* come back—were Uncle

Ben and Bucky" (qtd. in Reisman). These two characters have tragic stories that define other, more important characters. They exist for the purpose of someone else's story. Famously (as depicted in multiple blockbuster films in addition to countless comics), Uncle Ben dies when Peter Parker, freshly powerful after that fateful spider bite, lets a small-time criminal escape because Parker does not think him worth Spider-Man's time. That small-time criminal ends up killing his beloved Uncle Ben.

For Cap, losing Bucky was a sign of his personal failure, something he needed to amend. Importantly, Bucky's death also represented the end of an innocence, a time where a superhero seemingly required a teenaged sidekick. Batman debuted with Robin in 1940 and Cap and Bucky followed a year later. According to Sanderson, Bucky was about wish-fulfillment: "let's give the kids someone to identify with" (qtd. in Reisman). The readers were predominantly young and the writers felt that teen sidekicks were a path toward accessibility. The teen sidekick was emblematic of the Golden Age of comics—a way to get the young target audience to see themselves in the comic adventures (without taking the main hero role away from the adult white male hero). Some of those characters matured into the main hero role (such as Kid Flash/Wally West's promotion to being the eventual Flash), some became heroes in their own rights (like Robin Dick Grayson as Nightwing), and others became tragic figures that symbolized loss and untapped potential (like Bucky).

Captain America was reborn in Stan Lee's Marvel Comics world of the 1960s and, at the time, Lee was focused on realism in comics, something that teen sidekicks contradicted. In an interview with Renee Montagne on NPR's *Morning Edition* in 2006, Lee states, "I hated teenagers in comics because they were always sidekicks. And I always felt if I were a superhero, there's no way I'd pal around with some teenager." While the sidekick concept originates from writers wanting "wish-fulfillment" characters, its decline occurs because of writers who did not see realism in the existence of such characters. Bucky was a sacrifice the maturing era demanded. Well before Gruenwald's time on the comic, Stan Lee's choice to kill Bucky begins that division between Cap's contemporary life and that distant World War II past. When Cap is forced to recall Bucky's life (and death), he is forced to consider that long past war and, subsequently, he is brought back to a more innocent time.

Horrors of World War II

The idea of the 1940s being a "more innocent time" is ironic because that period is defined by the most horrific war ever fought. Estimates claim that between 70 and 85 million people (civilians and military) were killed during this war, a staggering 3 percent of the world's population at the time ("World War Two Casualties by Country"). In comparison, World War I estimates conclude that 20 million deaths (civilian and military) occurred during that conflict though, like with the World War II statistics, it is impossible to get 100 percent accurate numbers ("World War I Casualties"). These estimates certainly provide a clear insight into the scope of this war. The contemporary perspective of the war is often that it was a simple, straight-forward affair of good vs. evil where eager and enthusiastic men fought for the good cause and then came home to cause a Baby Boom. This is not to say that the trope shown in Captain America's origin story of the young soldier desperate to serve overseas is completely false, but in reality, 61.2 percent of Americans serving in World War II were drafted ("Research Starters: U.S. Military by the Numbers"). The narrative of young American men enthusiastically bounding overseas for war is a vast simplification of truth. *Captain America* comics (from any era) comics are not interested in depicting the horrors of war in any authentic or graphic fashion, but it can be argued that the lack of specific conversation from Gruenwald about the war can be seen as an unwillingness from Cap to fully jump into recollections about it. Indeed, Bucky's death is about more than just Stan Lee's dislike of teen sidekicks—it is about recognizing a reality about that war (and all wars) that the artists creating *Captain America* at the time of the war were unwilling to do.

Simon and Kirby were, of course, writing pro–American propaganda when they first created the character and, if their goal was to generate further pro–America, pro-war attitudes from young readers, depicting the horrors of war would be no way to accomplish that. When Lee brings back Captain America in *Avengers #4* in 1964, he does not include Bucky but does not specify Bucky's death. In *Avengers #56* from September 1968, writer Roy Thomas goes farther than simply not having Bucky around—he specifically reveals the character's death in World War II.

The Vietnam War and Captain America

The need to protect the image of American military might is obviously not the concern in 1968 that it was during World War II. The year 1968 saw the onset of the Tet Offensive during the Vietnam War, with American casualties growing throughout. The week of February 11, 1968, saw most American deaths during a single week during the conflict with 543 ("Vietnam War Timeline"). The protests that followed "sparked the most intense period of anti-war protests to date" ("Vietnam War Protests"). The climate toward war in 1968 was not the same as it was in 1942, and the comic world reacts accordingly. As public outcry against the Vietnam War increased, Lee had no interest in sugar-coating war overall and, significantly, he had no interest in creating a Captain America who is merely propaganda.

Cap has to deal with Bucky's death because, unlike the narrative drive of the original Kirby and Simon comic, Lee does not pretend that war is simple. It is indeed hell. Captain America is, at most points in his times as a modern Marvel Comics character, trying to avoid reliving World War II. Under Gruenwald, he is in no constant struggle to get past the war, but he is also clearly uninterested in rehashing it. The Red Skull is less concerned about such things, even if he is not exactly outward about revisiting the war either.

Modern Depictions of the Red Skull

The Red Skull can be classified in two ways in the modern Marvel catalogue from the 1960s to Gruenwald's run in the 80s and 90s—there is the Gruenwald version and the pre–Gruenwald version. While the Gruenwald version is a cunning and ruthless businessman (though his fascist Nazi ideology is still intact), comparing that iteration of the character to the earlier (but still post–World War II incarnation) gives us a clearer sense of Gruenwald's intentions. The pre–Gruenwald figure is often decked out in a green smoking jacket with white gloves. The Gruenwald Red Skull favors something less German aristocratic in the form of business suits. The pre–Gruenwald Red Skull lives in castles (including the previously discussed Skull-House), ornately decorated, often communicating with his minions from purple velvet chairs; the Gruenwald Skull is obviously still accustomed to finer things, but his tastes in décor are much more contemporary—business offices and modern five-star hotels. Gruenwald's Red Skull is obsessed with image and perception.

While he is in no way disavowing his Nazi ideology, he does not want to be defined by that ideology either. While he does go back to Skull-House on occasion in these issues, it is in times of desperation and not a normal occurrence (as seen in issue #370 when the Red Skull, nearly dead, asks to return to his house in order to either die or, as it turns out, be revitalized). The Red Skull wants to position himself as a modern man, not because that is necessarily how he feels, but because it is the persona that he thinks will gain him the most success. Again, he does not disown the Nazi ideology; he just knows there are more modern ways to gain power.

The Skull's dialogue differs in these two incarnations as well. It evolves from the pre–Gruenwald Red Skull's typical and banal villain posturing to something more psychologically menacing. For an example of the pre–Gruenwald Red Skull, we can turn to June 1977's *Captain America* #210 (written and penciled by Jack Kirby). In this issue, Skull's minion Armin Zola reports to Red Skull that he has captured Captain America. After breaking off the communication with Zola, Skull's response (spoken aloud in solitude and not simply conveyed through chain thought bubbles) show us an over the top villain in the classic mustache-twirling tradition:

> At Zola's prison, Captain America is literally in my hands!! Fate has chosen in my favor! Showdown Day! Old scores, hotly fought must seek a final end! It is karma!—Kismet! Destiny! How fleeting are the years! How immovable is the hatred! Enemies, like friends, become inevitably inseparable! Only death can part them! Death—in the form of artful—vengeance! [17].

The dialogue is choppy and erratic, far removed from the more calculating Red Skull Gruenwald will construct. Of the 21 punctuation marks in this above passage (including commas, dashes, and apostrophes), twelve of them are exclamation points. He is manic (and those three dashes add to this feeling as well). Though it is lacking in cohesive thought, it does make this villain feel less calculating and more primal. The frantic ranting here feels almost comical. His insistence that "karma" has brought Captain America into his life just so one of them can finally die shows other aspects of the character—an insistent belief in his own righteousness (something the Gruenwald Red Skull, so aware of his own evil, is less inclined toward) to the point that karma would be firmly on his side. This Red Skull has a belief in mystical powers outside of his own ability. The Gruenwald Red Skull is shown as a ruthless and practical man. That is not the case with this earlier version, still ruthless, but also a visceral and physical being, driven solely by revenge and destruction.

A Gruenwald-era example provides a linguistic and behavioral contrast. In the Gruenwald-written #364, Red Skull is contacted by Crossbones. Crossbones alerts Skull that he has apprehended Captain America, assuming that Red Skull would be happy to know his archenemy is captured. Instead, Red Skull is angry. Skull orders: "You fool! Let him go! You are my secret weapon, Crossbones! I do not want you to get mixed up with him unless I order you to do so! Now drop what you're doing and return to me at once! Understand?!" (15). In this exchange, Red Skull is calculating and practical. He is not underestimating Captain America (and Cap is, in fact, escaping Crossbones' trap as Crossbones speaks to Skull). He has a longer game to play and is uninterested by immediate gratification. Further, his dialogue is still animated with exclamation points (he is yelling at Crossbones, after all), but the words themselves are more calculated and collected than within the dialogue of the 1970s example.

Ultimately though, the two Red Skull incarnations are more similar than, perhaps, we might expect. The more modern version does not flaunt his Nazi ideology (though he certainly has not disowned it), but he hides it with Capitalistic attire and flourishes. In #350, after resurfacing as the mastermind behind the manipulations that removed Steve Rogers from the position of Captain America, he reintroduces himself by establishing his Nazi ideology as he alludes to his new cloned body of Steve Rogers: "I need never soil my Aryan hands again" (36). The Red Skull is always a Nazi and always an ideologue. Gruenwald does not hide this fact. His version of the Red Skull is simply politically savvy enough to not let that overshadow the perceptions everyone else may have. The pre–Gruenwald version has no desire to build a personal brand that makes his Nazism more palpable to others. Gruenwald's version is more careful with public perception of his ideology (though his grotesque face will still create a clear perception of that ideology). He is content operating from the shadows, moving his pieces of chaos around in secrecy.

Red Skull vs. Magneto

Of course, there are people who know of his World War II Nazi past, and Red Skull does nothing to assure them that those views are in the past, though he is not always flaunting them in public as he may have done before. Again, he is not ashamed to be a Nazi—he just knows, for business purposes, it is not prudent to flaunt it. One of the most fascinating aspects of the Gruenwald reimagining of Red Skull is how he is viewed not just by Captain America and other heroes, but how he is viewed by his fellow villains. He is on his own plane of evil. His Nazi beliefs establish him into a level of villainy beyond most of his villainous contemporaries. On two occasions during Gruenwald's run, Red Skull crosses paths with major Marvel villains and, each time, the depths of his personal evil makes the other villain he encounters (specifically Magneto and Kingpin) look sympathetic even when the other villain is doing heinous and barbaric things (Magneto vengefully leaves Red Skull for dead and Kingpin is running a destructive heroin operation). In each case, the Red Skull's tension with that other villain comes about because of Skull's Nazism. Through these interactions, Gruenwald is establishing a chain of villainy amongst Marvel villains that solidifies Nazism as the least forgivable sin.

Red Skull's specific conflicts with Magneto and Kingpin are each unique in motives and execution. Magneto's backstory as a Holocaust survivor and his role as a mutant freedom fighter rather than a comic book symbol of evil (as is Red Skull) makes Magneto's tension with Red Skull predictable (though Magneto's desire for vengeance and the severity of what he inflicts upon the Skull is still a bit shocking). The interaction between Red Skull and Magneto occurs during "Acts of Vengeance," a storyline that spreads through a number of Marvel comics in late 1989-early 1990 in which supervillains essentially "trade off" their rivals in order to have a better chance of actually winning (instead of fighting the same foes repeatedly and always losing).[14] After the major villains involved in this operation (Magneto, Red Skull, Kingpin, the Mandarin, the Wizard, and Dr. Doom) have met to discuss their strategies in issue #366, Magneto questions the seemingly non-threatening facilitator who helps organize the villains (and is later revealed to be the very non non-threatening Loki) on whether the Red Skull who attended the meeting was indeed the original World War II Red Skull. The disguised Loki answers, "As far as I know, he is," with a smirk (4) that shows that inter-villain tension is clearly part of his plan.

While this interaction reveals Magneto has potential reservations about working with the Red Skull (and "reservations" turns out to be an understatement), the Skull himself is upset about having to associate with any of these other villains, in part because he is convinced that they will "all conspire against" him (5). Red Skull, defined by a paranoia over others being either jealous of his accomplishments or angry about his ideology, is constantly convinced that everyone is out to destroy him, including his fellow villains. While he is paranoid about it, he does not seem to begrudge it either. He assumes everyone wants to destroy him, but he also seems to understand their instincts. His ideology and actions in World War II (and after) make these perceived adversarial reactions from others likely, and he seems to embrace the metaphorical target that has long appeared on his back.

Beyond his general sense of paranoia, he also dismisses each conspiring villain individually. In issue #367, he mentally goes through each villain in the "Acts of Vengeance" inner circle and dismisses each in turn: Dr. Doom is "mad," The Wizard is "an idiot," The Kingpin is "petty," The Mandarin is "a poor man's Fu Manchu," and, most significantly for our discussion, Magneto, is a "mutant miscreant" (4). His insult of Kingpin as "petty" will be relevant to the Red Skull/Kingpin dynamic to be discussed presently. These dismissals show us Red Skull's arrogance and racism, but the Magneto slur is the most important to dissect because it gives us the greatest insight into both his mindset in the storyline and how it plays into his World War II past.

Magneto is a Jewish holocaust survivor, something established in the comics by Chris Claremont in 1981 (Morton). This is the reason why the tensions that exist in these issues are manifested and why Magneto behaves as he does in this storyline. The Red Skull does not call him a "Jew miscreant," despite having just racially dismissed The Mandarin. Why not? Exploring Red Skull's anti–Semitism in 1990 in that direct a way might have been dicey for Marvel and Gruenwald. Perhaps that would feel too real, too heated. Gruenwald, however, is working from a template established by Stan Lee of incorporating Jewish elements into the comic without being wildly overt. As Ariel David discusses, Lee's use of the X-Men and "mutants" in general was based on the persecution of Jews: "Another aspect of Lee's work that connects to Jewish values—particularly those of progressive Jews—is characters who served as metaphors for victims of anti–Semitism or racism, such as the oft-persecuted mutants of the X-Men comics." When "mutant" is stated by the Red Skull, it is difficult not to hear the word "Jew" sliding out of the Red Skull's mouth alongside it. Magneto's motivations are clear, but Gruenwald replaces Red Skull's blatant anti–Semitism over for a more Marvel-appropriate anti–Mutant sentiment, but it still encapsulates Red Skull's predictable anti–Semitic response. The anti–Mutant mentality is still very on-brand for Red Skull and it fits with his Nazi background—because mutants are stand-ins for Jews.

Morton, discussing Mutants in the Marvel universe, states that they begin their lives as normal people, but as they get older, some mutation manifests itself. He adds that regardless of their other identity markers, "they are all mutants first. The ethnic, social, sexual, gender, political, or religious markers are secondary identities the larger society imposed upon them before they established their mutant hood." While we do not doubt Red Skull's enduring Anti-Semitism, we also see him developing era-appropriate discrimination and, in X-Men comics and Marvel comics in general, anti–Mutant sentiment is a symbolic way of discussing a variety of bigotry (especially after Claremont diversified the X-Men in the mid-'70s). Therefore, Red Skull's labeling of Magneto as mutant first and Jew second is a viable reaction for someone trying to become a more modern purveyor of evil (which Gruenwald's business-oriented Red Skull most certainly is trying to be). Red Skull does not just use the term "mutant" against Magneto in internal monologues. When they meet face-to-face a few pages later, Red Skull says it directly to him. Not only does he say it, but Gruenwald also provides him with a pause (represented here with ellipses) to emphasize the slur (6). This gives the slur the offensive weight that Skull clearly desires.

Magneto crashes (quite literally) into the Red Skull's office with an ominous request to meet. Magneto is depicted in this panel by Kieron Dwyer in a powerful pose, arms extended, floating through the debris as he controls metal to destroy Skull's office. Magneto's face is covered with his helmet, but even though his helmet does not completely block his face, in this image, his face is covered in shadows. On the other hand, the Red Skull is turning his grotesque face from the destroyed wall, cowering a bit at Magneto's arrival (5). Magneto is clearly the figure in power in this dynamic. After Magneto fully enters the now-partially destroyed office, he asks the Red Skull if he is indeed the World War II version. Red Skull concedes he is. Magneto then declares his dedication to avenging his own and his family's holocaust horrors during World War II. While conceding that the Red Skull was not involved directly in his family's tragedy, Magneto confronts him over his World War II experiences: "You willingly served the most barbaric despot of this century and committed countless atrocities to advance your twisted regime!" (7). Skull says nothing of Hitler in immediate response (though he brings him up later when making a comparison to Magneto). Gruenwald's version of the Red Skull here is not one to too closely align himself with Hitler; he would see himself as a greater purveyor of his cause than Hitler (and certainly the one who endures longer).

Gruenwald is instead forging Skull on a new path of villainy. Red Skull does not deny Magneto's sentiment, instead conceding that while he does support a "master race," he turns it back to Magneto by claiming that Magneto also wishes for a conquest by a "master race" (obviously, in Magneto's case, mutants) (7). He continues to confront Magneto over what he calls Magneto's "sanctimonious posturings [sic] of moral superiority." Magneto's own actions and ideologies, Red Skull claims, show a willingness to take actions not unlike those taken by Hitler and Red Skull himself.[15] Magneto's decades as an antagonist to the heroic X-Men provide myriad examples of his villainy, but the reader cannot fully side with Red Skull's assessment because Skull is depicted as being much worse. Unlike Magneto's, Red Skull's backstory is in no way sympathetic. He is also wholly deceptive and corrupt. Skull proposes a truce and a handshake with the sole intent to lure Magneto close enough to poison him with the smoke from his toxic cigarette. Magneto wisely refuses the gesture, shouting with bold all-caps in Jack Morelli's lettering, "THE DEVIL WITH THAT, NAZI SCUM!" For Magneto, despite his own criminal actions and ideologies, World War II still endures. At this moment, Magneto diverts himself away from his own ambitions to seek revenge. For Magneto, Nazi atrocities are something that, when given the opportunity (even when presented with a plan to eradicate his more traditional adversaries), must be avenged.

Whereas Cap defeats the World War II demons he needs to defeat (both literal and emotional) and manages to forge a clear path away from the war, and the Red Skull is able to put the war behind him in order to reestablish his villainy for a new generation, Magneto is trying to end the war in this moment, seeing a clear and tortuous and painful defeat for the

Red Skull as the clearest path for he himself to be done with his own World War II demons. Red Skull is not defeated easily, of course, and his willingness to run away from a fight is a clear example of his personal cowardice. Skull captures Magneto in a force field and, unsure of how long it will hold, runs away, delivering a "Heil Hitler" arm raise before disappearing down an elevator, showing both his true ideological colors and his willingness to troll an adversary (9).

Magneto immediately escapes the force field and pursues the Red Skull, who continues to flee. Magneto relentlessly destroys all of the robot guards (including several robots that look like the Red Skull himself) as well as weapons designed to slow him, showing how strong is his dedication to this vengeance and possible freedom from the chains of that decades-old conflict (as well as emphasizing his mutant power of magnetism to a *Captain America* reader that might not be as familiar with his skill set). If there was any doubt of Magneto's obsession, that is eradicated when Magneto eventually does capture the Red Skull. He takes him to an underground bunker with no way out (the only door is well above Skull's reach) and gives him only limited water. He leaves him to "suffer" and ponder the things he has done (18). Magneto exits and leaves the Red Skull alone in the dark of the bunker, depicted in the final few panels of the story by Dwyer with a growing darkness that shadows Red Skull's face until the final panel is completely dark. Aside from a single panel in issue #368 to follow his shift to an issue of another comic, *Avengers West Coast* (18), Magneto then moves on from *Captain America*, his goals having been achieved.[16]

Magneto confronts Red Skull on his Nazi ideology, captures him, punishes him, and then disappears from the comic completely. It ends up being difficult to not see Magneto as a device to provide therapeutic comeuppance against the Red Skull (and a device that vanishes from the story when no longer needed). Obviously, Cap himself would be capable of apprehending Red Skull, but Cap's moral code makes him an ill-suited adversary to give Red Skull what he really deserves. While sympathetic in this particular storyline, Magneto's morally ambiguous moral code allows him to apprehend and torture the Red Skull in the fashion he does without the reader feeling that a moral aspect of the character's basic sense of self was being violated (which the reader would assuredly feel if Cap treated any enemy, even the Red Skull, in a vindictive fashion). More than that, Cap has made amends with World War II, his role in the conflict, and both what he did and what happened to him. Magneto, in no way, has come to terms in the same fashion and is still trying to "win" a war that saw him and his family tortured and so much of his family murdered.

Red Skull vs. Kingpin

Kingpin is also used to present Red Skull and his World War II atrocities in a clear and glaring light. After orbiting around each other for several issues during the "Streets of Poison" storyline,[17] the Kingpin and Red Skull meet face-to-face over a drug turf war in issue #378. The way this confrontation fits into a larger philosophical discussion of drug distribution takes place in Chapter Nine, but this scene from the storyline fits into the current conversation because of how Gruenwald chooses to frame the animosity between the two men. After Red Skull makes Kingpin an offer to combine their efforts to extend their drug operations, Kingpin immediately rejects him, saying, "I am an American businessman, Skull, and I cannot stomach Nazism…. Despite your recent assumption of the veneer of a capitalist, you still have the heart of a Nazi" (3). The Kingpin, like Magneto (though perhaps less so), has been shown to be a sympathetic character prior to this (Frank Miller's *Daredevil: Love and War* from 1986, for example, paints Kingpin as a man driven to extremes out of love), but it is still striking to see him as the more heroic figure in a showdown.

For Kingpin, the lingering stench of Red Skull's World War II past is impossible to overcome. While Kingpin is often shown as a pragmatist, he is not rejecting the Skull's offer on pragmatic terms—it is pure pathos. Denied in his attempts at negotiation, Red Skull proposes "hand-to-hand combat" against Kingpin with control of the New York crystal meth operation on the line. Kingpin agrees, knowing he is the superior fighter, though he does not trust Skull—"this arch-fiend," he calls him internally (5)—to fight fairly. The reader would sympathize with Kingpin in this perception (despite Kingpin's own tendencies to eschew fair fights himself).

During the ensuing battle, Kingpin refers to Red Skull as a "Nazi" four times (and again refers to Red Skull as a "Nazi" to Cap after the fight when Kingpin is explaining what has happened). Much like Red Skull's repeated refrain of "Mutant" to Magneto, this repetition of "Nazi" shows us how Kingpin views the Skull. At one point, Kingpin announces, "Let me show you how an American fights!" (10). Against the Red Skull, even Kingpin can come across as a patriotic figure. Red Skull loses the fight but hardly seems defeated, gloating at Kingpin as he leaves the scene, calling him a "criminal" (16). Just as Kingpin cannot see Red Skull as anything other than a Nazi (and the repeated refrain of the term during their fight shows this), Red Skull cannot see Kingpin as anything but a "criminal" (and a "petty" one, as he labels him in issue #367).

If "Nazi" is the pejorative term for Red Skull that Kingpin favors, "Criminal" is the same for Red Skull. Skull, so ideologically driven, in no way see himself as a criminal, whether we are discussing the present day (1990) fight with Kingpin or World War II. He knows he is evil, certainly, but he also knows his work is so much more significant than being merely that of a "criminal." He is driven by a cause to undermine America, even in his "veneer as a capitalist," and so to insult Kingpin as a "criminal," ultimately petty and driven only by greed, denotes the lowest form of villain that Red Skull can comprehend. Skull is a mastermind with much loftier goals than mere acquisition of wealth.

When it comes to villains he admires, he is more impressed with someone like Viper, a clear nihilist (and discussed in Chapter Six), than a man he sees as a representation of bloated American greed. Whether or not the Red Skull ever has any thought of besting Kingpin in hand-to-hand combat is unclear (though Skull knows enough of adversaries—and for him, everyone is an adversary—to likely know he was overmatched), but considering his stated objective with his drug endeavors is to create chaos and corruption throughout the United States in a long term attempt to bring the nation to its knees, it ultimately does not matter to him who actually controls the drugs, just as long as they are there. In Skull's mind, it is better to leave such an undignified job to a "criminal" and let a true mastermind like himself rearrange the chess pieces after they have fallen off the board.

Evil with Any Face

The Red Skull sees himself as a true visionary, regardless of the era he lives within or the face he happens to be wearing. In a back-up story in *Captain America* #383 (an issue billed as the 50th anniversary of the Captain America character), Gruenwald writes a story that takes place after Red Skull's rebirth into a cloned body of Steve Rogers, but before Red Skull reveals himself to Steve Rogers in issue #350 (and subsequently inhales his own poison smoke to become permanently disfigured with the visage of the Red Skull). This story depicts a Johann Schmidt who, while not exactly child-like, is getting accustomed to his new body and surroundings. He is impatient with inaction. Later in the story, his ally Armin Zola (a Nazi scientist whose consciousness and face appear in the stomach of a robot) internally admits that Schmidt has been in the new cloned body for less than half a day (54), so he truly is a child becoming accustomed to his own body (though his comprehension is more sophisticated than that).

He is with his Zola in the Swiss Alps, preparing to leave for the United States shortly to begin the Skull's new life as a handsome American businessman. A number of masked men attempt to infiltrate Castle Zola and, instead of killing them, Skull wants to talk to the survivors, especially one whose tenacity has piqued Skull's interest (and this is revealed in the story to be Red Skull's eventual ally Crossbones). These men explain that they were hired to infiltrate the castle by Red Skull, something which the actual Red Skull responds to with incredulity (and violence). In order to get more information out of these men, Zola (smiling at the act) hands Schmidt a Red Skull mask in an effort to extract more information.

Schmidt, perhaps not fully embracing the grotesque mask, is reluctant. After Zola suggests wearing it, Schmidt, putting it on, shares a definite lack of enthusiasm: "perhaps," he says, as he is about to put it on, and "we shall see" as he is actually wearing the mask (53). While fate will force him to wear this mask in permanent form, he is slow to don it here because he is already forging the American businessman persona for which the mask would be an unnecessary addition (and a callback to an era that is slipping in relevance). However, when he does put on the mask, he changes from a relatively tepid man who wants to leave for the U.S. and only wants information from these invaders to someone barbaric and ruthless. After he dons the mask, he immediately kills one of the prisoners and states, "that [murdering of the prisoner] was … delectable. It seems this mask does bring out the best in me" (54). While the Skull does not want to be too attached to the World War II elements of his persona, he also realizes that the most effective Red Skull is intimidating and ruthless. The Skull spares Crossbones his life after besting him in battle, acknowledging that the Red Skull of old would not do such a thing but that he is not "bound by the way [he] did things in [his] prior incarnation" (56). Much like Cap's acknowledgment of the darkness and evil found within the Red Skull's eyes, Crossbones also recognizes the evil visible within, stating that he sees a "black spark" (55) within Red Skull's eyes.

Perhaps Red Skull does change for the evolving times during Gruenwald's era, but the ideology and evil do not change. Neither Cap nor the Gruenwald-era Red Skull are, as characters, interested in continuing the battles of World War II, but battles of some sort must be carried on. The Red Skull wants power and to cause destruction; Captain America must stop him. Even if World War II is not the main narrative drive for their conflict, they are very much the same people they were from the war—Rogers is still wholly decent and Red Skull possesses a palpable evil (and Skull hates Rogers). So even if these particular characters are not going out of their way to continue World War II—and if Captain America and the Red Skull are both working consciously to become more vital and aware of their contemporary world of the late 1980s and early 1990s—their respective conflicting ideologies make a repeat of that conflict as inevitable as the evil that is always present deep in the Red Skull's eyes.

SIX

The Ideological Enemy
The Gruenwald Vision
of Captain America's Antagonists

In the letter page of issue #325 from 1987, editor Don Daley responds to a reader's question about what the reader saw as a de-emphasis on Cap as a character in the first years of Gruenwald's tenure. Daley writes, "Gruenwald admits that his first year's worth of Cap tales were spent strengthening the ranks of Cap's nemeses and refurbishing Cap's modus operandi more than delving into Cap's character" (24). This is a logical creative move to strengthen the storytelling of the series—many of Cap's villains (though not all) prior to Gruenwald's era are post–World War II Nazis, robot monsters, and forgettable one-offs. In the two years prior to Gruenwald's run as writer (issues #284–306), Cap's primary adversaries are the Red Skull and his allies (Mother Night, Baron Zemo, and Helmut Zemo among them) and adversarial corporations, including Obadiah Stane and Stane International (typically an Iron Man adversary), the Brand Corporation (also often featured in *Iron Man*) and Roxxon Oil (which has had an adversarial relationship with a number of heroes). The stories themselves, while featuring extremely notable confrontations with the Red Skull and crossovers with Deathlok and the Avengers, often lack villains that feel ideologically equal to Cap himself (not counting the Red Skull and his allies).

Obviously, Gruenwald looked to change that and (considering Daley's quote) wanted to do it immediately. If indeed the first year (of what turned out to be ten) was dedicated to strengthening Cap's rogues' gallery, what did that effort provide? In those first twelve issues, we are given the following villains: Madcap (first appearance in issue #307), Armadillo (who makes his first appearance in #308 and returns in #316), Dr. Malus in #309, Serpent Society (first appearance as a team and first appearance for some members in #309, though not all), Scourge of the Underworld (a villain recently created by Gruenwald who had appeared both in *Captain*

America and other Marvel comics and appears in multiple issues during this period, including *Captain America* #311 and #318–320), Awesome Android (who first appeared in *Fantastic Four* #15 in 1963 and is featured in #311), Flag-Smasher (first appearance in #312), MODOK (another longtime villain who dies in his appearance in #313), Mink, Remnant, Pinball (enemies of the Squadron Supreme and featured in a crossover issue in #314), the Death-Throws (first appearance as a team in #317, featuring some members who make their first appearances), and Blue Streak (a Cap villain from the '70s who dies in his appearance in #318). While these are by no means all relevant villains throughout Gruenwald's run, it is fascinating to see not just how many varied villains appear but how many are new. Several of the more established characters are used to reinforce either newer characters or storylines. For example, MODOK's appearance and death helps the reader see the threat of the Serpent Society, Blue Streak's death reinforces the threat of Scourge of the Underworld, and the Awesome Android's appearance provides the impetus for Cap to set up his Hotline network.

Many of these villains (new or introduced elsewhere) are ideologically driven or are otherwise representative of a specific theme. As an example, Madcap represents chaos and anarchy, Armadillo embodies the beauty and beast story and is symbolic of love (and when his wife is unfaithful, we see where heartbreak can lead), Dr. Malus shows us the corruption of science, the Serpent Society represents American labor unions (discussed in Chapter Seven), the Scourge of the Underworld is a symbol of vigilantism (discussed in Chapter Eight), and Flag-Smasher serves as a counter to Captain America's patriotism by representing a radical view of anti-nationalism. These villains, disparate as they are from one another, represent a clear objective for Gruenwald—provide Captain America with villains that represent some aspect that can run in contrast (and conflict) to Cap's own ideology. In this way, Gruenwald is presenting a sort of mission statement for Captain America with the adversaries he has created (or otherwise chosen to use). Each significant villain that Cap stands at odds with during this ten-year run somehow further helps us define Cap as the character Gruenwald wants him to be. This chapter looks specifically at four characters: Red Skull; the aforementioned Flag-Smasher; Viper, an anarchist who briefly takes over the Serpent Society and revises their mission statement as was established by Sidewinder; and Batroc, a French mercenary who has been a long-standing adversary in Captain America comics, well before Gruenwald's time. By discussing these four specific adversaries, we can see how Gruenwald uses antagonists in this title, not merely to create tension and action (though that certainly occurs), but to give the reader and Captain America himself a better understanding of what he personally represents. These characters help us understand one of the central questions of Gruenwald's run on this title—is Captain America heroic simply because of his ideology or is there something within him personally that creates a heroism that transcends the ideological? The focus overall will be not just on the villains themselves but on what they symbolize and why that is ultimately crucial for a greater overall understanding of the Captain America character.

The Red Skull's Ideology (or Lack Thereof)

The Red Skull is, of course, not a Gruenwald creation, but he is used in a way that delves into aspects of his villainy that diverts from previous incarnations. The '60s and '70s era Red Skull is ideological, but is most often guided simply by vengeance (and not explicitly by ideology).[1] For example, in the first issues of *Captain America* (which begins its numbers with issue #100), Stan Lee and Jack Kirby unleash a very Nazi-era villain (despite the comic's 1968 release). However, his evil is defined not by ideological words but by diabolical actions. Issue #101 revolves around the launch of the Fourth Sleeper and Skull's mind is solely on its unleashing (and the subsequent destruction it will cause). He plots for his victory, more out of vengeance than ideology: "How doubly glorious will be my triumph now—now when the unsuspecting world thinks me dead and gone!!" (7). After that declaration, he revisits his previous battle with Cap that left Red Skull defeated. While Skull's recollection of his defeat (and subsequent secret escape) revolve around the practical aspect of his survival, he does state that his "destiny is not yet fulfilled!" (7). While not expressing a specific philosophy, this declaration indicates that he sees an ideological reason for his survival (beyond just simple survival).

When Skull does explain his goals, they are vague and menacing. They revolve around power and control. In issue #103 (written by Stan Lee), Skull states his interpretation of Nazi objectives: "Those who serve the Skull are motivated by a far stronger emotion than love! As Nazis, we pay homage to hatred, and tyranny!" (6). When it comes to Nazi philosophy, Skull is generally ambiguous. Ultimately, this is a deliberate technique to convey a foreign evil without equating it too clearly with either an outdated threat (as Nazism would be seen in the 1960s and 1970s) or an actual American threat with which some readers may sympathize. In his book *Captain America and the Nationalist Superhero*, Jason Dittmer discusses that the '60s and '70s Skull's villainy has less to do with actual Nazi ideology than with his non–Communist brand of anti–Americanism:

> While the 1966 return of Nazism as a threat to the United States seems rather far-fetched, it makes narrative sense as a symbolic other for Americanism.

During the 1960s (and later), counterpointing Captain America with communism or other "real world" threats to the United States would be unpalatable to vast swaths of the young, radical audience [97].

During this era, the Red Skull's ideology is less important than the evil he represents. If he has an ideology at this point, that ideology is evil for the sake of evil. This allows Captain America to be patriotic and heroic without alienating that radical audience Dittmer mentions. The main symbolism of the Red Skull is, therefore, defined not by his own ideology, but by the ideologies he opposes.

When Gruenwald reintroduces the character, that premise is still firmly in place, but Gruenwald is quick to make sure the reader is aware that the Skull's modus operandi has changed from his inevitably failing schemes of the past. When Steve Rogers (under the guise of The Captain) meets up with Red Skull (in a cloned Steve Rogers body) in issue #350, it has been a full fifty issues since their last battle. Red Skull has seemingly learned from his past failures. Skull explains to Rogers, "I'm going to stamp out freedom, justice, democracy—all of your idiotic little ideologies!…I've learned from the errors of my past life. I no longer put all my eggs in one basket. I no longer live from one grand scheme to the next" (37). Skull exists to serve as *other*—his ideology comes not necessarily from anything that philosophically emanates from within him personally, but for what he opposes. While Stan Lee and the earlier interpreters of the character try to give him motivation, it usually feels incomplete—just vague declarations of tyranny. Here, his adversarial relationship with Captain America is not just based on vengeance. It is focused on both opposition to Captain America's ideology and well as Red Skull's own pathological desire to inflict punishment and torture.

In issue #350, before John Walker's shield takes out the Red Skull's legs and ends his speech, Skull tells Rogers, "I want you to know I am here. I want you to know what I am up to. I do so like torturing you, don't you see?" (37). Here, the Red Skull's preferred torture is psychological. It does not remain as such and his desire for torture is not limited to even torturing others. For the Red Skull, the quality he most admires in others is sadism.[2] While he enjoys inflicting pain (psychological and physical) on others, that is not where it ends for Red Skull. He also enjoys being physically tortured himself. In issue #397, when he is attempting to convince Viper to work with him, he allows her to inflict torture upon him. He tells her, "pain can be a spectator sport, but I prefer to participate. I believe that you cannot truly become proficient at inflicting pain without knowing how to endure it" (12). This serves as a means of testing her personal sadism, determining if she can be trusted (as Viper herself theorizes) and, we can infer, as a method of sexual fore-play between the two.[3] The device in question is the "Wheel of Sorrow." Skull calls it "an ingenious device for inflicting discomfort by means of strategically-placed retractable needles and electrical current" (13). He locks himself into it and leaves himself to her mercy, eager to feel the type of torture he so readily inflicts upon others. We never see the conclu-sion of the torture (when we next see either character, in it is the follow-ing issue's B-story where they are together on a couch, Skull's arm around her),[4] and it merely ends with Viper wanting to show how "extreme" she is while Red Skull screams from off-panel: "NNNNYAAAAHH!" (13). The Red Skull's villainy is defined by both his opposition to Captain America's ideals (without needing to emphasize or define his own ideology beyond generalization) and his propensity toward pain and torture.

Flag-Smasher

If Red Skull is an ethos-driven villain whose ideology comes in large part to opposition to Cap's own beliefs, Flag-Smasher is the idealized form of the Gruenwald ideologically driven Captain America adversary and, when discussing Gruenwald's first-year mission statement to populate Cap-tain America's landscape with symbolic and ideological villains, he is the prime example. The depiction of this character is unsubtle and direct, he stands in ideological opposition to Cap, and he sees himself in clear ideo-logical terms. The significance of Flag-Smasher's intended symbolism is obvious from Paul Neary's cover of the first issue in which he appears (issue #312). Flag-Smasher (a character who had not appeared previously) is shown leaping through the burning center of a giant American flag, arms up with a smoking weapon (responsible for the damage to the flag) in his hand. Though an unknown figure to the audience, he is imposing—he is absurdly large with a black and white costume that stands in contrast to the red, white, and blue of the flag (as well as the traffic light green of the back-ground, a color that creates a sense of activity that amplifies the already very active looking Flag-Smasher).

In contrast to Flag-Smasher's bold leap into the audience's perspec-tive on the cover is Captain America's presence. Cap is forced to acquiesce the main action of the cover to Flag-Smasher. Instead, Cap is awkwardly moving out of the way of Flag-Smasher's leap. Not fighting back or defy-ing the villain, he is instead twisting his body to give Flag-Smasher, his ideological and symbolic counterpoint, space. He does not give too much space, of course—Cap is moving his upper body out of the way, but his feet (especially his right foot) remain firmly planted near the spot where Flag-Smasher is likely about to leap. Cap is shown surprised by Flag-Smasher's action but not backing down. This is a good representation of the encounter within the issue itself—Cap is willing to have an ideological discussion with Flag-Smasher, but he will not hesitate to stop the villain's ability to create chaos. While the cover has Cap twisting away from his adversary (but in no way backing down), Cap has no problem with substantial conversations about ideology with Flag-Smasher, as is shown in the body of the issue.

The first panel of Flag-Smasher's first appearance establishes not just the symbolic intentions of the character but also the character's own awareness of his symbolism. On the first page of issue #312, we see Flag-Smasher on his sky cycle, in shadows, flying above the United Nations building (2). To emphasize the symbolic significance of the about-to-be-introduced character, the reader's main focus in the full-page panel penciled by Paul Neary is not the shadowy Flag-Smasher image, though he looks intimidating with his billowing cape and mace held high in the air. No, it is the bright sequence of flags (the flags of Germany, the United States, the United Kingdom, Canada, Japan, Hungary are clearly shown[5]) that move in a horizontal line with a slight curve across the page, their colors popping against the blue of the building and the purple of the night (2).

The next page begins with Flag-Smasher and his sky cycle out of the shadows and into action. With a blow from his weapon, Flag-Smasher does what his as-of-yet unrevealed name promises—he smashes a flagpole to bring down the Japanese flag. He continues down the line, pontificating about his "crusade" against organized nations, dramatically saving the American flag for last (3). After bringing down the American flag, we are given a panel of it falling to the ground while Flag-Smasher continues to monologue (aloud, it is important to note but, considering he is alone during this act of vandalism, to no one in particular). He himself uses the term "symbolic victory" to describe his vandalism (3), thus emphasizing the symbolism he gives the act and the value he sees in the act itself. His actions could lead the reader to believe that Gruenwald holds globalism in contempt and moments like this destruction (and later acts of violence) will not refute that, but Gruenwald gives Flag-Smasher enough of a voice to bring that conclusion into debate. If Gruenwald clearly opposes global liberalism (and Flag-Smasher's depiction as a villain who desires to end borders would qualify), Gruenwald might not work to give Smasher a rational voice (and a message that Cap himself has to contemplate). This depiction stands in direct counter to the aforementioned Red Skull (who never has a point of view worth considering).

While he will later to be shown to be unafraid to inflict pain and personal harm upon others, Flag-Smasher is obsessed with symbol (not unlike

Cap himself). In this scene portraying the destruction of the U.N. flags, he is also immediately laying out his ideology. While he is violent (and this act is a precursor to much more violent and dangerous acts both in this issue and beyond), he does not see himself as a villain.[6] He is, in his own mind, a person capable of liberating the world from its chains. He uses violence as a tool, not because he enjoys it (unlike a character like, say, Viper or Red Skull) but because he has no other choice. He chastises but does not outright villainize the leaders of the world's nations. He describes the United Nations as a "farce" but also acknowledges that the people responsible for it are "good men with good intentions" (4), and he merely wants to show them the error of their methods.

Obviously, as is often the case with many a self-righteous supervillain, his liberal use of force and violence hides any message of unity he wants to project. After the United Nations guards have spotted him, he drops an explosive device atop the fallen pile of flags and announces his name to the guards who leap away from the explosion he has created. Later in the issue, continuing his symbolic acts of vandalism and destruction, he breaks into a flag factory and sets fire to rows of American flags, leaving the building in flames as he continues to espouse his anti-nationalist rhetoric high in the night sky (to no one who could ever hear his words). In the final panel of the factory attack, Neary gives us an image of Flag-Smasher looking backward at the fiery building, not just admiring his work, but taking in the symbolic nature of it. In the portion of the speech he is giving in that moment, he twice states how much the world will "thank" him for his actions (9). Clearly, Flag-Smasher is a character driven to violence for a cause he believes in and, crucially, also believes the world will eventually unify behind.

He is established immediately not as a villain who wants to conquer a country or world, or wants to destroy as much as possible for personal gain, but as a person who believes in a liberal cause to unite the people of the world. He truly feels that eliminating nations will benefit all people and end wars and conflict. He is a type of villain who is truly a deviation from the norm of conquest and vengeance (though a villain of this type is not particularly a deviation in Gruenwald's writing). He is driven not by greed or destruction but by an ideology he truly believes will improve humanity by bringing people of the world together without the influence of nationalistic tendencies. For Flag-Smasher, there is no line between patriotism and nationalism—it is all toxic. He envisions the power of a single united world and sees that as a clear ideal. He is clearly the type of villain who can make Cap look a hero in contrast because Cap does not firebomb flag factories (and instead fights and apprehends those who do), but it provides an ideological opportunity to contrast their respective ideologies. Flag-Smasher's rhetoric is something Cap can verbally retort.

Flag-Smasher wants to verbally spar with Captain America—possibly more than he wants to physically fight him—because he is so convinced of the righteousness of his mission. In a scene in which Flag-Smasher (out of uniform) is speaking to a picture of his deceased father, he announces how he wants to confront Cap in order to "crush him and the ideals he stands for!" (11). While we can see this as a desire to literally "crush," his desire to debate his ideology with Cap (thus the emphasis on Cap's "ideals"), makes it reasonable to conclude that, while physically defeating Cap would be wonderful, proving his own ideology superior to Captain America's patriotic ideology would be better. This is a unique progression for a Captain America villain. Flag-Smasher would like to best Cap in battle (the word "crush" clearly emphasizes that), but for him to point out the "ideals" makes it clear that he intends to voice his ideology publicly (which he does later in the issue, albeit through violence and the threat of firing upon a large crowd).

While this type of violence is nothing out of the ordinary for a Captain America villain, the ideological reason is unusual. Flag-Smasher is an early attempt by Gruenwald to normalize the ideologically driven villain motif. Flag-Smasher genuinely believes he has the moral high ground on ideology. His objective is "peace and unity" (12) and, while acknowledging the life of his diplomatic father and his father's failed attempts to push his own anti-nationalistic ideology (a philosophy Flag-Smasher has clearly inherited), Flag-Smasher concludes that the only way to achieve his goal of "peace and unity" is to use the "universal language of violence"[7] (13). The reader is aware of the warped sense of priorities present here, but Flag-Smasher's objective of "peace and unity" is honorable and deserves a debate. In contrast, Red Skull has no inclination toward potentially honorable ideas and does not deserve an ideological debate. Flag-Smasher feels the only way to earn such a debate is through force. Could someone less prone to violence who still possessed Flag-Smasher's ideology have proven to be a less adversarial foil to Cap? Could Cap have accepted someone with whom he engages in philosophical debates but ultimately fights alongside for the betterment of the world? Perhaps a pairing more akin to Denny O'Neil and Neal Adams' work on Green Lantern and Green Arrow team-ups in which the Green Arrow represents a liberal revolutionary counter to Green Lantern's establishment persona (Bondurant). In that comic, Green Lantern was challenged by an "angry, liberal-minded Green Arrow and was presented with arguments of social injustices from more than one side" (Sacks 22). Alas, none of that happens between Flag-Smasher and Captain America because, while Green Lantern and Green Arrow (and Cap for that matter) are honorable and understand the necessity of force only to protect lives, Flag-Smasher does not. Flag-Smasher's methods to get that philosophical debate with Cap make him a dishonorable villain, albeit one with values that can engage the reader toward contemplation of his perspective.

Reader Paul Weissburg observes in a letter in issue #318 that he sympathizes with Flag-Smasher's ideology but does not feel like that ideology was given the opportunity to resonate with the reader: "You never even try to give each side an equal chance." Editor Michael Carlin responds by stating that the reader (and Cap) are calling Flag-Smasher a villain without that description being necessarily shared by all: "It's perfectly possible for an anti-nationalist to be heroic or a patriot to be villainous, by today's standards" (24). The question is not whether Flag-Smasher's ideology is potentially heroic—it is whether Gruenwald wants that interpretation to be made and if Flag-Smasher's embrace of globalism complicates his villainy. For instance, reader Roger Z. Cadenhead's letter in issue #318 expresses a sympathy toward Flag-Smasher's philosophy (and a criticism of Cap's response to Flag-Smasher): "I…think Cap was incorrect to some degree when he said that Flag-Smasher was wrong. Fierce nationalism can set up the inferiority-superiority situations among people that make it possible for crimes like fascism to exist. Pride in one's own country is fine as long as it is not at the expense of another country" (24). Editor Michael Carlin writes in response that "Cap would agree with you that nationalism should not be used as an excuse for intolerance." Additionally, Cap's behavior toward other countries is respectful, thus not indicating a nationalism that disrespects other nations.

As #312 progresses, Flag-Smasher's opportunity to make his verbal manifesto public is at the expense of Captain America, who is giving a rare public statement at an outdoor theater to announce his hotline, a phone number that will allow Cap to be reached by citizens who have spotted danger that local authorities are unable to handle. In his speech (prior to Flag-Smasher's narratively telegraphed interruption), Cap speaks of the uniqueness of the United States and how much he cares about the American people and how, without the American people, "this land is no different from any other … and this government cannot exist" (15). This is fascinating because Cap is already offering a counterpoint to Flag-Smasher's argument before he even becomes aware of Flag-Smasher's existence. Even the issue's narration helps establish Cap's own position and ideology.

As Cap is going to the stage to make his announcement, the narrator muses not just on his symbolism, but also his celebrity, explaining that "his fame is a mere byproduct of his mission to give America an enduring symbol of its highest virtues—freedom, justice, dignity, and opportunity for all" (14). This reflection of Cap's celebrity does not originate with Gruenwald, but he uses it effectively at moments like this one.[8] While Gruenwald often takes these moments through his run to remind us of Cap's symbolism and overall mission, it feels especially purposeful here, as if to position the philosophies of the figures who will engage in debate into the proper places on the gameboard.

While Cap does engage in conversation with Flag-Smasher, he is not as rhetorically focused as he could be because he has to prioritize safety for the people attending the event. When Flag-Smasher is addressing the audience about his beliefs, Cap is less listening to the specifics of his message and more planning on how and when to disarm him. Flag-Smasher is ultimately able to be disarmed in this conversation because he *is* more rhetorically focused. He has waited, one would assume, a long time to be able to finally address a captive audience so he needs to get the words right. He presents himself as not being anti–American, but anti-nationalistic in a more general sense: "I am not against America in particular! I am against all countries.... I am against the very concept of countries!" (19). He is trying to be somewhat diplomatic with his words (though the fact he is holding a weapon on the crowd, forcing them to listen, certainly negates any linguistic diplomacy he might employ), but he expresses frustration with the audience's ultimate lack of understanding. After Flag-Smasher expresses his philosophy, Cap carefully counters him, acknowledging Flag-Smasher's seemingly positive objective, but calling him out on his methods. For Flag-Smasher, the ends justify the means; Captain America disagrees.

The crowd (represented by a few people standing behind Cap) immediately fall in line with Cap's rhetoric, showing their dedication to his personal ideology (these are, after all, people who specifically came out to watch Captain America make an announcement, so they are already predisposed toward him), but they also show a lack of understanding of Flag-Smasher's message—one member of the crowd, reflecting the Cold War tensions of the time, shouts, "Go back to Russia, ya Commie!" (19). Flag-Smasher seems surprised and, arguably, hurt by the comment because it is such a misrepresentation of his message: "What? I'm not a Communist. Weren't you people listening?" (19). The purpose of his violence, threats, and interruptions is to get his message conveyed to a larger audience, but when he manages to get an audience, that audience is not necessarily going to be receptive.[9] He has planned out this moment to broadcast his message, but the audience is not interested or understanding, thus his message is not as appreciated as he expected it to be. This is difficult for Flag-Smasher to comprehend. Considering the audience incorrectly equates Flag-Smasher's message of global unity with Communism further underscores the urgency he feels his message should convey.

Flag-Smasher's Respect for Steve Rogers (Not Captain America)

Flag-Smasher makes sporadic appearances during the first half of Gruenwald's run[10] and an appearance worth examining here comes in issue #348. In the opening pages of this issue, he is being pursued by his own U.L.T.I.M.A.T.U.M. agents without prelude or any explanation. As his agents attempt to apprehend him, they make extremely vague accusations and Flag-Smasher offers to explain to them why they are mistaken in pursuing him, but they refuse the offer, and continue their aggressive pursuit. Flag-Smasher realizes that they will never be able to "understand" why he feels as he does after he has "pegged the identity of U.L.T.I.M.A.T.U.M.'s true founder and financial backer" (3). This financial backer is ultimately revealed to be the Red Skull, and Flag-Smasher resents Red Skull's fascism, Nazism, and desire to separate mankind. In fact, he resents Red Skull as much as he resents Captain America's patriotism (though given that he enlists Cap to assist him in sabotaging Flag-Smasher's own already established plan to thwart the Red Skull's ambition, perhaps he resents the Red Skull more).

Flag-Smasher flees his former associates in order to fulfill his goals: "it's not only a matter of world security—but also of my honor as an anti-patriot!" (5). The reader might see Flag-Smasher as a character of little-to-no honor, but he does not see himself this way—his ideology does not waver, nor do his ideals. Obviously, having his operations funded by someone of infinite resources would be something most villains would eagerly accept, even if they are morally or ideologically opposed to that benefactor, but for Flag-Smasher, Red Skull is simply not an acceptable source of funding. Most villains would perhaps be less scrupulous (though Magneto's and Kingpin's disgust with Red Skull as outlined in Chapter Five reveal two other villains who opt not to associate with him), but Flag-Smasher's ideology is such that he is unwilling to sacrifice his values, even if maintaining his integrity puts him into conflict with his own allies. In fact, Flag-Smasher is so dedicated to his values, he is willing to ask for assistance from an enemy if he feels that said enemy is less a threat to his ideology than another (and he feels that the lesser enemy is honorable enough to actually help him). Therefore, he asks Captain America for help. Captain America quickly flies to Flag-Smasher's location to answer his call.

Unfortunately for Flag-Smasher, when that call is answered, it is not the Captain America he expects it to be. Instead of Steve Rogers (and the moral compass and care for human life he possesses), the Captain America at the time when Flag-Smasher issues his call for help is the far less morally pristine John Walker (and Walker and Flag-Smasher have had no previous interactions). Flag-Smasher is shocked by the change (indicated by the hesitation and emphasis): "You … you're not Captain America! You're an imposter!" (17). Flag-Smasher is expecting his ideological counterpoint in Steve Rogers (and someone the reader would see as a moral superior, but whom Flag-Smasher would see only as a moral equal), but he does not get that counterpoint. He does not spend a great deal of time determining the merit of this new Captain America—Flag-Smasher says he does not "have time for such foolishness!" (17)—and immediately attacks John Walker's Cap with clear intent to kill (he tells him to "prepare to die!" and then lunges at him with his giant spiked weapon).

Flag-Smasher repeatedly fixates on the fact that this Cap is not the one he expects. Flag-Smasher calls him a "lying cretin," a "fake," "a stand-in," and an "imposter" four times over six pages (18–23), emphasizing how upset he is about Walker's presence. Why is it such a point of contention for Flag-Smasher? It can be argued that Flag-Smasher, as much a symbol of anti-nationalism as he sees himself to be, is ultimately a personality-driven villain, and not as symbol-driven as he would think. While he believes deeply in his mission (and that does not seem debatable), he also values both his capability and value as an individual and the actual people he is opposing (and not simply their uniforms). He is not reaching out to Captain America in general—he needs Steve Rogers (even if he does not even know Steve Rogers' actual name).

One fascinating aspect of the fight between Flag-Smasher and Captain America in this issue is that, while one would assume Cap (John Walker) would be the combatant with whom the reader would have the most investment (as well as a rooting interest), it does not really work that way. In context, both Walker and Flag-Smasher are people the reader has seen perform heinous acts of murder and violence—Smasher typically in service of an ideology (though he clearly goes well beyond what a typical reader would find acceptable) and Walker mostly out of rage and a sense of duty the reader can see as misguided. Flag-Smasher enters this fight with a larger purpose of avoiding a massive crisis. "All of civilization is at stake!!" Flag-Smasher announces as he initially pounces on Walker (17), making the urgency of his situation—and the agency with which he personally takes it—clear. Walker is following orders from a governing body in which he has no faith (they attempt to fire him earlier in the issue). Walker is doing his job in as passive and non-committed a way as possible, and Flag-Smasher has more motivation to fight and win.

In context, Flag-Smasher is the more sympathetic figure. In execution, Gruenwald writes it in such a way that the reader would feel more invested in Flag-Smasher as well. First, Gruenwald makes it feel logical that Flag-Smasher would be confused and feel betrayed by another man arriving in the suit. He needs Rogers and not getting Rogers is a massive impediment for his plan. The reader can sympathize with his urgency and subsequent panic over the "wrong" Captain America arriving.[11] Second, the narrative structure emphasizes Flag-Smasher's perspective over Walker's. Their confrontation in this issue spans seven pages and those seven pages have 28 panels depicting their conflict. In those 28 panels, we get five occurrences of chain thought bubbles for Flag-Smasher and none for Walker.[12] Flag-Smasher, ostensibly the villain of the issue, is made far more sympathetic (and this is clearly by design) because of his unwillingness to waver from his ideology (and his trust in Rogers, the true hero of the series), even if it puts him in alliance with a character he ideologically opposes against the Red Skull, a character that a reader would see as a far greater evil. Red Skull's identity is officially unrevealed until issue #349, though if the reader does not know exactly who the threat is, they know the threat is an aggressively malevolent one. When Flag-Smasher does reveal this information in #349, Steve Rogers refuses to believe it (a trope discussed in more detail in Chapter Five). Flag-Smasher, however, never doubts the truth of what he has uncovered. He is a character of unshakable ideological values.

Flag-Smasher himself even laments his own idealism. In issue #349, Flag-Smasher has captured John Walker Captain America and is waiting on the arrival of Steve Rogers (known during this period as "The Captain"). As he is waiting, Flag-Smasher thinks, "If only I weren't such an idealist—and it did not matter to me where the funding for my anti-nationalist activities came from" (9). He has a self-awareness of how being an "idealist" is potentially leading to his self-destruction, but his adherence to ideology will not let him waver. Finally, Steve Rogers arrives at the base and finds Flag-Smasher in battle with his own agents of U.L.T.I.M.A.T.U.M. and Rogers expresses confusion: "nothing you do makes sense to me!" (16). This line represents the ideological gap between the two masked figures—there exists such a substantial rift between the two ideologically, it is impossible for them to truly understand one another.

Flag-Smasher then explains that U.L.T.I.M.A.T.U.M. is working on a Doomsday Machine that will render all electronic equipment inoperable, but once he realized where his funding is coming from, he knew he needed to destroy it: "to use a device funded by a Nazi—even to save the world—would be the height of hypocrisy!" (16). Rogers assesses that Flag-Smasher seems "earnest" and agrees to help him destroy the machine. There is never a point at which Flag-Smasher seems dishonest, during this storyline or any other appearance. Neither Flag-Smasher nor Rogers are particularly comfortable with their temporary alliance, but stopping the Red Skull is a place at which their ideologies and missions meet.

Not only is Flag-Smasher always driven by his ideology, he is also always ready to explain the value of his position. In one desperate moment when he and Rogers are together attempting to stop the Doomsday Machine with only minutes to spare, Rogers tells Flag-Smasher that he doesn't "even want to know" what this device would do to benefit Flag-Smasher's goals. Flag-Smasher (again, with only minutes before this destructive machine activates) says, "I will tell you anyway!" and begins to explain his purpose before the Captain cuts him off, telling him, "stow it, Mister" (19). Cap realizes the urgency and, while Flag-Smasher clearly does too (why else would he employ the assistance of an enemy?), he still cannot avoid articulating his goals and ideology. Flag-Smasher cannot stop delivering ideology about his ideology. He is a villain so confident in his positions that he cannot stop talking about those positions.

The Nihilism of Viper

While Flag-Smasher is driven by his potentially sympathetic ideologies, there are other villains who have no such potential sympathies. One of those is, of course, the aforementioned Red Skull, but worth noting and discussing individually is Skull's similarly-minded (though notably quite different) ally Viper. She is an anarchist and nihilist, hell-bent on destroying anything she can potentially destroy. Mikhael Bakunin, 19th-century German philosopher, described the tenets of what would be seen as Nihilism: "Let us put our trust in the eternal spirit which destroys and annihilates only because it is the unsearchable and eternally creative source of all life—the passion for destruction is also a creative passion!" (qtd. in Pratt). For a nihilist, there is an art to destruction.

Accordingly, Viper's plans are destructive and chaos-creating on a scale that she believes are aesthetically beautiful and would create chaos that could never be overcome. She only creates plans that will spread destruction on an irreversible scale. She infiltrates the Serpent Society in order to use it for her chaos-spreading needs (specifically to spread a poison throughout the United States that would turn all Americans into mindless snakes), and she later aligns herself with the Red Skull in order to increase her opportunities for chaos. He ultimately breaks off his ties with her because he does not see sufficient results for the anarchy she is interested in unleashing. He also does not want her to follow through on her most ambitious plans lest he have no world left to rule over if her plans of destruction are fulfilled. Her ideology is nihilism and anarchy.

According to Constancio, "Nietzsche defines 'nihilism' as the attitude of a will to truth that prefers 'an assured nothing' to 'an uncertain something'" (287). Mikhael Bakunin's early nihilist movement eventually "deteriorated into an ethos of subversion, destruction, and anarchy" (Pratt). If there is both a tragic perspective using the lens of the meaninglessness of life (and perhaps the work of Camus and Samuel Beckett capture this perceived meaninglessness) and a destructive state of seeing a meaningless world, Viper represents the destructive side of the philosophy. Bakunin's discussion of the state fits much more neatly with her perspective: "If there is a state, there must be domination of one class by another and, as a result, slavery; the State without slavery is unthinkable—and that is why we are enemies of the State" (qtd. in Fiala). Her hatred of the state drives her to destroy it (and her plan to turn all Americans into mindless snakes seems only to affect Americans, thus emphasizing the state to which she is most inclined to see herself as an enemy).

Bakunin's idea of rebelling against the state to destroy it (and the slavery inherent within) is a potentially heroic narrative. It is a call for a rebellion to free people from slavery. There is nothing heroic about Viper—she kills without regard to class or status and, in issue #395, when the Red Skull invites her into his hot tub so they can "brainstorm new evils together" (6), she immediately unrobes and joins him. Unlike Flag-Smasher, who would abhor the label of "evil," she embraces it (as does the Red Skull). In #344, after Viper escapes capture by D–Man and Nomad while she is in the midst of completing her master plan of turning Americans into snakes, Gruenwald depicts her in the chaotic streets of Washington, D.C., heavily armed and gleefully firing guns in into the air. As she walks past burning cars and people transformed into snakes, she cackles, "Hya-ha-ha-ha! Burn, Washington, burn!" (15). She starts firing upon already damaged cars and exclaims, "I am the viper coiled at the nation's breast! America is weak and decadent—its people are materialistic automatons—its institutions oppressive and obsolete—its leaders shameless charlatans and capitalist tools—!" (15). It is destruction driven by ideology, but it is ultimately not about burning it down to rebuild. It is just about burning it down. She is using the ideology of anarchy to destroy. She is using the ideology of nihilism to justify destruction for its own sake.

In issue #394, Red Skull orders Viper broken out of prison. This is a logical alliance in many ways—both are ideologues and creators of chaos. However, they are in no way the same, and Red Skull's allies are immediately aware of this fact. When Red Skull orders his allies to break Viper out of prison, Crossbones questions it. He tells Red Skull, "The dame's a full-time loon" (12). Red Skull, not one to take being questioned, fires him on the spot. Crossbones' assessment is shared by others, but they are too intimidated by Red Skull to speak up (and they have already witnessed Crossbones, Skull's most trusted henchmen, be fired for questioning his plan at this point). When Mother Night goes to Crossbones' quarters to share Red

Skull's orders to clear out his possessions, she tells Crossbones (in regard to Viper), "she's insane. Everyone knows that. She'll betray him first opportunity she gets" (13). If Red Skull is aware of this, he does not let on right away. After Viper has been freed from prison, the Skull explains that he wants to give her "the opportunity to fulfill [her] wildest nihilistic fantasies!" (18). At this point, he understands and values her nihilism. He, however, makes the mistake of miscalculating the depths of her nihilism. In #395, Skull further explains that he wishes to "finance ... whatever subversive activity [her] heart desires" (6). He praises their shared "genius for subversion" and their common goal of contributing "to the deterioration of the decadent society in which we live" (6). However, whatever affection exists between the two is forced to be short-lived.[13]

Predictably, their partnership fails, though not because of a betrayal by Viper that Crossbones and Mother Night found so inevitable, but because their ideologies are not as compatible as the Red Skull anticipates. In issue #419, Red Skull laments the failed potential of their partnership, putting the blame squarely on Viper's shoulders. He states that she has "one fatal flaw, and he elaborates this by explaining the differences between their philosophies: "I believe in fomenting chaos in order to bring a new order—while you believe in fomenting chaos for the sake of chaos" (2–3) He further adds that "The Red Skull is many things, but a nihilist is not one of them" (3). It is unclear why the Skull miscalculated the effectiveness of their partnership, though he was justified in not heeding concerns about her potential betrayal (considering that is not how the alliance ends).

If nihilism is indeed the idea that everything is valueless and "nothing can be known or communicated" (Pratt), that is indeed a far cry from what the Red Skull believes. He does believe that certain things possess value. Ultimately, the Red Skull cannot maintain the partnership with Viper because of the severity of her plans. He recruits her to cause anarchy, but she is so good at it, he realizes that her "talents" will not help him. He acknowledges that she has undertaken a plan that will "bring about a cleansing purge of this corrupt and decadent society ... but it is a purge from which recovery cannot occur in my lifetime!" (3). Skull wants the "cleansing purge of this corrupt and decadent society" (3), but he needs to be the one to clean it up and rebuild it in his name. If everything is simply burnt to the ground, there is no world left for him to rule.

Cap's responses to these characters indicate the threats they possess, of course, because he is a master tactician and therefore would be capable of assessing any enemy quickly, especially if he has had prior interactions with said enemy. When Cap encounters Viper after she and her minions have invaded the Serpent Citadel (in issue #342), he notes that "this little raid was just a prelude to something really sinister" (23). She is an ideologically driven villain whose *ideology* is the main threat—the combination of nihilism and anarchism is inherently dangerous in someone willing to act out that ideology. With Flag-Smasher, the threat is not really with the ideology—it is with the level of dedication to the ideology (and this willingness to use violence on behalf of a cause that could otherwise be supported and endorsed civilly). Both Viper and Flag-Smasher are absolutely dedicated to their ideology in a narrowly focused way. Ultimately, Viper's goals are destruction. There can be no debate between Cap and Viper about her goals (and Cap debates Flag-Smasher on several occasions) because she is not interested in convincing anyone of the righteousness of her ideology (unlike Flag-Smasher)—she just wants to kill.

Batroc's Sense of Honor

Another villain, however, has an ideology that does less to lead them toward their sinister undertakings as much as it works to protect their honor from being too compromised by their actions. Batroc, a French mercenary skilled in kickboxing, is a villain that, unlike Flag-Smasher, but similar to Red Skull and Viper, is not original to Gruenwald. This villain, a longstanding threat to Cap prior to Gruenwald, represents a sense of honor that is unique amongst Cap's villains. His defining feature (outside of his over-the-top French dialect) is that he abides by an honor code, despite his often ruthless methods. He can be read as a representation of Masculine Honor Beliefs, a system of beliefs that "contends that aggression is sometimes appropriate, justifiable, and even necessary, especially when used as a response to provocation and/or in the protection of others" (Saucier et al. 7). While this might seem an apt description of multiple characters in this title (including Captain America himself), Batroc is a clearer emblem, especially when we look at the belief system in more detail.

One study found correlations between levels of aggression and sexism, as well as "social desirability, conservatism, and self-esteem" (Saucier et al. 9), traits that all seem arguably possible with Batroc. They also could be representative of John Walker, especially in light of research that men from the southern United States (like John Walker) are "more concerned with masculine reputation" (Barnes et al. 1020) and often fit clearly into this honor ideology. For southern men, failure "to respond aggressively would not only result in a loss of honor, but could endanger one's livelihood and family" (Stratmoen et al. 152). Despite his hailing from France, rather than Walker's Custer's Grove, Georgia, Batroc is a clearer example because, while we also see patriotism and fury embodied in Walker, with Batroc, we see little else beyond a textbook representation of masculine honor ideology.

Even when he has been hired to obtain a rare and valuable artifact (as is the situation depicted in "The Bloodstone Hunt," a multipart series that runs from issue #357 to issue #362), he is willing to risk the success of the mission in order to maintain his personal honor and integrity. The storyline follows an adventure quest in which Baron Zemo is searching for the magical Bloodstones (small gem fragments) in order to resurrect his father. Zemo hires Batroc and his mercenary associates Zaran and Machete[14] to travel the world and track down the stones. In #357, Diamondback has been observing them and accidentally gets herself caught by Batroc and his associates (and physically assaulted before they identify her). When she is spotted in full, Batroc (he of the rigid honor code, something Diamondback would not have expected) is immediately apologetic for knocking her out: "Zut Alors! It ees a woman! A thousand pardons, mademoiselle!" while his allies are unmoved by her gender (22). Saucier et al. proposes that "higher levels of masculine honor includes the protection of others … masculine honor would be associated with higher levels of benevolent sexism" (9). Batroc stands out here because his colleagues do not share the same philosophy of benevolence in their sexism. Machete explains that he "caught the witch eavesdropping" (21) and the word "witch" feels like a clear stand-in for "bitch" in a family-friendly comic book. Batroc's honor code encourages this condescending "benevolent sexism" (as if Diamondback, a lethal adversary, could not possibly handle herself in battle because of her gender) and he, accordingly, treats Diamondback differently than the others treat her, establishing that Machete and Zaran possess a more malevolent sexism.

Diamondback, who has a transmitter device that can contact Cap, uses it to alert him of her situation, and he comes to save her after she has been left for dead in issue #357. Upon assessing the situation, he quickly joins the search for the Bloodstones himself. In #359, Cap goes underwater to find one of the Bloodstones and Batroc and his allies already there. Instead of being concerned about the presence of his adversary and its implications for his success, Batroc, in a thought chain bubble, says "Captain America! Ha-ha!" (16) as if relishing a fight (and adhering to the desire for noble conflict within his ideology of honor). Cap notices, however, that Batroc immediately swims away from Cap and toward the surface, something Cap notes is unusual for someone like Batroc who would never flee a fight. Batroc, heading toward the surface, regrets his lack of involvement in the fight and then kills a shark that is on its way to attack him. This act attracts many other sharks and those sharks end up pursuing Cap, Batroc, and the others.

This is completely a mistake on Batroc's part, but in issue #360, Cap assesses it to be part of a twisted plan. Cap tries to escape the shark by entering the enclosed cockpit of a plane at the bottom of the ocean, but

Batroc and his allies have occupied the area first and therefore are able to prevent him from entering. Batroc, who prevented Cap from entering the cockpit just moments earlier, then realizes Cap's hopeless situation when he sees Cap battling the sharks. Batroc then takes one of Machete's knives and leaves the safe confines of the cockpit (completely confusing his allies), killing the shark attacking Cap. Cap does not understand why Batroc does it, but the act does allow Cap to escape, and Cap has survived enough life-and-death situations to not begin questioning his fate. Batroc thinks, "I can do no more for zee Capitan without jeopardizing my own worthless hide! I hope it was enough!" (12). He abides by his honor code to not see his respected adversary die at the hands of the beast, but he is too insecure to confess this truth to his allies. He knows that Cap is a more worthy warrior than is he, so he risks his own mission (and his "own worthless hide") to save Cap's more valuable life. Considering only his mission, allowing Cap to be killed by sharks would have been ideal for Batroc and his allies. Certainly, Machete and Zaran have no qualms about Cap's seemingly inevitable fate. For Batroc, though, the dishonor of dying, not in battle to a warrior of equal standing, but to a merely instinctual creature, is unfair for a competitor of Captain America's prestige.

Zaran and Machete's response to Batroc's action shows us another side of the masculine honor belief system. In #361, after the rescue, Batroc's allies question his motives. Batroc says, "I only aided him last time in order to clear a way past the sharks" (8), something the reader knows is a fabrication. Zaran questions Batroc by accusing him of "going sweet on the American," and this accusation of homosexuality causes Batroc to attack and subsequently threaten Zaran to "nevair call Batroc anyzing but a ladies' man—if you weesh to keep a full set of teeth" (8). This overreaction to his sexuality being questioned is a clear aspect of the masculine honor belief ideology: "men with a greater adherence to masculine honor beliefs also have a greater likelihood of perceiving slurs that threaten their masculinity ... as being more offensive, and are also more likely to indicate that they would respond physically to such slurs" (Saucier et al. 14). While readers think of Cap as an archetype of honor, Batroc shows us the potential darker side of honor (much like Super-Patriot is a darker reflection of patriotism). Batroc's honor does not prevent him from undertaking a mission for a madman (which Zemo clearly is), nor does it prevent homophobia (in fact, it seems to provoke it).

Issue #443, Gruenwald's last issue as writer of Captain America, features a conversation between Batroc and Cap that greatly emphasizes the honor inherent within the character. In this issue, Captain America is dying. His body is decaying and he can only move thanks to a suit of armor created by Tony Stark. Further, Cap is told by the Black Crow, a man who describes himself as "something of a mystic" (3), that he has had a "vision" that Cap is going to die in 24 hours. He tells Cap that he feels he should know, and then transforms into a bird and flies out. Cap is left with only the knowledge of his impending death and the day ahead of him. While Cap internally considers his distrust of mystic elements, he also feels certain that Black Crow is correct. He heads off into the rainy night to live his last 24 hours. He has a number of conversations, including with Jack Flag and Free Spirit, his young protégés; Fabian Stankowitz and Zack Moonhunter, his trusted associates; his partner Falcon; his old friend Arnie Roth, a man dying of cancer (who dies as Cap leaves his bedside); Ram, his biggest fan and supporter; and even Crossbones, his vicious enemy (in order to see if his theory that everyone can possibly be redeemed is true, a theory Crossbones does not validate). He looks at photographs of Sharon Carter and Bucky Barnes, loved ones lost.

Finally, he gets a surprise visit at the Avengers Mansion from the aforementioned Batroc, who has gotten himself caught by Avengers security devices. Batroc has come to ask for help with an assassin who has been killing a number of costumed villains, including Batroc's friend Machete. Cap informs Batroc that he has already defeated that killer (named Zeitgeist) and Batroc needs not worry. Batroc thanks Cap and offers to buy him a drink. Cap brusquely declines. Batroc, in a moment of intimacy between adversaries who have battled, but always with honor, puts his hand on Cap's shoulder and asks Cap directly why he has chosen to wear the metal suit instead of his traditional costume. Again, Cap is direct and tells Batroc to leave. Batroc says that he can tell Cap needs to talk and persists in his earlier invitation: "Can we not mourn together?" (20). Cap relents and, as Cap puts it in his narration of the story, "Nine and a half hours to live and I'm having tea with Batroc in the Avengers library" (21). It is an absurd development, of course, but Batroc's honor code makes him a logical partner. In these moments, they are not enemies who have battled so many times— they are some of the only people on Earth who understand this life of adventuring (and, Batroc, unlike Crossbones, respects Cap enough as a person and adversary to have a meaningful dialogue).

Cap confesses that he is about to die and Batroc looks shocked and sincerely hurt. After their conversation (which Cap states went on for hours), Batroc admits his feelings upon hearing the news: "I will ... miss you, mon ami. You are zee only man I have nevair beaten" (21). Batroc's admiration for Cap comes from his intense respect for him as an adversary. Batroc has never bested Cap, so he cannot help but see him as a person deserving of his respect. It is a form of masculine honor beliefs—because Cap is Batroc's combat superior, he earns Batroc's complete respect. Batroc's example shows us that the masculine honor code is a potentially destructive ideology that can be used to rationalize sexism and homophobia (and romanticize violence), but it is also a philosophy that makes Batroc a much more desirable partner for tea and conversation than any other Captain America villain.

Ideology in Contrast

Gruenwald emphasizes villain development over his first year (and as Red Skull, Viper, and Batroc prove, continues throughout his ten years) on this comic because he felt that only by understanding Captain America's adversaries could he understand Cap himself. In a 1995 interview with comic-art.com that was conducted as his time on the comic was reaching its end, Gruenwald acknowledge the overall development of villains as one of the most effective changes he provided:

> I think when I inherited [Cap], he had maybe only two good villains: Red Skull obviously, and The Viper. And I think I've bolstered his ranks of his rogues' gallery quite significantly during my ten or so years on the book so now he's finally got at least ten good villains with different agendas and whatnot, so that's one thing that I think was an accomplishment.

Gruenwald needed to know not only why Cap does what he does (and that is well-defined in the comics and discussed in Chapter Two and elsewhere), but also what motivates his adversaries. Cap's enemies are not just criminals who happen to run into Cap while committing crimes and are thus defeated. From this perspective, this type of villain could be stopped by any equal hero and the reader would have had the same experience. Instead, these are villains who see Cap as a symbol in their way, representing something they need to defeat in order to fulfill the goals of their ideology. Cap is not just an obstacle—he is, in some ways, the reason they exist. These are villains who cannot become their most complete selves until they defeat Cap. Cap's purpose is fulfilled by consistently defeating each of them. Cap's villains are symbolic representations of the threats Cap faces and only by defeating them can he feel that he is fulfilling his objectives. The idea of a great hero needing a great villain is just a start—for Gruenwald, a great ideology needs a counterpoint in order to fully validate its greatness.

SEVEN

The Serpent Society
The Working People's
Supervillain Team

Generally, when a group of supervillains in a comic book form an alliance, their goal is either destroying a specific nemesis that cannot be handled alone (such as The Masters of Evil against the Avengers, the Sinister Six against Spider-Man, Brotherhood of Evil Mutants against the X-Men, or the Frightful Four against the Fantastic Four) or to take over the world (Apocalypse's Horsemen fit this description, though a group can fulfill both above goals). The Serpent Society is different. Although Captain America ends up as a persistent rival to their criminal aspirations, their alliance is not about defeating him or any other single adversary (or collection of adversaries). While criminals, their objective is not about world domination—they simply want wealth. Their best chance at such wealth is in collaboration with one another. The unifying link of all Society members having snake-themed nicknames and skillsets is objectively silly, but what Gruenwald is getting across with this team is anything but silly. He creates a supervillain team that functions as a labor union, with each member getting specific objectives, consistent payments, overall stability, and increased job security.

The job of being a supervillain is a dangerous one, and the Society provides added protection for its members[1]—they often work in pairs to increase security and are frequently shown protecting one another. This team gives a reader the rare opportunity to see villains supporting one other (while so many other villain teams consist of either bickering villains all trying to be in charge or a single authoritative leader who eliminates conflict through power and sheer will). While humanizing villains would become more commonplace as time progressed in the comics world and certainly the norm in the current wave of Marvel films (even Thanos is depicted as having a sympathetic reason for committing mass genocide in

2018's *Avengers: Infinity War* directed by Anthony and Joe Russo), Gruenwald does something in 1985 that made readers, if not sympathize with, at least understand the life and working conditions of a professional supervillain and the traditional societal way of navigating those professional hazards that the team adopts. Analyzing the Serpent Society as an organization allows readers to understand the potential for long-form storytelling for a group of villains in a traditional superhero comic and the way labor unions function and their potential for good, even when crime is the objective.

Air Traffic Controllers' Strike

On August 5, 1981, President Ronald Reagan fired over 11,000 striking air traffic controllers after they refused his order to return to their jobs (Glass). This action was perceived as "a warning to future strikers, and a sign of the weakness of a labor movement which in the thirties and forties had been a powerful force" (Zinn 49). With this defiant move, some critics argued that Reagan "had turned his back on eight decades of labor progress ... from industrial democracy to collective bargaining" (Dray 636). Reagan was using his presidential power to take power away from unions and devalue their potential to improve their ability to negotiate their contracts, not just for air traffic controllers, but for all unions looking at the same actions.[2] Despite the harshness of Reagan's actions (including banning the government from hiring the fired workers again), 59 percent of Americans approved the job he did in handling the situation, and 51 percent were more sympathetic toward Reagan than the striking workers during the confrontation, as opposed to 40 percent who were more sympathetic toward the striking air traffic controllers (Rosenthal).

In terms of public perception, Reagan successfully made the argument that the union was violating the law (and was slowing vital air travel): "They are in violation of the law, and if they do not report for work within 48 hours, they have forfeited their jobs and will be terminated" (qtd. in Craig). By 1985, public approval for labor unions was 45 percent, a low that would climb briefly over the ensuing decades before dropping to 40 percent in 2010 ("Labor Unions Seen as Good for Workers, Not U.S. Competitiveness").[3] While the Republican party was determined to lessen union powers, by the 21st century, the Democratic party was not the labor ally that it was mid 20th century: "the party of Roosevelt had long ago ceased being a reliable companion" (Dray 642). The public was soured on labor unions and the idea of taking something unpopular in the general populace (as labor unions were in 1985) and that was being soundly villainized by the Republican Party over and, ultimately, beyond the decade (and was not as vehemently defended by the whole of the Democratic party as it was in earlier generations) was a reasonable choice for creating a team of villains. Applying the motif of a labor union to an actual supervillain team is a sound idea, especially considering Gruenwald's interest in creating symbolic villains that can help construct and idealize Captain America's ideology (as is discussed in Chapter Six). However, Gruenwald does little to criticize labor unions in this depiction and, if anything, depicting the Serpent Society as a labor union functions as a Trojan Horse that unexpectedly provides a more sympathetic view toward the union structure than one would expect.

The Snakes of the Labor Movement

To a critic of labor unions, depicting them as organizations consisting entirely of "snakes" would be apropos. The members of the Serpent Society are not only snakes, but they are snakes who are recruited to the Society by the promise of removing consequences for their criminal acts and by playing on their greed. In issue #309, when we first meet the group (though nothing of the group is particularly formal at this stage), we see three specific incidents of recruiting. The first two are examples that play on the negative connotations for labor unions rampant at the time (specifically that they are greedy or criminal—and potentially both): first, we see Sidewinder literally break Cobra out of prison, and second, the silent Death Adder hands a card with a message promising "great wealth" to Princess Python in order to recruit her (11). According to David Macaray, writing on the topic of labor union criticisms, those heard most widely are that "(1) they are self-serving and corrupt, and (2) they've ruined the American economy by pricing themselves out of the market and forcing employers to relocate overseas." Sidewinder breaking Cobra out of prison is a clear example of corruption, and Princess Python being lured into the Society by the promise of wealth is an appeal to her self-serving nature. As for the second criticism, the Society is mostly successful in their efforts toward wealth throughout Gruenwald's run, and there is little indication of them "pricing themselves out of the market" (and when their successes decrease, it is attributed mostly to Cobra's less-than-successful leadership). These tropes lend themselves clearly toward a negative stereotype of unions and the leaders they serve.

What is most interesting here is that Gruenwald does not use the Serpent Society to merely vilify unions. The benefit of unions is their ability to "give workers a fair shot at achieving a semblance of economic equality" (Macaray). While the first two examples of recruiting highlight those negative perceptions, it can be argued that the third example shows the assistance to a struggling blue-collar community that unions can provide. This third recruiting scene in #309 begins with a narration informing us that the scene takes place in Pittsburgh, Pennsylvania, and provides an establishing image of the "Shamrock Bar," a working-class destination advertising "Iron City Beer" and "a fight every night" (11).

The Shamrock Bar is an obvious allusion to the Irish history of the city, and that history is built on a mistreatment of the Irish that improved with unions protecting workers, specifically immigrant workers. In 1832, fifty-seven Irish immigrants died of cholera because, even though they were working in railroad construction, they were denied health care because of "prejudice against Irish Catholics" ("Timeline of Labor History in Pennsylvania"). While this example takes place in Eastern Pennsylvania, it represents the truth of historical mistreatment for the region as a whole. The bar's front window's promise of "a fight every night" is also a callback to the city's roots. According to "Labor History Sites in the Pittsburgh Region," "'Depression Boxers,' literally fighting for a better life, lifted the city's boxing status to tops in the world (1938–1942)," thus showing this bar's ties to the city's working-class (and heavily union) roots. This bar is not a place for the weak or soft. Clearly, this exterior is portraying the difficult path to the mid–1980s for a union town as well as the hardscrabble reality that defines the region. While the reader does not know simply through this exterior who is waiting to be met inside the bar, Gruenwald and artist Paul Neary have established a narrative of the type of life that has perhaps led someone there.

The Constrictor (out of uniform) sits alone at a table at the bar, wearing a simple white t-shirt and nursing a beer. He looks like any other physically fit working-class man, though perhaps one hitting hard times. The look Paul Neary gives him in his first panel appearance shows a sullen man, one perhaps thinking of difficult times who stares ahead without appearing to look at anything in particular. Though the reader will soon learn that this is a person with a criminal persona and past (and future), he appears at first to be any working-class individual lost in his own thoughts. Anaconda, a large woman with strange gill-like growths on her face, appears suddenly and sits next to him with a proposition to talk to an "associate" of hers about "work" (11). While we can imagine, because of both the context of this conversation in a superhero comic book and the individuals involved (and the two interactions that precede this one), that the offer is criminal (and that is correct), the offer of "work" is less incriminating than an offer of great wealth. The setting of this interaction differs greatly from a prison. Anaconda is appealing to Constrictor less through the promise of excess and more with the hope of stability.

The Serpent Society is a criminal organization, obviously, but it is a criminal organization that understands real-world needs (something that will become even more clear when Sidewinder's daughter is in need of medical care later in issue #424). These characters perhaps are being courted through the promise of money and potential wealth, but it is not through an arrangement of vengeance or power (as drives other similar villainous supervillain organizations) and that paints them as more opportunistic than evil.

Sidewinder's Objectives and Leadership

There are three characters who assume leadership of the Serpent Society at various points during Gruenwald's run. They are Sidewinder (the aforementioned founder and original leader of the group), Viper (who infiltrates and takes over the group for her personal nefarious purposes), and Cobra (who also refers to himself as King Cobra; he takes over after Sidewinder leaves the group following Viper's infiltration). Each of these characters has unique leadership qualities that can be discussed as part of a larger discussion of the general qualities of union leaders. Sidewinder's inherent respect for unions is complimented by Cobra's acquired appreciation for the concept and countered completely by Viper's utter disregard and disrespect for it.

Sidewinder is the founder and first head of the Serpent Society, and his words and ideas reflect someone with a clear respect for union values and history. In issue #310, He gathers all of his recruits for a discussion (and, including him, his first meeting features twelve prospective members).[4] After the Serpent recruits have gathered, Sidewinder discusses his intentions: "to form a permanent society for our kind—a guild, a labor union, a talent pool..." (9). Technically, the terms "guild" and "labor union" are different—a "guild" refers to a "collective bargaining organization for independent contractors" while a "union" is "a collective bargaining organization for employees" (Schiller). For Sidewinder, the differences are irrelevant in this context—the Serpent Society may more closely adhere to the technical description of a guild, but ultimately it does not matter and merging the terms emphasizes that point. Sidewinder is proposing a version of a labor union and, unlike other incarnations of supervillain alliances that are more informal collections of like-minded villains, this type of alliance is important to Sidewinder. He wants to create something that unofficially and informally mimics a very official and formal American institution.

As Sidewinder is talking, he is interrupted by Constrictor (recruited

in that Pittsburgh working-class bar discussed above), who expresses reservations about the arrangements (and lets those reservations be known
with a stern fist smack upon the table). He questions the need for a union
by explaining that, as an independent contractor, he has done "just fine for
[him]self" and he does not want to join "a bunch of jerks [he's] never heard
of unless there's something in it for" him (9). When the reader discovers
Constrictor in the Shamrock Bar, he is not portrayed in any way as someone doing "just fine," and he represents someone who, based on life circumstance, would be the ideal benefactor of a labor union but has been
soured on labor unions through political rhetoric. Sidewinder explains that
the "something in it for you" aspect is freedom from incarceration because
of Sidewinder's teleporting abilities. Constrictor, acting unimpressed with
Sidewinder's abilities (though his thought bubble after he witnesses his
teleportation shows he is impressed a bit), calls the group "bozos" who
"think yer the greatest thing to come along since the AFL-CIO" (10).[5] This
comparison further establishes Gruenwald's intentions of putting labor
unions at the forefront of the reader's mind. Constrictor then leaves the
meeting and immediately calls the Avengers to report the Serpent Society's existence, not to be a good Samaritan, but instead to "make sure this
little group never gets off the ground" (11). He infiltrates the meeting with
at least some interest but immediately turns to union-busting to protect his
perceived self-interest (because he rationalizes that an organized group of
criminals will take away business opportunities from an unaffiliated independent contractor like himself).

Constrictor calls the Avengers with an anonymous tip and Captain
America follows the lead. He soon finds three members of the Society—
Anaconda, Cobra, and the Rattler—stealing equipment from a shuttered
warehouse. Cap arrives and defeats Anaconda while Cobra and Rattler
escape (16–20). Sidewinder retrieves the defeated Anaconda and, by the
end of the issue, Cobra and Anaconda seek out Constrictor for retribution (correctly assuming he was responsible for notifying Captain America). Anaconda beats him nearly to death. Cobra emphasizes this point in
shocked stuttering: "Aw geez, Anaconda. It-it looks like you k-killed him!"
(23). This brutality emphasizes negative stereotypes of labor unions and
violence.[6]

Speaking specifically of the Teamsters Union (though all labor unions
can be seen through this perspective), it can be said that a reputation for
"violence and intimidation is well-established" ("The Past" 12). A presidential commission investigation in 1969 claimed, "The United States has
the bloodiest and most violent labor history of any industrial nation on
Earth" (qtd. in "The Past" 12). Anaconda's attack on Constrictor is about
revenge, yes, but it is also about violence and message-sending. It also is

further proven after she has beaten Constrictor nearly to death and she tells him, "It ain't healthy to go crossin' the Serpent Society" (22). Constrictor, at this point, assuredly cannot hear this message—he is unconscious in a pile of trash in an alley behind a bar, but perhaps the message is not just for him, but for any implied "double-crossers" (including the visibly shaken Cobra who observes the attack). Constrictor himself has received the message through Anaconda's powerful punches and did not need to heed the literal words. Cobra (and the others who will hear of this vicious attack) will also get the message.

Cobra's hesitation toward Anaconda's attack deserves discussion. If Gruenwald would have had both members of the Society equally involved in the brutal beating, it would be an undeniable message that this aspiring labor union of supervillains would play into the basest stereotypes of union violence. Instead, Gruenwald gets to have it both ways. Anaconda's actions represent the violence associated with union intimidation and violence (which would have been a perception present in the 1980s when this comic was published), and Cobra's horrified reaction allows readers to know that this is not the norm. Otherwise, Cobra would not have been so visibly horrified (had this been the kind of attack Cobra would have anticipated, he may have still disproved, but would not have been shocked). Cobra, also, is a character who eventually assumes (through a mutually-agreed-upon transition of power) leadership of the Serpent Society. The reader does not know that yet in issue #310, but having this knowledge in hand allows us to know that the patterns of normalized union violence perhaps can be stopped by future leaders who are less inclined toward it (though Anaconda can still represent the brutish union muscle oft associated with labor unions and Teamsters specifically). Ultimately, Cobra realizes that "proper" leadership requires violent displays of power, but this scene shows us that he did not start with this philosophy.

"Craftsmen of Our Particular Persuasion"

Sidewinder, Viper, and Cobra each possess unique leadership qualities that can be discussed as part of a larger discussion of general qualities of union leaders. Sidewinder's vision for the organization is a mutually beneficial group of like-minded individuals. In issue #341, as he is pitching the organization to four new prospective members (who turn out to be associates of Viper as she is about to overtake the organization), Sidewinder explains, "In essence, the Serpent Society is a trade union dedicated to giving craftsmen of our particular persuasion the best pay, benefits, and work conditions possible!" (19). He goes on to explain that the group is highly successful, with each member bringing in "a million dollars alone each year." For a worker to join a labor union, that worker must typically be convinced that the organization will provide the worker with benefits they would not have on their own in order to justify the financial cost of joining the union.[7] Obviously, the shared organizational structure and resources provide plenty of benefits that the members of the Society would not have on their own, but Sidewinder also provides something else— the promise to the members of the Society to never be contained long in prison.

Thanks to his teleporting cloak, Sidewinder can teleport and subsequently free any imprisoned member of the society. Like any good union will provide, there is the clear promise of benefit, and Sidewinder's special power is a unique benefit his version of the Serpent Society can provide. However, a special ability is of no value if it is simply teased and not used. In just the first few appearances of the Serpent Society, Gruenwald shows Sidewinder's powers employed for the betterment of his allies on several occasions: he retrieves Cobra from prison in issue #309 (11), Anaconda from police custody in #310 (it is not directly shown, but heavily implied), an injured Bushmaster back to the Serpent Citadel for medical assistance in #313 (as in the previous example, Sidewinder states he is going to do this, but the comic does not explicitly show it, though it obviously occurs) and, in issue #315, he retrieves Death Adder, Rattler, and Cottonmouth from a holding cell while they are being questioned by Captain America (23). He does not just promise the use of his skill set to protect the others—he proves it in execution several times. His leadership is strengthened because the rest of the group can trust him for protection (unless they have violated a tenet of the Serpent Society, as will be seen below).

Beyond the promise (and illustration) of his willingness to protect the others, Sidewinder is engaged in the administrative side of leadership. In #341, he is shown in bed pouring over paperwork and prospective jobs. We find him mid-thought, indicating that he has been working on this material for a while: "...still owes from Sumatran affair ... have to send Anaconda to collect ... hmm ... this offer from Hydra sound promising ... might be up Bushmaster's alley!" (21). This is a brief private look at Sidewinder's leadership approach—it is built on his preparation and respect for the members of his group to complete their stated goals (and that respect is reciprocated). The other members of the Society are aware of his effort and respect him for that. He does not put himself into the direct missions (expect for post-mission retrieval, but his teleporting abilities make that risk minimal), leaving the rest of the team for those responsibilities. In #424 (an issue discussed in more detail below), he reveals that he formed the Society to lead from an administrative position and not risk putting himself in direct physical danger (he states this in interior monologue on page 10 and again to Diamondback on page 13).

Thanks to his administrative acumen and his fulfilled promise to protect and retrieve, Sidewinder's cowardice is never stated as a concern for the rest of the group's membership. Sidewinder's external confidence and his intimidating costume would make the rest of the group quite unaware of this truth. Instead, they praise his skills often. Black Mamba,[8] for example, while being tortured into joining Viper's incarnation of the Society in issue #342, tells Viper that she is a "fool to think [she] can run the society as smoothly as Sidewinder did! The man was a business genius!" (14). The thoughts in Sidewinder's head while he sits upon his bed working through the team's finances and prospects also serve to emphasize that. While Cobra was upset by Anaconda's attack on Rattler, Sidewinder understands and values her approach (demonstrated by his willingness to send her out to collect money in an enforcer role). Also, this is a criminal organization, and Sidewinder's enthusiasm over an offer from Hydra, a clear terrorist organization, shows he is concerned solely with financial gain and moral interests are less important. Despite the appeal of the group's commitment to protect one another, they are indeed a criminal organization and Gruenwald lets the reader into their inner workings while still showing enough critical aspects to not let that reader gain too much admiration for the group. Sidewinder and the group's dedication to the union model, however, prevents his incarnation of the Serpent Society from feeling one-dimensionally evil very often.

Sidewinder is singularly dedicated the Society. When Viper infiltrates the group in #341, she poisons him with a toxin. He is with Diamondback, a member of the group loyal to Sidewinder when he cries out, "S-s-save the s-s-society … get … helllpnnnghh!" (24). Though he is dying (or at least thinks he is dying), his conscious thoughts are all on the survival of the Society. He built the organization and considers it his legacy. The "help" he is asking for is not literally for himself (Diamondback has already administered a cure); he is asking for help for the organization overall. In issue #342, Diamondback begins to worry about the impending arrival of Viper's team and she does indeed call outside for help (reaching out to Captain America) but she expresses her concerns to the barely conscious Sidewinder when she screams at him in an attempt to revive him, "Sidewinder! If you don't get it together, this Society—and you—are doomed!" (9). Sidewinder's obsession with preserving the Society is not limited to him personally—he has managed to encourage some of the other members to feel the same level of ownership and loyalty. His life and sanity, at this moment, need to be saved because, without him, the Society cannot be sustained.

Sidewinder's Ruthless Leadership

This is not to say he is a passive leader. He does lead through intimidation and retribution. Princess Python is a member of the group who is assigned to kill MODOK, but she is intimidated by MODOK's power and ruthlessness and runs away from the mission. In issue #315, Sidewinder apprehends Princess Python and she is attached to an electrified machine where he tortures her for abandoning her assignment. He pulls a switch that causes an obviously large amount of electricity to course through her body. Sidewinder appears to inflict this torture reluctantly. He explains that she should have contacted him in advance to express her trepidation, but he is left with no recourse but to "make an example of [her] to the others—lest they get any ideas" (7). As he activates the machine and tortures her with it, he does apologize ("I'm truly sorry, dear woman"), but he also lets her know, even though he has been called abruptly away from torturing her, that he intends to complete the process: "When I'm done, you'll never be able to betray the Serpent Society again!" (7). He is obligated to punish her but, despite his reluctance, he still performs the act. He expresses remorse, but also enacts torture.

Later, the brutish Anaconda suggests she simply "snuff" Princess Python rather than risk another betrayal, but Sidewinder calmly declines the offer and instead tells Anaconda to take Princess Python back to the "confinement chamber" to continue her "debriefing" (13), explaining that he hopes to ransom her off to a group of her former allies, a suggestion that Anaconda appreciates. She does not see him as a coward for not killing Princess Python (and Anaconda's tendencies toward violence and a lack of empathy make it possible she would see him as weak for sparing Princess Python's life) and, in fact, compliments him on the idea: "Gotta hand it to ya, Sidey—yer noodle's always thinkin' green" (13). He has earned respect from these allies because of his effectiveness at what he does and, while his contribution to the organization does not involve his physical involvement in conflicts, the membership does not mind because of his overall responsible leadership and the trust he has earned (and his financial success).

While the audience would see his punishment of Princess Python as barbaric, for the sinister intentions of the Society, it is an act that helps further establish him as a strong leader. Robbie Kunreuther, a former labor relations specialist, asks, "What defines a 'good' or 'effective' labor organization and its leadership? Is the best union leader the one who takes no prisoners and fights for every inch of employee rights and convenience?" While Kunreuther's question is rhetorical, Gruenwald's characters provide even further insight. Unlike an actual labor union, of course, the Serpent Society is not negotiating with an employer. Instead, when Sidewinder is fighting for the betterment of the Society, the opposition standing in the way of increasing the Serpent Society's status are, besides law enforcement officials and Captain America, the members themselves. Instead of a leader who "takes no prisoners" while sitting at the bargaining table, Sidewinder "takes no prisoners" when it comes to setting a tone for the other members.

Eventually, Sidewinder leaves the group after he is forced out of power during Viper's coup. Following Viper's defeat, he decides to resign from the Society because of how much it hurt him to see so many members of the Society betray him (and what the Society stands for) to join what quickly becomes Viper's terrorist incarnation of the Serpent Society. For his labor union philosophy to be realized (and this occurs several times over his run as leader), the group must trust one another and work cohesively. The first missions he gives the team in #310 are intended to gauge each member's trustworthiness. He states, "I do not know if some of you are team players. It is of paramount importance in an organization such as ours that everyone knows how to cooperate" (12). When he finds members that do not live up to that paragon of cooperation, he feels he must implement punishment (like with Princess Python).

When he sees multiple members of the group join up with Viper when she assumes control, he feels like the loyalty he cultivated is lost, and he therefore walks away from the group completely. He turns over leadership to Cobra but does not do so before negotiating an escape clause. As Cobra recalls in an internal monologue in *Captain America Annual #10*, "In exchange for a 25% cut of all of the organization's future earnings, I place all of the society's assets under his management" (39). This deal establishes two things—Sidewinder's business acumen and Cobra's desperation to accomplish something (revealed by his willingness to give up a significant portion of earnings to someone who, while indeed the founder, would not be contributing to the profitable missions). While the Society under Cobra's leadership proves less profitable than while under Sidewinder's guidance, there is no way to know that at the time the deal is arranged and if, at the peak of the group's success, each member was bringing in a million dollars a year, this deal (which would require no effort from Sidewinder) could lead to millions for Sidewinder. The image accompanying this text (penciled by James Brock) depicts Sidewinder and Cobra shaking on the agreement, though one would assume that a person of Sidewinder's business acumen would want such a deal made official in writing.

Sidewinder and Hillary Clinton

However, considering Cobra's initial lack of financial success while leading the Society (and his subsequent arrest), that 25 percent (if Cobra was good for it), does not amount to much. When we see Sidewinder in *Captain American* #424, he is unable to pay for a medical procedure that will help control his daughter's seizures (because, as his doctor explains, Sidewinder's insurance has lapsed). Sidewinder tells the doctor to continue with the procedure and he will find a way to get the money (4). Knowing his criminal tendencies, the reader makes quick assumptions as to what will happen next, but those expectations are subverted. Sidewinder does not immediately commit a crime to procure the money. Instead, he contacts Cap and arranges a meeting where he asks Cap to help him get the necessary funds—Sidewinder adds that he is specifically choosing not to "commit crimes to procure it" because he "is trying to live a lawful life these days" (8). As head of the Serpent Society, Sidewinder is willing to show force in order to set examples for the members, but out of that role, he seems to legitimately want to go straight, even when his daughter's health is on the line.

In this 1994 comic (issue #424), Sidewinder tells Cap, "Until Hillary's national healthcare program goes into effect, I have no medical coverage or insurance" (8). He adds that his "credentials" make such things "hard to get." It is not hard to acknowledge two aspects about this reference to then-First Lady Hillary Clinton and her early-to-mid-nineties efforts to spearhead a new national health care program—first, the parallels to the health care situation of the United States when Clinton was the Democratic nominee for president (rather than the First Lady) in 2016 (over twenty years after this issue was published) are hard to ignore in hindsight and, more importantly, Sidewinder seems completely genuine in his confidence that she will accomplish this goal. There is no sarcasm in Sidewinder's dialogue (though whether Gruenwald was playing with dramatic irony is certainly a valid question).

The Democratic party is certainly the party more affiliated with positive perceptions (though, as discussed above, that enthusiasm and loyalty to unions waned over time) for labor unions and Sidewinder's sincere admiration for labor unions is undeniable at any point. Therefore, Sidewinder showing tendencies and loyalties toward the Democratic party and the party's presidential leadership is quite plausible. Having him express his confidence (and implied support) of Clinton helps frame his labor union support more fully. This is key for Gruenwald because he wants the Serpent Society (starting with its founder) to be completely genuine about its protective intentions. This is not just a quick and passing comparison—the union influence of the group is what matters about it ideologically. When that ideology is stripped and someone who cares not at all for union values takes over, the contrast is striking enough to leave the reader still thinking about those labor connections that Sidewinder establishes even when he is gone.

Viper's Leadership

Through a violent coup, Viper takes over leadership of the Society, first covertly installing her own loyalists into the organization and then forcing the preexisting members to pledge loyalty to her lest they be executed. As a leader, Viper is authoritarian and vicious, and her mission goals for the organization are anarchistic rather than materialistic. Therefore, her leadership techniques do not fit into a conversation of traditional union leadership.

While Sidewinder founds the organization on a clear series of principles to which each member is privy and each member agrees, and Cobra is granted leadership through a logical (and potentially legal) sequence of transfer, Viper takes over the leadership position forcefully and does nothing to promote the cooperation of labor unions instilled by the others. She is authoritative as a leader and unwilling to share her plans for the group with the members (whereas Sidewinder is very clear about telling the group what they are attempting to accomplish and who they are working for in any given mission).

With Viper, the Serpent Society ceases to function as a mutually beneficial organization and becomes a terrorist organization led by an anarchist. She realizes that the Society could have provided different benefits had her personal ideology not dictated her decision. In issue #343, she states, "Leadership of the Serpent Society would have given me choice operatives for future campaigns, but I may have no need for future campaigns if this one succeeds!" (15). She realizes the assets of group leadership, but she is not someone looking to secure multiple financial scores over time—she wants to cause a single mass destruction so great that no subsequent plans are needed.

When Sidewinder and Cobra are in charge of the Serpent Society, they plan and coordinate multiple income streams with a variety of members within the Society; Viper is always going for the one big job—the job that, as she states, will make other potential jobs obsolete (and, for Viper, these are never about financial gain). While Sidewinder is leader, Cap often interferes with the Society in order to stop their missions, but they keep enough of a low profile to stay mostly off his radar (the group is financially successful under Sidewinder, so Cap is clearly not thwarting their every effort). Viper, however, lacks such subtlety. Cap, based on prior encounters, realizes this too—Cap is aware that Viper's objectives make the Society a much greater threat than when their goals are simply financial. Cap knows Sidewinder's Society is criminal and he wants to apprehend Sidewinder and shut the Society down,[9] but he does not possess the same imperative to stop him as he does with Viper. He cannot lose track of Viper or she will potentially destroy the world. Viper's involvement makes the Serpent Society a high-risk operation that must be stopped at the risk of lives being lost. With Sidewinder, Cap wants him off the street and the Society stopped, but he does not have to prioritize it as a life or death situation.

Of course, in Gruenwald's world, she always fails. Narratively, Sidewinder's and King Cobra's respective incarnations of the Serpent Society can be successful criminal operations, mainly because their crimes are financial and not as world-endangering as Viper's. Sidewinder and King Cobra are villains, of course, and if life is lost in the balance, neither would likely be overly concerned, but that loss of life is never the objective as it is with Viper. If Sidewinder or King Cobra succeeds in a typical mission, money is stolen (and while Cap typically defeats them when he faces them, Sidewinder's reports of the group's success indicate that he is unaware of their criminal dealings most of the time). If Viper succeeds on a typical mission, the world would be destroyed.

Even Viper herself is aware of this reality. In issue #419, long after her failed efforts to use the Serpent Society to throw America into chaos, she orchestrates another massive and potentially destructive plan. Thinking she is victorious (and acknowledging the failure of her past plans in the process), she boasts: "At long last one of my schemes has achieved fruition! Nihilism reigns!" (24). However, Captain America and Silver Sable have thwarted her plan before she has even realized it. Nihilism fails to reign. She is aware of her limitations and seems surprised in this moment where she might actually succeed (and Gruenwald plays the subsequent moment of her failure for laughs). Because of her ambitious plans, of course, she would only need to succeed in a single mission for her anarchist plans to be fulfilled, but from a narrative perspective, she must be defeated lest too much chaos reign.

When she takes over leadership of the Serpent Society, the original members of the Society cannot help but compare her leadership style to Sidewinder's. When Captain America learns of her plan, he infiltrates the Serpent Citadel and pursues her, and she leaves the rest of the Society behind to be captured. Unlike the labor union tradition of each person working together toward similar goals, Viper is self-oriented. In issue #343, Rattler, upon being left behind by the fleeing Viper, wonders why he aligned with her and thinks, "Sidewinder never would've left any of us behind!" (6), something proven by Sidewinder's actions as leader. In the same issue, Cobra further expresses regret: "Why did I throw in with [Viper's ally Copperhead] and the Viper? ... She's as sick as they come" (15). She pales in comparison to the prior leader due to the perception of his loyalty to the cause and his higher ethical standards (for a criminal).

In issue #344, Cobra, upon seeing the humans infected by the snake toxin tearing through the streets is appalled by the nihilism: "I just don't see the point of it" (6). In response, Copperhead tells him, "The Viper doesn't need a point. She's a nihilist!" When she takes over the Society, her ideology (discussed in Chapter Six) also takes over the group. She is uninterested in the ideology of labor unions because her personal values and goals have nothing to do with labor unions. The deviation between Viper and Sidewinder (and later Cobra's) incarnations of the Serpent Society comes with Cobra's reaction in #343 to the plan of poisoning the Washington D.C. water supply: "I just don't see where the money is in poisoning a city!" (15). For Cobra, the Serpent Society is a job, not necessarily an ideology (though Sidewinder is clearly dedicated to the concept of labor unions). When he takes over leadership from a disillusioned Sidewinder after Viper's defeat and imprisonment, he tries to model Sidewinder's leadership style.

King Cobra's Insecure Leadership

Cobra is a character with deep roots in the Marvel universe, debuting as an adversary of Thor's in 1963's *Journey in Mystery* issue #98. He is introduced as a rank and file member of the Serpent Society in *Captain America* #309. Upon Sidewinder's resignation as leader, Cobra (the member with the most criminal experience) assumes leadership, but this leadership is initially, especially in Cobra's own mind, a failure. His failures as a leader are created by his own personal insecurities. The group is not as successful as it was under Sidewinder, and he is not commanding the same level of respect. Issues #364–366 feature back-up stories (shorter stories that run after the main story) that feature Cobra in a starring role. In this story, he picks a fight with Mister Hyde, his powerful former partner, in an effort to instill self-confidence in himself.

He has long harbored a fear of the powerful Mr. Hyde and has convinced himself that only by defeating Hyde can he prove his personal worth to himself. Indeed, in issues #366 and 367, he does ultimately best Hyde in combat, spitting in his mouth and pretending it is a poisonous solution. At the onset of the story (in issue #365), he admits in a chain thought bubble that he is insecure: "What's wrong with me? I'm the leader of the world's most successful group of super-mercenaries! I've got … power, resources, and respect … and yet I don't feel I'm doing as good a job as my predecessor" (21).

The Society, at this time, behaves in a less motivated fashion than under Sidewinder. In #365, Rattler, for example, is shown with his feet carelessly and disrespectfully propped up on the group's conference table during a formal meeting (20). Cobra theorizes that the reason for his lack of success in the position is because he is "not providing aggressive enough leadership!" (21). Following his victory over Mister Hyde, Cobra triumphantly returns to address his Serpent Society, suddenly filled with much more self-confidence than prior. In issue #367, he admits that he has failed as leader. When he is about to make an announcement to the assembled Society, Puff Adder thinks that maybe he is going to resign because he "ain't cuttin' it" (23). Instead, Cobra admits his failure: "I have been doing a less than spectacular job leading the Serpent Society…. I have never earned the fear and the respect that felons no stronger or brighter than I manage to acquire!" The confidence from defeating Mr. Hyde drives him to become a more self-assured leader (though he still deals with those basic inadequacies). He tries to make himself a more intimidating figure by changing his name (he rebrands himself "King Cobra" in #367) and tries to create a fiercer public persona to increase the effectiveness of his leadership.

By issue #434, King Cobra has relocated the Serpent Society to fictional Sandhaven, Arizona (far removed from the luxurious New York locale of the Serpent Citadel). While the mansion that is the Serpent Citadel is representative of Sidewinder's ideal of luxury (an east coast ideal of traditional inherited wealth), King Cobra remakes the Society into his own ideal of luxury—King Cobra and the Serpent Society are frequently depicted lounging poolside and working very little. For King Cobra, his idealized locale and life embody relaxation (not only is he often poolside, he offers Mister Hyde the same possibility of peacefulness when Hyde arrives to seek revenge on King Cobra). In #435, he explains that Sandhaven is his representation of the criminal's dream: "I fashioned Sandhaven to be what many in our profession have dreamed about for years—a place to relax, a place to spend our ill-gotten gains, a place to enjoy the finer things in life free of persecution" (17). He further confides in his former partner Mister Hyde (who, after defeating in battle, he no longer fears) that he lives in constant fear that it will be taken away from him.

This life is an essential element of success to King Cobra because it is his idealized life. As he and Hyde fight a physically compromised and vulnerable Captain America in issue #436, Cobra tells Hyde, "We must kill him! Or he will ruin my dream—my American Dream—of living a life of leisure!" (4). Sidewinder expresses reservations about his confidence in battle, but that awareness is articulated long after his time as leader. King Cobra, even after adopting a more confident persona and relocating the team to his version of the American Dream, cannot live with the pressure of failure. His leadership is less economically effective than Sidewinder's because King Cobra is less able to push back his fear of failure. That fear of failure is never far from Cobra's mind. With Captain America prone and motionless on the ground, Cobra goes in for the kill, but he is stopped by security devices on Captain America's new armor. Cobra's defeatist tendencies emerge after he is defeated: "Oh ... why does this always have to happen to me? Don't I ever deserve a single lousy break? Why do I always have to be the loser? Why me-?!?" (14). This lack of self-confidence prevents effective leadership.

Models to Evaluate Serpent Society Leadership

One way to examine union leadership qualities is through the lens of what Sayles and Strauss in their book *The Local Union* call "administrators" and "social leaders." Sidewinder and Cobra certainly fit into these categories, though neither do so neatly. As articulated by Miller et al. in *The Practice of Local Union Leadership*, "The 'administrators' ... are described as problem-oriented in approach to their positions, efficient, and liking to deal in abstractions, but lacking warmth in relationship with rank-and-file members." As for the "social leaders," their leadership makes up that lack of warmth by being "primarily interested in personalities and social relationships rather than problem and issues [and] were relatively inefficient in routine matters and union functioning" (Miller et al. 13).

Cobra's early failures can be attributed to an overly "social leader" approach. Viper is an absurd rendition of the "administrator," giving the members specific tasks but being so purposefully vague as to not provide the members information about the task's objective. The members react differently to Viper's leadership style—as discussed above, Copperhead is nonchalant about it, and Cobra is conflicted. Sidewinder is the best balance of the two, managing the group with a clear head toward administrative leadership and a very "by-the-numbers" approach, though he also is willing to let the group know exactly what the outcomes of certain jobs should be (and develops genuine friendships within the group).

In the 1920s, labor unions were squashed throughout the country, and business owners frequently used violent and dangerous methods to stop their employees from unionizing: "independent labor organizations were replaced with farcical 'company unions,' under a system called, significantly, the American Plan" (K. Baker 252). The American Plan was an attempt by employers to equate American Labor Unions with Germans and Bolshevism in order to paint a negative light on American unions ("American Plan"). Through government-sanctioned efforts for decades, efforts were made to discredit unions in regard to their methods, their necessity, their leadership, and their general membership. As a result of both these sustained campaigns against unions and those that are supportive of labor unions and overcompensate in their defense, the story of labor unions has become wildly skewed and inconsistent over time. With the Serpent Society, however, Gruenwald creates a band of villains who convey a surprisingly well-rounded vision of labor unions and it is not a depiction that exists in a vacuum—instead, it takes the cultural impressions of the time and creates a fully fleshed vision that exists in spite of the potentially limiting guise of snake-themed supervillains.

PART III

DEATH AND DISTRACTION

Tony Stark/Iron Man's greatest enemy, it can be argued, is not the Mandarin, Titanium Man, Fin Fang Foom, or any other external threat. As depicted in both the comics and film versions of the character, Tony Stark's personal addictions and hubris end up thwarting his attempts at heroism as often as any super-powered villain. In *Iron Man* #120–128 from 1979, David Michelinie and Bob Layton penned the seminal storyline entitled "Demon in a Bottle" that centers around Stark's alcoholism. Comic critic Henry Northmore describes the arc as "the quintessential Iron Man story, showcasing Marvel's strengths in flawed heroes with real-world problems." Stark's personal battle with addiction is an internal fight that has defined the character.

Captain America, however, is less often depicted as a superhero who faces his greatest obstacles from within. On the contrary, Cap is a character who responds heroically to the external—adapting and adjusting to these threats. While he is able to respond effectively to his villainous antagonists, some of his greatest challenges are the threats of a changing world. While his status as a barely aging fictional character benefits him, Cap must respond to a dangerous world that, occasionally, forces him to consider his own mortality. In these final three chapters, Cap's place in that evolving world of the early-to-mid 1990s is examined, specifically how he responds to the celebration of violence occurring in society during this timeframe and the proliferation of illegal drugs. In the final chapter, Gruenwald shows readers a Cap who does have to look internally when his body finally begins to betray him. Cap's own mortality is the external threat hovering over the entirety of "Fighting Chance," the 12-part story that (along with its epilogue and follow-up issues) serves as the denouement for both Gruenwald's time on the comic and his definitive take on the titular character.

EIGHT

Justice vs. Justice

Challenges to Captain America's Code of Honor

Compared to where they were in the 1960s and 1970s, comics are in the midst of significant change by the mid–1980s when Gruenwald begins writing *Captain America*. Artistic creativity is exploding, both inside and out of the comics mainstream. In 1986 (a year after Gruenwald's run begins), the following were all released: Art Spiegelman's *Maus*, Alan Moore and Dave Gibbons' *Watchmen*, and Frank Miller's *The Dark Knight Returns* and *Daredevil: Born Again*, among others (Ramsey). These graphic novels and titles are not just critically praised (*Maus* would earn Spiegelman a Special Award in Letters from the Pulitzer Committee in 1992), but they are also darker in tone and content than perhaps what a more idealistic superhero title like *Captain America* would provide. Comics were not just becoming acceptable reading for sophisticated adults, they were becoming literature worthy of analysis and study.[1] The rise of more mature interest in comics facilitates a rise in more mature characters and themes. While it is perfectly reasonable to think that some comics would be geared toward different audiences (and there would be different expectations from different titles), an obvious tide was turning toward not just more adult-oriented content, but also more aggressive anti-heroes, such as Cap's fellow Marvel comics characters Wolverine, Punisher, and Ghost Rider, among others. The tide toward emphasizing more adult themes and violence was strong, affecting many comics and readers of this era. These trends were obvious through the comic book universe.

In 1993, DC presented the "Knightfall" series in which Bane, a super steroid-enhanced criminal, breaks Bruce Wayne/Batman's back. Wayne is replaced as Batman by Jean-Paul Valley/Azrael[2] who is able to avenge his mentor by defeating Bane. Valley's more vicious and violent personality presents "a radical change that fit a new generation of comics readers" (Sacks and Dallas 113). While Gruenwald does not allow Steve Rogers to show an anti-hero side during this period, he does allow Captain America to do so, in the form of the much more aggressive John Walker. When Walker takes over the title, Gruenwald is able to instill a "Rambo" like quality to the character, something Gruenwald himself was often encouraged to do by fans looking to see Cap adopt a harder edge, as was becoming popular at the time. The incorporation of the aggressive John Walker into the comic as an aggressive Captain America was a calculated move aimed at increasing lagging sales. As Gruenwald states in an interview with Joe Field, "I still couldn't get people to read it who weren't already reading it so I knew I had to do something spectacular and out of the ordinary" ("Mark Gruenwald Interviewed by Joe Field"). Inspired by public trends toward aggression, Gruenwald's *Captain America* is often punctuated by this tension between Steve Roger's straight-arrow "truth and justice" embodying hero and the comic public's growing desire for justice of a more aggressive sort.

Representative Aggressive Captain America *Characters*

Multiple characters and storylines during Gruenwald's run embody a desire for a swifter and more authoritative style of justice than Steve Rogers is comfortable distributing. The most important characters Gruenwald creates to represent this idea of the anti-hero are the Scourge of the Underworld and the character of Americop. The Scourge character has multiple appearances in a variety of comics, but this discussion concerns Scourge's appearances in *Captain America* and the *U.S. Agent* miniseries (also written by Gruenwald). Americop is a character who appears in the mid–1990s, relatively late in Gruenwald's run, and represents the vigilante trope in that era of comics (and analyzing the character will show that trope works in the context of Cap's heroic sense of justice).

By looking at how Gruenwald uses these two characters, the reader can understand how the behaviors of these characters in *Captain America* have less to do with capitalizing on the anti-hero craze of the time, and more to do with solidifying Cap's character in contrast to those with far more ambiguous moral codes. This era is not just about darker storylines and misguided vigilantism. The 1990s especially marked an era of decline in the creative work of the industry and the public's perception of it, with an emphasis on sex and violence to generate more sales. A more cynical public became less interested in brightly illustrated depictions of good versus evil in part because certain people were more interested in what was subjectively considered "cool" and in exploiting the industry for profit. Accordingly, the comics industry in the 1990s hit a wall of creative dearth, flailing sales, and overproduction that almost destroyed it, culminating in the collector's bubble that nearly ruined the industry.

Superhero Justice

In order to contrast Captain America's traditional superhero sense of justice with the more aggressive styles of Scourge and Americop (as well as popular characters of the time, including Punisher), this concept of morally sound superhero justice should be explored in more detail. The type of idealized moral justice practiced by Captain America is about stopping the perpetrators of harm, but not necessarily doing so with ensuring that a punishment would fit a crime (as would the Punisher or Scourge). Cap stops the criminals and leaves them in the hands of the American justice system (which Cap sees as capable of issuing just punishments). In defining and discussing "justice," David Miller looks at the moral purity associated with justice:

> Aristotle also noted that when justice was identified with "complete virtue," this was always "in relation to another person." In other words, if justice is to be identified with morality as such, it must be morality in the sense of "what we owe to each other" (see Scanlon 1998). But it is anyway questionable whether justice should be understood so widely. At the level of individual ethics, justice is often contrasted with charity on the one hand, and mercy on the other, and these too are other-regarding virtues. At the level of public policy, reasons of justice are distinct from, and often compete with, reasons of other kinds, for example economic efficiency or environmental value.

So, from this perspective, Cap's sense of mercy and charity leads him to not be the one to administer a sentence upon even the most deserving, but leaving said punishment to "public policy" and not himself. Regardless of the potential biases of the American legal system, Cap can maintain his sense of moral purity by divesting himself of the challenges inherent within the process of levying justice. Cap is endlessly "other-regarding." He is not a hero seeking vengeance or celebrity. He simply wants to stop those who are committing crimes.

Superman is likely that character that comes to mind first in this discussion of "other-regarding virtues" amongst comic book heroes, due in no small part to his well-trod defense of "Truth, Justice, and the America Way." Mark Waid, who has written comics for both Cap and Superman,[3] in an essay "The Real Truth about Superman: and the Rest of Us, Too," describes Superman as being "as close as contemporary Western culture has yet come to envisioning a champion who is the epitome of unselfishness. The truest moral statement that can be made of Superman is that he invariably puts the needs of others first" (3). While emphasizing this moral purity of the character, however, Waid pulls the rug from the reader by following the above passage with a simple question: "Or does he?" Waid expands upon that contrarian query by questioning the character's relevance in the evolving age, wondering what Superman's motivation really is.

Waid ultimately discusses the moral depiction of various heroes through the generational lens of his younger readers who have, perhaps, a more cynical view of the world-at-large. Waid, in this 2001 essay, writes,

> Comic book superheroes were created as, and always have been at root, an adolescent power fantasy. As literary constructs go, they don't need to be terribly complex; in their primary-colored costumes, fighting gaudy villains and hyper-dramatic menaces that aren't terribly subtle, they're intended to excite the imaginations of children.... But, to kids today, as the stars and profile of Batman, Spider-Man, and Wolverine have risen, Superman has become increasingly irrelevant. As a pop-culture force, he enjoyed his greatest impact nearly a half-century ago. ... [T]he Gen-X and Gen-Next audience I cater to as a comics writer perceive the world around them as far more dangerous, far more unfair, and far more screwed up than my generation ever did. To them, and probably more accurately than the child in me would like to believe, their world is one where unrestrained capitalism always wins, where politicians always lie, where sports idols take drugs and beat their wives, and where white picket fences are suspect because they hide dark things [5].

Captain American and Superman are characters that both creators and readers expect to be written with a sense of moral decency and that can require a sense of justice that feels outdated at best and naïve at worst. According to Jessica Del Prete Mainer in the article "Modern Heroes: Classical Mythology and Classical Values in the Contemporary Acquis, the Case of Captain America," "Captain America is an essential element in the constitution of American morality and identity, a role prefigured by the heroes of the classical world, who similarly served to embody the ideals and moralities of their communities." If "American morality" is a relevant concept, it is "essential" that Captain America and Superman be proponents of it. Accordingly, the quintessential depictions of these characters (including Gruenwald's) maintain this sense of decency in regard to justice. As Waid observes in his essay on Superman, however, the changing world has the capacity to invalidate the potentially outdated moral codes these well-established characters possess.

"Who reads 'em?"

Gruenwald's *Captain America* is in no way immune to darker storylines[4] but, by 1994, the magnitude of the public's interest in darker stories, vigilante heroes, and a profit-first approach to comic books was working its way into the comic so directly that Cap himself is forced to deal with it in a brief interlude involving the attempted theft of several comic books. An interesting interaction in this world of comics and culture occurs in the first issue of the "Fighting Chance" storyline (issue #425), where Steve Rogers' body begins to suffer from what we are told is the "inevitable degradation of the super-soldier serum" (7). Rogers, out of uniform and out for coffee with Rachel Leighton (Diamondback, his villain-turned-hero partner and love interest) at an outdoor café, witnesses the aftermath of a robbery in which a kid steals a handful of comics from a comic book shop. Seeing the kid charging past him (and hearing the comic shop merchant shout "thief") motivates Rogers to reach over the short barrier in the outdoor area of the coffee shop and grab the kid to stop him (18). When the comic shop vendor reaches the scene where Rogers has apprehended the kid, the vendor mostly laments about the monetary value of the comics, threatening the kid retribution if "any of these are damaged" (19). Rogers, upon seeing a *Captain America* comic fall out of the kid's attempted bounty, asks to see it.

Rogers sees the thief's *Captain America* comics as the path toward reaching him. This meta relationship between the fictional world of Captain America and in-universe comics based on his adventures is well-established—early in Gruenwald's run, Rogers is, in fact, hired as an artist on *Captain America* (#311). Grunwald presents Marvel (and Cap's comic books) as canonical within the Marvel universe. The comic vendor agrees hesitatingly to let Rogers look at the comic under the condition he not remove it from its protective casing. Rogers uses the *Captain America* comic to try to teach the kid about the values and messages of the comics. For Rogers, Cap's adventures are a moral lesson. While holding the *Captain America* comic (which, in an even more meta-move, looks a bit like a small scale crude version of the cover of #425, the issue in which this scene appears), Rogers asks the boy, "How can you read these and get the idea that it's all right to steal from others?" To Rogers/Captain America, these adventures are moral lessons. He is genuinely confused that someone could possibly look up to Captain America enough to read his comics, yet not learn from Cap's heroism.

In the comic world, it is established that Cap gives permission to Marvel Comics to publish his adventures—as is explained in *Captain America* #310, Jarvis, the Avengers' butler, supplies Marvel with summaries of their adventures and also has final approval over what content from Avengers' missions appears in Marvel comics (6). Cap does not license the rights to his adventures simply for profit or to increase exposure for himself or the Avengers. He sees his example as one that leads to a clear definition between right and wrong. However, the boy in issue #425 explains (and Dave Hoover's artwork provides the boy with a constantly grimacing face and arched eyebrows to indicate his insolent nature) that he does not read them. In fact, the boy states, "who reads 'em? I just collect 'em so I can resell 'em when they're worth a lot of money!" (19).

The kid represents the collector who sees comics as a potential pathway to money and not an artistically valuable medium. By scripting the kid to say, "who reads 'em?" Gruenwald is issuing a harsh critique toward those who are more interested in profit than art (and also implying that others in this kid's peer group feel the same). Not only is the kid misguided and greedy, he is not just an isolated person expressing this view—he is representing others of his generation by implying that he does not know anyone who actually reads comics, though many of his peers might collect them for future profit.

In the early 1990s, the comic industry was seeing temporarily increased sales that, ultimately, would cause the industry to implode. Jean-Paul Gabilliet discusses this era in *Of Comics and Men: A Cultural History of American Comic Books*. He discusses a "speculative bubble" that first carried the trading card industry and then later infiltrated the comic book world:

> After the collapse of the speculative bubble that had carried it for several years, the trading card industry branched into comic books, which seemed to be an industry ripe for speculation. While numerous stores that had previously specialized in trading cards mutated into comic book stores, the sale of books experienced greater growth than the actual increase in the number of new buyers [149].

Gabilliet then explains the tactic of using alternative covers to lure collectors into buying multiple copies of single issues (as well as producing comics filled with bonus trading cards and promotional material). The publishers increased the number of copies in a print run and "comic book stores increased their preorders accordingly" (150). Readers became collectors who became speculators. The industry grew beyond its abilities, not just in terms of overpublished, overproduced individual comics, but publishers as well—24 new publishers debuted by 1993, and very few of those made it past 1996 (McCallum). Creators saw a potential opportunity for a business boom in the comic book industry, but the reality was different. This oversaturation of comics was ultimately a massive problem. Too many people were convinced that special event comics (such as those with alternative covers as mentioned above) like the "Death of Superman" storyline were going to be wildly valuable. Speculation saturated the market. At the start of the decade, there was reason to think the market was primed to explode in sales and profit.

Eventually, by the mid-1990s, the bubble burst. Those who survived that burst were trying to hold on: "As 1995 began, retailers could only reminisce about the comic book boom of a few years earlier. The downward sales slide that began in 1993 continued unabated two years later" (Sacks and Dallas 164). By 1995, the sales numbers had stabilized, but the influx of new publishers that emerged earlier in the decade were no longer viable (Gabilliet 150). The collapse affected Marvel greatly. In 1991, Marvel published nearly half of the comics sold in America; that number dropped to less than 32 percent in 1994 (Sacks and Dallas 165). Marvel was attempting to branch out in various markets at this time to stop their decline (including acquiring trading card company SkyBox in 1995 along with their 1991 purchase of the Fleer trading card company[5]), their comic book wing was being cut back dramatically. Not surprisingly, Gruenwald, a creator so deeply attached to the success of Marvel, was devastated by the decline, not just in the industry, but to Marvel specifically. When he passed away in 1996, *Captain America* was being handed off to a "third party" writer (Rob Liefield), who led the title to criticism and further decline.[6] Marvel, overall suffered: "Gruenwald *was* devastated by the terrible turn of events at the company he loved so much" (Marks and Dallas 204). The industry was not just changing—it could be argued that, even in the early 1990s when sales were strong, signs were already clear that it was all falling apart.

After 1992's *Superman* #75 (featuring Superman's much-hyped death) was a runaway success—it made $30 million for comic shops in a single day ("1992 Comic Book Sales to Comic Shops")—the market became overly saturated with "event comics." Suddenly, many people saw themselves as collectors and any "event" comic book could be as potentially valuable as the public assumed *Superman* #75 would be. Comic publishers saw this potential as well and published a number of "event" comics (including extended storylines with multiple characters, unique covers, and reboots). As Stillman notes, amateur collectors bought these highly hyped titles and "stuck the collectibles in their white boxes in the basement, bagged and boarded, with the promise that in 20 years they could put their kid through college." Even the successful issues failed to do that—as successful as *Superman* #75 was at the time, a quick look at the available stock at online comic vendor mycomicshop.com shows multiple copies available starting at $37.95. That is an increase of thirty times the cover price, but it is not getting anyone through college. Superman's (complicated) return in *The Adventures of Superman* #500 was also a sales success (though not at the level of *Superman* #75), but (based on personal and admittedly anecdotal experience), within a year of #500's 1993 release, bagged collector copies were available in retail bargain bins at a third of the original retail price (and five of those copies sit in a comic box in this author's own collection, never maturing into the financial value so many assumed notable "collector's" comics would achieve). As for the available prices of *Adventures of Superman* #500, on mycomicshop.com, the going price for a bagged collector copy starts at $1.70, under the original newsstand $2.95 price.

As the scene of the attempted comic theft in *Captain American* #425 would indicate, this possibility of wealth being gained through comic collecting (without regard to the comics themselves) was both present and worth vilifying. Readers looking back at this scene of a thwarted comic book theft some decades after Gruenwald wrote it can at least take solace in the fact that, even had this kid gotten away with his 1994 comics, they likely would not be worth much now.

"The more violent they are, the better I like them!"

After apprehending the would-be comic thief in #425 and subsequently discouraged by the kid's lack of enthusiasm for the moral messages of the comics themselves, Rogers turns his attention to the comic shop retailer and asks him about his feelings about comics. Rogers is hoping that, although the young thief had a cynical profit-based view of comics, the store owner would appreciate the moral lessons present within the comics. The comic vendor replies that he does indeed read comics and, in fact, "love[s] superheroes" (19). Rogers' momentary hope is short lived. The comic vendor's vision of the ideal superhero archetype differs greatly from what Steve Rogers has dedicated himself to representing over his lifetime as a hero. The comic shop owner explains that if he knew any of his favorite superheroes, he would "have the Punisher break this punk's hands or have Wolverine carve the word 'thief' on his forehead" (18). The vendor then explains that "the more violent [heroes] are, the better I like them!" Rogers is crestfallen. When Rogers asks the shop owner if he wants to press charges, the owner says, "Nah ... the law will let him off anyway. That's why the best heroes take the law into their own hands" (18), thus repudiating Rogers' entire philosophy on justice. The scene ends and Rogers is left wondering if his sense of "values are hopelessly outdated" (19) and therefore incompatible with the contemporary world.

This encounter is an illustration of where a comic like *Captain America* stood in the mid-'80s to mid-'90s. While the top-selling individual comics of 1994 were primarily issues of *Spawn* and *X-Men* titles (comics that predominantly feature more aggressive heroes than Cap), no issue of *Captain America* appears anywhere in the top 300 selling issues of that year ("1994 Comic Book Sales to Comics Shops"). *Captain America* is not alone in this ignominy—none of the *Avengers* line of comics make the list either (including *Avengers*, *Thor*, or *Iron Man*). These were low-selling comics during a period defined by low sales. This is a period not looked at as a peak creative and popular era for these *Avengers* titles[7] and one can get a tangible sense of Gruenwald's frustration over his titles (and, considering he was the editor and writer for other non-top selling comics, this is not just about *Captain America)* not generating the same amount of attention. Gruenwald addresses these frustrations in these issues by incorporating anti-heroes and having them painted as villains in no small part to contrast them with Captain America as a character.[8] Captain America's morality and sense of lawful justice are always portrayed as being an admirable part of his heroic make-up, but audiences were not as responsive, especially by the end of Gruenwald's tenure, in part, because the end of the Cold War made America's global might less essential.

Through the entirety of his run on the title, Gruenwald created a version of Cap that was less focused on stopping foreign adversaries because of priorities in the U.S. from coast to coast, but the potential casual reader perhaps saw Cap as passé. As Richard Hall writes in "The Captain America Conundrum," "Without the unifying threat of Soviet communism, the weaknesses within American culture and society itself were made more manifest. On the world stage, America reigned supreme. Within, America was more and more at war with itself" (287). The changing global political climate left America without a natural global enemy and, while Gruenwald shows minimal interest in creating foreign stereotypes to serve as antagonists, those perceived "weaknesses within American culture" as Hall writes, certainly detract from the potential urgency readers would detect in the character.

Comics in the 1990s are looked at today, through a very general lens, as being defined by their excess: "Everything had to be more violent, more sexy, more gritty" (Dean). Captain America, as he has long been defined, is a character whose basic principles would be compromised to fit into these trends, though Gruenwald is aware enough as a writer to know not to ignore the trends of the era. He just does not let trends adversely shape Steve Rogers. Punisher and Wolverine, the characters mentioned by the comic shop owner, are two who were objectively more popular in 1994 than Captain America (both in terms of cultural cachet within the comic reading universe and sales). They also became synonymous with the era of the late '80s and early '90s because of their popularity and violent intensity. Both characters are typically depicted as being violent toward their adversaries and uninterested in sustaining a dialogue with someone who is seen as a threat. Comic book magazine *Wizard* ranked Wolverine #1 on its 200 Greatest Comic Book Characters of All Time list from 2008 (Cap ranked a strong #7). While *Wizard* is a magazine known best for its 1990s heyday,[9] the list is a 21st-century artifact, though the placement of Wolverine at the top (and Punisher was #38) shows the celebration of the aggressive, violent hero.[10]

Both Wolverine and Punisher accrue massive body counts in their respective adventures but neither man would be looked at as a "villain" despite those fatalities because of the more obvious villainy of those they oppose. The vigilante behavior and body counts tallied by the Punisher and Wolverine in their own comics (and Scourge and Americop in *Captain America*, as discussed below) are justified in those characters' minds by the fact they are only pursuing and eliminating criminals. This behavior is furthered rationalized by an audience desensitized by violence: "Much violent behavior is socially acceptable to large numbers of Americans" (Foer 107). Foer was writing in the late 1970s, thus elegantly easing into the era of Gruenwald's work. With generations of wars and violent media, many readers (both today and in the 1970s-1990s) can easily accept violent storylines and characters. Gruenwald's depictions of violence and purveyors of violence are almost always negative—he is not amongst that "large number of Americans" who are casually romanticizing violence.[11] These violent characters are portrayed as authority figures—powerful people who deserve to get their way. If Americans are finding violence more "socially acceptable" (as Foer states above), Americans are even more willing to condone these types of acts by people in power: "Violence by persons in authority ... even when unprovoked, is considered by many to be permissible conduct" (Foer 107). While Wolverine and Punisher's methods might be seen by some as uncouth (and Gruenwald seems to be in this camp based on the negative way he is depicting the comic shop owner who revers these violent characters), far more people see this as "permissible" and, in some cases, something to celebrate.

Cap's Self-Reflection

After this exchange with the comic shop owner, Cap is forced to wonder about how he personally fits into this contemporary superhero landscape. He is not the type of "hero" who would carve initials into someone's head or break a child's hands (as the comic shop owner sees as an ideal form of both punishment and heroism). Cap's methods are marginalized by both the characters within the story (who serve as stand-ins for the evolving comic book reader) and the sales figures for the title (which were floundering in comparison to the best-selling titles of the time period). Would the citizens he has sworn to protect see him as less effective because of his strict moral code? The reader is not necessarily being led to believe that Cap himself is questioning whether he should abandon his own moral code, but he does question whether the public will question his effectiveness. When Cap shoots and kills an U.L.T.I.M.A.T.U.M. agent in *Captain America* #321, it triggers a several issues arc in which Cap is haunted by his actions.[12] If Punisher does the same thing, neither the character nor the reader would be bothered. An event such as that would be followed by no soul-searching character arc. For the Punisher character, the context of his killings are justified, and he is therefore still seen as heroic by the reader (though certainly not by Cap and other heroic peers). Cap's moral code is a significant aspect of this title—it affects his relationships with other characters and the process of his adventures. This exchange with the comic vendor and would-be thief gives the reader the impression that Gruenwald himself worried that such a morality code on a comic in the mid–1990s would do less to create valuable modeling of good behavior for young readers and more to establish the comic as a well-intentioned but out-of-touch title not bold or contemporary enough with which to be bothered.

Gruenwald addresses this tension head-on by not pretending *Captain America* exists in a vacuum where the popular vigilante heroes of the era do not exist. Instead, Gruenwald embraces this conflict by having Cap himself deal with this debate and, significantly, oppose adversaries who embody that vigilante mentality. The two vigilantes primarily in question in this discussion, Scourge of the Underworld and Americop are, ostensibly, on Cap's side in the fight against crime. This is said with an awareness that, while the Scourge's identity and purpose are occasionally complicated, his basic goals of killing criminals fits the discussion. While Scourge is a presence in this title many times over Gruenwald's run, the incarnation with which this discussion will focus is from Gruenwald's first two years and Americop appears in Gruenwald's final year as writer. Therefore, we will be able to trace how vigilantism influences affect this title during two very different times of comics (albeit in the same title by the same writer).

"Justice Is Served"

Captain America, in a speech to Flag-Smasher from issue #322 (discussed in detail in Chapter One), explains that one of the things that drives him is his dedication to "justice." Obviously, this idea of justice for Cap is not about inflicting punishment as a means of violent retribution, but to behave in a just manner to represent well the things he values (and let the American judicial system function as it should). When the Scourge of the Underworld shouts "Justice is Served!" after killing a costumed villain, something that occurs multiple times, not just in *Captain America* but in *Iron Man* and other Gruenwald edited titles (among other Marvel titles from the era), it is clear that "justice" in this context means something different, something more akin to vengeance than Cap's sense of justice. Vengeance is enacting retribution in order to fulfill a vendetta or resolve a personal dispute. Cap is uninterested in vengeance of this type.[13]

Scourge's history is a complicated one to trace since several known people have adopted the Scourge persona (and have done so for different reasons), but the most relevant incarnation for the purposes of the present conversation is the Scourge (or Scourges) who appears in *Captain America* #311 to #320.[14] In issue #320, after Cap finally unmasks the Scourge and sees who he is (and it is a person Cap has never met), Scourge is shot and killed by some unseen assailant who shouts the Scourge catchphrase and flees. In the *U.S.Agent* miniseries written by Gruenwald, it is revealed that "Scourge" is really a team of assassins founded by an elderly former hero known as the Angel. The purpose of the Scourge operation is to bring violent justice to the world and, in his own words in issue #4 of the series, the Angel explains that he's "improved the quality of life in this nation" (19). Those involved in this operation genuinely feel that they are doing a great amount of good by eliminating costumed criminal threats. "Good" in this context means eliminating villains through quick and swift judgment (that falls well outside the standards of law and order). By this rationale, the Scourge program produces far more "good" than Captain America (or U.S.Agent, more violent than Cap but far less likely to kill his adversaries at this point than during his stint as Captain America) are able to do, operating within the rules of law and decent society as they do.

At another point, Scourge is shown to be an operative under the Red Skull's employ (revealed in *Captain America* #394), something that could be explained either as a ruse by the Skull to use the Scourge in a way separate from the Scourge Operation described later in the *U.S.Agent* miniseries (to say that Skull employs people dressed in the Scourge costume to cause havoc and make Captain America's life miserable), or that Red Skull is ultimately the one in charge of everything do with the Scourge operation (regardless of the Angel's confession in *U.S.Agent* #4). For the purposes of this discussion, we should look at both the Angel's confession and the Scourge's confession in #320 as genuine sentiment by men who are unknowingly being manipulated by the Red Skull.[15]

In Scourge's earliest appearances, the reader is led to believe it is a lone male, so thinking of it in these terms (that the Scourge Cap apprehends and unmasks in #320 is a representative version) simplifies this analysis. Scourge's dedication to stop masked villains seems wholly sincere. After this original Scourge is apprehended by Cap, he tells his story of why he has committed these murders. His brother had become a costumed criminal and disgraced Scourge's family; in order to get over that shame, he put on a disguise and killed his brother so he would "stop disgracing himself" (23). Scourge's story may or may not be legitimate (in the issue, it certainly appears to be), but the reader is led to believe it is legitimate and that is what matters most. Believing that, we can see the moral righteousness that the character has deluded himself into believing to rationalize these murders.

Batman vs. Joker

When it comes to this idea of "moral righteousness," it is worthwhile to look at a comic dilemma that argues moral superhero behavior ultimately serves as a detriment to society at large. Batman refuses to kill Joker even though, inevitably, Joker will return after exile or imprisonment to kill again. Batman adheres to a nonlethal philosophy so, regardless of the inevitably of Joker's future atrocities, he cannot kill him. Cap also follows this philosophy of not killing his enemies,[16] but Cap's enemies are not typically psychotic murderers like Joker. During Gruenwald's time as writer, even the murderous Red Skull would not kill thousands of people without reason. His reasons would be invalid to any rational individual, but he would not kill so many people lest he have no one left to reign over when he achieves his ultimate victory. In addition, Cap rarely gets easy opportunities to confront the clandestine Red Skull, while Batman's opportunities with Joker are more frequent.

There are many explanations as to why Batman refuses to kill Joker. In an article entitled "Why Doesn't Batman Just Kill the Joker?" author Jesse Richards hypothesizes that it is because Joker's objective is to force Batman into Joker's darkness: "The Joker wants Batman to kill him because [Joker] perfectly embodies chaos and anarchy and wants to prove a point to everyone that people are basically more chaotic than orderly. This is why he is so scary: we are worried he may be right." Batman's control (and the same can be said of Cap) is a defining feature of his heroism. If these heroes cannot control their emotions, then the morality and control that help define them as heroes are gone.[17] Richards continues, "If the Joker can prove that Batman—the most orderly and logical and self-controlled of all of us—is a monster inside, then we are all monsters inside, and that is terrifying." Would Batman save lives if he simply killed Joker when given the opportunity? Batman's humanity is too important to him to do it. If Batman gives in and kills Joker, who is to say that he would not descend into the same pit of inhumanity? While readers would not think such a path for Batman would be possible, Batman himself is less sure.

The Bar with No Name

While Punisher's frequent kills are an essential part of his "heroism," Scourge's actions are never depicted as heroic. There is no moment where Gruenwald allows us to entertain the thought that what he is doing might be an overly aggressive but still justifiable (and heroic) response. These types of body counts cannot be heroic in a comic where Captain America is the protagonist—that would be condoning this level of retribution and vengeance. For instance, at the end of *Captain America* #319, eighteen low-level supervillains (or supervillains attempting to reform) meet in secret at a supervillain bar known only as "The Bar with No Name." Their objective is to discuss their options about how to deal with the recent rash of killings perpetrated by Scourge (a figure who has caused justifiable fear in the supervillain community). According to Gary Gilbert (the former costumed criminal known as Firebrand and organizer of the group), Scourge is a "master of disguises" whose "typical victim" is "someone who's encountered a 'super hero' at least once, been convicted for some crime or other, and uses unusual weapons or powers…" (22).

While Gilbert and the assembled group argue about what to do to protect themselves, the bartender at "The Bar with No Name" quickly and quietly pulls out two guns and shoots every single person in the bar dead, proclaiming after the act and after he has removed a mask that has hidden his identity (even though his face remains covered in shadows to the reader), "Dead—all eighteen of them! Justice is served!" (23). These villains who become Scourge's victims are not depicted as ruthless and destructive antagonists who must be killed in order to stop the threats they pose. Instead, Gruenwald shows them as scared and desperate. These villains are not the ruthless types who often appear in the pages of *Captain America* as a major threat to the protagonist—instead, they are low-level villains, some of whom are unintimidating at best and a bit goofy at worst.[18] Among those killed in the massacre at the Bar with No Name, for example, is Turner D. Century, a villain who travels on a flying bicycle and uses a fire-throwing umbrella.[19] These are not, as a rule, fiendish villains the audience is desperately waiting to see get their deserved comeuppance. There is nothing cathartic about watching Scourge kill everyone in the room. This is different than, say, how vigilante acts are depicted when committed by someone such as the Punisher. With that character, the context of the storylines would justify the act and the reader would be satisfied by the violence.

The Scourge storyline works through *Captain America* and other comics in 1985 and 1986. At the same time, in 1985, *The Punisher* four-issue limited series was on newsstands. On the first page of the first issue of that series (written by Steven Grant and drawn by Mike Zeck), we see Frank

Castle (the Punisher) being led down the corridors of Ryker's Island Prison while other prisoners talk in whispered tones about him. Castle, in an interior monologue, states, "I'd like to blow them all away" in reference to his fellow prisoners and, seemingly (though unlikely), even the guards leading him down the hall (2). While Punisher is not typically depicted simplistically as a cold killing machine (in these pages, Zeck's pencils often depict him in moments of conflict and confusion), his dismissiveness of (unworthy) human life is certainly a character trait. In his own head, he is so hell-bent on revenge, he cannot be caught up in sentimentality. It is a trait a reader is willing to support because Punisher's adversaries are mob stooges and mob bosses depicted with zero humanity. That is not what Gruenwald does with the eighteen villains gunned down by Scourge (nor with many of the other Scourge kills prior to this in a variety of comics). These characters are depicted sympathetically because they seem scared and quite human. Gruenwald could have made their deaths feel deserved. He did not.

In the issue that follows the massacre (#320), Cap meets up with Water Wizard, a similarly low-level and obscure villain who has something he wants Cap to see. Cap immediately notes that Water Wizard "seems really nervous" (5), making Water Wizard immediately sympathetic to the audience, even though he attacked Cap without warning to start the issue. The surprise attack is something Water Wizard can justify—it is a tactic to make sure Cap is truly who he claims to be and not the Scourge in disguise. The reader would assuredly see this as a reasonable thing to do (and Cap is never in any real danger in this brief conflict though he is somewhat annoyed by the attack). Water Wizard subsequently leads Cap to The Bar with No Name and invites Cap to enter first. The reader knows what Cap is going to see, of course, because of the concluding events of issue #319, but Gruenwald still builds suspense by moving slowly and building tension.

The scene moves slowly, and the reader cautiously moves from panel to panel. Cap, prior to entering the room where the massacre has occurred, mentally notes, "it's as quiet as a church in here. And that strange smell..." (6). For Cap to acknowledge that "strange smell," which is the as-of-yet-undiscovered smell of eighteen corpses lying in a room, makes it clear to the reader that a massacre on this scale is foreign to even a hero who has had to deal with tragedies and criminals for the entirety of his adult life. All of this makes what Cap is about to see carry weight and consequence. It is easy to say that killing eighteen people at once would always have consequence, but the growing wave of "heroic violence" of the era could subvert the once-anticipated expectations.

Readers during this era were desensitized to violent acts, primarily from film, television, and news. These things clearly work themselves into the comics medium as well. In the 1985 film *Commando*, for example,

Arnold Schwarzenegger plays a special agent named John Matrix who must rescue his kidnapped daughter. In doing so, he kills 102 people during the 90-minute runtime ("Commando"). An audience can be desensitized to killings (Schwarzenegger's film catalog in the 1980s is a clear illustration of that), but Gruenwald does not allow full desensitization. Instead, after building this uncomfortable tension as Cap arrives on the scene, he shows us the scene of the massacre. Penciller Paul Neary draws the scene (which is shown in a large three-quarters portion of the page) in shadows so that the murdered characters are shown dead and shadowy green, making their presence dark and morbid (6).

As the reader looks over Cap and Water Wizard's shoulders, seeing the horrifying scene from their perspective, the reader notices the two living characters are shown in full color, further emphasizing the dark and haunting image in front of them. In fact, throughout the scene in which Water Wizard and Cap visit the massacre, the bodies are always shown in shadows. It, perhaps, tones down the potentially graphic nature of the scene, but it also emphasizes the distance between the murdered villains and Cap (and Water Wizard). Gruenwald and penciller Paul Neary do not want to make this massacre feel commonplace. This scene is purposefully off-putting and the color differences effectively reinforce the differences between the living and dead.

After realizing what has happened, Cap is shocked and sickened by the sight, saying only, "Good Lord!" in an effectively understated moment that emphasizes the true horror of the moment but resisting an overstated, rehearsed response from Cap. It is not hard to think of MCU Captain America's final words in 2018's *Avengers: Infinity War* after Thanos has successfully wiped out half of life across the universe. At that moment, Cap (played by Chris Evans) utters an understated "My God."

In issue #320, after taking in the supervillain massacre, Cap immediately pivots to protecting a terrified Water Wizard and finding Scourge. He tells Water Wizard, "After I find a safe place to hide you, I swear I'm going to track down that killer and bring him to justice!" In response, a visibly distraught Water Wizard tells Cap that he instinctively trusts his words (8). Cap's use of the word "justice" is intentional in contrast to Scourge and his "Justice is served!" battle cry. Cap and Scourge are two characters with two very different perceptions of justice. For Scourge, justice is killing. For Cap, an eventual punishment is not for him to decide. Cap is consciously inverting Scourge's perceptions of justice. Cap has, unfortunately, heard Scourge's battle cry before and he is hoping to retake ownership of "justice" away from Scourge's co-opting of the term into something violent.

Water Wizard's reception to Cap's words presents a valuable contrast between a vigilante who thinks he is doing a hero's work and an actual hero. Thanks to his reputation (and the way he handles himself amongst so much death, danger, and uncertainty), Cap's words carry enough weight to comfort the Water Wizard. Cap is the real hero in these pages, even if Scourge fancies himself in a similar role. The issue's narration, a normally objective tool for Gruenwald, further paints a self-delusional sense of Scourge—the reader is shown the Scourge's van and the narration informs us, "its owner is not a hero—save perhaps in his own mind" (8). Again, there is no point in this storyline that we should see him as a sympathetic and heroic figure. Even the objective elements (like a neutral narrator) refuse that reading of Scourge. When Scourge realizes that Captain America is pursuing him, he thinks, "Although he and I are on the same side—my methods are so much more effective than his—he opposes me!" (19). For Scourge, Cap is noble but ineffective.[20] He sees the two as pursuing the same objectives but views his "methods" as superior.

When Scourge is alerted by Domino, his well-informed contact, that Diamondback[21] of the Serpent Society is recovering from injuries at a hospital, he quickly acts upon eliminating her. Upon arriving at the hospital and seeing Cobra helping her escape (and Cobra is highly motivated by fear after Scourge's execution of their Serpent Society ally Death Adder), Scourge excitedly states (and it is with a speech bubble as opposed to a chain thought bubble to show how eager he is to express the sentiment) that he could eliminate both at once. When he fails, he rationalizes that "justice will win in the end" (13).

In his discussion of the moral lessons derived from Captain America, Mark B. White defines "justice" in Captain America's world as "making sure every person gets what he or she deserves in interactions with other people, in terms of both individuals and society as a whole" (182). "Deserves" could be interpreted in a number of ways, but for Cap, he has no interest or involvement in figuring out what a criminal "deserves." His job is not to pass sentence on criminals—his job is to stop their criminal efforts and let someone else inflict a fair punishment (and he trusts the judicial system enough to believe that will happen). These more aggressive vigilante "heroes" take the role of executor themselves. While White argues that Cap's world is one in which "every person gets what he or she deserves," Cap himself is not the one to determine that. He needs to apprehend Scourge (and other villains), not to convey punishment. If a vigilante is one who takes actions into their own hands without the support of the state then, at this point in comics (late 1980s), Cap is a vigilante. He is not an agent of S.H.I.E.L.D. (or otherwise associated with that organization) nor is he a police officer (as he was for a short while in the 1960s).[22]

Perceptions of Justice

Philosopher Noam Chomsky clarifies that there are different types of justice systems at work in any given system and, just because the state regards something as criminal or unjust, that does not necessarily mean an individual would feel the same ("Chomsky & Foucault—Justice vs. Power"). Cap sees the state as a reasonable enforcer and decider of punishment for violations of laws (again, because in his mind he can be neither a judge nor a conveyer of punishment).[23] Michel Foucault, to whom Chomsky made this remark in a 1971 debate, later states that justice is a concept created by the oppressed to articulate their struggles and "justice" would be invalidated in a classless society, points to which Chomsky disagrees. Foucault sees justice as a necessary tool to deal with hostile situations. Eliminating justice would mean eliminating oppression and Foucault sees that as a positive outcome.

Chomsky sees it as something more evolving and personal than that. Mostly, Chomsky is more *American* than that. Bruce Robbins, discussing Chomsky's views on cosmopolitanism, states that critics often find concern with Chomsky's overly American perspective on issues: "Chomsky puts the United States at the center of virtually all his judgments" (551). Captain America's perspective on justice is one tied to fairness and individual freedoms. Scourge's perspective on justice is about class—the oppressed class, in his mind, are crime victims and, for him, justice is about both equaling the field and, perhaps more significantly, earning retribution on behalf of the oppressed. Following Chomsky's thought, if an individual can determine whether an action is just or unjust, judgment is dependent upon the individual. Scourge can be completely righteous in his methods because he believes his executions of these criminals are justified. Captain America does not feel the same. A reader could sympathize with Scourge's efforts because of perceived shortcomings in the justice system, but two things make him a clear antagonist in these comics—the brutality of the killings and Cap's opposition to his methods.

Later in *Captain America* #320, Cap takes the identity of one of the criminals killed in The Bar with No Name massacre and then tricks Scourge into pursuing him. Eventually, Scourge realizes that Cap is indeed the criminal and realizes that Cap intends to apprehend him. Scourge is morally torn. Scourge thinks, "What do I do? That's Captain America, one of the biggest names in crime smashing" (20). Scourge is conflicted. He mentally assesses his options. He thinks, "but If I don't stop him, he'll stop me!" (20), and he cannot bring himself to kill Cap because, as he rationalizes, Cap does not "deserve" it (unlike the others he has shot in cold blood). Scourge is faced with a moral dilemma. Cap and Scourge fight. Cap knocks Scourge off his feet and Cap loses possession of his shield in the process. Scourge still has his gun and Cap in sight. With ease, Scourge (a known murderer) could fire his gun and end Cap's life, but he does not shoot (even Cap himself is surprised by that). Scourge, dealing with a moral dilemma, chooses not to shoot and kill Captain America, even knowing that doing so would save himself and allow him to carry on with his mission. Scourge passes on this opportunity to kill Cap because he didn't want to "be as bad as the criminal scum" he has hunted (22).[24] Clearly, there is a moral code at work and a willingness to sacrifice the mission rather than eliminate someone who is not (in Scourge's mind) a justifiable target.

After Cap has apprehended and unmasked the Scourge (and revealed him to be nobody he can recognize), the vigilante explains his backstory, identifies himself as a "hero" (22) (something Cap finds baffling), claims the "lenient" U.S. justice system forced him to act, and is then shot by someone possessing the same characteristics of the Scourge (same armor-piercing exploding bullets), and the same use of "Justice is Served!" (23).

This is, of course, not the last of the Scourge. As mentioned above, Scourge is in the line-up of villains in the Red Skull's employ in issue #394 in 1991. Later Gruenwald deals with the Scourge storyline in full once again in 1993 with a four-part miniseries called *U.S.Agent*, featuring Jack Daniels, the hero who is known previously in these pages as John Walker (Super-Patriot and the replacement Captain America). The important aspect is that the Scourge, even when depicted through speeches uttered by unmasked figures justifying their behavior, is not portrayed sympathetically (save maybe when he refuses to shoot Cap in #320), and the idea of the Scourge as "heroic" is roundly rebuffed by the heroes (first Captain America and later U.S.Agent). U.S.Agent, especially, is forced by Bloodstain and Caprice, two agents with the Scourge operation,[25] to relive his memories and face his own violent past. We gain more sympathy for U.S.Agent because of his regret for his past actions as contrasted by the remorselessness shown by those operating as Scourge. Even though each Scourge sees themselves as a hero, Gruenwald's use of the Scourge characters as a contrast to Captain America and U.S.Agent always leaves the hero (including the occasionally hard to like U.S.Agent) more sympathetic.

"You have the right to remain silent—forever!"

Scourge is not the only vigilante who fashions a hero persona (despite the narrative's clear push back against that reality). Americop, a vigilante character with a considerably less convoluted origin story than Scourge, also fulfills this persona. A relatively late addition to Gruenwald's cast of characters, Americop debuts in issue #428 (released in June 1994) and is a murderous figure who, like Scourge, can rationalize his behavior because of the criminal nature of his victims (and, unlike Scourge, has a pretense of "arresting" the criminals), but that step of the justice process is pretty quickly bypassed by Americop into direct punishment. The first appearance of Americop functions differently than most of what we see with Scourge. While the villains who are pursued by Scourge are so afraid they become sympathetic (regardless of past deeds), Gruenwald does not give Americop's victims the same treatment. The first pair of criminals pursued by Americop are very clearly made not to be sympathetic. They are depicted as swearing (shown in Joe Rosen's letters as indecipherable scribble), driving a stolen car, and transporting a person in the trunk. We get no sense we should care about their well-being. This could be an era-influenced choice, showing us a darker and grittier reality that would have been less likely in the mid–1980s. It also works to make readers feel immediately relieved that someone is going to stop them (which Americop's excessive violence then works to undermine).

When Americop approaches the car, the criminal in the passenger seat immediately shoots him in the face. Indeed, there is no nuance to the way these criminals are depicted. While this may incline us to see Americop sympathetically, that immediately turns due to his own brutality. After shooting Americop, the criminals attempt to get away. He quickly recovers and, in a robot-type internal monologue—with "officer's log" entries (4) in the form of chain thought bubbles shown to be more artificial than those generally used to convey Captain America's thoughts[26]—he assesses the situation, shoots out their car tires and, then, brutally, kills both men while their bodies dangle out of the car windows. Upon executing the two men, he shouts, "You have the right to remain silent—forever" (3), a catchphrase that lacks the simplicity of Scourge's "Justice is Served!" but certainly feels similar. It is also a catchphrase that emphasizes the victim by starting with "you." Therefore, while Scourge's phrase emphasizes the act, Americop's phrase emphasizes the fault of the victim.

Americop is also a speaker of much more reservation and restraint than most. In an issue (#428) that features 81 exclamation points overall, Americop uses only eight of those (tallying 10.1 percent of the total number of exclamation points), even though, of the speech and thought bubbles employed in the issue, Americop uses the most, tallying 26.7 percent of the speech and thought bubbles featured in the issue, which is similar, but still more, than Cap's 24.9 percent and far more than Diamondback, the character we hear the third most from in the issue, and her 12.6 percent. This is relevant because it emphasizes Americop's rational and uneasily calm persona throughout the issue, coldly working his way through the criminals he encounters. It plays up his calculating and robotic personality. He is also far less sympathetic toward "fellow heroes" than is Scourge. When Scourge faces off with Captain America in #320, he refuses to kill Cap, sacrificing his entire mission as a result of his refusal. In #428, when Americop encounters a similar challenge from Cap, Americop also hesitates and does not kill Cap even when it is possible, but his reasons are less morally driven and more duty-driven (Americop declines to shoot Cap once he hears sirens and knows "agents of the law enforcement establishment are imminent") (22). Instead of seeing Cap as being on the same side of the law (as does Scourge), Americop sees Cap as a "sad instrument of liberal dogma" (21). To Americop, Cap is not a similarly-minded peer—instead, he is a weak-willed "instrument" who is responsible for crime by not doing enough to stop it (and "liberal" in this context is tying back to the long-standing motif of liberal democrats being "soft" on crime).

Police Brutality in the 1990s

The Americop issue was published on June 10, 1994, two days before the murders of Nicole Simpson and Ron Goldman. O.J. Simpson would be accused of these murders and his defense was built upon perceived racial bias, police corruption, and general ineptitude. Race relations became a nationwide conversation as the Simpson defense team claimed racism affected the perception of certain officers investigating the case. While this particular issue of *Captain America* was released before the event that would bring extensive scrutiny to the police force (thus cannot be seen as a commentary upon it), it serves as a reminder of how much this perception of police brutality was already in the public consciousness.

While Gruenwald would not have a perspective of the current 21st-century American climate, where police shootings and beatings of African Americans feel more commonplace, these assaults are is not a new phenomenon. Martin Luther King Jr., in his 1963 "I Have a Dream Speech," specifically calls out "unspeakable horrors of police brutality," and Gruenwald would have been shaping the character of Americop in the shadow of the 1991 Rodney King beating, a police assault of an African American man that was videotaped by a bystander and subsequently became a significant national story. Those four officers were brought to trial and each was acquitted on all counts with the exception of an assault charge against one of the officers that was undecided by the jury (Serrano and Wilkinson). A day after the verdict was announced, an ABC News/Washington Post poll showed 92 percent of African Americans surveyed (and 64 percent of whites) felt the officers should have been convicted (Sigelman, et al.). Americans were skeptical of police brutality and this character is Gruenwald's attempt to articulate the validity of those concerns, though he is unwilling to put it in directly racial turns. Americop (who is white but well-concealed) is shown as an equal-opportunity aggressor, executing and beating victims portrayed as both African American and white. Gruenwald, it can be argued then, is making a statement about police brutality without emphasizing race.

In his next appearance in #429, Americop once again targets criminals with absolutely no redeeming qualities, but his brutality leaves the reader uncomfortable with the interaction, no matter how much the perpetrator deserves some sort of retribution. We see two men walking out of a video store having just rented writer/director Neil Jordan's *The Crying Game*, a 1992 film that was a key moment in LGBTQ+ representation during the decade and "showed audiences that [LGBTQ+] identities do not have to be defined by our biology but instead are merely a factor that we choose to incorporate (or not) in the self that we construct" (Kurtis). By showing two men walking out of the video store excited to see the film—one answers with an enthusiastic "*The Crying Game* of course" when the other asks what film he wants to watch first (3)—Gruenwald gives the reader a direct cue about their sexuality.

The two men are immediately approached by a group of four men who confront them and, uninvited, look through their rented films. The bullied men are too taken aback to respond. Upon looking at the films in their bag, the leader of the men who have accosted the couple says, "My, my! These vidayos are all about fancy men!" He then immediately physically attacks the men, explaining that he has to assault them because of their sexuality: "if you was [fancy men], I'd have to kick you in the pansy-pants—like so!" (3). The assault is unprovoked and brutal—one panel shows the video store couple being kicked while sprawled on the ground. The attackers' dialogue is so broken it is almost incoherent; it takes away humanity from the characters.

Americop arrives quickly on the scene and, though the attackers plead with him to stop, he knocks them all over and shoots them—"How fast do you think you'll be with artificial kneecaps?" he asks them (5) after informing them that their future "hate crime" victims will be spared. The two actual sets of criminals Americop stops in these two issues are heinous—kidnapping and hate crimes—but his brutality is still not depicted as heroic or justifiable. Gruenwald is depicting these scenarios and defying the reader to sympathize. Perhaps some readers, those sympathetic toward the Punisher's adventures, for example, would disagree, but in the pages of a comic with a protagonist as unflinchingly just as Captain America, that depiction does not resonate. Gruenwald is reacting against the trend of vigilante heroism by depicting one in a context that strips away the sexiness and desirability from the trope.

The Punisher

The Punisher does not specifically appear in Gruenwald's *Captain America*, though his influence is clear. He and Captain America do team up in *Punisher/Captain America: Blood and Glory*, a limited series from 1992 that was written, not by Gruenwald, but by D.G. Chichester and Margaret Clark. The one deliberate interaction between the characters was one that did not involve Gruenwald himself. Frank Castle AKA The Punisher, like Scourge and Americop, "sees crime as a non-nuanced aberration of civil order that needs to be brought to justice" (Allen) but, unlike the moral code that the Scourge often follows, Castle is willing to execute whoever gets in the way of his idea of justice. The Punisher's exploits have transcended comics and come to represent a significant portion of American gun culture, embodying the "only way to stop a bad guy with a gun is a good guy with a gun" motif—SEAL Team 3 has co-opted his logo as a sign of allegiance to Punisher's characterization (NerdSync). So, the Punisher is depicted as "heroic," but this type of "heroism" is very much context-based.

While he does not directly appear in Gruenwald's *Captain America*, when he is mentioned, it is typically done to emphasize a contrast with Captain America that leaves Punisher looking like an amoral antithesis to Cap (such as the above-mentioned reference to Punisher from the comic shop owner and the time that Cap goes undercover in the "Streets of Poison" storyline in issue #372 and is mistaken for Punisher).[27] Predictably, Cap is typically depicted as being "repulsed by the Punisher's *weltanschauung* and has referred to him as a 'fascist'" (Worcester). While there might exist a very general and simplistic similarity to their goals, Cap himself would never want to associate with the Punisher and his methods (though the Punisher himself insinuates, in *Civil War* #6, long after Gruenwald's run, he respects Captain America too much to fight him). Castle can look up to him in that regard, but that does not mean that Rogers would return the favor. Obviously, his warped sense of justice, even if inspired by Cap's heroics, is not something of which Cap himself would approve.

Cap has to figure out how he fits into a world that, if it is not increasingly violent, as least is more desensitized toward violence. This acceptance of violence is nothing new to Cap and it is nothing new to society at large. Vigilantism and justifiable violence are not new things, and the effects of this approval of otherwise problematic violence have been present for centuries. According to Richard Maxwell Brown in his book *Strain of Violence:*

Historical Studies of American Violence and Vigilantism, not only are these behaviors tied deeply into American consciousness, they are subsequently uniquely interwoven with America's origins:

> Going back to the colonial period and patriotic resistance to the British mother country, "the American," observed James Truslow Adams, "had developed a marked tendency to obey only such laws as they chose to obey.... Law which did not suit the people, or even certain classes, were disobeyed constantly with impunity." Perhaps in the long run, the most important result of vigilantism has been the subtle way in which it has persistently undermined our respect for law by its repeated theme that law may be arbitrarily disregarded—that there are times when we may choose to obey the law or not [132–133].

This "arbitrary disregard" stands in direct and dramatic contrast to Captain America himself, a character who rarely wavers from his moral compass, regardless of the challenge faced. Cap does not believe in inflicting "justice" himself because of his respect for laws and the judicial system. If vigilantism has indeed been working for decades to "undermine" Americans' "respect for law," Captain America represents an important counter to that—the hero that stands in opposition to the rushing torrent of acceptance for violent methods.

Ultimately, the most important point about these vigilante figures is that their presence in the pages of Gruenwald's *Captain America* (or even their mere mention) creates a different context for them than it might in a comic that features a character with a less consistent moral center. In this world, instead of a vigilante character like Scourge or Americop looking like a darker alternative to Captain America, they end up (because of the moral light Cap possesses) simply looking like villains. Crucially, Steve Rogers is also never tempted by these characters.[28] Gruenwald's Cap never, even for a moment, considers the prospect of adopting a harder edge to his persona (and the mind-altering impact of the crystal meth that affects his moral code is an aberration).

If anything, these interactions strengthen Cap's personal resolve that his personal methods are the most appropriate. This also shows Gruenwald's personal resolve to maintain the integrity of the Steve Rogers character and his unwillingness to compromise his moral code, even when the violent hero is the more popular character type of the time. Gruenwald responds to the desperate and trend-chasing comics of the 1980s and (especially) 1990s with characters and storylines that address the changing worlds of comics. Gruenwald allows Cap to be timeless in a way that transcends such trends. The vigilante trope might play in a positive way in other '80s and '90s comics, but there is not room in *Captain America* for it to succeed, not with Steve Rogers' moral inflexibility providing the beating heart of the comic.

NINE

Fire and Ice

The Presence and Consequence of Drug Abuse

The "Just Say No" era was alive and well at the onset of Gruenwald's run on *Captain America* and the simplistic approach to discussing drug use (and abuse) seen in the pages of *Captain America* reflects that era. In 1982, American First Lady Nancy Reagan took the issue of drug abuse among children as her own and championed the "Just Say No" campaign and the phrase (and its zero-tolerance policy mentality) became an inescapable part of '80s culture, both in schools and in media.[1] Any type of illegal drug use was looked at as a social faux pas and, potentially, a massive criminal offense—Los Angeles Police Chief Daryl Gates said, "casual drug users should be taken out and shot" (qtd. in Newman). These policies would lead to mass incarceration, and jail time for "nonviolent drug violations increased from 50,000 in 1980 to more than 400,000 by 1997" (Newman). That *Captain America*, as a comic, falls in line with this "Just Say No" mentality, especially early in Gruenwald's run, is not a surprise considering the comic series is such a product of its era.

However, there are moments later in his time as writer on this title where things get, perhaps not exactly nuanced, but at least more fully discussed, especially when Gruenwald gets to the "Streets of Poison" storyline in which Cap is first confronted by the potential hypocrisy of his anti-drug philosophy despite the Super Soldier Serum that granted him his physical abilities. In this storyline, he is exposed to drugs and subsequently suffers a personality change when the drugs affix to the Super Soldier Serum in his body, in turn increasing the drug's effects (this occurs beginning in issue #372). While this does not necessarily produce a conversation about drug use that feels particularly sophisticated, it does lead us to see drugs as something more than a plot contrivance that can be used to easily vilify an antagonistic character.

Earlier in the run, Cap confronts the strength-enhancing process of the Power Broker (Curtis Jackson), a character who puts many other characters (including both heroes and villains) through a strength augmentation process that changes the client's body to increase muscle mass and provide unthinkable strength. The process is highly unnatural and comes with great risks (as do the augmentation process' real-world equivalent, anabolic steroids). The ways in which Cap responds to the use of these drugs during these storylines give us a clear understanding of Gruenwald's perspective on the issue at the time, and it is hard not to feel the cultural influence of "Just Say No" even when Gruenwald is pushing somewhat back upon the philosophy.

Captain America and 1980s Recreational Drug Excess

When drugs are brought up in the issues published during Reagan's presidential term, "Just Say No" is the approach. In an adventure from early 1987, for example, Cap and Nomad tangle with a crime boss called The Slug, and this character's villainy is portrayed both through his grotesque obesity and the excesses of drugs he has available on his yacht. The references to drugs are not specific. Nomad is on the Slug's yacht because he is helping a woman named Priscilla look for her estranged brother. Nomad finds the brother and tells him about his sister's concern, but the brother, smoking a cigarette, pokes Nomad aggressively on the chest and tells him that he does not want to leave because he "belong[s]" with the Slug and his crew thanks to, in part, "good drugs" (10). We know the comic wants the reader to determine the brother is of low moral character (and we do not mourn him much when he seems to die later in the issue) because Gruenwald has established his drug use as a character trait (as well as his cigarette smoking and aggressiveness toward Nomad). Again, it is a simplistic (and highly unfair) approach to a complicated matter, but it is a comic that is intended for an audience of children and possesses a moralistic responsibility to teach right from wrong that is lacked in harder-edged comics. Captain America sees himself as a role model and, accordingly, Gruenwald treats conveying that moral responsibility as a key part of his role as creator.

Later in issue #325, after his interaction with Nomad, Priscilla's brother sneaks into Nomad's room with another of the Slug's lackeys and injects Nomad with a syringe of "horse," translated to "heroin" for the reader by the editor's notes at the bottom of the panel (13). Nomad is immediately incapacitated by the heroin and subsequently tossed into the ocean to die. Captain America, after being notified by Priscilla that Nomad might be in danger, finds him floating on the ocean's surface. Nomad tells Cap that he was "shot … full of drugs" and explains that he believes the drug to be heroin (15). Cap posits that the Super Soldier Serum in Nomad's body helps negate the drugs.[2] This is a plot device often used to explain why Cap (and, in this situation, Nomad) reacts differently to some foreign influences and, in this case, how Nomad manages to survive.

This is not a particularly accurate account of heroin use. Heroin would not just incapacitate a person and leave them prone and unable to fight back (especially a person at peak physical condition like Nomad), but the issue does not want to provide any positive connotations. Typically, a heroin user would experience a "rush" very quickly after an injection ("seven or eight" seconds after injection) and that rush can last from "45 seconds to a few minutes" though the effects can "generally last for three to five hours depending on the dose" ("Heroin"). We are told only that Slug's lackeys inject a large amount into Nomad. While there is a period of sedation that typically follows the rush, there seems to be no reason to think it would simply tranquilize a person in order to easily toss them in the water, as seems to be the thinking here. It is a simple impression of "all drugs are bad" and "all drugs do bad things." The injection of heroin has the effect upon Nomad as would an injection of a tranquilizer (which, narratively, could be a side effect of Nomad's Super Soldier Serum).

Augmentation and Steroids

In issue #328, Cap investigates the Power Broker's augmentation process, and the drugs in question go from the illicit narcotics such as heroin on Slug's yacht to performance enhancing drugs and procedures that are not specified as steroids, but certainly have similar strength increasing properties. Like illicit narcotics, performance-enhancing steroids were also topical in the mid-to-late 1980s. In 1985, *Sports Illustrated* published William Oscar Johnson's in-depth account of the steroid problem in sports, including an interview with NFL player Steve Courson who claimed that "75 percent of the linemen in the NFL are on steroids and 95% have probably tried them" and, in the late '80s, baseball players such as Mark McGwire and Jose Canseco were generating whispers that steroids were being more used in baseball (and those whispers would turn to shouts by the next decade and beyond).

The public did not become concerned with the issue of performance-enhancing drugs in sports until it became clear in retrospect that steroids were being used when McGwire and Sammy Sosa battled over the single-season home run record in 1998 (Bishop). Testimonies like Courson's, the aforementioned NFL player, never faced the same public scrutiny. While not credibly viewed in the same way as the NFL or MLB, the World Wrestling Federation (now World Wrestling Entertainment) was facing definite scrutiny for steroid suspicions during this era, culminating in a 1993 trial over steroid distribution. At the center of the trial was George Zahorian III, a urologist from Harrisburg, Pennsylvania, who was charged for distributing steroids to wrestlers. Vince McMahon, the owner of the WWF, was especially scrutinized for his willingness to allow rampant steroid use to occur. Zahorian would be convicted. McMahon would later face trial in 1994 on charges of steroid trafficking and be acquitted ("A Promoter of Wrestling is Acquitted"). The comic in which Cap investigates the Power Broker occurs years earlier (in 1987), but the suspicions of steroid use in professional wrestling were already a clear black eye. In an article from *Sports Illustrated* from the time of the Zahorian trial, wrestling journalists Dave Meltzer and Richard Demak write,

> The more muscular wrestlers, like [Hulk} Hogan, Lex Luger and The Ultimate Warrior, are promoted, while less muscular types, like Ric Flair and Bobby Eaton, are being phased out. The WWF and WCW haven't just turned a blind eye to the use of steroids. By making stars of certain wrestlers, the promoters have actually encouraged the use of steroids. "McMahon has made a lot of guys very rich," says Terry Funk, a former pro wrestling champion, "but he may also be taking years off their lives" [9].

While McMahon was not convicted of distributing steroids, it is obvious from Funk's comments that wrestlers themselves knew who was going to be placed higher on the card based on particular body types and, therefore, the steroid use was quietly encouraged.

Courson further explains that "steroids are a different realm of drug from speed or painkillers. They enhance your natural ability. They are a building block." This is not particularly different than the description given of the Power Broker's augmentation progress. In *The Thing* #35, written by Mark Carlin (and edited by Gruenwald), Sharon Ventura[3] seeks out the Power Broker/Curtis Jackson in order to undertake the augmentation process (with the understanding that she will use her augmented body and strength to compete in the Unlimited Class Wrestling Federation). When Ventura approaches Jackson (while he is covered in darkness and she is blinded by lights to conceal his identity), he explains the process:

> First, our trained staff will treat you with a small dosage of radiation … which will raise your body's natural abilities to their highest levels. Then you must receive an injection of certain stabilizing enzymes which will help your body combat possible side effects of the treatment! Lastly, you will be submitted to a

second treatment to bring your strength up to the level needed to compete in the Unlimited Class Wrestling Federation [8].

In this storyline, the wrestlers in the UCWF (a wrestling league that the Thing[4] joins) are depicted, not directly as steroid-enhanced beasts, but strength-augmented beasts. In this world, the augmentation process is in clear parallel to steroid use. Here are comments from an interview with Larry Pfohl, better known as professional wrestler Lex Luger (mentioned above by Meltzer as an example of an overly muscular wrestler more likely to be promoted to the top of a wrestling organization), talking about his days as a football player (thus prior to his pro wrestling days):

> So I had to gain weight quick—the unethical, cheating shortcut. Guy in the gym said, "Buddy, these little blue pills are called Dianabol." And I took four a day, five milligrams apiece. You get on these steroids and you train better, eat more. And you retain water from them. So I gained 15 pounds in about two months. I jumped on it and it worked.
>
> And it is the same old thing: Once you do something one time, it leads to another. And then I started in the offseason, where I would do one cycle for 12 weeks. A friend of mine was an exercise physiologist. She monitored my blood [levels]. I never took it in-season. I'd just take it in the offseason to build as much strength as I could [qtd. in Fish].

The parallels are clear. The goal seems reasonable—performing at an elite level in a professional sport. The methods are, to a degree, controlled. Luger has a physiologist checking blood levels; Power Broker enlists the help of "trained professionals." The scientific explanations behind both add credibility to the situation, making the user comfortable in thinking things are controlled and safe (though Luger's comment about "unethical cheating" provides his hindsight perspective).

But these processes are very much unsafe in both cases. In *The Thing* #35 and *Captain America* #329–330, the protagonists face off against the failed augments. The creatures are no longer human and are instead freakishly strong and disfigured, striking ahead with nothing more than instinct. When Ventura sees them in *Thing* #35, she immediately connects them to the procedure she undergoes earlier in the issue, fearing that these horrific transformations could befall her or "maybe it still could!" (15). She and Cap (in separate adventures) witness the horrors directly. In *The Thing* #35, we also see Dennis Dunphy (Cap's future partner D–Man) struggle with withdrawals as he tries to give up the drugs that he has been using following his augmentation process.

With Power Broker's procedure, the side effects include permanent dependencies and potential disfigurement into a mindless monster-state. With anabolic steroids, the effects are not as comic book-appropriate as potentially becoming a sewer-dwelling monster but, according to "Androgenic Steroids," side effects can include cancerous liver and kidney tumors (thus increasing chances of death) as well as negative physical transformative conditions such as jaundice and severe acne. Gruenwald is creating a comparable type of performance-enhancing process in order to accentuate the problems inherent within the real-world process. Considering the troubled state of the wrestling industry's relationship with steroids, the fact that the majority of those enhanced by Power Broker's process are brought into professional wrestling is deliberate, not only illustrating the dangers of steroids but also pointing out the business type most likely to see performers succumb to the side effects and dangers.

As a reference point, Wrestlemania III, the WWF's (now WWE) premiere wrestling event of 1987 (the year *Captain America* #328–330 were published), featured 38 wrestlers in in-ring competition ("Full Wrestlemania III Results"). As of mid–2020, 15 of those competitors are dead (39 percent) and those 15 men died at an average age of 56.7. According to a report from the National Center for Health Statistics, the average age of an American male at death in 2017 was 76.1 years (Tinker). Only one of these 15 wrestlers reached the age of 76 (Harley Race, who died at 76 in 2019). For further comparison, using information compiled on *Baseball Reference*, 48 players competed in the 1987 World Series. Of those, four are dead as of mid–2020 (8 percent of the baseball players who participated in the World Series vs. 39 percent of competitors at Wrestlemania III). Carlin and Gruenwald were clearly predictive to equate the dangerous augmentation process with the dangerous world of professional wrestling, and the knowledge of the mortality rates for professional wrestlers adds insight as to the dangers illustrated in these issues.

Cap has the opportunity to complete the full augmentation procedure but turns it down, not because of conflict over using illegal substances, but because of his own personal confidence in himself, his awareness in his body, and his constant pursuit of challenges; he states in #328, "Great strength alone is no guarantee the fights will get any easier. In fact, it could throw off my fighting technique … cause certain other battle-skills to become weaker…. I guess I enjoy the challenge of beating the odds against me too much to change my approach this late in the game" (22). He already sees himself as an ideal physical specimen and, considering how well he knows the potential and limitations of his own body, Rogers can reason that any enhancement would perhaps require him to relearn things he already knows about physical combat. He does wonder though, asking himself, just two panels after explaining why he is choosing against the process, "Have I just made a bad decision?" (22), thus emphasizing his self-doubt.

The Super Soldier Serum

It is impossible to engage in the overall discussion of physical augmentation in a comic featuring Captain America without thinking about how Steve Rogers became Captain America. In 1941's *Captain America Comics* #1 by Joe Simon and Jack Kirby, the scrawny Steve Rogers is part of a top-secret American government experiment and "allows himself to be inoculated with [a] strange seething liquid" (6). This injection then immediately causes him to transform into a perfect physical specimen. Professor Reinstein (later known as Dr. Erskine), the doctor who injects the serum, explains, "the serum coursing through his blood is rapidly building his body and brain tissues, until his stature and intelligence increase to an amazing degree" (7). In this original telling, it is not simply a drug that allows him to reach physical perfection; it also provides mental perfection (an aspect discarded in Gruenwald and other contemporary storytelling, writers instead crediting Rogers with his own mental and intellectual capabilities).[5]

In later retellings (including 2010's film *Captain America: The First Avenger*), the Super Soldier serum is augmented by "Vita-Rays." In the film, Steve Rogers (played by Chris Evans) is first injected with a series of "micro-injections" that will create "immediate cellular change." Obviously, this is not dissimilar to the single injection process from the comic in 1941, but to counter the sports-related stigma of a player illegally injecting substances to improve performance, the film showcases a series of "micro-injections" to make the process seem more fantastical and less like a simple example of single syringe injection. Dr. Erskine (played by Stanley Tucci) then explains Rogers will be "saturated with Vita-rays" to "stimulate growth." This is another effort to make the process feel less like a simple steroid injection.

Importantly, the film also gives agency to Steve Rogers himself—the process in the film is portrayed as being very harrowing and difficult. The scientists conducting the process consider shutting it down to protect Rogers, but he himself (from inside the metal cocoon-like device in which he is undergoing the process) calls out to Erskine and the others in the room, saying that he can indeed endure the process. That gives Rogers agency in the transformation (as opposed to passively receiving an injection and subsequently physically changing as is depicted in the 1941 comic). Regardless of the methods depicted in various comics and media, however, the reality is that Steve Rogers becomes Captain America as a result of a science experiment gone right—he was given a substance (and/or undergoes a process) that gives him extraordinary power in entirely the expected way.[6] Considering the rampant use of steroids in various professional sports, it is not unfair to say that the Captain America transformation process was one made possible by "performance-enhancing drugs."

Humanizing Drug Abuse

One place where this conversation about Cap's artificial augmentation does not happen, however, is in *Captain America*, at least not prior to the "Streets of Poison" storyline that runs from *Captain America* #372–378. The multipart series begins in issue #372 with another simplistic depiction of drugs and street-level violence. Cap is patrolling the city in his sky cycle when he sees Boomslang, a member of the Serpent Society, on top of a building. Cap tries to get his attention to find out what he is up to and Boomslang runs away, ultimately running toward a street gang that immediately shoots him repeatedly (2–4). Cap, angered by what he identifies as "senseless violence" (5), attacks the street youth in order to apprehend them. He, of course, subdues the gang easily and, after the police have taken them in and he walks back to his sky cycle, he ruminates on the list of crimes perpetrated by the gang: "attempted murder, unlawful weapons, controlled substances…" (7). "Controlled substances" is last in that list for a reason.

As in issue #325, when Nomad is questioning Priscilla's brother about working for the Slug and the brother lists the aspects he enjoys about being in the Slug's employ, the last thing in Cap's mental list of the crimes committed is drug-related. In both cases, the drug reference comes at the end of a list and after an implied pause. It is a place to emphasize the drug reference—to make it linger in the air a bit and make the audience think about the significance. For Captain America, drugs are the crime (or indulgence, depending on the situation) with the most significant long-term consequence, and Gruenwald makes sure to emphasize it as such. This is especially clear narratively in the situation with the gang members because the storyline that follows deals heavily with drug addiction.

Cap, now forced to deal with the drug-riddled criminal youth of his city, thinks, "Welcome to the future," sardonically as he flies into the night (7) and heads back to Avengers headquarters. Cap, a character typically optimistic about young people, is showing rare cynicism thanks to what he sees as a drug infestation. When he arrives back at headquarters, he is told to check on Fabian Stankowicz, a one-time minor Avengers foe who Cap employs as an Avengers in-house inventor, because of Stankowicz's recent strange behavior. When Cap arrives in Stankowicz's workspace, he finds it more chaotic than usual and, when he approaches Stankowicz, Cap finds him in a nervous and jumpy state. Cap points out that he looks thin (Cap estimates Stankowicz has lost thirty pounds in a matter of weeks) and Stankowicz deflects the question and begins acting in defensive and paranoid ways.

Stankowicz shouts, "The Masters of Evil planted a bio-bug in my ear—now they can hear everything I'm thinking! They broadcast my thoughts to everyone! Now everyone knows! Can't you hear my thoughts, Cap? Can you?" (8). Cap immediately tries to comfort him by assuring him that, while what he says might be true, it likely is not. Stankowicz suddenly shouts at Cap, accusing him of being an imposter "sent by the Masters of Evil to ruin [his] work" (9). Cap asks Stankowicz if he's "on something" (and Cap does so delicately, pausing after he says his name, establishing a likely warm and comforting tone considering the situation). Stankowicz denies it initially but eventually admits that he's on "ice." Stankowicz explains that it's "like crack ... but it lasts a lot longer," and he started taking the drugs to build up his self-confidence to work with Cap and the Avengers (9). He describes how it allows him to work longer, faster, and ultimately feel more confident.

It is notable that, in this issue, which was published in 1990, Gruenwald is willing to explain why someone might take an illegal drug (unlike the quick dismissal of the drug users on Slug's yacht), thus humanizing the user. Stankowicz is a character the reader has known and liked, so this familiarity further cements the humanization process. After confessing, Stankowicz is terrified of being forced to leave the Avengers, and Cap tells him he feels forced to suspend Stankowicz until he completes a treatment program. Cap does not fire him outright but tells Stankowicz that, since "the Avengers are role models to the nation, we simply cannot tolerate unhealthy, illegal abuse to go on among us" (10). This is a very mid-eighties, "Just Say No" response—Cap cannot fathom the idea of an Avengers staff member's drug usage, but he supports that user enough personally that he is unwilling to completely cast them aside.[7]

"That's ... uh, different"

As mentioned earlier, this issue is not from the Reagan era. It is from 1990 and, while "Just Say No" has not faded from public consciousness at this point, Gruenwald's willingness to confront drug use has evolved; he is willing to approach things more directly. After the situation has defused and Cap and Stankowicz are walking away (with Cap's arm comfortingly on Stankowicz's shoulders), Stankowicz asks hesitantly if the Super Soldier Serum is not also a drug. Cap, so verbose in his dialogue moments earlier when confronting Stankowicz about his drug use, is suddenly at a loss for words: "That's … uh, different" (10). Then, implying Cap can say nothing else, Gruenwald ends the scene.

In a scene later in the issue, after Cap has left Stankowicz's company, he reflects on how Stankowicz's question is something he's never "really thought about before" and then further reflects about what the substance is and what it did for him, conceding that the Serum is a drug "in the technical sense" (12). He starts to ponder if the serum is a "forerunner" of anabolic steroids and other performance-enhancing drugs, but then reassures himself that the serum is indeed different because it "hasn't shown any harmful side effects," as opposed to other types of steroids and drugs. It is a fascinating oversight in the history of *Captain America* that this had not been considered a potential dilemma before this moment, either for Cap as a character or, one would assume, for any of Cap's writers.[8] For Gruenwald, this is especially noteworthy because the Power Broker strength augmentation storyline mentioned above would have been an ideal opportunity to explore this question several years prior, but it never crosses Cap's mind (and Gruenwald is generous throughout this run with providing Cap's internal thoughts, so the reader would have known).

So why did Gruenwald wait five years into his time as writer to provide this story? Editor Ralph Macchio's response to a reader letter in issue #378 gives us insight. It is based on a reader suggestion from Faiz Rehman, who suggests that he would "like to see a story where Cap is accused by a junkie of being the same as him" (23). Macchio responds to the letter by stating that they did indeed take the suggestion seriously. Gruenwald has opportunities to incorporate the "Cap as Drug User" motif, but until a reader makes the suggestion, it is not pursued. Perhaps Cap's inherent righteousness makes such an observation impossible to see when a creator is so deeply in Cap's head (as would be the case with Gruenwald).

In addition, such as storyline would be complicated for a character as morally unambiguous as Cap. A story dealing with this would have to delicately function to make sure the reader's perceptions of Cap are not altered in a negative way. When the moment of Cap being forced to face this possibility of his own dependencies arrives, Cap is blindsided by the insinuation from Stankowicz though, honestly, Stankowicz makes a fair point that Cap perhaps should have considered prior to this moment. Perhaps the way that Cap is blindsided reflects the fact that the storyline has to come out of a reader suggestion—both Cap and Gruenwald were too deep in the expectations of what Cap should be to see the reality of his origins.

Captain America Delves Into Drug Culture

Cap, following his quick dismissal of the suggestion that he does, in fact, owe his abilities to performance-enhancing drugs, turns his attention to internet research and studies up on drugs, specifically "ice." One panel (with art by Ron Lim) depicts an over-the-shoulder view of Cap looking at a computer screen reading the basic definition and characteristics of "ice" (12). With Cap himself covered in shadows, the reader's eye is drawn toward the screen and its informative text. This storyline about drugs begins by teaching the reader about the dangers of drug use, sure, but Gruenwald does not do this in as quite the simplistic fashion as in the Slug storyline discussed above. Instead, it is adding the layer of Cap himself learning about these dangers along with the reader. By confronting Cap with this particular limitation (lack of illegal drug knowledge), it changes Cap's perceptions of the world. We find there are things about which Cap is not confident.

It is important to note that Cap's lack of knowledge of the drug is not the reader's only opportunity to learn about the drug in the storyline. Several issues later in #377, Red Skull (who is behind the overall operation)[9] reconnects with his associate Crossbones and takes him to an illicit drug warehouse (that appears from the outside to be an ice cream factory) and explains the manufacturing operation. He tells Crossbones that the best thing about manufacturing crystal methamphetamines is that "none of the chemicals that make [it] up are in themselves illegal," and he, therefore, does not have to deal with the illegal substances that make up other drugs (14). This is notable because it is an example of Gruenwald giving us background into the drug itself but, while Cap is learning about it from a technical perspective and giving the reader information based on scientific research, Red Skull is giving us information that is ultimately practical and gives us a further understanding of the criminal mindset. The story is not just about a dramatic narrative revolving around certain types of illegal drugs—Gruenwald also approaches it as a teaching opportunity about what these substances are and where they come from.

Typically, Cap is not a character who changes easily or recognizes his own limitations because, frankly, he does not have many limitations. In this case, he both recognizes something he could improve (his understanding of the drug problem in the United States) and then does something about it. Cap, illuminated by the glow of the computer screen (and thus illuminated literally by previously unknown information), realizes he has to do more to address "the nation's number one problem" and he then decides that he will start to rectify that "right now," (12). When he resolves to address the problem, we only see Cap's left eye in the panel, and that eye is narrowed and focused. Lim's artwork in this specific image of Cap allows the reader to understand Cap's purpose and determination. The eye shows the narrow focus Cap truly possesses on this topic of drug abuse (especially since he witnesses its consequences directly). This depiction leaves the reader firmly convinced that Cap is going to do something about this problem, though that reader might be unsure of how one man in a red, white, and blue flag uniform can solve a problem that affects millions of Americans as does substance use disorder.

Cap is shown throughout his many incarnations as someone who, above all else, knows how to strategize himself through a battle, and he therefore wastes little time making his initial move. He finds Stankowicz, who assumes that Cap is ready to send him to rehab. Stankowicz, it should be noted, seems very much his old self after Cap has talked to him about his addictions earlier in the issue. The storyline reflects a simplistic view of drug abuse and recovery. Stankowicz is going through a drug-related mental breakdown until Cap knows what is happening and subsequently talks to him. At that point, Stankowicz immediately reverts to normal (though we may assume this is only temporary, the comic does not explicitly state that fact). Based on how Stankowicz reacts to Cap's intervention, perhaps readers should feel comfortable with Cap's ability to handle the nationwide crisis—his mere presence makes things better.

Cap on "Ice"

Cap can only improve the situation if he himself is at his full capacity, and Gruenwald introduces the narrative tactic of removing the constant that is Captain America's mental stability. Cap asks Stankowicz the identity of his dealer and, after assuring Stankowicz that he is not interested in simply busting the dealer but instead thwarting the entire operation, Stankowicz provides that information. Cap then goes undercover as a hairy homeless man who flashes a lot of cash in front of the dealer in order to get the dealer to reveal his supplier. The story then immediately cuts to Cap and the dealer meeting the supplier and Cap, who the dealer and supplier think is the Punisher, forces the supplier to show him where the drugs are manufactured (15). Cap's plan moves the story very quickly through the various stages of the drug process.

While progressive minds in the era suggested that decriminalizing drugs would establish a pathway toward alleviating the problem, Cap takes a much more Reagan-centric position—punish the criminals and take out their supplies, regardless of the inevitability of those supplies resurfacing. Solutions in the middle ground of these philosophies existed too, including the "Ultimate Drug Solution" program Gordon Browne wrote about in 1996 (several years after this particular adventure, but certainly soon enough after the publication of the comic that Cap could have researched and discovered a similar situation had Gruenwald envisioned such a storyline). This particular solution would propose that "the United States government would purchase illegal drugs and give them free of charge to registered addicts in the controlled and closely regulated environment of a drug distribution center" (46). If the options are to either provide decriminalized, government ownership of drugs to allow safer and regulated distribution or to ambush the suppliers and destroy the manufacturing process, it is obvious that Captain America in 1990, still influenced by the Reagan era anti-drug movement, is not going to take a nuanced approach to the problem. He is going to ambush the suppliers. For one, a "Just Say No" education cannot allow for any possibility of addiction and illness being the problem over the drugs themselves.

It is not like the first half of the 20th century, and World War II specifically, did not have drug abuse problems, but Cap himself was likely sheltered and focused on the battlefield during the war.[10] It could be speculated that Cap himself (based on his clear moral code, something established to be well in place prior to his transformation into Captain America) would have had minimal to no exposure in his youth. While drugs, especially amphetamines, were used widely by American soldiers during World War II (Tackett), Cap would not have been working with the typical American soldier on the ground. While amphetamines were provided by the government, it is likely that, considering how pivotal Captain America is as both a practical and symbolic figure during World War II, the military and government may have gone out of their way to "protect" him from outside influences. After he is thawed out of his accidental suspended animation,[11] Cap enters modern society. Illicit drugs were likely something found outside of the Avengers community (and Tony Stark's alcoholism is simply dismissed as a problem unique to Stark and is a personal shortcoming).

When Cap arrives at the warehouse in #372, he embodies a desire to stop a massive and complicated issue in as quick and hands-on a manner as is possible. He meets a man who calls himself "Napalm," and Napalm immediately blows up the warehouse with him and Cap still inside (18). As the next issue in the series begins (#373), John Jameson, Cap's driver and pilot at the time, witnesses the explosion and is unsure of Cap's fate. He immediately calls the Avengers for help, and Peggy Carter, in charge of communications for the Avengers, notifies both Black Widow and Diamondback (Cap's love interest at the time) of the event. Outside the scene of the explosion, Jameson and Diamondback fear the worse. They embrace, preparing themselves for mourning.

Cap's Drug-Induced Personality Shift

Suddenly, Captain America arrives, unscathed. In the panel in which he returns, Ron Lim draws him with a yellow star-like background emerging from behind to emphasize the energy Cap brings, but even in this first panel, there seems to be something off. Cap's expression in this panel is off, ever so subtly—instead of a warm smile upon seeing his friends, Cap is frowning. Diamondback immediately embraces him across his chest and Cap's facial reaction remains dour (in obvious contrast to Diamondback's and Jameson's wide smiles). At this point, Diamondback and Jameson (and the reader) likely do not suspect anything different in his behavior—they are so happy to see him alive that the frowning has likely not been noticed.

Gruenwald then makes things more obvious by writing Cap to kiss Diamondback in a passionate and wholly unexpected way. Cap's romantic relationship with Diamondback has, to this point, been portrayed as mostly chaste (save, perhaps, a goodnight kiss in issue #371). Diamondback spends a great deal of time pining over Cap, while Cap himself internally acknowledges that he is more interested in her than he should be[12] but doing little to share his feelings or act upon them. As Cap returns from the explosion, those reservations are dismissed. Diamondback herself is at a loss, asking herself, "Did he just do what I thought he did?" Jameson is shown scratching his head in befuddlement and asking Cap if he feels all right. Cap responds, "never felt better" (5). Cap is never a character who needs a confidence boost, but this exchange shows us that when he does receive a confidence boost, his arrogance, something always present but sincere and somehow charming, becomes less charming. His confidence also manifests itself in a way that, at least in this exchange, it never does elsewhere—sexually.

Cap explains he escaped the warehouse by jumping out of the window and making it to the street. When Jameson asks why Napalm would blow himself up, Cap dismisses the question by simply saying, "it takes all kinds" (6). In Lim's drawing, as Cap says this, his face is covered partially in shadows, his eyes darkened completely, and his smile (thanks to his darkened eyes) drawn as being somewhat sinister. In all other situations, Cap is methodical and detail-oriented (and most issues contain a plethora of his thought bubbles, something less present here). Gruenwald makes sure all of those traits are undone in this storyline after this point. Cap refuses a suggestion for paramedic assistance, insisting that he has "never felt better."

After returning to the Avengers compound for a shower, Cap immediately orders his team to "move out" and investigate the people behind the warehouse explosion. When Jameson questions the wisdom of moving forward without a plan, Cap dismisses him and says they will think of something eventually (10). Jameson and Diamondback know that this lack of thorough preparedness is an indication that something is up. Diamondback theorizes in #374 that Cap has been exposed to the same drugs as Stankowicz (and the drugs in Cap's system have bonded with the Super Soldier Serum to become something more powerful and unique), but in #373 (and later, even after Diamondback's theory is introduced), the reader can only observe Cap's erratic behavior and note how certain traits (like confidence and frenetic bursts of energy) described prior by Stankowicz are manifesting themselves and, after so many issues of portraying a specific personality for Captain America, how striking it is to see Cap's changed behavior. It gives the reader a stronger sense of the stability of Cap's typical behavior by pulling that stability away so abruptly.

Later that evening (in #373), Cap and Diamondback investigate the scene of the explosion by watching from a nearby rooftop to see if any activity transpires. Diamondback questions the wisdom of such a tactic and Cap, without explaining his methods, tells her to leave if she is bored (12). He is not particularly rude as he says this, but it is not the tenor the reader expects from him. He is just, again, enough outside of his character for a reader to mentally recognize it without feeling like Gruenwald is making Cap so different that the mystery of what has happened to him fades away. Cap is typically rigid in his beliefs, values, and personality depictions. For Cap to undergo a personality transformation is not common in the comics.

While comic characters are temporarily "turned to evil" by external forces with some regularity, Gruenwald (and other writers during this period) avoids this with Cap. To note, this is not counting storylines in which a character is acting within the purview of their character but doing things that are perceived as villainy by others (so as simply illegal but, in the hero's mind, justified), such as Iron Man's actions in the "Armor War" storyline where he works ruthlessly to stop people who have stolen his tech. Instead, this is referring to a personality shift within a character brought on by nefarious outside influence.[13] When Gruenwald does write deeper personality changes into Steve Rogers as a character, it is something we can look at as a significant development. Transforming Steve Rogers' personality into something more sinister is not done lightly; clearly, the changes that occur in "Streets of Poison" are of major import.

Diamondback is certainly aware of these changes and is concerned about them, thinking about how his erratic behavior has been potentially caused by the explosion. Her thoughts escalate from thinking, "I think that explosion shook you up a lot more than you let on" on page 12 of issue #373 to thinking, "What the %#$& is wrong with him!?!" on page 14 after he leaps off the sky cycle they were on together and that he was piloting. He leaves her to pilot it by herself (without any training on the vehicle). In issue #374,

Cap yells at Peggy Carter about calling in Black Widow to check in on him, leaving Peggy to ask, "What's wrong with him? He's never spoken to me like that before!" (11). As the story progresses, the changes to Cap's personality become more obvious, and his friends and allies acknowledge those changes.

The long-term effects of "ice"/crystal meth as described by the National Institute on Drug Abuse include a number of consequences that clearly are observed in Stankowicz's behavior, including extreme weight loss, anxiety, paranoia, hallucinations, and sleeping problems. The shorter-term effects, as detailed in the Alcohol and Drug Foundation, displayed in Cap's behavior include: "feelings of pleasure and confidence, increased alertness and energy, [and] ... increased sex drive" ("Ice"). In issue #374, Diamondback theorizes Cap's condition, listing his newly developed traits ("manic energy ... compulsive behavior ... heightened libido ... and uncharacteristic paranoia"), and she posits that it "adds up to one thing: Cap's on drugs" (17). Jameson finds it initially unlikely because of Cap's behavior history but Diamondback further theorizes that the explosion exposed him to the drugs and they subsequently bonded with the Super Soldier Serum to create a major dramatic effect (which is exactly what has happened). When his body is inspected by Dr. Kincaid, an Avengers doctor, in issue #377, the doctor notes that the behavior could have been caused by the fact Cap was awake "for at least four days straight" (8), thus showing us other traits that link his behavior to drug use.

Cap also displays a short temper and extreme levels of irritation. His actions are aggressive, both to his friends and the drug distributors. Thanks to his exposure to the drugs, Cap is violent in his attempts to stop the drug problem. He refuses help in his crusade against the drug problem and instead functions independently, acting violently and shouting aggressive quips. In #374, he pulls a drug buyer out of his limousine and tells him, "Every time you buy drugs you are financing murder" (16). After he threatens and yells at the man, he leaves him behind thinking, "I think he got the message," a smug smile covering his face. Cap does nothing to turn these criminals over to the authorities and instead intimidates them with violence and antagonistic words.

In issue #375, he is violent, both to enemies (the street-level drug criminals) and allies (he is quick to turn aggressive against Daredevil) and is uncharacteristically arrogant and threatening with Kingpin—Cap sits uninvited at Kingpin's restaurant table and deliberately eats the food in front of him. In issue #377, after being subdued by Black Widow, Cap is strapped to a medical table as medical professionals (and scientific geniuses like Hank Pym) figure out what to do. At one point, Cap begins to suffer from hallucinations that force him to mentally confront his own drug dependency. The dependency in question is not about his recent battle with "ice," however, but something that has been in his system for much longer.

Cap's Internal Battle with Drugs

In #377's "dream sequence,"[14] Cap moves from the modern muscular Captain America prone on a table to the skinny pre–Captain America Steve Rogers, also upon a doctor's table (but the reader, knowing Cap's history, knows we have delved deep into Cap's past). As the skinny Rogers lies on the table, in the forefront (in shadow), Ron Lim draws a most ominous hypodermic needle. In the caption above the image, we get a monologue from Cap stating, "I never noticed before how much it looks like a junkie's needle" (11). The connection between the modified memory and the main drug storyline is made explicit here. Then young Steve Rogers looks up at Professor Erskine, about to administer the serum, and asks, cautiously, "your serum is a drug … isn't it?" and Erskine, bathed in red, and looking down at Rogers, is depicted as nearly demonic (11).

In the next panel, Erskine looks even more demonic and terrifying, losing his original facial features and slowly merging into features that mimic those of the Red Skull. This Red Skull/Erskine amalgam screams at Rogers, "You owe your very life as Captain America to a drug!" Rogers shouts back that Captain America is something he has created from within, not from a syringe. Rogers argues, "The drug may have made me strong, but it did not make me brave! It may have made me agile, but it did not give me skills! … Those things make up Captain America—not your drug!" (11). Is Rogers' argument valid? He concedes that, yes, the drug did give him abilities he would not have otherwise possessed, but his values and dedication make Captain America what he is.

Is it possible that an athlete on performance-enhancing steroids could argue the same? A person with no ability or understanding of baseball could not take anabolic steroids and expect to break a Major League Baseball home run record. Therefore, baseball player (and admitted steroid user) Mark McGwire could reasonably say that the drug helped him but did not teach him how to hit a baseball. In fact, in a 2010 interview with Bob Costas, McGwire concedes that he took performance-enhancing drugs, but the ability to hit home runs was already within him: "the only reason I took steroids was for health purposes" ("McGwire Apologizes to LaRussa and Selig").

Is McGwire's rationalization so much different than Cap's? Erskine fully morphs into the Red Skull and mocks Cap over his dependency upon the serum, telling him, "You are nothing without the drug!" (12).

Cap argues that others have undergone the procedure and taken the Serum, but only he has become a true hero. "Why?" he asks, "Because none of them have had my ideals! None of them have had my drive and determination! ... I'm a man who believes in something! I believe in freedom!" (12–13). Gruenwald is attempting to get the reader to see that the person within the suit is what matters most and, from a strictly narrative perspective, that is successful (especially paired with Cap's subsequent decision to remove the Serum completely in order to remove the drug), but it also pinpoints how complicated the larger issues of substance abuse truly are.

Gruenwald deserves credit for taking on a complicated and vast problem, but the inconsistencies of Cap's rationalizations show us that our changing knowledge of substance abuse (including what has evolved since Gruenwald's time) make some previous storyline motifs (including the injection of the Super Soldier Serum) feel out of touch. Cap is dedicated to not being reliant upon the Super Soldier Serum, if even just for his own mental sake, and resolves to test his body's abilities and endurance once the Serum is removed. After Hank Pym and the doctors give Cap a total blood transfusion, they remove the Serum from his blood stream. Cap is at peace with this, though clearly concerned that it means the end of Captain America. As he, against doctor's orders, suits up to battle crime, he explains to Peggy Carter, "I've got to find out if what really counts is the drug ... or the man" (17). Needless to say, the story resolves to show us that, indeed, in this case, it is "the man" that truly counts.

Red Skull vs. Kingpin

While Cap resolves his personal crises, his future crises are anticipated within the storyline. It is revealed that the saturation of ice into the New York market is happening because of efforts by the Red Skull (who, after issue #350 where the Red Skull returns, is often the revealed as the secret leader behind machinations against Cap). He and Kingpin (and their respective subservient henchman) subsequently do battle over who has the ability to sell drugs on what turf. At the onset of issue #377, Bullseye (in the employ of Kingpin) breaks into a hotel where the Red Skull and his allies are meeting and immediately shoots him in the head. It is quickly revealed that this Red Skull is not the flesh and blood version, but a robot decoy equipped with Skull's consciousness. Bullseye is convinced he has killed the Red Skull, but when he reports to Kingpin, Kingpin himself fails to share his enthusiasm. Kingpin's associate Typhoid Mary reminds him of how ideal the Red Skull's death would be because his footing in the drug scene would be easily taken, but she quickly realizes that Kingpin has no doubts that Red Skull is not dead: "Not on your life," Kingpin says (and repeats for emphasis) (10). There is no one more capable of understanding the resourcefulness of a supervillain to maintain survival than another supervillain.

The very much alive Red Skull then asks Crossbones to set up a meeting with Kingpin to discuss the turf war that has developed between the two criminal masterminds. That meeting happens at Yankee Stadium and, while the World War II/Nazi aspects of this confrontation are discussed in Chapter Five, the important points for the purposes of this conversation are the way the two villains discuss drugs and drug distribution. Red Skull offers a working business arrangement in issue #378. Red Skull presents his argument to Kingpin: "You are motivated by profit and power. I am motivated by ideology and power. Is it possible we can work together?" (3). Kingpin, citing Red Skull's Nazi ideology, refuses. Red Skull then offers Kingpin the opportunity to "buy out" his ice operation and Kingpin mocks him, reminding him that moments earlier he implied he was not motivated by profit. Skull explains his drug operation exists primarily to maintain his ideological objectives. He is in the drug business because drugs allow him to accelerate his plan to make America a "morally bankrupt country" by increasing the number of addicts in the country. Subsequently, this will cause the country to "crumble from corruption and violent crime." He further states that his business "is the destruction of American society" and asks Kingpin to admit that he is in the same business. Kingpin disagrees and sees drugs as something that will prey upon only the weakest Americans, thus eliminating those weakest portions of the populace and therefore strengthen the country overall (4). After the simplistic discussions of "solving" the drug problem earlier in this series (and, in the pages of an action-oriented superhero title, that mostly involves violence and intimidation), Gruenwald introduces a compelling different perspective—that of the criminals (who happen to be supervillains) who have ideologically driven different perspectives on drug abuse, with Kingpin rationalizing that rampant illegal drug use is, in fact, a benefit to society as a whole.

Drug Influence Past, Present, and Future

While this is not part of the comics history, but something limited to actual world history, the villains Captain America was originally created to fight, the Nazis, were motivated to use drugs to find ways to create more perfect and destructive soldiers. In *Steroids and Doping in Sports: A Reference Handbook*, David E. Newton writes that "Nazis made use of sex hormones ... providing drugs to members of the military with the objective of making German soldiers stronger, more aggressive, more violent, and better suited to prevail in combat" (56). According to the article "The Third Reich Was Addicted to Drugs," "In Germany in 1937, a 'variant of crystal meth' was available without a prescription—even sold in boxed chocolates—and was widely adopted by all sectors of society" (Loudis).

The idea of Captain America battling soldiers abusing performance-enhancing hormones and driven by crystal meth is a much older tradition than just Gruenwald's work in the 1980s and 1990s. Captain America's perspective on drugs does undergo some evolution throughout Gruenwald's run, moving from mostly obliviousness (with the Power Broker's augmentation process and his lack of understanding of the 1990s drug abuse problem) to simple vilification (encapsulated by the depiction of drug dealers in the "Streets of Poison" series) to an eventual humanizing of the epidemic (when Cap himself is exposed to a drug transformation).

The removal of the Serum from his body forces Cap to push himself farther and it affects the character throughout the rest of Gruenwald's run. By the early 1990s, Cap is a character who is both well-established and unflinching in his behavior. Not much changes Captain America—during Gruenwald's tenure, he becomes (and unbecomes) a teenager[15] and a werewolf[16] with no long-term consequences. The influence of illegal drugs during "Streets of Poison," however, leaves an impact that helps this quintessential American hero better understand the America he has so dedicated himself to protect.

TEN

Mark Gruenwald's "Fighting Chance"

Cap Faces His Own Mortality

When Captain America #425, the first issue of the twelve-part "Fighting Chance" storyline that would serve as the beginning to the conclusion of Gruenwald's tenure on the title, was first published in April 1994, it preceded Gruenwald's own death by a little over two years. Gruenwald himself would not know this, of course, ultimately the victim of an unforeseen heart attack, but the themes of death (and preparation for death) that define this series are difficult to read now without thinking of Gruenwald's own death so shortly after the completion of this series. Considering there is an epilogue issue to this twelve-part series and six connected subsequent issues that follow that epilogue, the "Fighting Chance" storyline itself does not technically end his run, but the issues that follow it are so tightly tied to the events of "Fighting Chance," it can be argued that the storyline does not end until Gruenwald completely leaves the title. "Fighting Chance" and its aftermath are the climax and coda of Gruenwald's writing career on *Captain America* and its story of a man facing mortality and finding ways to continue fulfilling his life purpose is a fitting conclusion to a writer whose love and dedication to the character of Captain America kept him creating memorable and important stories until the final months of his life.

In the letters page of #442, aware of Gruenwald's impending departure from the title,[1] reader Ben Herman reflects upon Gruenwald's tenure. After praising his overall work on the comic, Herman writes, "Mark deserves credit for sticking with it as long as he did." Editor Ralph Macchio responds that Gruenwald did so "out of love for the character and the endless stream of stories that kept coming out of that fertile noggin of his. No one knows Cap and the other Marvel heroes as deeply and truly as Mark does" (31). He had trouble leaving the comic because he could not stop coming up with storylines that would satisfy his interpretations and expectations for the character. He did this out of loyalty and commitment to the character. On the letters page of his final issue, #443, Gruenwald provides a goodbye letter to readers that included the following explanation of his intentions. After listing out how many more issues he had written than any of his predecessors, he writes, "If there's any hero in all of comics who has the drive to go the distance, it's Cap, and it struck me as odd that he never had a writer willing or able to do the same. I wanted to be that writer" (24). This was published in 1995 and, in an interview from 1988 with Joe Field, Gruenwald also discusses the same issue of a lack of consistency amongst Cap writers. The length of his tenure is a point of pride for Gruenwald because it emphasizes his dedication to a character who embodies dedication.

Gruenwald's widow Catherine Schuller-Gruenwald explains, "He was made for fantasy. He had the capacity to think abstractly, to understand science, astronomy, nature, politics, systems, etc.… It was fantasy, but not convenient manipulation of the facts. It had to make sense at all time" (qtd. in White). His fantasy comic book world works because he cared about so many different things. He cared about his characters being consistent, with the worlds he created fitting into different disparate worlds. He cared about what his readers were experiencing, and he cared about their reactions and their emotions. There is an inherent decency that Gruenwald conveys in these pages and that is ultimately one of the most important aspects of both the comic and of him as a writer overall. It is not always Cap himself who is modeling decency—often it is someone else who has learned decency from Cap and is able to become better because of his influence. "Fighting Chance," with its introduction of young and honorable protégées, dedicated allies and friends, and Captain America's own unflinching desire to push himself to protect others (even when it is destructive and foolhardy to do so), is a fitting final mission statement for the stories Gruenwald had spent a decade crafting. Cap himself is not always the perfect paragon he strives to be and Gruenwald lets him—not just Steve Rogers, necessarily, but Captain America as well—be human.

"Fighting Chance"—Conceit and Structure

"Fighting Chance" showcases this willingness to let Captain America become human. Cap's decisions within the storyline favor duty and commitment over his own well-being (thus potentially risking himself even though so many more friends rely on him emotionally than he realizes). The storyline has a broad overarching conceit of Cap learning of his declining health and fighting a variety of various villainous threats and meeting new allies (and losing a key ally along the way).[2] Significantly, the key trope of "Fighting Chance" is transformative change. Cap must deal with his changing and devolving body along with a changing team of allies. Even his antagonists (aside from Americop, who is entirely new and Kono the Sumo and Damon Dran, who Cap had not interacted with until these adventures) may wear familiar costumes or bear the name of criminal organizations Cap has faced before, are still quite different. For instance, he faces a new Super-Patriot and a revamped (and refocused) Serpent Society (lead by King Cobra). Additionally, he fights old foe Baron Zemo who, in addition to being newly married (with 25 stolen and brainwashed children), has a new face.

This is a storyline of transitions. Cap transitions from his normal level of physical ability prior to the storyline to feeling discomfort with a limited ability to recover to ultimately 95 percent paralysis over the course of the storyline. He goes from his traditional uniform to a Fabian Stankowitz-designed vest and holster.[3] The changes he endures are internal and external, and they are both small and wildly significant. There is very little transition that Cap does not endure over this storyline (and its follow-up), but the adventures themselves remain true to the exciting and adventurous character-building stories Grunwald had been writing for years.

Logistically, the twelve-part storyline is comprised of four trilogies. The first trilogy features a new Super-Patriot and his associate Dead Ringer out to get revenge on Cap (issues #425–427). The second presents, among other challenges, the threat of Americop (#428–430). The third introduces Cap's new ally Free Spirit who joins his side to face off against Baron Zemo (#431–433). Finally, the fourth trilogy introduces another new ally, Jack Flag, who has infiltrated the Serpent Society and needs Cap and Free Spirit's help (#434–436). The trilogies that comprise the official storyline are followed by an "epilogue" where Cap mentally fights for control of his 95 percent paralyzed body while Tony Stark tries to find some way to assist him (#437). In #438, Cap is given a suit of armor by Stark that allows him to continue to serve. The final five issues feature adventures in which Cap is wearing that mobility-saving armor while inching closer and closer to his likely demise. It all culminates in #443 where Cap is visited by the Black Crow,[4] who tells Cap that he has but 24 hours to live. This issue revolves around Cap's efforts (some of which are futile) to help inspire those in his life. It ends with his apparent death and subsequent disappearance.

Fateful Diagnosis

The focus of #425, the first issue of the "Fighting Chance" series, is Cap's compromised physical state, but the issue does not begin directly with that revelation. Instead, it starts with one of the villains who will plague Cap in this first "Fighting Chance" trilogy. We find the new Super-Patriot[5] in the process of obtaining a shield so that he can fulfill what he describes as a "personal crusade … against Captain America" (3). The scene ends with a full-page image (penciled by Dave Hoover) of this new Super-Patriot holding his duplicate of Captain America's shield high in the air. In these issues, Super-Patriot imitates Cap in order to discredit him. The irony Gruenwald infuses into the story is that, while Super-Patriot wants to discredit Cap morally (by making him look immoral and criminal), this entire series compromises Cap physically. While Super-Patriot wants to represent Cap as a shell of what he really is, the real Cap is so physically compromised, he truly *is* a shell of what he was.

The scene in #425 then shifts to Captain America training on a rooftop with lifelike robotic adversaries.[6] While fighting combat robots, Cap is in deep thought about his recent physical challenges: "Something's out of whack with me lately. My coordination's been off[,] I've been experiencing muscle cramps, and I'm not up to my usual speed" (4). As he fights through the challenges in the combat simulator, Cap literally feels his body betraying him: "Nnnh—shoulder aches where I hyperextended!" (6). Cap has always been in peak condition and these physical ailments are more than just a bother—for Cap to lose a sense of control over his body means that he is losing a key sense of what makes him extraordinary.

As Cap continues to ponder what is wrong with him, Doctor Kinkaid[7] shuts off the training session to give Cap his test results. He explains to Cap,

> The inescapable fact seems to be that your body is experiencing some maladaptive degradation of the Super-Soldier Serum … every day of your life you crowd in what for anybody else would be a month's worth of physical activity…. Well, it seems like you've finally overtaxed the serum's limits—its ability to repair cells that become damaged or worn through use!

In interviews (and in the stories themselves[8]), Gruenwald consistently explains that Steve Rogers' work ethic is the reason he is Captain America and not the Super Soldier Serum. In an interview with comic-art.com, Gruenwald states, "It's my contention that even without Super-Soldier Serum that Steve Rogers, by the strength of his own character, would have [found] some way to be Captain America." It can be argued that in Gruenwald's world, the Serum (along with Rogers' innate character and other internal qualities) is merely a tool and not the reason for his greatness.[9] Steve Rogers is great and that is why Captain America is great. In this particular storyline, the serum evolves to become something much more sinister—the curse that will kill Cap (or render him paralyzed).

Cap then demands the doctor provide the "bottom line." Dr. Kinkaid tells him, "if you keep up your current level of high adrenaline activity, you will experience total muscular paralysis in about a year … if you restrict your activities to normal human levels, you could probably maintain mobility and muscular usage for the rest of your natural life" (7). Therein lies the set-up of the greatest battle of Cap's life. He is pitted against both his duty and his body. The only way to win the battle against his body is to give up the duty and responsibility of Captain America (and, likewise, maintaining the duties of Captain America will cause him to lose the battle against his body). The first thing Cap does after Dr. Kincaid leaves him alone on the rooftop (after Kincaid tells him to avoid unnecessary activity) is pick up one of the training drones and throw it aggressively across the sky (with a "RAAAGH!" to further emphasis the aggression and frustration). He then goes back to his Brooklyn Heights secret headquarters and confides his situation to Diamondback (after deliberating as to whether doing so is the right move). When she asks him what he plans to do, he is at a loss: "I don't know. Being Cap is what I do best" (12). This idea of "being Cap" embodies so much for Steve Rogers. "Being Cap" is about safeguarding the country and globe and being a symbol that properly represents the values of his country. It is also a reflex—Steve Rogers cannot fathom life without Cap because of how organic it is to his very identity.

Imitation

While the series and its seven follow-up issues focus heavily on Cap's mortality, his potential death is merely one way the series looks at death. One of the key antagonists in both the first trilogy and issue #439 (an issue that comes soon after the conclusion of "Fighting Chance") is Dead Ringer, a villain with the ability to absorb the powers and appearances of dead bodies through touch.[10] In #439, he explains that he finds the bodies of "powerful" people in order to take on their extraordinary attributes. He further admits he collects "obituaries of superhumans who died" in order to exhume their bodies (16). This character helps establish two important themes in these late-period Gruenwald issues—imitation and death. Dead Ringer is a key example of imitation, but he is not alone in Gruenwald's focus on imitation. Dead Ringer aligns himself with a new Super-Patriot[11] and both men imitate others—Super-Patriot imitates Captain America and Dead Ringer imitates a number of dead supervillains. While this story occurs after "Fighting Chance," issue #442 is the penultimate issue on Gruenwald's run and it features another villain (Larry Elker, AKA Zeitgeist

AKA Everyman) who imitates other heroes in order to eliminate superhumans.[12] Steve Rogers is Cap, and there is no trickery or imitation inherent within that but even he is an imposter after his diagnosis because he is not capable of living up to the standard of Captain America that he has previously established.

When he attempts to stop the Serpent Society in #435, for example, he is first confronted by Jack Flag. Flag, while infiltrating the Society, dons King Cobra's uniform (yet another example of imitation), so Cap, logically, sees him as an enemy. Once they realize the situation (and that the man in the King Cobra uniform is really an ally), Cap "allows" Jack Flag to beat him up and take him prisoner. Flag assumes that it is simply the plan, but the reality is that Cap has very little ability or courage to fight back. Cap *must* let Jack Flag defeat him just so he could replenish his diminished physical reserves and possibly have a chance at defeating the real King Cobra and his allies. As Cap considers after Flag has encouraged him to fight a little bit harder to make their staged fight a bit more convincing, "I'm trying to keep my energy level low to avoid stimulating my adrenal glands. Adrenaline triggers my muscle seizures according to Doc Kincaid!" (15). Cap cannot function as he did before, so he must plan out his attacks more strategically. In this way, he is not the Captain America he seems to be (and who both allies and enemies expect him to be) and he cannot, for fear of giving his enemies too much of an advantage, reveal the ruse.

These multiple examples of imitation serve to highlight the uncertainly and confusion of Captain America's future. When he is focused on an adversary, he is not confused, but when he starts looking forward to what he can do long term, it becomes more of a challenge. He is misrepresented by Super-Patriot in an attempt by Super-Patriot to sully Cap's pristine reputation, but Captain America's own performances in battle are doing far more to damage the public perception of the character. In fact, in issue #426, Super-Patriot (in Cap's costume) attempts to rob an armored car in order to make Cap look like a criminal when he and Dead Ringer (using the body and abilities of the Night Flyer) are attacked by Cap's old nemesis the Resistants, a militant mutant group.[13] Thanks to Dead Ringer's ability to switch bodies and powers, they not only survive the attack but apprehend the Resistants and allow law enforcement to arrest them. This is not Super-Patriot's plan, but he and Dead Ringer are able to do it. The irony, of course, is that Cap himself might not have been able to stop the villainous group given his compromised physical state. The imitation to discredit Cap backfires because Super-Patriot is able to accomplish something that Cap himself, because of his declining health, cannot do.

Representations of Death

What makes Dead Ringer so important in this storyline is that he represents both imitation and death. He gains his ability from the dead, absorbing their bodies and abilities into his own. He is a villain who, while not able to resurrect the dead, can use the dead for his own nefarious means. In issue #439, Bernie Rosenthal finds a box of fingers in Dead Ringer and Super-Patriot's hideout, a horrific discovery that appropriately appalls both Rosenthal and Super-Patriot. When Super-Patriot expresses disgust, Dead Ringer responds calmly, "I can assume the shape of a dead person I've touched only once, unless I touch them again. That's why I take souvenirs." Super-Patriot is outraged, reminding Dead Ringer, "You told me you were grossed out by having to touch dead bodies … now I find— this! What else have you lied to me about?" Dead Ringer, again calmly, tells Super-Patriot to "Get a grip," adding, "I do what I have to, so do you. It's not like it's my freaking hobby" (12). In this instance, Super-Patriot is referencing an earlier conversation that takes place at a graveyard in issue #426 when Dead Ringer tells his partner, "If there was any other way to absorb these bodies' powers and skills—I'd jump at it" (3). As he says this, he is in the process of absorbing their powers, and although he is expressing discontent at the process, he does not feel enough discontent to altogether refrain from it.

Introducing Dead Ringer early in this storyline is a deliberate nod to the comic book mentality of death. In this particular genre (filled with countless resurrections), death is not necessarily permanent and, even in death, the dead shall rise. Captain America's dilemma in this series is not about death, but it might as well be. Captain America would see a deterioration of his physical capacity to be the death of the character. Cap could choose to retire from crime-fighting and take it easy, but that choice is never really one he contemplates.

After receiving Dr. Kincaid's diagnosis in #425, he briefly debates whether he should confide in Diamondback, his partner and love interest. He decides to do so (lest he prevent her from ever being open with him if he does not do the same for her), but his explanation is less dramatic than Dr. Kincaid's. While Dr. Kincaid warns of "total muscular paralysis," if Cap overextends his activity, Cap tells Diamondback only that "I may really mess up my health" (11). Death is not specifically mentioned, but it does not have to be. If Steve Rogers cannot commit to rigorous activity, he might not die, but Captain America would undeniably be dead. While Rogers' death is not assured by the diagnosis, Dead Ringer makes the reader think of death regardless—and in Dead Ringer's eyes, death is a job. Perhaps, as he says in #426, he does not get his "jollies" from touching dead bodies (3), but he is still matter-of-fact about the process. While some readers of the comic may have (ultimately wrongly) anticipated Steve Rogers' death at the end of this storyline, Gruenwald uses death as an inevitably, but it is not to be dreaded. It is an inevitability and even the supervillains who make their trade in death can disconnect themselves from it.

In issue #438, Cap dons an armor designed by Tony Stark to make movement possible. Cap thinks, Stark "then rigged an exoskeleton to do the movement that my recalcitrant musculature no longer could" (2). The cover of the issue features artwork by Dave Hoover in which Captain America is wearing the exoskeleton (appropriately mimicking the design of his traditional uniform), lunging from the sky and into action. The caption on the cover's lower right-hand corner reads, "Without his new armor he would lie paralyzed! With it, he intends to go out in a blaze of glory!" The phrase "blaze of glory" refers to significant events at the end of one's career or life, thus the cover is anticipating the end, at best, of Cap's career.

Blaze of Glory

In the twelve issues of "Fighting Chance," even without the armor, Cap only considers that "blaze of glory" option. While Cap does contemplate his two options (retire or paralyze himself through adrenaline-inducing action), his debate is minimal. Perhaps in his own mind, Cap thinks he is seriously considering walking away from the life of adventuring, but it never feels particularly sincere. The reader knows he is incapable of stopping. In #425, as he is having lunch with Diamondback, he feels his morals and philosophies are outdated in a changing world: "Maybe it won't be such a terrible thing for me to stop being Cap..." (20). At the end of that same issue, he admits to Diamondback, "I don't know what I'm going to do. I've always been a fighter, but this time it seems ... the harder I fight, the faster I'll lose everything" (32).

In #426, the debate of retiring is barely mentioned (Cap is distracted by Super-Patriot's efforts to disgrace Cap's image). In #427, he asks Quicksilver to help him capture Super-Patriot. Quicksilver is confused by the request (though he obliges), wondering why Cap would not just do it himself. Quicksilver wonders, "Is Captain America going soft?" (10). Cap is trying to have both worlds—moderate his effort while using his Avenger connections to apprehend criminals. When Cap does appear to fight Super-Patriot, he strives to defeat his enemy quickly as to not "expend needless energy—" (19). He does not stop completely, despite doctor's orders. The reader is given no reason to believe Cap does not believe Dr. Kincaid's diagnosis. It also cannot be argued that Cap does not care—he thinks about his physical limitations often and strategizes how to work around the problem. It is simply a matter of him not being able to stop. Additionally, he has the available resources to address these challenges with help. Considering the "help" he has at his disposal is the Avengers (and other superhero allies), Cap could manage these threats without "expend[ing] needless energy." However, asking Quicksilver is depicted as not being easy for him.[14]

In the letter page of issue #439, reader Robert Moraes writes, "Steve should ... realize that his reluctance to rely on others is a real weakness on his part. He must come to terms with himself that sometimes it's okay to ask others for help. That's what you do with friendships and with people you care deeply about" (30). Cap cares about his friends and allies, but he cannot stop overvaluing his own abilities, even when those abilities are compromised. Moraes calls this a "weakness" and that is ultimately a fair assessment. This storyline is significant because Gruenwald is willing to depict Captain America, a character who is rarely shown as possessing any flaws, as possessing a weakness that could lead to his death (and, depending on the moment his body was to completely give out on him, potentially the deaths of countless others).[15]

In #429, Cap's arms tense up while simply piloting his sky cycle and not exerting himself much (12), which leads him to consider asking Dr. Kincaid to test him again to further test his limits. At this point, Cap is not contemplating retirement (and his quick consideration of the idea allows the reader to conclude that he never takes the idea seriously). At the conclusion of #430, he has allowed the crazed vigilante cop Americop to kill several criminals in a helicopter and failed to stop a situation with criminals peacefully. At the conclusion, he thinks to himself, "My incompetence here was staggering ... unbearable. I didn't accomplish one thing! Everybody had to cover for me. What am I going to do now that I can't cut it anymore?" (22). Considering his friends Diamondback and Zach Moonhunter were rescued from criminal Damon Dram, Cap certainly did accomplish things that could not have happened without him, but it simply is not good enough. He wonders, "what am I going to do," but this many issues into "Fighting Chance," it is clear that Cap is incapable of sitting out these battles. The question of what he will do is not about retiring but is instead about how he can keep everything the same as it has always been (but without paralysis). The storyline sets this up as an impossible option.

When he meets with Dr. Kincaid in issue #431, Cap assures Kincaid that he "tried" to restrain from activity, but "it was simply impossible." He continues, "When I see an injustice.... I just can't stand idly by!" (3). Cap's attempts to restrain have often been defined by trying to defeat a villain quickly, not avoiding the situation altogether. Cap's actions in these stories make it clear that Gruenwald does not envision him as a potential mentor or hero who can contribute in a supporting capacity. Cap's "tries" to reduce physical activity are purposefully insufficient. Steve Rogers simply could not be Cap if he would be willing turn away from "injustice." He has also done little to avoid these instances of "injustice." For instance, in #431, the injustice he "sees" is an alert that Baron Zemo has kidnapped children in Mexico. He and Diamondback fly off to investigate (15). Could another Avenger have taken on this mission?[16] For Cap, the answer is no. He always expects himself to win a given battle, even when he has no real reason to have that confidence. In this situation, that confidence is even less grounded than usual.

In issues #432 and #433, Cap has a few moments where he laments his limitations, but he has minimal time to debate his actions. After all, in both of these issues, he is battling Baron Zemo and his minions. Ambushing Zemo's castle is entirely Cap's call and Cap in no way debated the decision, so he had no time to consider the consequences. In #434, after saving the children kidnapped by Zemo, he is feeling more confident: "Maybe I'll be able to come to terms with my declining abilities" (5). Despite the doctor's warning and his own physical failure, Cap is rationalizing. While sparring with Free Spirit, he becomes temporarily paralyzed (ending with the insinuation that he is going to let Free Spirit in on the information about his health condition). The consequences of his physical activity are clear, but Cap continues to push himself forward regardless.

Issue #435 begins not with Cap's recovery but well after it. Moonhunter is retrieving Cap and Free Spirit from Castle Zemo in Mexico when Cap reroutes them to Arizona to investigate a tip about the Serpent Society. In the panel in which Cap orders Moonhunter (who is unaware of Cap's condition) to go to Arizona, Dave Hoover pencils Free Spirit as looking sternly at Cap, but this is as close as we get to her reaction following the news of his health delivered off-panel at the end of the previous issue (and the image of Free Spirit is small in a small panel and, considering her masked face, it is potentially debatable that it is not a look of disgust at all). Cap heads off on another mission that will potentially leave him paralyzed or worse, and he does not debate not doing so (even after falling paralyzed after sparring with an amateur).

In #436, Cap's unflinching confidence flinches. After being apprehended by the Serpent Society, he is dispatched into the desert to be ambushed by King Cobra and Mr. Hyde. Upon seeing them, Cap thinks, "They've followed me out in the desert to finish me off! With my muscles cutting out on me whenever I exert myself too much ... there's a good chance they might just succeed!" (3). If Cap questions his chances in battle prior to "Fighting Chance," it would be easy to read it as false modesty. That is not the case here. Hyde and King Cobra are significant threats with murder on their minds.[17] Despite being pummeled to the point of immobility, Cap survives through luck (and Fabian Stankowitz's clever weaponry). Hyde and King Cobra are both unable to kill the prone-on-his-back Cap because of the automatically activated armaments emerging from Cap's battle vest. Cap is momentarily paralyzed, but he fights himself to mobility in order to move King Cobra out of the direct heat lest he die of exposure. Cap uses what little he has left to protect the enemy that, moments earlier, was on the brink of strangling him to death in cold blood. This is a reminder that Cap is not just any superhero. He is, as Cap himself thinks to himself in a thought chain bubble, "Captain Freaking America!" (17). He tells himself that he has "never given up before! Never!" and pushes himself harder and harder until he simply collapses in unconsciousness and paralysis. Gruenwald does not let Cap walk away from the superhero life. Allowing Cap to do so, even as an act of self-preservation, would be a betrayal of the character.

In the essay, "'Captain America Must Die': the Many Afterlives of Steve Rogers," Dave Walton describes "Fighting Chance" as "the next logical step in Gruenwald's concern with external and internal molders, turning to Steve Rogers' failing body as an ambiguous speaker, separating his creative vision for Captain America from the reality of his legacy" (170). While there could be a desire to elevate Captain America to the heights of relevance and popular culture prominence, the character is nowhere near that. Cap's declining body is a tool that allows Cap as a character to reassess his legacy, but instead it focuses Cap on his own personal failings. While "Fighting Chance" is ambitious in its length and conflict, Gruenwald keeps the story unambitious in scope when it matters. The story stays rotating in a familiar orbit of Cap allies and villains, all the while reworking the status quo to show readers the most enduring of characters as he faces the end (of either his life or relevance).

Reader Reactions to "Fighting Chance"

Captain America and Mark Gruenwald were not the only ones facing the end; readers were also reluctant about where the title and character were heading during this series and its aftermath. Prior to the opening issue, this series was hyped up to the point of creating genuine concern amongst the readers as to Steve Rogers' place on the title. Those concerns elevated throughout the publication of subsequent issues. In the letter page of issue #428, reader Harry Simon asks, "Would it ultimately be futile to request that Steve Rogers retains the role of Cap after this upcoming saga?" This letter from Simon was written *before* "Fighting Chance" even started. The hype for this storyline was obviously effective. Issue #424, the issue immediately before the first issue of the 12-part series, features this teaser in its letter page: "So take a deep breath and let it out one month from today when our double-sized extravaganza 'Fighting Chance' marks a bold new chapter in the life of Marvel's hero of heroes!" (24).

In addition to hype created from within the comic, the reader belief that Rogers would no longer serve as Cap likely also comes from the tendency for radical change of the era. "Fighting Chance" begins in 1994 and, in just the few years prior to that, Superman had died and been resurrected (1992–1993) and Bruce Wayne's back had been broken and he was replaced as Batman (1994). Massive change was so common in the era that fans would no longer be surprised when such change was planned.

Accordingly, the covers of the issues of the series themselves are filled with hype. Issue #425 alerts the reader: "It All Starts Here! Witness the Most Startling Event in the life of America's Greatest Hero!!" Issue #426 promises "The Most Crucial Storyline in Cap's History!" Issue #435 promotes itself by stating, "The Battle That May Kill Cap Starts Here!" And, issue #436, the final issue of the storyline (though not Gruenwald's final issue overall) states boldly: "Fighting Chance No More!" It also puts the word "finished!" underneath the title of the comic (to spell out "Captain America Finished!"), featuring artwork by Dave Hoover of Cap on the ground, contorting in pain while the rattle of a rattlesnake sits in his unclenched hand. The cover is promising the end of the storyline and, seemingly, the end of Cap's life.[18]

Many of the reader letters during the storyline follow this pattern of nervous speculation. The letters page of issue #429 contains a litany of concerns from various readers. Reader George Becnel writes, "I have a gut feeling the future role for Steve Rogers is that of an older mentor to a new Captain America." Reader Adam Moreau writes, "I have heard rumors that Cap was going to die and the Punisher (now reformed) would become the *new* Captain America." Reader Omar Hussien adds, " It looks really bad for Cap now, and I sincerely hope you guys don't kill him off or anything insane like that." In #438, reader David Hofstede agrees with the above reader sentiment and laments the future: "Younger readers, those reared on the Punisher[19] and his concept of justice, will probably approve of a 'new' Captain America … if you lose some of us 30+ dinosaurs, it won't make much of a dent in your sale figures" (31).

It can be argued that these concerns are not about clinging to the past or nostalgia, but a worry that changing Cap into a Punisher-like figure would be a betrayal of what the Captain America character represents.[20] These reader responses do not necessarily paint a picture of nostalgia-driven fans unwilling to part with an important character of their childhoods—they are worried about Steve Rogers' values being dismissed in favor of something less morally instructive. For some of these readers, perhaps these feelings are driven by a concern that the moral teachings they have derived from Captain America will not be available for future young readers if Steve Rogers is no longer the hero in the uniform.[21]

As. Richard J. Stevens discusses in *Captain America, Masculinity, and Violence: The Evolution of a National Icon*, "One of the stereotypes of 1990s comic books narratives is that they involved the escalation of violence, increased use of firearms, and rampant portrayals of violent vigilantism. The 1990s Captain America, however, largely resisted those trends and was even used by his writers to critique them." Indeed, these letters express a worry that the Gruenwald (and other potential Cap readers) would rather find a way to inflate sales than stay true to the character, but those readers were perhaps letting their personal concerns divert them away from Gruenwald's mission to "critique" the tropes that were infiltrating other comics (rather than bringing in the Punisher as a replacement).

The Journey

Additionally, while readers were concerned with Cap's ultimate fate and where this twelve-issue series was going to *end*, the comics themselves are much more interested in the journey toward that fate than any end result. "Fighting Chance" is uniquely structured twelve-part story. It does not have a singular storyline that builds up but instead has an overarching problem with which Cap deals, mostly by himself. It also does not feature constant cliffhangers to lead the reader from one issue to the next, not even within the four "trilogies" that make up the twelve issues. In fact, several of these issues conclude with the word "end," typically representing something more climactic than it does here. This is not a storyline built on intensity and suspense. It is about following Cap as he comes to terms with the seemingly irreparable changes threatening his life and mission.

The storyline itself concludes with part twelve, but it is perhaps one of the least satisfying endings of the twelve issues and assuredly one of the more prominent cliffhangers, but even this ending is more morose in its lack of ending than it is suspenseful. In issue #436, Hank Pym (under the guise of Giant-Man) finds an alive but paralyzed Cap in the Arizona desert. Pym lifts him up, lamenting, "Even if I can save your foolish life, there'll be nothing I can do to restore your body anymore. You'll live out the rest of your days unable to move!" (22). This storyline is not about where it ends. That holds true for the final panels of Gruenwald's run overall, where the Avengers enter a room expecting to find Cap's dead body but instead find an empty bed. While those readers who wrote letters worrying of Cap's fate were fixated on the destination, these issues show that Gruenwald's priority was firmly on the journey. Even these moments of death and paralysis were soon followed by new opportunities. Gruenwald resists the urge to provide too much of a conclusion because, again, this is not a story about endings, no matter how much it might seem like it along the way. It is a story about how change infiltrates and influences people and circumstances, regardless of the individual facing that change.

"Fighting Chance," while filled with action sequences and battles, is methodical. It weaves between multiple villains and challenges while always keeping the reader in Cap's thought process as he works his way through each obstacle. Obviously, being introspective is not a new way for Gruenwald to depict Cap, but his introspection here often deals with his own fate in a way that is not common to earlier self-reflections.[22] There are plenty of battles, but as they get more intense (as they do throughout the series, culminating in a battle against the Serpent Society and Mister Hyde), there is never doubt that a full-strength Cap would defeat his adversaries. The threat is always about how he must contend with his body first. In this way, this story is not about the ending but about how Cap can mentally deal with these limitations and the ultimate betrayal of his own body along the way toward that ending.

After "Fighting Chance," Gruenwald winds down his tenure on the comic with action and, ultimately, poignancy. In order to save their paralyzed ally in issue #437, Tony Stark and Hank Pym battle through Cap's psyche in order to revive his consciousness. Stark then equips Cap with a suit of armor that will allow Cap to resist paralysis and continue his adventuring although, as Cap admits to his friends in #438, the armor is ultimately a high-powered Band-Aid because his "heart could go at any minute" (22). Through "Fighting Chance" and its aftermath, Cap's mentality only leads him to fight, despite the inevitability of his demise as a result. His thoughts of retirement are, if not insincere, unlikely. The title "Fighting Chance" is ultimately appropriate because "fighting" is the only way Cap can see himself surviving a problem (even one made tangibly worse through the physical exertion of fighting).

"The Character Should Not"

Made for battling the Axis armies in World War II, Cap is a character who is battle-born. More than any other superhero, his origin story is tied to a specific place and time. Superman and Batman were created in a similar era, but their stories could transcend time in a way that Cap's (so entrenched in the conflict of World War II) could not. Cap is also depicted often, prior to Gruenwald, through the "man out of time" lens. While there are still moments in these pages in which Cap feels like an "other," his otherness by the '80s and '90s comes from his sense of morality rather than cultural differences. Ultimately, Gruenwald saw the chance to present Cap in this contemporary era as an opportunity to try something new—not because of what the '80s and '90s could do to Cap, but what he could do for that era. In an interview with comic-art.com from 1995, Gruenwald is asked if Cap should make a "sort of reflection of the time in which he is being published?" Gruenwald responds,

> The book obviously has to be set in the time period in which the readers are reading it but Captain America's values are timeless.... Okay, so while the stories have to be set in the time period in which they're coming out, Captain America's ideals are timeless. I mean they go back to our founding fathers and if you go back even further than that, they go back to, you know, the birth of democracy itself, which I guess was in ancient Greece, you know, they started the democratic ideals, you know, what democracy, government by the people is about. So I actually think … that Captain America is more interesting now than in the forties because in the forties everyone was patriotic. He was just more patriotic than most. Now, very few people are patriotic and very few people believe that the government and its ideals are the solutions to anything and so it's that contrast, that relief from the environment that makes Captain America more interesting today. So, the farther America in reality gets from America the ideal, the more interesting Captain America is.

At the beginning of this answer, Gruenwald explains that, while the comic itself should be a reflection of the era in which it appears, "the character should not." By the end of the run, Cap is given a more '90s look (initially with his battle vest adorned with pouches and later armor), but that is as far as the modern makeover, externally or internally, goes. Gruenwald's Cap adapts to eras but is not compromised by them. Over the course of these ten years, Gruenwald presents Cap against a backdrop of a strange and difficult world. He presents Cap with challenges related to changing geo-political realities, drug usage, and society's increased tolerance and desire for violence. Gruenwald makes Captain America essential for this decade precisely because the way Cap sees these challenges is different than it would be for any other hero.

Gruenwald ends "Fighting Chance" with Cap's full paralysis and ends his run with Cap's disappearance and, while Cap's death seems inevitable during Gruenwald's final year and a half, that inevitability is not fulfilled. It is as if Gruenwald left that responsibility to someone else, some later writer who was willing to try it.[23] Not Gruenwald. In the same 1995 interview, Gruenwald explains why Cap has always been Rogers and, in his mind, always should be:

I don't think there's anything you could replace that with which would be res-
onant and compelling as Steve Rogers, so everyone else is doomed to just be
a replacement. He's got the primal connection that's the basic concept, so at
least by my way of thinking, no one could replace him forever if you want to do
something called Captain America.

This is why, at the end of Gruenwald's run, Cap's absence says so much. His
allies assume the end for Steve Rogers is nigh, and they do not know how to
face a world without Steve Rogers. Perhaps either does Gruenwald, hence
leaving the issue for another writer to resolve.

On the last page of issue #443, the final *Captain America* comic Gruenwald wrote, penciller Dave Hoover draws the collected Avengers entering
the room where a paralyzed Cap has been left alone in his quarters. After
Avengers butler Edwin Jarvis discovers Cap motionless (and apparently not
breathing), the Avengers have entered the room expecting to find his dead
body. They do not. Steve Rogers is gone, and only his Stark-designed exoskeleton battle armor is left upon the bed. The collected Avengers (and Jarvis, who discovers the scene) are shown heads down and sobbing. In the
last three panels, Quicksilver runs to an open window and, after finding
out from Jarvis that it was not left open earlier, sees an eagle flying into the
New York sunset. The final panel moves from inside the room to outside,
Hoover's pencils showing us Quicksilver looking out the window from the
view of the bird. In this panel, the curtains are billowing and the Avengers
are suddenly small and in shadows.

The Avengers, larger than life as they are, are suddenly smaller than
the possibilities of Captain America's future (or simply his legacy). Quicksilver then delivers the last lines Gruenwald writes in a *Captain America*
story: "What has happened to Captain America? Does his disappearance
mark the end of an era?" (22). To answer Quicksilver's final question, it
does mark the end of an era. For Captain America himself, his disappearance was resolved over the next few issues by Mark Waid, the writer who
took over writing duties. No, the era that ended was the era of Mark Gruenwald. He would still serve as a key editor at Marvel before his August 1995
death, but the end of his tenure marked a change. Due to the speculator
bubble collapsing in the mid–90s (as discussed in Chapter Eight), among
other factors, the industry was already changing, but the impact of Gruenwald's work on this comic was significant both in terms of future Captain
America stories, comic writing overall, and the current wave of superhero
culture, too. Gruenwald valued humor and honor. He respected his characters and he respected his audience. He created comics of dynamic energy
and enjoyment. Mostly, he helped readers understand, through a character
who could seem so far above the rest of us in terms of abilities and moral
standing, what it means to be human.

Chapter Notes

Introduction

1. Perhaps this mainstream critical acceptance began in earnest when Moore and Gibbons' *Watchmen* won the 1988 Hugo Award, a nod toward the artistic merit of superhero comics. Art Spiegelman's *Maus* was awarded the Pulitzer Prize in 1992.

2. "Streets of Poison," the 1990 saga that runs from *Captain America* #372–378, is an example. Cap takes on the drug problem and Gruenwald depicts drug turf battles. Ultimately, though, the saga stays focused on character beats and fight scenes more than a larger commentary about drugs, but it does not shy away from discussing drugs. This saga is focused upon in detail in Chapter Nine.

3. For example, the Red Skull can be described as a Nazi madman, Flag-Smasher an Anti-Nationalist Terrorist, and Armadillo a, well, giant armadillo (who represents the "Beauty and the Beast" motif).

4. Falcon's presence is often of a man between two worlds, fully appreciated in neither. He quits the Avengers because he feels he would be a token member in *Avengers* #184, but he is also repeatedly criticized by members of Harlem's black community for being an "Uncle Tom," both as the Falcon in *Captain America* #151 and as Sam Wilson in #143 (to cite just two examples of a recurring motif).

5. "Retcon" is short for "retroactive continuity," and it is a way of describing the act of rewriting "a current origin or introduction of new information as if it had always been that way" ("Retcon (Concept)").

6. According to Gruenwald, "A closed crossover is conceived of as involving specific titles where each title is equally important in advancing the storyline," as opposed to an "open crossover" in which there is a single main storyline and then tangential storylines that appear in other comics and, while those issues are related to the main storyline, they are not essential in understanding the main story ("Mark's Remarks").

7. The role of Thor is fulfilled at this time by a character previously known as Thunderstrike.

8. Four years of published comics is not the same as the time that passes within the comics themselves, but this is still a significant amount of time for this tension to linger.

9. Sharon Carter is obviously a key recurring romantic figure for Cap in the '60s and '70s, but Rosenthal was an effort to "normalize" his relationships by having him be involved with a regular citizen rather than a S.H.I.E.L.D. agent.

10. This motif begins with the first MCU movie when, in *Iron Man*, Robert Downey, Jr.'s Tony Stark announces to a gathering that he is Iron Man. Thus started a cinematic trend of heroes either being "unmasked" (as in *Iron Man* and *Spider-Man: Far From Home*) or forgoing secret identities altogether.

11. While Iron Man and Cap fight multiple times during Gruenwald's run and have an extended icy relationship, Mark Millar's 2006–2007 *Civil War* crossover comic event features full-on fatal battles between Cap's and Iron Man's teams.

12. While Tony Stark's character arc in the MCU movies sees him evolving from a self-serving billionaire to a hero willing to

sacrifice himself for a greater good (nearly doing so in *Marvel's Avengers* and then doing exactly that in *Endgame*), Steve Rogers needs no similar arc. In *Captain America: The First Avenger*, young Steve Rogers (not yet Captain America) lunges on what he thinks is a live grenade in order to sacrifice himself for the sake of others. Rogers has already shown his willingness to sacrifice himself for others.

13. Quoting Salinger seems highly appropriate considering that J.D. Salinger's son Matt plays Cap in the 1990 film *Captain America*.

14. Red Skull (ultimately revealed to be fake) states that they were "inconveniently wrenched from [their] affairs on earth" by "alien abductors" (11).

15. Though Cunningham does begrudgingly admit Gruenwald's status as the "largely … definitive version for most modern comics readers" (178).

16. This is further discussed in the preface.

Chapter One

1. Symbols include the bald eagle, the Liberty Bell, the Statue of Liberty, Uncle Sam, and the White House, just to identify a few. Each of these above symbols is seen at some point in the pages of Gruenwald's *Captain America*.

2. Interest in the film was massive. Its November 20, 1983, debut ranks as the 16th most-watched television program of all-time, trailing, among other television events, the final episode of *M*A*S*H* and nine Super Bowls ("Top 100 Rated TV Shows of All Time").

3. Cap even fights a reptilian Ronald Reagan in the Oval Office in *Captain America #344*.

4. He does develop a personal vendetta against—and respect for—Steve Rogers (despite not knowing Rogers personally). In *Captain America #348*, when he expects Steve Rogers in the Captain America uniform and instead gets John Walker, he refuses to acknowledge Walker as Cap.

5. According to the U.S. Flag Code (Title 4 of the United States Code), section 8, clause D, "The flag should never be used as wearing apparel." Section 8, clause J reads, "no part of the flag should ever be worn as a costume or athletic uniform." This establishes Cap's mere uniform as problematic (qtd. in "U.S. Flag Code").

6. Gruenwald does work to give Walker a redemptive story arc over time.

7. The interpretation of the poem's meaning is challenged today. In 2019, acting director of U.S. Citizenship and Immigration Services Ken Cuccinelli was asked if Lazarus' poem ("give me your tired, your poor") was still "part of the American ethos." Cuccinelli responded with, "They certainly are: 'Give me your tired and your poor who can stand on their own two feet and who will not become a public charge'" (Nichols), thus rewriting the text and sentiment for political objectives.

8. This has not always been a steadfast rule for Cap, but Gruenwald depicts Cap as if it has been. During the 1940s comics, Cap was frequently depicted with a sidearm (as was the case in director Joe Johnson's 2011 *Captain America: The First Avenger* film).

9. Abraham Lincoln believed in God without adhering to Christianity. Lincoln wrote: "That I am not a member of any Christian Church, is true, but I have never denied the truth of the Scriptures; and I have never spoken with intentional disrespect of religion in general, or of any denomination of Christians in particular" (qtd. in Little).

10. Reader Ali T. Kokmen comments in the letters page of issue #395 from 1991 (during the Gulf War) that these figures of American legend lack Cap's ethos: "Even now, with our nation at war, Uncle Sam has not remerged into the national consciousness. If there is an American spirit, these men do not quite catch it (or no longer do) because they are so absent from Americans' thoughts. Cap is different, though … Cap resonates within all Americans, not just soldiers, or planters, or cowboys, or railroad workers, or loggers" (31).

11. Walker's parents are killed in *Captain America #345* in a targeted terrorist attack after Walker's true identity is revealed to the public, thus showing that Walker indeed did need to be concerned with that practical reason for wearing a mask.

12. Cap has a long history of reforming supervillains; Hawkeye, Quicksilver, Scarlet Witch, and Black Widow, just to name a few, are Cap's Avenger allies who were once criminals he helped reformed.

Chapter Two

1. While various images are used in this box over time, the particular image that is replaced here is in place from issue #304 to #331.

2. Both the shield and uniform vanish unexpectedly. Rogers is surprised by the loss of the shield but fights on. When he loses the uniform, he is quickly defeated. He is left literally wearing only a pair of America flag-inspired boxer shorts, exposed and vulnerable in a way never seen elsewhere in Gruenwald's run.

3. When the giant adopts Rogers' face, that Rogers tells our Rogers, "You're the one who got you into this mess!" (5). This establishes the guilt and blame Rogers is putting on himself at this point in the storyline for his decision.

4. This would be changed in 1991 to "Strategic Homeland Intervention, Enforcement and Logistics Division," and this full name is the one used in the MCU. In the first episode of ABC's television series *Agents of S.H.I.E.L.D,* Maria Hill asks Agent Grant Ward, "What does S.H.I.E.L.D. stand for?" Ward answers in full. When Hill asks him what that means to him, he answers, "It means someone really wanted our initials to spell out S.H.I.E.L.D."

5. This is an acronym for "Underground Liberated Totally Integrated Mobile Army to Unite Mankind."

6. The augmentation process is a clear reference to steroid abuse and is discussed further in Chapter Nine. D-Man is a former professional wrestler and the ties between the Augmentation process and professional wrestling are clear. This storyline takes place in 1987. The World Wrestling Federation (known now as World Wrestling Entertainment) was beseeched with drug issues and rumors at this time and a 1991 trial would convict Dr. George Zahorian of providing steroids to professional wrestlers. In 1993–1994, the WWF/WWE and its head Vince McMahon would be on trial for drug distribution (and would subsequently be acquitted).

7. Under Gruenwald, Steve Rogers as Captain America is extraordinarily self-reflective, deliberating heavily on decisions but typically standing by a decision once it is made.

8. Shroud is Max Coleridge, a heroic vigilante. The Night Shift were a group of villains he covertly led while working undercover in Los Angeles.

9. While North and others were indicted and sentenced, those punishments were largely vacated, including President George H. W. Bush's pardon of North.

10. In the letters section of 1987's *Captain America* #333, reader Hurricane Heeran presents the question of Cap's political leanings, a topic of much discussion in earlier eras, adding that this was likely a question "that maybe every reader of *Captain America* has an opinion on": "What type of politics would Cap most likely follow? Would he be a liberal because Captain America started during the administration of Franklin Roosevelt? Or would he be a conservative because that's the beat of the current president? (One might note that Ronald Reagan was a Democrat during FDR's terms and changed parties during the Kennedy administration)." Editor Don Daley (we can assume, speaking for Gruenwald's perspective) argues, "We've always seen Cap as adhering to no political party or position since to represent America, he has to represent the entire spectrum of opinion, publicly at least. As far as his deep-down privately held beliefs, who can say?"

11. These two political scandals were different in scope and influence. The Watergate scandal, focusing on a presidentially authorized break-in of the Democratic National Committee's headquarters in 1972, would ultimately lead to Richard Nixon's resignation and leave a lasting mark of public distrust in elected officials. The Iran-Contra affair involved the sale of arms to Iran to fund Nicaragua's right-wing Contras in the mid-1980s. While President Reagan would eventually apologize, he did not suffer the same consequences as did Nixon, nor was his involvement ever as clearly verified as was Nixon's. Among many others, Reagan's secretary of Defense Caspar Weinberger was indicted for his involvement (and others were convicted) but was pardoned (along with several others) in 1992 by President George H. W. Bush.

12. While Watergate is never mentioned by name in *Captain America* #175 (when Nixon is revealed to be Number One), it is mentioned in the lead-up to the issue. In #174, it is mentioned twice—once by Number One (Nixon) when he mentions it as "fortuitous" as a means of hurting America and secondly by Moonstone, a

villain pretending to be a hero with aspirations of replacing Captain America (equating Watergate and Captain America as factors "pulling this nation apart").

13. As of these 1974's *Captain America* issues, Cap and Sharon are romantically entwined. Peggy is Sharon's older sister (later, her aunt) and Cap's 1940s love interest. Peggy, who has aged normally since the 1940s while Steve has kept his youth thanks to his decades-long artic hibernation, is revealed to have been a long-time prisoner of the villainous Doctor Faustus in 1973's #161–163 before Cap and Sharon rescue her (and subsequently keep their relationship secret as to not upset Peggy's fragile emotions as she recovers).

14. Though Rogers will not admit that the man confessing to the plot is indeed the genuine Red Skull. Rogers' unwillingness to admit this point, despite all evidence pointing to its truth, is discussed in Chapter Five.

15. This is a result of Skull accidentally inhaling his own poisoned cigarette, Skull's weapon of choice (besides hired muscle) during Gruenwald's era.

16. To provide additional context, in 1996, the earliest presidential election year following Gruenwald's time on *Captain America*, the *1996 Democratic National Platform* mentions "Freedom" 12 times, "Equality" once, "Justice" three times, and "Opportunity" 28 times (the occurrences of "Justice" and "Opportunity" as exactly the same for 1998 and 1996). *The 1996 Republican National Platform* mentions "Freedom" 27 times, "Equality" twice, "Justice" 15 times, and "Opportunity" 26 times.

Chapter Three

1. When Walker is reborn as U.S. Agent in *Captain America* #354, he is also given a new name—Jack Daniels. Both Johnny Walker and Jack Daniels are popular types of American liquor, so Gruenwald is clearly asking the reader to see additional differences between Rogers' pristine non-drinking persona and Walker's harder edge.

2. Rogers' use of the word "pal" when addressing Walker is something that surprises Walker himself.

3. When speaking to the other "Buckies," in #327, Lemar Hoskins (the future Bucky/Battlestar) warns of approaching students at the International Student House: "Here come the campus Khaddafies to admire our work" (4). While one could argue that Walker's allies are committing the hate act primarily to frame Captain America for the act, the use of a racial slur in a private moment between allies makes it obvious that these feelings are sincere.

4. Farm-Aid started in 1985 as a benefit concert for American family farms. It was organized by, among others, Willie Nelson, who is depicted as being onstage at the benefit concert in these pages.

5. The Red Skull, notably, is a shadowy version of Captain America, both similarly created to represent different nations and ideologies, Flag-Smasher, also, is a shadowy version of Cap in regard to globalism vs. patriotism/nationalism.

6. At an October 2018 rally in Houston, Trump told the crowd of supporters: "You know what I am? I'm a nationalist, O.K.? I'm a nationalist. Nationalist! Use that word! Use that word!" (qtd. in Baker).

7. Two of the most popular Marvel characters of the late 1980s were Wolverine and Punisher, two characters who romanticized violence and aggression. Creating a Captain America that operated in this capacity was clearly following contemporary trends.

8. Batroc the Leaper is a long-time nemesis of Captain America's. His role as a villain with a sense of masculine honor is discussed in Chapter Six.

9. Reader reactions to the Watchdogs varied. Reader Jeff Hilderley criticizes Gruenwald's characterization of a later use of the group in *Captain America* #398 by saying, "The pro-decency movement as defined by your writing is embodied by unremorseful renegade terrorists using high-tech equipment to trespass and vandalize at night. Not quite, Gruenwald … you have thrown together one of the worst, most unimaginative stories I've ever read." On the same letter page, Dan Jennings writes, "The Watchdogs are exactly the kind of villain Cap should be taking on. Not only are they making a mockery of traditional Christian and American values, the 'Dogs are also quite clearly a cadre of fascist stormtroopers, and fascism is what Cap was created to fight in the first place" (31).

10. A reader letter from Jeff Melton in Wilmington, NC, from *Captain America* #339 reveals animosity over Walker's characterization: "Super-Patriot is a stereotype.

In case you are unaware of this fact, not all Southerners are conservative fools who voted for Reagan. I hate writers—or those claiming to be writers—who insist upon showing Southerners as being fools who carry around their NRA membership card." Editor Ralph Macchio, after explaining that the letter was edited to remove "more abusive passages" (though thanking him for signing his inflammatory letter) explains that the depiction was meant to be "provocative" and not stereotypical (23).

11. As discussed in the Introduction, "Bucky" is a racist term, and Hoskin's codename was changed to "Battlestar" (along with a uniform change). Gruenwald was unaware of the racist connotation of the term and renamed the character (and Hoskins was advised to change the name by an older African American character).

12. This is implied early on but is not shown as often as inferred. Walker's depiction as a man who rarely shows outward emotion prevents us from seeing much of this eventually gained respect.

13. Professor Power is Anthony Power. According to Walker in #338, he "used to be some kind of high muckamuck political scientist and adviser" who tried to get the U.S. into a nuclear war" (4).

14. Additionally, both men's youth were shaped by formative wars. Rogers sees World War II as a success of global outreach since it involved diverse countries successfully stopping a threat. Walker loses his older brother in the Vietnam War, thus emphasizing the failures of international intervention, perhaps creating a mindset of isolationism.

Chapter Four

1. Unsurprisingly, there is some variance here. The 1920 date comes from *The Adventures of Captain America*, written by Fabian Nicieza in 1991 (during Gruewald's era). The MCU Captain America was born in 1918. Other versions have him born in 1922 and one has 1917 (WondyGirl). One consistency, though—when a birthday is mentioned, it is always July 4th.

2. Moore's work, including *Watchmen*, *V for Vendetta*, and *Batman: The Killing Joke*, expects much more maturity from an audience than does Gruenwald's.

3. Claremont's *Uncanny X-Men*, while narratively more complex than *Captain America*, was not necessarily aimed at an audience more mature based on the advertising content featured in both (which would have been the same).

4. Or, in the above case of Spider-Man, the character may age very slowly.

5. This is seen by his willingness to forfeit the title of Captain America in issue #332.

6. Gruenwald's interpretation of Cap abstains from alcohol, but earlier versions were less concerned. In #261 from 1981, J.M. Dematteis writes a scene in which Steve Rogers and Sam Wilson get drunk on sangria (and Rogers admits to being drunk on "only [his] third glass" (2). When Rogers and Wilson have to unexpectedly fight some criminals, Rogers thinks, "tonight's the last time I ever put so much liquor in my system!" (4). In the MCU film *Captain America: The First Avenger*, it is explained that the Super-Soldier Serum negates the effects of alcohol.

7. While the 1960s youth culture (composed of Baby Boomers) was reliant on teamwork to fulfill goals in achieving cultural change, the narrative shifts as they approach later life in the 1970s and 1980s (when the moniker "Me Generation" becomes widespread).

8. For each generational designation, there is some discrepancy as to the range of years encompassed. For example, Pew Research Center uses the years 1901–1927 as the range while Strauss and Howe designate the years 1901–1924.

9. As soon Cap leaves, a new antagonist, Blistik, the Urban Avenger, arrives to violently force the young people to turn down their music.

10. This is especially interesting considering he includes the mass-murdering terrorist Viper in the same company as his allies Silver Sable and Diamondback.

11. Considering that these moments of frustration accompany his declining health, that can also be considered.

12. When Cap is revived by the Avengers in *Avengers #4*, he wakes up still living the exact moment when he was frozen (as proven by his cry of "Bucky—Bucky! Look out!" upon awakening).

13. Though arguing that Gordon Gekko is also a madman is not a particularly difficult reach.

14. While Gruenwald updates the character for the era, the Red Skull is still more fascist than capitalist. Red Skull's adoption of the capitalist veneer is simply out of convenience for further plans of mass destruction and is not out of desire for wealth. Red Skull is a fascist and never a capitalist.

15. Gruenwald does not provide a specific birth year for Walker and he was too young to participate in the Vietnam War, but he is old enough when his brother dies to know that he was not born after 1965 and thus be a member of Generation X. He might be a young Boomer, but as of his introduction and subsequent appearances in Gruenwald's *Captain America*, he qualifies as a Boomer.

16. These distinctions are challenging because of the use of a floating timeline. By 1995 (at the end of Gruenwald's tenure), Falcon and Diamondback, for instance, would technically be Gen X, but earlier they are not. Even if they are not Boomers by the closing years of Gruenwald's tenure, the obvious youth and enthusiasm of a Gen-X character (like Free Spirit) contrasts with the world-weariness of Falcon and Diamondback.

17. The slacker label was not new to Gen X (younger generations being looked down upon for their laziness and strangeness is nothing new), but Gen X took ownership in a way that is more unique (seen in media and characters that the generation was drawn to such as *Heathers*, *Benny and Joon*, and *Reality Bites*, among others).

18. Superia is a genius-level supervillain who Gruenwald first introduces in *Captain American* #390 during "The Superia Stratagem," a six-part storyline in which Superia leads an army of women in an attempt to take over the world.

19. Much like the Red Skull takes on the guise of a 1980s business professional to push his fascist agenda, Zemo is using the current political rhetoric of the time to do the same. Zemo is a fascist, not a capitalist (and certainly not a representative of any American political party), but Zemo uses this language to mock American political rhetoric.

20. "Stars and Stripes" is the name of the group that Cap helped organized to help him answer calls for help that were made to his national hotline.

Chapter Five

1. Roy Thomas is a comics legend and former editor-in-chief at Marvel Comics who had, prior to this particular issue, written issues #215 and #217 of *Captain America* and served as editor for issues #215–220 (in 1977–1978).

2. For example, there is a brief reference in #320 when Cap says that a massacre of supervillains is like nothing he's seen "since the war," (8) emphasizing the gravity of the massacre. So, when Gruenwald does reference World War II, it is often to give context to something that Cap is experiencing in the moment.

3. Gruenwald was obviously involved with the comic at the time. He does write one of the back-up stories for the issue thus showing his involvement with both the character and the monthly comic at this point. This annual came out in 1991 and that fits directly into Gruenwald's tenure.

4. "The Sleeper" was the name of five destructive robots created and used by the Red Skull. These menaces are always stopped by Cap and his allies, culminating with the Fifth Sleeper's defeat in the Gary Friedrich-written *Captain America* #148. Gruenwald incorporates the Sleeper into his rogue's gallery when Machinesmith, a villainous master of robotics, uses the Fourth Sleeper as part of Red Skull's team of villains known as the Skeleton Crew (*Captain America* #368).

5. Additionally, Baby Boomers were the generation most impacted by the Vietnam War and members of that generation were leading this creative charge as a way to reflect upon the impact of that conflict and era.

6. Though both in Gruenwald's era and in previous eras, the Red Skull is often depicted as a behind-the-scenes deus ex machina villain when a secret mastermind is present (as seen in Gary Friedrich's #143 from 1971 when the Red Skull is revealed as the secret mastermind behind a movement to create race divisions and in Gruenwald's #350 (and beyond) when Red Skull is revealed to be behind virtually everything menacing Cap over the previous 40 issues.

7. Cap's pre-Gruenwald encounters with the Red Skull often have that sense of a continuation of the war. While Gruenwald writes Red Skull as a fascist and racist madman, his Red Skull is wise enough

to hide those tendencies in public. In earlier incarnations, he is unable to push down these deplorable qualities. In *Captain America* #185, Red Skull is unable to properly enjoy a victory over Captain America and his allies because of something he "cannot chase..from [his] mind"—Gabe Jones (an African-American S.H.I.E.L.D. officer) in a romantic relationship "with this white woman [Peggy Carter]!" Skull is so outraged by this that he changes his thus far successful plans to "crush these two 'lovers'" (5).

8. Skull-House is the location of the Red Skull's apparent death in #300. Captain America subsequently monitors the house closely after issue #300.

9. While *Captain America* would typically come out once monthly during this era, the number of issues per year is skewed higher here because a handful of issues during this timeframe were released twice monthly.

10. Viper is clearly the most "evil" of these non-Red Skull enemies and, accordingly, one that does indeed ally herself with the Red Skull.

11. The Red Skull is in this physically and mentally compromised state because of his time with minimal water and no food in an isolated underground bunker courtesy of Magneto (which begins in *Captain America* #367).

12. Diamondback, in this exchange, theorizes to Cap that he is leading them away from Skull-House and that he is leaving because he was waiting for more evidence and could conceivably "come back any time." Cap ignores her at first before solemnly admitting that indeed the Red Skull they have encountered is the genuine Red Skull.

13. Bucky's return as the Winter Soldier takes place in Brubaker's *Captain America, Vol. 5* that runs from 2005 to 2009.

14. This storyline was an "open crossover" in which a reader did not need to read every single comic in the cross-over to follow the story. While the "Acts of Vengeance" storyline aspects most relevant in *Captain America* deal with Magneto vs. Red Skull, other comics in the series featured such unusual match-ups as Daredevil vs. Ultron (in *Daredevil* #275 and #276) and Thor vs. Juggernaut (*Thor* #411 and #412).

15. Red Skull specifically references the time Magneto killed "hundreds of men by sinking a submarine a few years back" (6), a callback to *X-Men* #150, in which Magneto sinks a nuclear Soviet sub.

16. *Captain America* #369 does feature a battle between Cap and a Magneto robot created by Machinesmith in a failed attempt to potentially lure Magneto out in the open so Red Skull's remaining allies can apprehend him and learn of the Red Skull's whereabouts. So even though Magneto is not literally in the flesh in the comic after he fights Red Skull, his impact remains.

17. "Streets of Poison" is a multipart story that runs in *Captain America* #372–378 in which Cap fights back against the influence of dangerous narcotics being distributed in New York.

Chapter Six

1. Often Red Skull will shout vague declarations of purpose, but they are not necessarily about furthering any specific philosophies as much as words demonstrating his general villainy. In issue #101, he shouts, "Where Hitler failed—we shall succeed!" and, when speaking of his allies The Exiles, he states, "they are fearless fanatical fighting machines—ready to die for tyranny!"(4).

2. In issue #397, Viper asks the Red Skull if he is bothered that Blackwing and Jack O'Lantern got away after trying to rob him, and Skull compliments their "viciousness" and then decides to hire them in his own employ (4).

3. Something alluded to both by their intimacy and implied sexual relationship and the innuendo inherent within their dialogue exchanges. After Skull reveals his desire to endure pain in issue #397, Viper (looking away from him) says, "This is a side of you I did not suspect, Skull. Tell me more" (12).

4. This short B-story in #398 follows Mother Night, a Red Skull ally who is deeply in love with him. In the story, she confesses to Skull that she was found by Captain America (who therefore knows that she and Skull are alive, despite what was previously thought). To punish her, Skull beats her mercilessly while she begs him to beat her further. This shows the inherent sadism working its way through Red Skull and each of his allies.

5. Oddly, the last flag in the sequence seems to be a variation of Japan's "Rising Sun" battle flag.

6. Again, this stands in contrast to every depiction of the Red Skull, who always knows he is representing evil.

7. This issue, from 1985, comes during the Cold War and, while America could be seen by some as a country emphasizing diplomacy, others would look at American aggression as being used more often to deal with other nations. In addition, some nations like the Soviet Union and China could easily be seen as speaking that "universal language of violence" more than diplomacy.

8. In the Roger Stern–written issue #250 from 1980, Cap contemplates running for president. In the issue's opening scene, the narration elevates Cap from man to myth: "teeth gritted in determination, this living legend speaks not a word … launching himself forward with a speed that causes the room's occupants to gasp in awe and wonder!" (2). As in #312, this description emphasizes the awe-inspiring effects Captain America has on the public.

9. In a letter published in issue #318's letter page, Norman Breyfogle writes, "Cap's final speech was insightful, but I doubt everyone was listening to him, either!" (24). Ultimately, the crowd was interested in spectacle more than rhetoric.

10. This includes the storyline from issues #321–322 in which Cap is forced to kill one of Flag-Smasher's minions with a gun in order to protect a group of hostages.

11. When Walker arrives, Flag-Smasher presents a blend of pleasantries and threats, as if performing a dance the two had often performed. Upon sight of Captain America, Flag-Smasher says, "Captain! Good to see you again!" It is difficult not to read the remark with sarcasm after he adds, "Now drop your weapon or I will use this sniveling scientist's brains for paint!" He says this because he knows what Steve Rogers' next move would be—diplomacy. When Walker simply says, "no," Flag-Smasher is at a loss (16).

12. Battle Star, who is serving as backup for Walker outside the science facility in which the fight is taking place, even gets a chain-thought bubble during a brief look-in during the battle (22).

13. In issue #404's letter page, reader Chris Cerza asks if Red Skull is falling in love with Viper. Editor Ralph Macchio humorously responds, "You ask him—we're too afraid" (25). Skull seems a figure too filled with hate to feel what another person would call love.

14. This group is known collectively as Batroc's Brigade.

Chapter Seven

1. Again, the underlying requirement for entry into the group is that all members must be criminals and have snake-related names and abilities.

2. Reagan himself served as leader of the Screen Actors Guild and, in 2017, was inducted into the Labor Department's Hall of Honor. American Federation of Government Employees Local 12 President Alex Bastani wrote to the Labor Secretary expressing "shock and disappointment" over the decision (Davidson)

3. This long-term shift in public opinion was not just politically influenced. Negative and violent media depictions of unions have been prevalent in film for years. An article from 1981 by Ken Margolies entitled "Silver Screen Tarnishes Unions" starts by discussing the negative portrait of a union leader in *On the Waterfront* and walking through the history of the negative depictions back to the beginnings of film.

4. Those in attendance for the first meeting of the Serpent Society in #310 are Sidewinder (who identifies as the "host"), Constrictor, Black Mamba, Death Adder, Princess Python, Cottonmouth, Diamondback, Bushmaster, Cobra, Asp, Rattler, and Anaconda (8–9).

5. The AFL-CIO is the American Federation of Labor and Congress of Industrial Organizations. At the time of this issue in 1985, virtually all unionized laborers in the country were represented by the AFL-CIO.

6. This does not mean that Gruenwald's portrayal of labor unions is negative—it merely represents the effort he is taking to represent a ton of labor aspects within the membership of Serpent Society. Anaconda represents that stereotypical brutality, while some of the other members recoil at the thought of using violence in this fashion.

7. Constrictor's rejection of

Sidewinder's invitation is an example of an individual who is not convinced of a union's offer.

8. Black Mamba is also shown to be in a romantic relationship with Sidewinder, thus showing potential biases toward Sidewinder but also reflecting her genuine affection. In issue #341, Viper knocks out Black Mamba while she is getting ready for a romantic interlude with Sidewinder and takes her clothes (a revealing maid's outfit) to secretly infiltrate Sidewinder's living quarters (21). Before Sidewinder realizes it is Viper (and not Black Mamba), he affectionately calls her "darling." This romantic interaction stands in clear contrast between the sadistic pain-based relationship between Viper and Red Skull as seen in issues #395–397.

9. Cap takes Sidewinder's actions personally, but his actions to apprehend Sidewinder lack the urgency he possesses when pursuing Viper. In issue #315, Cap is talking to three apprehended members of the Society when Sidewinder teleports in to ensure their escape. After Sidewinder has disappeared, Cap says, "I promise you this—one day I'm going to get you!" (23). He is focused on Sidewinder's apprehension, but he still says "one day" for the time of Sidewinder's capture (rather than something more immediate).

Chapter Eight

1. While these particular works helped create more mainstream credibility for comics, there were efforts in the decades prior by universities and professors to use comic books academically. One professor was using copies of *Fantastic Four* #46 in an English class in 1966, and the first college class entirely dedicated to comics was taught in 1972 at Indiana University (Letizia).

2. According to reviewer Andrew Asberry, Azrael "was a real head-case that was far too brutal with Gotham's criminals." Despite how well Azrael represents some of the aggressive superhero trends of the time, he in not, as Asberry points out, fondly remembered. He describes him as a character "who most folks don't like."

3. In fact, Waid's term on *Captain America* immediately follows Gruenwald's. In addition to his many runs as writer

for many characters and comics, perhaps Waid's most definitive tenure was an eight-year run on *The Flash*.

4. The death of John Walker's parents in issue #345 and the massacre of multiple supervillains in #319 come immediately to mind.

5. As discussed by Gabilliet, the trading card industry was also facing a speculative bubble. Marvel's acquisition of Skybox (along with a prior acquisition of Fleer) gave them a once-promising card company that was facing the same bleak future as Marvel itself. Marvel bought Fleer in 1991 and Skybox in 1995 for a combined $490. In 1999, they sold both for $30 million.

6. Rob Liefield's run on *Captain America*, Vol. 2 was widely panned. It was one of several post-"Onslaught" titles under the "Heroes Reborn" banner (Onslaught was a 1996 crossover event that left Captain America, the Avengers, and Fantastic Four "dead" and eventually "reborn") and, according to JPRoscoe, *Captain America* "was the weakest of the lot." A reviewer on Goodreads named Todd described the twelve issues as "so terrible," while Jdetrick called Liefeld's work "ugly and disjointed."

7. This trend would eventually be upended. By 2006, *Civil War*, in which Cap and Iron Man do battle, Avengers comics would take up all of the top five spots on this list, and Ed Brubaker's *Captain America* #25 would be the top-selling comic of 2007.

8. Wolverine appears in 1992's storyline "Man and Wolf," which runs through *Captain America* #402–407. In it, Gruenwald makes Wolverine a mind-controlled minion for the main antagonist, forcing him into battle with Cap. Doing so negates Wolverine's antihero popularity. In these issues (until his inevitable recovery), Wolverine is not the charismatic and mysterious violent hero and is instead an obstacle for Cap to fight (though Wolverine's very popular visage gets to appear on the cover to potentially increase sales). Gruenwald refuses to let this more popular character outshine Cap.

9. Gabilliet places a significant amount of blame for the inflation of the speculative bubble that nearly ended the industry on *Wizard*: the magazine's emphasis on potential profit from comics "transformed readers into speculators by hammering them

with the idea that the market for new comics was an untapped source of speculative profits" (149).

10. Cap, not typically thought of in the same aggressive vein, is depicted on the cover of this celebratory issue in a montage with the other featured characters. Uncharacteristically (and certainly not something we see often during Gruenwald's era), Cap is drawn with a very aggressive scream, tying him into the aggression celebrated with their top pick and elsewhere.

11. While his job as comics writer is one that requires some insertion of violent circumstances, it is typically neither exploitive nor particularly graphic (though exceptions, like the Scourge storyline, do exist).

12. As discussed in detail in Chapter Five, Cap would have a history of violence during World War II, but Gruenwald is mostly unwilling to make Cap address those experiences, thus allowing Cap to fixate on his rare contemporary acts of violence without getting bogged down in his WWII experiences. By avoiding WWII completely in this storyline in which he guns down the U.L.T.I.M.A.T.U.M. agent, he allows the focus to remain on that situation without diluting it with stories (however potentially relevant) from Cap's distant past. In addition, on the letters page of issue #327, editor Don Daley addresses a reader comment that Cap would have carried guns and fought enemies with the intent to kill: "Neither Cap nor [his allies] the Invaders ever carried guns behind enemy lines during the War. They were never actively engaged in combat with the Axis *militia* but concentrated their efforts against Nazi super-agents and their leaders. All this is to say that Captain America never sought to kill anyone on the battlefield. It probably happened that soldiers who shot at Cap were hit by their own ricocheting bullets, but that's not the same as Cap shooting someone" (24).

13. Though, obviously, Captain America is synonymous with the "Avengers," a team name notably connected to "vengeance." In the first *Avengers* comic from 1963, when the group is deciding upon a name, Wasp offers "Avengers" because the name "should be something colorful and dramatic" (23), thus feeling like the name is less about its meaning and more about "dramatic" branding. This is not to say all individual

Avengers are against "vengeance." In the same issue, Thor tells Loki: "You have committed some foul deed, knowing I would come to avenge it! And avenge it I shall!!" (17).

14. This is the same Scourge, ostensibly, as the one inflicting similar murders in other titles during this period, or at the very least, this Scourge is operating under the same modus operandi as the other Scourges since there is no way to identify who is actually playing the part at a given time.

15. The *U.S. Agent* miniseries is from 1993 and the issue of *Captain America* in which Scourge is revealed to be in Red Skull's employ (*Captain America* #394) is from 1991. Either the Angel is completely lying to cover up the Skull's involvement, Gruenwald devised the 1993 story as a retcon for the 1991 story, or (most likely), the Skull employed copycat Scourges in order to control the operation, while the Angels operation was still functioning.

16. The Scourge storyline is defined by Cap working to save the lives of super-villains. While villains die (including MODOK in *Captain America* #313, among others), only in #321 does he kill an enemy (an U.L.T.I.M.A.T.U.M. terrorist) to protect innocent lives. The act tortures Cap for many subsequent issues.

17. Richards argues: "This self-control is Batman's superpower."

18. Indeed, the villains are so inconsequential, the act of Scourge's mass murder could be discounted. In the letters page of issue #325, reader Paul Carbonaro writes, "The menace of Scourge really *is* more of a joke on your part than serious dramatic action ... Killing off eighteen characters in one panel is nothing short of laughable and obviously of no real importance in the Marvel Universe (24). In response to the letter, editor Don Daley wrote that Carbonaro's opinion was not shared by the majority of letter writers.

19. He first appeared in *Spider-Woman* #33 in 1980.

20. This is a sentiment shared by Punisher.

21. This is before Cap and Diamondback operate as partners and become romantically involved. At this point, she is merely a villainous member of the Serpent Society.

22. Cap goes undercover as a police

officer in the Stan Lee written *Captain America* #139 from 1971 and apparently stays on the force (though it is not a constant factor in the comics) until #180 in 1974.

23. While Cap's enemies are typically of the super-powered variety, Cap still does not believe in lethal means of apprehension. In the case of the Red Skull, a villain whose death would leave the world a much safer place, Cap knows the futility of attempting to kill him anyway. In *Captain America* #394, Cap finds Red Skull (and his Wrecking Crew associates) all murdered. Cap, however, does not believe them to be dead. Cap thinks, "This looks way too contrived. I've seen the Skull get out of better deaths than this" (10). Of course, Cap is right.

24. Which is a concern for Batman in the above-discussed dilemma of whether Batman should kill Joker.

25. Bloodstain pretends to be the long-deceased brother of John Walker/Jack Daniels in an attempt to pull Walker into the Scourge operation.

26. This technique of speech bubbles also indicates to a reader that Americop has a robotic voice that would help conceal his normal voice.

27. Both Captain America and Zach Moonhunter, Cap's pilot/driver, maintain the charade to infiltrate the New York drug scene.

28. Whereas, in the *U.S.Agent* limited series referenced above, U.S.Agent is temporarily fooled into thinking that the Scourge program is government-sanctioned, and he does indeed entertain the idea of becoming a Scourge.

Chapter Nine

1. In 1991, Marvel Comics (and the Federal Bureau of Investigations) published two issues of *Captain America Goes to War Against Drugs*, giveaway comics aimed toward preventing childhood drug use.

2. Jack Monroe/Nomad has a convoluted history, debuting as "Bucky" as a sidekick for the deranged 1950s Captain America (a man so obsessed with Captain America he had plastic surgery to look like Steve Rogers and changed his name to Steve Rogers). In writer Steve Englehart's *Captain*

America #155, it is revealed Jack Monroe/ Bucky and 1950s Captain America injected themselves with a Super Soldier Serum created from a formula found in Nazi file. Without completing the rest of the process as did Rogers in the 1940s (including exposure to Vita-rays), the Serum leaves both men mentally unstable.

3. Sharon Ventura is introduced as a friend of the Thing who undergoes the Power Broker's augmentation process to gain great strength. She becomes Ms. Marvel at one point and, later, mutates in the same fashion as The Thing, becoming known as She-Thing.

4. The Thing/Ben Grimm is a founding member of the Fantastic Four. He is defined by his immense strength and rocky orange exterior. During this particular era, Thing has left the Fantastic Four to figure out his life on his own, traveling the country and going on adventures (including becoming a professional wrestler)

5. In *Captain America* #155, written by Steve Englehart, it is revealed that two people injected themselves with a version of the Super Soldier Serum in order to turn themselves into the 1950s versions of Captain America and Bucky. While the original telling of Steve Rogers/Captain America depicts injections as the sole means of becoming Captain America, that is retconned over time by adding Vita-rays to the process. The 1950s Captain America and Bucky go insane because they only got the injection and not the Vita-rays.

6. In all versions of Captain America's origin story, Dr. Erskine (originally known as Dr. Reinstein) is shot and killed. He is the only one who knows the formula for the Super Soldier Serum, so the prospect of more Super Soldiers dies with him. While the scientific aspects of Cap's origin go according to plan, obviously the entire episode does not go as expected.

7. Though likely Cap would not cast anyone aside, especially a friend.

8. Although, admittedly, this would shift Cap's focus on external threats to a very internal threat (his very body). That would have been a much different struggle than what was focused upon by previous *Captain America* writers. This storyline inches us toward the idea of Cap either reconsidering or outright battling his body and the processes that give him his physical abilities—a concept that culminates for

Gruenwald in the "Fighting Chance" storyline that begins his concluding run on the comic.

9. There are very few operations presented over the course of Gruenwald's time on the comic that either the Red Skull or one of his allies are not secretly (or overtly) directing.

10. Cap and his superpowered allies would have been most directly pitted in battle against their superpowered Axis equivalents, not fighting in the metaphorical trenches.

11. In *Avengers* #4, Stan Lee writes that Cap had fallen from a drone plane into the North Atlantic Ocean where he became frozen in a block of ice. He remained frozen in that ice for decades because eventually returning to society and joining the Avengers.

12. Diamondback is a former criminal, after all.

13. The trope of heroes turning villain (typically on a temporary basis) is an incredibly common one. Examples include Green Lantern Hal Jordan becoming the evil Parallax in 1994's *Green Lantern* #50 and the Fantastic Four's Sue Storms' transformation in Malice, Mistress of Hate in 1985's *Fantastic Four* #280 and #281. Both of these examples occur during Gruenwald's term.

14. The reader is made aware of the dream motif because of an unnatural yellow coloring and the wavy lines that form the panel boxes.

15. In *Captain America* #355, Cap is purposefully transformed into a teenager by the magical Sersei in order to investigate a rash of disappearing teenagers.

16. Cap is turned into a werewolf by Nightshade during the "Man and Wolf" storyline from *Captain America* issues #402–407.

Chapter Ten

1. Gruenwald's last issue on *Captain America* is #443.

2. The departed ally is Diamondback. She leaves Cap's side to work with the villain Superia in exchange for Superia's efforts to find a cure for Cap's condition.

3. Stankowitz is Cap's resident inventor. His battle-vest creation, laden with prominent shoulder accessories and

pouches, is very representative of 1990s superhero fashion.

4. Jesse Black Crow is a Navajo mystic who, among other abilities, receives occasional prophetic visions. In this situation, he describes his vision as a "dark vision" (3).

5. This is the second Super-Patriot, not to be confused with John Walker, the original Super-Patriot, who later became Steve Roger's replacement as Captain America and, still later, U.S. Agent.

6. The reader is not privy to the information that this is a training simulator (with robots serving as adversaries). That way, the reader does not realize that Cap is in no danger, despite his internal concerns about his physical condition.

7. Dr. Keith Kincaid was the official Avengers doctor at the time

8. The conclusion of the "Streets of Poison" storyline (*Captain America* #372–378) introduces this concept by removing the serum from Cap completely. There are countless examples of this trope, but a compelling one is a two-part story from issues #355 and 356 in which Cap has himself transformed into a non-powered teenager in order to investigate teen disappearances. Teen Cap manages to elude his enemies through wits and cunning, but he is ultimately on the brink of defeat when he transforms back into his adult self. This is an example of how the brains and the brawn coexist (but the character and heart of the character matter more because that was what gave Cap time to survive against overwhelming odds to have survived at all).

9. In the same interview, Gruenwald states, "It was only Steve Rogers, by strength of his personality and strength of his beliefs and his ideals that managed to take the Super-Soldier Serum and do something great with it and that is come up with the Captain America concept and really embody the ideals which he believes America stands for." Rogers is not the only recipient of the Serum, but he is the only one of the people who received the treatment to earn the right to be Captain America long-term.

10. He tells his partner Super-Patriot in issue #426 that the first body he ever imitated was his cat, Demelza. In #439, he describes touching his dead father and suddenly becoming "transformed into the exact likeness of [his] old man" (16).

11. This Super-Patriot is Mike Farrell,

an old college friend of Cap's former fiancée Bernie Rosenthal, who blames Cap for his life's problems.

12. After defeating him in #442, Cap explains Elker's motivation to Vormund (the former Hauptmann Deutschland): "Apparently he believed that the existence of superhumans somehow made a mockery of the achievements of the ordinary man. He wouldn't have been satisfied until he eliminated us all" (23).

13. The Resistants debuted in *Captain America* #343. In that issue, they also battled a Captain America who was not Steve Rogers.

14. Quicksilver does immediately arrive to help, but he expresses uncertainty as to whether or not he can at first and then, albeit in his own head, questions Cap's strength. While some Avengers would never hesitate at or question Cap's requests, Quicksilver is certainly among the most cantankerous of Cap's allies.

15. Avoiding this problem, when Cap's body does suffer complete paralysis in issue #436, Gruenwald makes it as isolated an event as possible, sticking Cap alone (with King Cobra and Mr. Hyde) in the Arizona desert.

16. When Cap gets the message about Zemo, he indicates that Vision is the one who has discovered the information, so the Avengers are obviously aware of this situation.

17. King Cobra vows that he and Hyde will kill Cap: "This is the end of the road! I swear to you you're not going to leave this desert alive!" (5). Does King Cobra actually believe he is capable of committing this act of murder? What matters is that he seems to think he can (and Cap is vulnerable enough to possibly allow it to happen).

18. While this is not always the case, Dave Hoover's art on the cover of #436

also properly represents content from the story itself (Cap does indeed lie prone in the desert when he is confronted by a rattlesnake).

19. If the Punisher character feels like a catalyst for Captain America fans, that is by design. As Cord says in his essay "The Alpha and the Omega: Captain America and the Punisher," "The character of the Punisher represents the antithesis of Captain America (Cap), but at the same time represents a darker part of the American psyche. He is the one willing to do anything necessary to rid the world of truly bad people" (125–126). The Punisher is presented by these readers as their worst-case scenario replacement because he is designed to represent things that Cap does not. Accordingly, the idea of him as a Cap replacement is a complete rejection of what Steve Rogers represents.

20. In the immediate future after "Fighting Chance" and Gruenwald's tenure, these worries were unfounded. Mark Waid took over the title on issue #444 and retained Steve Rogers as Captain America.

21. Based on his stories, Gruenwald himself seems innately aware of this. When Gruenwald did write a storyline in which Rogers was removed as Captain America (starting with Rogers' resignation in #332 and John Walker's subsequent appointment as the new Captain America in #333), Rogers stayed a constant presence in the title.

22. The two-part adventure in which Cap is transformed into a teenager (#355–356) has similar parallels. In both, a physically compromised Cap is forced to logically adapt to his new circumstance.

23. Eventually, that writer would turn out to be Ed Brubaker in 2007. Steve Rogers is assassinated in *Captain America* (volume 5) #25.

Works Cited

Abramson, Alexis. "Ten Important Baby Boomer Characteristic and Statistics." *Dr. Alexis*, 3 July 2018. https://www.alexisabramson.com/baby-boomers-characteristics-statistics/.

"Adventures of *Superman* 500." *My Comic Shop.com*. https://www.mycomicshop.com/search?q=adventures+of+superman+#500&pubid=&PubRng=.

Allen, Jesse. "Marvel Comics and New York Stories: Anti-Heroes and Street Level Vigilantes Daredevil and The Punisher" (2014). *CUNY Academic Works*, Oct. 2014. https://academicworks.cuny.edu/cgi/viewcontent.cgi?article=1401&context=gc_etds.

"American Plan." *Encyclopedia of Chicago*. 2004. http://www.encyclopedia.chicagohistory.org/pages/43.html.

"Androgenic Steroids." *LiverTox: Clinical and Research Information on Drug-Induced Liver Injury*, National Institutes of Health, U.S. Department of Health and Human Services, 10 Apr. 2014. https://www.ncbi.nlm.nih.gov/books/NBK548931/.

"Are You an American or a Democrat?" *Reddit*. 13 Nov. 2018. https://www.reddit.com/r/forwardsfromgrandma/comments/9wxd0d/grams_said_pick_one/.

Arnold, Mary Louise. "Stage, Sequence, and Sequels: Changing Conceptions of Morality, Post-Kohlberg." *Educational Psychology Review*, vol. 12, no. 4, Dec. 2000, Vol. 12, Issue 4, p 365–383.

Asberry, Andrew, et al. "Batman: Knightfall Vol. 2 Review." *Batman News*, 19 Aug. 2012. batman-news.com/2012/08/19/batman-knightfall-vol-2-review/.

Audi, Robert. "Nationalism, Patriotism, and Cosmopolitanism in an Age of Globalization." *Journal of Ethics*, vol. 13, no. 4, Oct. 2009, 365–381. EBSCOhost, doi:10.1007/s10892-009-9068-9.

Baker, Kevin. *America: The Story of Us*. A&E Television Network. 2010.

Baker, Peter. "'Use That Word!': Trump Embraces the 'Nationalist' Label." *New York Times*, New York Times, 23 Oct. 2018. www.nytimes.com/2018/10/23/us/politics/nationalist-president-trump.html.

Barnes, Collin D., et al. "Don't Tread on Me: Masculine Honor Ideology in the U.S. and Militant Responses to Terrorism." *Personality and Social Psychology Bulletin*. Vol. 38, No. 8, 1018–1029. 2012. DOI: 10.1177/0146167212443383.

Baseball Reference. Sports Reference, LLC. 2000–2019. https://www.baseball-reference.com.

Bellotto, Adam. "74 Years of Captain America: A History of Marvel's America-iest Superhero." *Film School Rejects*, 1 Apr. 2014. https://filmschoolrejects.com/74-years-of-captain-america-a-history-of-marvels-america-iest-superhero-9ed077efb670/.

Bennett, David H. *The Party of Fear*. Chapel Hill: University of North Carolina Press, 1988.

Bishop, Greg. "After Drug Revelations, Redefining '98 Home Run Chase." *New York Times*, New York Times, 4 July 2009. https://www.nytimes.com/2009/07/05/sports/baseball/05homers.html.

Bondurant, Tom. "Hard-Traveled Tales: Is Green Lantern/Green Arrow Still Relevant?" *CBR*, CBR, 8 Apr. 2017. https://www.cbr.com/green-lantern-green-arrow-still-relevant.

Brockell, Gillian. "The Statue of Liberty was Created to Celebrate Freed Slaves, Not Immigrants, Its New Museum Recounts." *The Washington Post*, 23 May 2019. https://www.washingtonpost.com/history/2019/05/23/statue-liberty-was-created-celebrate-freed-slaves-not-immigrants/.

Brown, Nina W., *Children of the Self-Absorbed*. New Harbinger Publications, 2001.

Brown, Richard Maxwell. *Strain of Violence*. Oxford University Press, 1975.

Browne, Gordon. "Time to Stake out a Middle Ground in the Drug War." *Alcoholism & Drug Abuse Weekly*, vol. 8, no. 46, Nov. 1996, 5. EBSCOhost, search.ebscohost.com/login.aspx?direct=true&db=asn&AN=9612050677&site=eds-live.

Byrne, John. "Tell Them All They Love Must Die." *Fantastic Four*, vol. 1, no. 280, Marvel Comics, July 1985, *Marvel Unlimited*. https://read.marvel.com/#/book/5922.

_____. "With Malice Towards All!" *Fantastic Four*, vol. 1, no. 281, Marvel Comics, Aug. 1985, *Marvel Unlimited*. https://read.marvel.com/#/book/5923.

Carlin, Mike, writer. "Power Play!" *The Thing*, vol. 1, no. 35, Marvel Comics, May 1986.

Chichester, D.G. "Call of Duty." *Captain American Annual*, Vol. 1., No. 10, Marvel Comics, 1991, *Marvel Unlimited*. https://read.marvel.com/#/book/38900.

Claremont, Chris. "I, Magneto…" *Uncanny X-Men*, vol. 1, no. 250, Marvel Comics, Oct. 1981, *Marvel Unlimited*. https://read.marvel.com/#/book/25962.

Clymer, Adam. "A Poll Finds 77% in U.S. Approve Raid on Libya." *New York Times*, 17 Apr. 1986. https://www.nytimes.com/1986/04/17/world/tension-libya-polling-american-public-poll-finds-77-us-approve-raid-libya.html.

"Commando." *IMDb*, 4 Oct. 1985. https://www.imdb.com/title/tt0088944/.

Conway, Gerry. "Panic on Park Avenue." *Captain America*, vol. 1, no. 151, Marvel Comics, July 1972, *Marvel Unlimited*. https://read.marvel.com/#/book/22223.

Crowley, Michael, and Hector Florin. "The New Generation Gap." *TIME Magazine*, vol. 178, no. 19, Nov. 2011, 36–40. EBSCOhost, search.ebscohost.com/login.aspx?direct=true&db=asn&AN=67102877&site=ehost-live.

Cunningham, Phillip L. "Stevie's Got a Gun: Captain America and his Problematic Use of Lethal Force." *Captain America and the Struggle of the Superhero*. Edited by Robert G. Weiner. Jefferson, NC: McFarland, 2009.

David, Ariel. "Stan Lee May Be Gone, but His Super-Jewy Superheroes Live On." *Haaretz*, Haaretz.com, 13 Nov. 2018. https://www.haaretz.com/us-news/.premium-stan-lee-may-be-gone-but-his-super-jewy-superheroes-live-on-1.6652039.

Davidson, Joe. "Perspective | Induction of Union-Busting Reagan into Labor's Hall of Honor Shocks Union." *The Washington Post*, 19 Sept. 2017. www.washingtonpost.com/news/powerpost/wp/2017/09/19/induction-of-union-busting-reagan-into-labors-hall-of-honor-shocks-union/.

Dean, Charles. "16 Superhero Trends from the 90s That are TOTALLY Unacceptable Today." *CBR*, CBR, 19 Oct. 2017. https://www.cbr.com/ridiculous-90s-comic-book-trends/.

DeFalco, Tom. "The Gentleman's Name is Juggernaut!" *Thor*, vol. 1, no. 411, Marvel Comics, Dec. 1989, *Marvel Unlimited*. https://read.marvel.com/#/book/21596.

_____. "The New Warriors!" *Thor*, vol. 1, no. 412, Marvel Comics, Jan. 1990, *Marvel Unlimited*. https://read.marvel.com/#/book/21599.

DeMatteis, J.M. "Celluloid Heroes." *Captain America*, vol. 1, no. 261, Marvel Comics, Sept. 1981, *Marvel Unlimited*. https://read.marvel.com/#/book/22843.

_____. "Yesterday's Villain!" *Spider-Woman*, vol. 1, no. 33, Marvel Comics, Dec. 1980.

DeMatteis, J.M., and Michael Ellis. "Das Ende!" *Captain America*, Vol. 1, No. 300, Marvel Comics, Dec. 1984. *Marvel Unlimited*. https://read.marvel.com/#/book/29613.

Dillon, Wilton S., and Neil G. Kotler, eds. *"The Statue of Liberty Revisited*. Smithsonian Institute, 1994.

Dray, Phillip. *There is Power in a Union*. New York: Doubleday, 2010.

Drier, Peter, and Dick Flacks. "Patriotism and Progressivism." *Peace Review*, vol. 15, no. 4, Dec. 2003, 397–404. EBSCOhost, doi:10.1080/1040265032000156816.

Eagan, Kevin. "Comics for Academics: How Critics Approach the Language of Comics." *Medium*, Critical Margins, 27 June 2017. criticalmargins.com/comics-for-academics-how-critics-approach-the-language-of-comics-c3f19f6a24a5.

Englehart, Steve, writer. "Before the Dawn!" *Captain America*, vol. 1, no. 175, Marvel Comics, July 1974. *Marvel Unlimited*. https://read.marvel.com/#/book/5370.

_____. "Beware of Serpents." *Captain America*, vol. 1, no. 163, Marvel Comics, July 1973, *Marvel Unlimited*. https://read.marvel.com/#/book/22242.

_____. "Captain America Must Die!" *Captain America*, vol. 1, no. 176, Marvel Comics, Aug. 1974. *Marvel Unlimited*. https://read.marvel.com/#/book/5371.

_____. "The Coming of the Nomad." *Captain America*, vol. 1, no. 180, Marvel Comics, Dec. 1974. *Marvel Unlimited*. https://read.marvel.com/#/book/5377.

_____. "If he Loseth his Soul!" *Captain America*, vol. 1, no. 161, Marvel Comics, May 1973. *Marvel Unlimited*. https://read.marvel.com/#/book/23129.

_____. "The Incredible Origin of the Other Captain America!" *Captain America*, vol. 1, no. 155, Marvel Comics, Nov. 1972. *Marvel Unlimited*. https://read.marvel.com/#/book/23129.

_____. "It's Always Darkest." *Captain America*, vol. 1, no. 174, Marvel Comics, June 1974. *Marvel Unlimited*. https://read.marvel.com/#/book/5369.

_____. "Nomad—No More!" *Captain America*, vol. 1, no. 183, Marvel Comics, Mar. 1975. *Marvel Unlimited*. https://read.marvel.com/#/book/5380.

_____. "Scream the Scarlet Skull." *Captain America*, vol. 1, no. 185, Marvel Comics, May 1975. *Marvel Unlimited*. https://read.marvel.com/#/book/5382.

_____. "This Way Lies Madness!" *Captain America*, vol. 1, no. 162, Marvel Comics, June 1973. *Marvel Unlimited*. https://read.marvel.com/#/book/22241.

Favreau, Jon, dir. *Iron Man*. Marvel Studios, 2008.

Fiala, Andrew. "Anarchism." *Stanford Encyclopedia of Philosophy*, Stanford University, 3 Nov. 2017. https://plato.stanford.edu/entries/anarchism/.

Fish, Mike. "Lex Luger's Confessions of a Drug-Abuse Survivor." *ESPN*, ESPN Internet Ventures, 13 Sept. 2007. https://www.espn.com/espn/news/story?id=3016179.

Flynn, Thomas. "Jean-Paul Sartre." *Stanford Encyclopedia of Philosophy*, Stanford University, 5 Dec. 2011. https://plato.stanford.edu/entries/sartre/.

Foer, Lois G. "Protection from and Prevention of Physical Abuse: The Need for New Legal Procedures" *Violence and Responsibility: The Individual, the Family, and Society*. SP Medical and Scientific Books, 1978.

Forsythe, David P., and Patrice C. McMahon. *American Exceptionalism Reconsidered: U. S. Foreign Policy, Human Rights, and World Order*. New York: Routledge, 2016. ProQuest Ebook Central. https://ebookcentral-proquest-com.dist.lib.usu.edu/lib/usu/detail.action?docID=4748601.

Foucault, Michel. *The Order of Things: An Archeology of the Senses*. London: Routledge, 1994.

Friedrich, Gary. "The Big Sleep." *Captain America*, vol. 1, no. 148, Marvel Comics, Apr. 1972, *Marvel Unlimited*. https://read.marvel.com/#/book/29121.

_____. "Power to the People." *Captain America*, vol. 1, no. 143, Marvel Comics, Nov. 1971, *Marvel Unlimited*. https://read.marvel.com/#/book/22822.

"Full Text: Trump's Comments on White Supremacists, 'Alt-Left' in Charlottesville" *Politico*, 15 Aug. 2017. https://www.politico.com/story/2017/08/15/full-text-trump-comments-white-supremacists-alt-left-transcript-241662.

"Full WrestleMania III Results." *WWE*, WWE, 11 Mar. 2013. https://www.wwe.com/shows/wrestlemania/3/results.

Gilder, Rodman. *Statue of Liberty Enlightening the World*. The New York Trust Company, 1943.

Glass, Andrew. "Reagan Fires 11,000 Striking Air Traffic Controllers Aug. 5, 1981." *Politico*, 5 Aug. 2008. https://www.politico.com/story/2008/08/reagan-fires-11-000-striking-air-traffic-controllers-aug-5-1981-012292.

Godin, Seth. "Watchmen and the Importance of Comics to Be Seen as Literature." *Medium*, Medium, 16 Feb. 2018. https://medium.com/@jaysonbrown/watchmen-and-the-importance-of-comics-to-be-seen-as-literature-4dd5e2539c44.

Goldberg, Beckian Fritz. "Poetry and Murder." *Planet on the Table: Poets on the Reading Life*, edited by Sharon Bryan and William Olsen. Louisville, KY: Sarabande Books, 2003. 167–178.

Golob, Sacha. "Subjectivity, Reflection, and Freedom in Later Foucault" *International Journal of Philosophical Studies*, 2015, Vol. 23, No. 5, 666–688. http://dx.doi.org/10.1080/09672 559.2015.1091029.

Grant, Steven, writer. "Circle of Blood!" *Punisher*, vol. 1, no. 1, Marvel Comics, 1985. *Marvel Unlimited.* https://read.marvel.com/#/book/9989.

Greene, Kate. "Statue of Liberty, New York City." *Discover*, vol. 33, no. 8, Oct. 2012, 22–23. EBSCOhost, search.ebscohost.com/login.aspx?direct=true&db=asn&AN=79697521&s ite=ehost-live.

Gruenwald, Mark, et al. "Q-S." *Official Handbook of the Marvel Universe.* Marvel Comics. Sept. 1983.

Gruenwald, Mark, writer. "After Blow." *Captain America*, vol. 1, no. 373, Marvel Comics, Late July 1990. *Marvel Unlimited.* https://read.marvel.com/#/book/30923.

———. "After Blow." *Captain America*, vol. 1, no. 375, Marvel Comics, Late Aug. 1990. *Marvel Unlimited.* https://read.marvel.com/#/book/30925.

———. "After the Storm." *Captain America*, vol. 1, no. 401, Marvel Comics, June 1992. *Marvel Unlimited.* https://read.marvel.com/#/book/5432.

———. "America the Scorched." *Captain America*, vol. 1, no. 339, Marvel Comics, Mar. 1988. *Marvel Unlimited.* https://read.marvel.com/#/book/23534.

———. "Asylum." *Captain America*, vol. 1, no. 314, Marvel Comics, Feb. 1986. *Marvel Unlimited.* https://read.marvel.com/#/book/5426.

———. "Baptism of Fire." *Captain America*, vol. 1, no. 335, Marvel Comics, Nov. 1987. *Marvel Unlimited.* https://read.marvel.com/#/book/23522.

———. "Baron Ground." *Captain America*, vol. 1, no. 432, Marvel Comics, Oct. 1994. *Marvel Unlimited.* https://read.marvel.com/#/book/19396.

———. "Basic Training." *Captain America*, vol. 1, no. 334, Marvel Comics, Oct. 1987. *Marvel Unlimited.* https://read.marvel.com/#/book/23521.

———. "The Beaten Path." *Captain America*, vol. 1, no. 429, Marvel Comics, July 1994. *Marvel Unlimited.* https://read.marvel.com/#/book/19392.

———. "Blood in the Sea." *Captain America*, vol. 1, no. 360, Marvel Comics, Late Oct. 1989. *Marvel Unlimited.* https://read.marvel.com/#/book/23257.

———. "The Body in Question." *Captain America*, vol. 1, no. 308. Marvel Comics, Aug. 1985. *Marvel Unlimited.* https://read.marvel.com/#/book/12853.

———. "The Bombs Bursting in Air." *Captain America*, vol. 1, no. 437, Marvel Comics, Apr. 1995. *Marvel Unlimited.* https://read.marvel.com/#/book/19401.

———. "The Bombs Bursting in Air." *Captain America*, vol. 1, no. 438, Marvel Comics, Apr. 1995. *Marvel Unlimited.* https://read.marvel.com/#/book/31180.

———. "Break-In." *Captain America*, vol. 1, no. 341, Marvel Comics, May. 1988. *Marvel Unlimited.* https://read.marvel.com/#/book/23063.

———. "Breakout." *Captain America*, vol. 1, no. 340, Marvel Comics, Apr. 1988. *Marvel Unlimited.* https://read.marvel.com/#/book/23535.

———. "Broad Stripes and White Stars." *Captain America*, vol. 1, no. 442, Marvel Comics, Aug. 1995. *Marvel Unlimited.* https://read.marvel.com/#/book/31184.

———. "Camptown Rages." *Captain America*, vol. 1, no. 356, Marvel Comics, Aug. 1989. *Marvel Unlimited.* https://read.marvel.com/#/book/29867.

———. "Cap Out." *Captain America*, vol. 1, no. 430, Marvel Comics, Aug. 1994. *Marvel Unlimited.* https://read.marvel.com/#/book/19394.

———. "Cap's Night Out." *Captain America*, vol. 1, no. 371, Marvel Comics, June 1990. *Marvel Unlimited.* https://read.marvel.com/#/book/30921.

———. "The Chasm." *Captain America*, vol. 1, no. 322, Marvel Comics, Oct. 1986. *Marvel Unlimited.* https://read.marvel.com/#/book/30900.

———. "Children of the Night." *Captain America*, vol. 1, no. 404, Marvel Comics, Early Sep. 1992. *Marvel Unlimited.* https://read.marvel.com/#/book/24449.

———. "The Choice." *Captain America*, vol. 1, no. 332, Marvel Comics, Aug. 1987. *Marvel Unlimited.* https://read.marvel.com/#/book/23518.

———. "City of Wolves." *Captain America*, vol. 1, no. 403, Marvel Comics, Late July 1992. *Marvel Unlimited.* https://read.marvel.com/#/book/24448.

_____. "Clashing Symbols." *Captain America*, vol. 1, no. 327, Marvel Comics, March 1987. *Marvel Unlimited*. https://read.marvel.com/#/book/30911.

_____. "Creatures in Love." *Captain America*, vol. 1, no. 316, Marvel Comics, Apr. 1986. *Marvel Unlimited*. https://read.marvel.com/#/book/30897.

_____. "The Crimson Crusade." *Captain America*, vol. 1, no. 394, Marvel Comics, Nov. 1991. *Marvel Unlimited*. https://read.marvel.com/#/book/31022.

_____. "Dances with Werewolves." *Captain America*, vol. 1, no. 405, Marvel Comics, Late Sep. 1992. *Marvel Unlimited*. https://read.marvel.com/#/book/24325.

_____. "Death Throws." *Captain America*, vol. 1, no. 317, Marvel Comics, May 1986. *Marvel Unlimited*. https://read.marvel.com/#/book/30898.

_____. "Deface the Nation." *Captain America*, vol. 1, no. 312, Marvel Comics, Dec. 1985. *Marvel Unlimited*. https://read.marvel.com/#/book/30895.

_____. "Diamonds Aren't Forever!" *Captain America*, vol. 1, no. 433, Marvel Comics, Nov. 1994. *Marvel Unlimited*. https://read.marvel.com/#/book/19397.

_____. "Don't Tread on Me." *Captain America*, vol. 1, no. 344, Marvel Comics, Aug. 1988. *Marvel Unlimited*. https://read.marvel.com/#/book/23549.

_____. "Enemy Fire" *Captain America*, vol. 1, no. 427, Marvel Comics, May 1994. *Marvel Unlimited*. https://read.marvel.com/#/book/19389.

_____. "Everybody Hurts Sometime." *Captain America*, vol. 1, no. 436, Marvel Comics, Feb. 1995. *Marvel Unlimited*. https://read.marvel.com/#/book/19400.

_____. "Falling Out." *Captain America*, vol. 1, no. 374, Marvel Comics, Early Aug. 1990. *Marvel Unlimited*. https://read.marvel.com/#/book/30924.

_____. "Falling Out." *Captain America*, vol. 1, no. 376, Marvel Comics, Early Sept. 1990. *Marvel Unlimited*. https://read.marvel.com/#/book/30926.

_____. "Field of Angels." *U.S.Agent*, vol. 1, no. 4, Marvel Comics, Sep. 1993. *Marvel Unlimited*. https://read.marvel.com/#/book/49626.

_____. "Forgive Us Our Trespasses." *Captain America Annual*, vol. 1, no. 10, Marvel Comics, May 1991. *Marvel Unlimited*. https://read.marvel.com/#/book/38900.

_____. "Gantlet." *Captain America*, vol. 1, no. 421, Marvel Comics, Nov. 1993. *Marvel Unlimited*. https://read.marvel.com/#/book/31162.

_____. "Going Ballistic." *Captain America*, vol. 1, no. 422, Marvel Comics, Dec. 1993. *Marvel Unlimited*. https://read.marvel.com/#/book/31163.

_____. "Grand Stand Play." *Captain America*, vol. 1, no. 378, Marvel Comics, Oct. 1990. *Marvel Unlimited*. https://read.marvel.com/#/book/30928.

_____. "Graven Images." *Captain America*, vol. 1, no. 426, Marvel Comics, Apr. 1994. *Marvel Unlimited*. https://read.marvel.com/#/book/19387.

_____. "The Hard Sell." *Captain America*, vol. 1, no. 315, Marvel Comics, Mar. 1986. *Marvel Unlimited*. https://read.marvel.com/#/book/29847.

_____. "The Hard Way." *Captain America*, vol. 1, no. 328, Marvel Comics, Apr. 1987. *Marvel Unlimited*. https://read.marvel.com/#/book/29579.

_____. "The Haunting of Skull-House." *Captain America*, vol. 1, no. 326, Marvel Comics, Feb. 1987. *Marvel Unlimited*. https://read.marvel.com/#/book/29634.

_____. "House Calls." *Captain America*, vol. 1, no. 370, Marvel Comics, May. 1990. *Marvel Unlimited*. https://read.marvel.com/#/book/22857.

_____. "I am Legend." *Captain America*, vol. 1, no. 383, Marvel Comics, Mar. 1991. *Marvel Unlimited*. https://read.marvel.com/#/book/31010.

_____. "Ice Cap." *Captain America*, vol. 1, no. 349, Marvel Comics, Jan. 1989. *Marvel Unlimited*. https://read.marvel.com/#/book/23546.

_____. "It Came from Outer Space!" *Captain America*, vol. 1, no. 398, Marvel Comics, Mar. 1992. *Marvel Unlimited*. https://read.marvel.com/#/book/718.

_____. "Justice is Served?" *Captain America*, vol. 1, no. 318, Marvel Comics, June 1986. *Marvel Unlimited*. https://read.marvel.com/#/book/22918.

_____. "Lair of the Living Mummy." *Captain America*, vol. 1, no. 361, Marvel Comics, Early Nov. 1989. *Marvel Unlimited*. https://read.marvel.com/#/book/23261.

_____. "The Last Operation." *Captain America*, vol. 1, no. 424, Marvel Comics, Feb. 1994. *Marvel Unlimited*. https://read.marvel.com/#/book/31179.

_____. "Leader of the Pack." *Captain America*, vol. 1, no. 406, Marvel Comics, Early Oct. 1992. *Marvel Unlimited.* https://read.marvel.com/#/book/24332.

_____. "The Little Bang Theory." *Captain America*, vol. 1, no. 320, Aug. 1986. *Marvel Unlimited.* https://read.marvel.com/#/book/23296.

_____. "The Long Road Back." *Captain America*, vol. 1, no. 337, Marvel Comics, Jan. 1988. *Marvel Unlimited.* https://read.marvel.com/#/book/23525.

_____. "Lord of the Wolves." *Captain America*, vol. 1, no. 407, Marvel Comics, Late Sep. 1992. *Marvel Unlimited.* https://read.marvel.com/#/book/24335.

_____. "Magnetic Repulsion." *Captain America*, vol. 1, no. 367, Marvel Comics, Feb. 1990. *Marvel Unlimited.* https://read.marvel.com/#/book/30092.

_____. "Man Trap." *Captain America*, vol. 1, no. 364, Marvel Comics, Dec. 1989. *Marvel Unlimited.* https://read.marvel.com/#/book/30192.

_____. "Mark's Remarks." http://www.oocities.org/mh_prime/9305.html.

_____. "Missing Persons." *Captain America*, vol. 1, no. 355, Marvel Comics, July 1989. *Marvel Unlimited.* https://read.marvel.com/#/book/29859.

_____. "Mission: Murder Modok!" *Captain America*, vol. 1, no. 313, Marvel Comics, Jan. 1986. *Marvel Unlimited.* https://read.marvel.com/#/book/30896.

_____. "Movers and Monsters." *Captain America*, vol. 1, no. 329, Marvel Comics, May 1987. *Marvel Unlimited.* https://read.marvel.com/#/book/30912.

_____. "Murder by Decree!" *Captain America*, vol. 1, no. 400, Marvel Comics, May 1992. *Marvel Unlimited.* https://read.marvel.com/#/book/1172.

_____. "Natural Calling." *Captain America*, vol. 1, no. 336, Marvel Comics, Dec. 1987. *Marvel Unlimited.* https://read.marvel.com/#/book/23523.

_____. "The Next Generation." *Captain America*, vol. 1, no. 431, Marvel Comics, Sep. 1994. *Marvel Unlimited.* https://read.marvel.com/#/book/19395.

_____. "Night of Sin"/"Bloodstone Hunt: Prologue/" *Captain America*, vol. 1, no. 357, Marvel Comics, Early Sep. 1989. *Marvel Unlimited.* https://read.marvel.com/#/book/29869.

_____. "Night Shift." *Captain America*, vol. 1, no. 330, Marvel Comics, June 1987. *Marvel Unlimited.* https://read.marvel.com/#/book/30913.

_____. "Nomad Madcap Cap..." *Captain America*, vol. 1, no. 309. Marvel Comics, Sept. 1985. *Marvel Unlimited.* https://read.marvel.com/#/book/30893.

_____. "The 100% Solution." *Captain America*, vol. 1, no. 377, Marvel Comics, Late Sept. 1990. *Marvel Unlimited.* https://read.marvel.com/#/book/30927.

_____. "Out of Commission." *Captain America*, vol. 1, no. 348, Marvel Comics, Dec. 1988. *Marvel Unlimited.* https://read.marvel.com/#/book/23547.

_____. "Overkill." *Captain America*, vol. 1, no. 319, Marvel Comics, July 1986. *Marvel Unlimited.* https://read.marvel.com/#/book/23295.

_____. "Policing the Nation." *Captain America*, vol. 1, no. 428, Marvel Comics, June 1994. *Marvel Unlimited.* https://read.marvel.com/#/book/19390.

_____. "Power Struggle." *Captain America*, vol. 1, no. 338, Marvel Comics, Feb. 1988. *Marvel Unlimited.* https://read.marvel.com/#/book/23532.

_____. "The Prowling." *Captain America*, vol. 1, no. 402, Marvel Comics, Early July 1992. *Marvel Unlimited.* https://read.marvel.com/#/book/24331.

_____. "Reawakening" *Captain America*, vol. 1, no. 354, Marvel Comics, June 1989. *Marvel Unlimited.* https://read.marvel.com/#/book/30918.

_____. "Red Twilight." *Captain America*, vol. 1, no. 368, Marvel Comics, Mar. 1990. *Marvel Unlimited.* https://read.marvel.com/#/book/30919.

_____. "Remote Control." *Captain America*, vol. 1, no. 366, Marvel Comics, Jan. 1990. *Marvel Unlimited.* https://read.marvel.com/#/book/30091.

_____. "The Replacement." *Captain America*, vol. 1, no. 333, Marvel Comics, Sep. 1987. *Marvel Unlimited.* https://read.marvel.com/#/book/23519.

_____. "Rogues in the House." *Captain America*, vol. 1, no. 395, Marvel Comics, Dec. 1991. *Marvel Unlimited.* https://read.marvel.com/#/book/31023.

_____. "Seeing Red." *Captain America*, vol. 1, no. 350, Marvel Comics, Feb. 1989. *Marvel Unlimited.* https://read.marvel.com/#/book/23541.

_____. "Serpents of the World Unite!" *Captain America*, vol. 1, no. 310, Marvel Comics, Oct. 1985. *Marvel Unlimited*. https://read.marvel.com/#/book/30894.

_____. "Shot in the Dark." *Captain America*, vol. 1, no. 397, Marvel Comics, Feb. 1992. *Marvel Unlimited*. https://read.marvel.com/#/book/31149.

_____. "The Skeleton Crew." *Captain America*, vol. 1, no. 369, Marvel Comics, Apr. 1990. *Marvel Unlimited*. https://read.marvel.com/#/book/30920.

_____. "Slippery People." *Captain America*, vol. 1, no. 343, Marvel Comics, July. 1988. *Marvel Unlimited*. https://read.marvel.com/#/book/23544.

_____. "Slugfest." *Captain America*, vol. 1, no. 325, Marvel Comics, Jan. 1987. *Marvel Unlimited*. https://read.marvel.com/#/book/30910.

_____. "Snake Bites." *Captain America*, vol. 1, no. 434, Marvel Comics, Dec. 1994. *Marvel Unlimited*. https://read.marvel.com/#/book/19398.

_____. "The Snake Pit." *Captain America*, vol. 1, no. 342, Marvel Comics, June. 1988. *Marvel Unlimited*. https://read.marvel.com/#/book/23540.

_____. "Snake, Battle, and Toll." *Captain America*, vol. 1, no. 435, Marvel Comics, Jan. 1995. *Marvel Unlimited*. https://read.marvel.com/#/book/19399.

_____. "Sold on Ice." *Captain America*, vol. 1, no. 372, Marvel Comics, July 1990. *Marvel Unlimited*. https://read.marvel.com/#/book/30922.

_____. "Soldier, Soldier." *Captain America*, vol. 1, no. 331, Marvel Comics, July 1987. *Marvel Unlimited*. https://read.marvel.com/#/book/30914.

_____ "Stop Making Sense." *Captain America*, vol. 1, no. 307. Marvel Comics, July 1985. *Marvel Unlimited*. https://read.marvel.com/#/book/30892.

_____. "Submission." *Captain America*, vol. 1, no. 365, Marvel Comics, Mid. Dec. 1989. *Marvel Unlimited*. https://read.marvel.com/#/book/30090.

_____. "Super Patriot Games." *Captain America*, vol. 1, no. 425, Marvel Comics, Mar. 1994. *Marvel Unlimited*. https://read.marvel.com/#/book/19386.

_____. "Super-Patriot is Here." *Captain America*, vol. 1, no. 323, Marvel Comics, Nov. 1986. *Marvel Unlimited*. https://read.marvel.com/#/book/30908.

_____. "Surrender." *Captain America*, vol. 1, no. 345, Marvel Comics, Sep. 1988. *Marvel Unlimited*. https://read.marvel.com/#/book/23553.

_____. "Television Blind." *Captain America*, vol. 1, no. 419, Marvel Comics, Sep. 1993. *Marvel Unlimited*. https://read.marvel.com/#/book/31160.

_____. "Through the Perilous Fight." *Captain America*, vol. 1, no. 439, Marvel Comics, July 1995. *Marvel Unlimited*. https://read.marvel.com/#/book/31181.

_____. "Twilight's Last Gleaming." *Captain America*, vol. 1, no. 443, Marvel Comics, Sep. 1995. *Marvel Unlimited*. https://read.marvel.com/#/book/31185.

_____. "Ultimatum." *Captain America*, vol. 1, no. 321, Marvel Comics, Sept. 1986. *Marvel Unlimited*. https://read.marvel.com/#/book/30899.

_____. "Wheel of Death." *Captain America*, vol. 1, no. 359, Marvel Comics, Early Oct. 1989. *Marvel Unlimited*. https://read.marvel.com/#/book/23255.

_____. "When Women Wage War!" *Captain America*, vol. 1, no. 390, Marvel Comics, Aug. 1991. *Marvel Unlimited*. https://read.marvel.com/#/book/31017.

_____. "Working..." *Captain America*, vol. 1, no. 311, Marvel Comics, Nov. 1985. *Marvel Unlimited*. https://read.marvel.com/#/book/29640.

Grygiel, Jennifer. "How Right-Wing Meme Slingers Weaponize a Toxic Patriotism." *Fast Company*, 7 Feb. 2019. https://www.fastcompany.com/90301007/how-right-wing-meme-slingers-weaponize-a-toxic-patriotism.

Hacker-Wright, John. "Philippa Foot." *Stanford Encyclopedia of Philosophy*, Stanford University, 17 Aug. 2018. https://plato.stanford.edu/entries/philippa-foot/.

Hall, Richard A. *The Captain America Conundrum: Issues of Patriotism, Race, and Gender in Captain America Comic Books, 1941–2001*. 2011. Auburn University, PhD dissertation.

Hart, Benjamin. "Reagan's Mental-Health Concerns Handled Very Differently Than Trump's." *Intelligencer*, Intelligencer, 14 Jan. 2018. nymag.com/intelligencer/2018/01/how-reagans-mental-health-concerns-were-handled.html.

"Heroes Reborn: Captain America." *BasementRejects*, basementrejects.com/review/heroes-reborn-captain-america/.

"*Heroes Reborn: Captain America* by Rob Liefeld." *Goodreads*, Goodreads, 6 Dec. 2006. www. goodreads.com/book/show/838930.Heroes_Reborn.

"Heroin." *CAMH*. https://www.camh.ca/en/health-info/mental-illness-and-addiction-index/ heroin.

History.com Editors. "Vietnam War Protests." *History.com*, A&E Television Networks, 22 Feb. 2010. https://www.history.com/topics/vietnam-war/vietnam-war-protests.

———. "Vietnam War Timeline." *History.com*, A&E Television Networks, 13 Sept. 2017. https://www.history.com/topics/vietnam-war/vietnam-war-timeline.

"Ice." *Alcohol and Drug Foundation*, 20 Feb. 2020. https://adf.org.au/drug-facts/ice/.

Inside the Magic. "FULL Marvel Phase 3 Announcement…" *YouTube*. YouTube, 29 Oct. 2014. https://www.youtube.com/watch?v=L2VoJuVfbjI.

"The Iran-Contra Affair." *PBS*, Public Broadcasting Service. www.pbs.org/wgbh/ americanexperience/features/reagan-iran/.

Johnson, William Oscar. "Steroids: A Problem of Huge Dimensions." *Sports Illustrated*, 12 May 1985. https://www.si.com/vault/1985/05/13/622442/getting-physical-and-chemical.

Johnston, Joe, director. *Captain America: The First Avenger*, Marvel Comics, 2011.

Kane, Sally. "Common Workplace Characteristics of the Silent Generation." *The Balance Careers*, The Balance Careers, 2 May 2019. www.thebalancecareers. com/workplace-characteristics-silent-generation-2164692.

Khan, Yasmin Sabina. *Enlightening the World: The Creation of the Statue of Liberty*. Cornell University Press, 2010. *ProQuest Ebook Central*. https://ebookcentral-proquest-com.dist. lib.usu.edu/lib/USU/detail.action?docID=3138081.

King, Martin Luther, Jr. "I Have a Dream by Martin Luther King, Jr; August 28, 1963." *The Avalon Project*, Yale Law School. avalon.law.yale.edu/20th_century/mlk01.asp.

Kirby, Jack. "Showdown Day!" *Captain America*, vol. 1., no. 210, Marvel Comics, June 1977, *Marvel Unlimited*. *https://read.marvel.com/#/book/5403*.

Kleingeld, Pauline. *Kant and Cosmopolitanism: The Philosophical Ideal of World Citizenship*. Cambridge University Press, 2011. *ProQuest Ebook*.

Kleingeld, Pauline, and Eric Brown. "Cosmopolitanism." *The Stanford Encyclopedia of Philosophy*, Stanford Center for the Study of Language and Information, 1 July 2013. https://plato. stanford.edu/entries/cosmopolitanism/.

Kunreuther, Robbie. "The Good and the Bad Union Representative." *FedSmith.com*, 10 Aug. 2015. https://www.fedsmith.com/2015/08/10/the-good-and-the-bad-union-representative/.

Kurtis, Luke. "Before We Knew Better: This 90s Movie Accepted LGBT People in a Way Society Hasn't Yet Been Able To." *Quartz*, Quartz, 5 June 2019. https://qz.com/1565594/ why-the-crying-game-deserves-its-status-as-a-classic-90s-movie/.

"Labor Unions Seen as Good for Workers, Not U.S. Competitiveness." *Pew Research Center for the People and the Press*, 24 Sept. 2018. https://www.people-press. org/2011/02/17/labor-unions-seen-as-good-for-workers-not-u-s-competitiveness/.

Lee, Stan. "The Badge and the Betrayal!" *Captain America*, vol. 1, no. 139, Marvel Comics, July 1971, *Marvel Unlimited*. https://read.marvel.com/#/book/29106.

———. "Captain America Joins…The Avengers!" *The Avengers*, vol. 1, no. 4, Marvel Comics, 1964. *Marvel Unlimited*. https://read.marvel.com/#/book/4206.

———. "The Coming of the Avengers!" *The Avengers*, vol. 1, no. 1, Marvel Comics, 1964. *Marvel Unlimited*. https://read.marvel.com/#/book/482.

Letizia, Anthony, and Anthony Letizia. "Anthony Letizia." *Geek Frontiers*, 9 Feb. 2020. geek-frontiers.com/geek-history/the-first-college-course-on-comic-books/.

Little, Becky. "Was Abraham Lincoln an Atheist?" *History.com*, A&E Television Networks, 24 June 2019. www.history.com/news/abraham-lincoln-religion-christian-atheist.

Loudis, Jessica. "The Third Reich Was Addicted to Drugs." *The New Republic*, 6 Mar. 2017. https://newrepublic.com/article/141125/third-reich-addicted-drugs.

Macaray, David. "Two Negative Perceptions of Labor." *Common Dreams*, 22 Feb. 2012. https:// www.commondreams.org/views/2012/02/22/two-negative-perceptions-labor.

Mainer, Vanessa Del Prete. "Modern Heroes: Classical Mythology and Classical Values in the Contemporary Acquis, the Case of Captain America." Journal of Comparative Literature and

Aesthetics, vol. 42, no. S1, 2019, 74+. *Gale Literature Resource Center.* https://link-gale-com. dist.lib.usu.edu/apps/doc/A597616359/LitRC?u=utah_gvrl&sid=LitRC&xid=c64f2679.

Margolies, Kevin. "Silver Screen tarnishes unions." *Cornell University ILR School*, Screen Actor, 42–52. http://digitalcommons.ilr.cornell.edu/articles/231/.

"Mark Gruenwald Interviewed by Joe Field 1988." Uploaded by FlyCoJoe, *YouTube*, YouTube, 13 Dec. 2014. https://www.youtube.com/watch?v=saD2pP-PvX0.

Marz, Ron. "Emerald Twilight, Part 3: The Future." *Green Lantern*, vol. 3, no. 25, DC Comics, Mar. 1994.

McCallum, Michael. "Revisiting the '90s Speculative Boom That Nearly Ended the Comic Book Industry." *Comic Booked*, 17 Jan. 2019. https://comicbooked. com/revisiting-90s-speculative-boom-nearly-ended-comic-book-industry/.

"McGwire Apologizes to La Russa, Selig." *ESPN*, ESPN Internet Ventures, 11 Jan. 2010. https:// www.espn.com/mlb/news/story?id=4816607.

Meltzer, Dave, and Richard Demak. "The Sham Is a Sham: A Trial Reveals Widespread Steroid Use in pro Wrestling." *Sports Illustrated*, vol. 75, no. 2, July 1991, 9. *EBSCOhost*, search. ebscohost.com/login.aspx?direct=true&db=asn&AN=57929873&site=ehost-live.

Michelinie, David. "Death on the Hudson!" *The Avengers*, vol. 1, no. 184, Marvel Comics, June 1979. *Marvel Unlimited*. https://read.marvel.com/#/book/12429.

Millar, Mark. *Civil War*, Vol. 1, No. 6, Marvel Comics, Jan. 2007. *Marvel Unlimited*. https:// read.marvel.com/#/book/5491.

Miller, Robert W., et al. *The Practice of Local Union Leadership: A Study of Five Local Unions.* The Ohio State University Press, 1965.

Molloy, Daniel. "Is Patriotism Good for America?" *Ozy.* Ozy. 2 Feb 2018. https://www.ozy. com/opinion/is-patriotism-good-for-america/83037

Montagne, Renee, host. "Stan Lee on Realism in the World of Comic Heroes." NPR, NPR, 27 Dec. 2006. https://www.npr.org/templates/story/story.php?storyId=6684820.

Moore, Alan, and Dave Gibbons. *Watchmen.* DC Comics, 2005.

Morgan, George W. *The Human Predicament.* Brown University, 1968.

Morton, Paul. "The Survivor: On Magneto, Mutants, and the Holocaust." *The Millions*, 26 May 2014. https://themillions.com/2014/05/the-survivor-on-magneto-x-men-and-the-holocaust.html.

Moser, John. "Madmen, Morons, and Monocles: The Portrayal of the Nazis in *Captain America.*" *Captain America and the Struggle of the Superhero.* Edited by Robert G. Weiner. Jefferson, NC: McFarland. 2009.

"Narcissistic Personality Disorder." *Psychology Today.* https://www.psychologytoday.com/us/ conditions/narcissistic-personality-disorder.

NerdSync. "The Psychology of the Punisher: Is Frank Castle Evil?" *Medium*, Medium, 4 Feb. 2018. https://medium.com/@NerdSync/the-psychology-of-the-punisher-is-frank-castle-evil-e96ddba07689.

"The New Colossus." *National Parks Service*, U.S. Department of the Interior. www.nps.gov/ stli/learn/historyculture/colossus.htm.

Newman, Tony. "Nancy Reagan's Role in the Disastrous War on Drugs." *Drug Policy Alliance*, 6 Mar. 2016. http://www.drugpolicy.org/blog/nancy-reagans-role-disastrous-war-drugs.

Newton, David E. *Steroids and Doping in Sports: A Reference Handbook*, ABC-CLIO, LLC, 2013. ProQuest Ebook Central. https://ebookcentral-proquest-com.dist.lib.usu.edu/lib/ usu/detail.action?docID=1682961.

Nichols, John. "Don't Let the Trump Administration Rewrite Emma Lazarus." *The Nation*, 14 Aug. 2019. www.thenation.com/article/archive/emma-lazarus-poem-ken-cuccinelli/.

"1994 Comic Book Sales to Comics Shops." Comichron. https://www.comichron.com/ monthlycomicssales/1994.html.

"1992 Comic Book Sales to Comics Shops." Comichron. https://www.comichron.com/ monthlycomicssales/1992.html.

"Noam Chomsky>Quotes>Quotable Quote." *Goodreads.* https://www.goodreads.com/ quotes/669518-to-begin-with-we-have-to-be-more-clear-about.

Nocenti, Ann. "False Man." *Daredevil*, vol. 1, no. 275, Marvel Comics, Dec. 1989, *Marvel Unlimited*. https://read.marvel.com/#/book/39208.

_____. "The Hundred Heads of Ultron." *Daredevil*, vol. 1, no. 276, Marvel Comics, Jan. 1990, *Marvel Unlimited*. https://read.marvel.com/#/book/39209.

"Nomad (Jack Monroe)." *Marvel.com*. https://www.marvel.com/characters/nomad-jack-monroe.

Parks, Tim. "Tim Parks by Scott Esposito." BOMB Magazine, 7 May 2015. https://bombmagazine.org/articles/tim-parks/.

"The Past. 'We Were at War': Labor Movement Violence and the Role of the Underworld." *Trends in Organized Crime*, vol. 7, no. 2, Dec. 2001, 12–39. EBSCOhost, search.ebscohost.com/login.aspx?direct=true&db=asn&AN=13293882&site=ehost-live.

Patrick, Neil. "The Baby Boomers Were Nicknamed the 'Me Generation' Due to Their Perceived Narcissism." *The Vintage News*, 5 Sept 2016. https://www.thevintagenews.com/2016/09/05/priority-baby-boomers-nicknamed-generation-due-perceived-narcissism/.

"Philosophy Overdose. Chomsky & Foucault—Justice vs. Power." *YouTube*, YouTube. 17 Jun. 2017. https://www.youtube.com/watch?v=J5wuB_p63YM&vl=en.

"Pilot." *Marvel's Agents of S.H.I.E.L.D.*, directed by Joss Whedon, season 1, episode 1, ABC Studios and Marvel Television and Mutant Enemy Productions, 2013.

"Pittsburgh's Labor History Sites—An Interactive Map." *The Battle of Homestead Foundation*. https://battleofhomestead.org/bhf/pittsburghs-labor-history-sites-an-interactive-map/.

Pratt, Allan. *Internet Encyclopedia of Philosophy*. https://www.iep.utm.edu/nihilism/.

"A Promoter of Wrestling Is Acquitted." *New York Times*, 23 July 1994. www.nytimes.com/1994/07/23/nyregion/a-promoter-of-wrestling-is-acquitted.html.

"Public Trust in Government: 1958–2019." *Pew Research Center for the People and the Press*, Pew Research Center for the People and the Press, 29 May 2019. www.people-press.org/2019/04/11/public-trust-in-government-1958-2019/.

Ramsey, Taylor. "The History of Comics: Decade by Decade." *The Artifice*, 5 Feb. 2013. https://the-artifice.com/history-of-comics/.

"RealClear Opinion Research." *RealClear Politics*, 22–26 Feb. 2019. https://www.realclearpolitics.com/docs/190305_RCOR_Topline_V2.pdf.

Reed, Patrick. "Today in Comics History: A Tribute to Mark Gruenwald." *ComicsAlliance*, 18 June 2015. comicsalliance.com/tribute-mark-gruenwald/.

Reisman, Abraham. "The Story Behind Bucky's Groundbreaking Comic-Book Reinvention As the Winter Soldier." *Vulture*, 6 May 2016. https://www.vulture.com/2016/05/bucky-winter-soldier-history.html.

Republican Platform 2016. Committee on Arrangements for the 2016 Republican National Convention. Cleveland, OH, 2016. https://prod-cdn-static.gop.com/media/documents/DRAFT_12_FINAL%5B1%5D-ben_1468872234.pdf.

"Research Starters: U.S. Military by the Numbers." *The National WWII Museum New Orleans*. https://www.nationalww2museum.org/students-teachers/student-resources/research-starters/research-starters-us-military-numbers.

"Restoring the Statue." *National Park Service*. 26 Feb. 2015. https://www.nps.gov/stli/learn/historyculture/places_restoring.htm. Accessed 18 August 2019.

"Retcon (Concept)." *Comic Vine*. comicvine.gamespot.com/retcon/4015–43566/.

Richards, Jesse. "Why Doesn't Batman Just Kill the Joker?" *HuffPost*, HuffPost, 7 Dec. 2017. www.huffpost.com/entry/why-doesnt-batman-just-ki_b_3686003.

Richardson, Heather Cox. "The Language of Patriotism." *New Republic*, vol. 249, no. 9, Sept. 2018, 4–6. EBSCOhost. search.ebscohost.com/login.aspx?direct=true&db=asn&AN=1316 22603&site=ehost-live.

Robbins, Bruce. "Chomsky's Golden Rule: Comparison and Cosmopolitanism." *New Literary History*, vol. 40, no. 3, 2009, 547–565. JSTOR. www.jstor.org/stable/27760275.

Rogers, Vaneta. "Is the Average Age of Comic Book Readers Increasing? Retailers Talk State of the Business 2017." *Newsarama*, 2 February 2017. https://www.newsarama.com/33006-is-the-average-age-of-comic-book-readers-increasing-retailers-talk-state-of-the-business-2017.html.

Rosenberg, Eli. "'Olliemania': The Stage-Worthy Scandal That Starred Oliver North as a Congressional Witness." *The Washington Post*, WP Company, 8 May 2018. www.washingtonpost.com/news/retropolis/wp/2018/05/08/the-nras-new-president-oliver-north-is-notorious-for-his-role-in-an-illicit-arms-deal/?utm_term=.863af54b8708.

Russo, Anthony, and Joe. *Avengers: Endgame*. Marvel Studios, 2019.

_____. *Avengers: Infinity War*. Marvel Studios, 2018.

Sacks, Jason. *American Comic Book Chronicles: The 1970s*. TwoMorrows Publishing, 2014.

Sacks, Jason, and Keith Dallas. *America Comic Book Chronicles: 1990s*. Raleigh, NC: TwoMorrows Publishing, 2018.

Salinger, J.D. *Catcher in the Rye*. New York: Little, Brown & Co. 2014.

Saltzstein, Herbert and Yoko Takagi. "Some Critical Issues in the Study of Moral Development." *International Journal of Developmental Science* 13 (2019) 21–24 DOI 10.3233/DEV-170244.

Samuel, Lawrence R. *The American Dream*. Syracuse University Press, 2012.

Sanders, Cheryl E. "Lawrence Kohlberg's Stages of Moral Development." *Encyclopædia Britannica*, Encyclopædia Britannica, Inc. https://www.britannica.com/science/Lawrence-Kohlbergs-stages-of-moral-development.

Saucier, Donald A., et al. "Masculine Honor Beliefs: Measurement and Correlates." *Personality and Individual Differences*, no. 94, 2016, 7–15.

Schiller, Christopher. "Legally Speaking, It Depends—Guild or Union." Script Magazine, 24 Aug. 2014. https://www.scriptmag.com/features/legally-speaking-guild-or-union.

Scott, Cord. "Alpha and the Omega: Captain America and the Punisher." *Captain America and the Struggle of the Superhero*. Edited by Robert G. Weiner, McFarland, 2009.

Serrano, Richard and Tracy Wilkinson. "All 4 in King Beating Acquitted." *Los Angeles Times*, 30 Apr. 1992. https://www.latimes.com/local/california/la-me-all-4-in-king-beating-acquitted-19920430-story.html.

Shen, Yanni, et al. "How Social Support Affects Moral Disengagement: The Role of Anger and Hostility." Social Behavior & Personality: An International Journal, vol. 47, no. 3, Apr. 2019, 1–9. EBSCOhost, doi:10.2224/sbp.7720.

Sigelman, Lee, et al. "Police Brutality and Public Perceptions of Racial Discrimination: A Tale of Two Beatings." *Political Research Quarterly*, vol. 50, no. 4, 1997, 777–791. JSTOR. www.jstor.org/stable/448986.

Simon, Joe and Jack Kirby, creators. "Meet Captain America." *Captain America Comics*, vol. 1, no. 1, Mar. 1941. *Marvel Unlimited*. https://read.marvel.com/#/book/1652.

Smith, Tom. "The Polls: American Attitudes Toward the Soviet Union and Communism." *General Social Survey*, NORC at the University of Chicago. https://www.google.com/url?sa=t&rct=j&q=&esrc=s&source=web&cd=3&ved=2ahUKEwjFqPGyxLzpAhUEVK0KHd8aBssQFjACegQIARAB&url=https%3A%2F%2Fgssdataexplorer.norc.org%2Fdocuments%2F798%2Fdownload&usg=AOvVaw2UT4pGGw4cg0LFj2-RjicI.

Stern, Roger. "Cap for President!" *Captain America*, vol. 1, no. 250, Marvel Comics, Oct. 1980, *Marvel Unlimited*. https://read.marvel.com/#/book/5417.

Stevens, Richard J. *Captain America, Masculinity and Violence: The Evolution of a National Icon*. Syracuse University Press, 2015.

Stillman, Jesse. "The Comic Book Crash of the '90s And Why Comics Are Safe Today." *Comic Booked*, 26 June 2018. http://comicbooked.com/comic-book/.

Stone, Oliver, director. *Wall Street*. 20th Century Fox, 1987.

Stratmoen, Evelyn, et al. "What, I'm Not Good Enough for You? Individual Differences in Masculine Honor Beliefs and the Endorsement of Aggressive Responses to Romantic Rejection." *Personality & Individual Differences*, vol. 123, Mar. 2018, 151–162. EBSCOhost, doi:10.1016/j.paid.2017.10.018.

Strauss, William and Neil Howe. *The Fourth Turning: What the Cycles of History Tell us About America's Next Rendezvous with Destiny*. Three Rivers Press, 1997.

"Superman (1987 2nd Series) 75D FN/VF 7.0." *My Comic Shop.com* Collect. https://www.mycomicshop.com/search?q=superman 75.

Sweet-Cushman, Jennie, et al. *Generations: Rethinking Age and Citizenship*, edited by Richard Marback, Wayne State University Press, 2015. ProQuest Ebook Central. https://ebookcentral-proquest-com.dist.lib.usu.edu/lib/usu/detail.action?docID=3446577.

Swift, Donald C. "Commenting on Generation X Goes to College." *Social Studies*, vol. 89, no. 5, Sept. 1998, 219. EBSCOhost, doi:10.1080/00377999809599855.

Tackett, Brittany. "The History of Drug Use in Wartime." *Recovery.org*, 7 Dec. 2018. https://www.recovery.org/addiction/wartime/.

Tarantino, Quentin, dir. *Kill Bill, Vol. 2*. Miramax, 2004.

Taylor, Ted. "Fleer/Skybox Sale Finally Goes Through." *Philadelphia Daily News*, 4 Feb 1999. Late Edition. *Timeline of Labor History in Pennsylvania*, 11 Aug. 2016. https://palaborhistorysociety.org/timeline-of-labor-history-in-pennsylvania/.

Thomas, Roy, writer. "Death, Be Not Proud!" *Avengers*, Vol. No. 56, Marvel Comics, Sept. 1968. *Marvel Unlimited*. https://read.marvel.com/#/book/4222.

———. "War Zones." *Captain America*, Vol. 1, No. 423, Marvel Comics, Jan. 1994. *Marvel Unlimited*. https://read.marvel.com/#/book/31178.

Thomas-Gregory, Susan. "The Divorce Generation." *Wall Street Journal*, 9 July 2011. https://www.wsj.com/articles/SB10001424052702303544604576430341393583056, accessed 28 Aug. 2019.

Tinker, Ben. "U.S. Life Expectancy Drops for Second Year in a Row." *CNN*, Cable News Network, 22 Dec. 2017. https://www.cnn.com/2017/12/21/health/us-life-expectancy-study/index.html.

"Trust in Government." *Gallup.com*, Gallup, 18 May 2019, news.gallup.com/poll/5392/trust-government.aspx.

"2007 Comic Book Sales to Comics Shops." *Comichron*. https://www.comichron.com/monthlycomicssales/2007.html.

2016 Democratic Party Platform. Democratic Platform Committee. Miami, FL, 8–9 July 2016. https://democrats.org/wp-content/uploads/2018/10/2016_DNC_Platform.pdf.

"U.S. Flag Code." Military.com, *Military.com*. www.military.com/flag-day/us-flag-code.html.

Virisasova, Inna. "The Problem of Freedom in the Works of Michel Foucault." *CEU Political Science Journal*, No. 5, 62–77. http://epa.niif.hu/02300/02341/00005/pdf/EPA02341_ceu_2006_05_64-77.pdf.

Vogler, Christopher. "Joseph Campbell Goes to the Movies: The Influence of the Hero's Journey in Film Narrative." *The Journal of Genius and Eminence*, Vol. 2, No. 2, 2017, ISSN: 2334-1130 print/2334-1149.

Waid, Mark. "The Real Truth About Superman: And the Rest of Us Too." *Superheroes and Philosophy: Truth, Justice, and the Socratic Way*. Edited by Tom Morris and Matt Morris, Open Court, 2005, 3–10.

Whedon, Joss, director. *The Avengers*. Marvel Studios, 2012.

White, Mark D. *The Virtues of Captain America: Modern-Day Lessons on Character from a World War II Superhero*. Hoboken, NJ: John Wiley & Sons, 2014. ProQuest Ebook Central. https://ebookcentral-proquest-com.dist.lib.usu.edu/lib/usu/detail.action?docID=1597378.

Will, George F. "Conservatives Favor Freedom, While Liberals Favor Equality." *Mercury News*, 30 May 2007. https://www.mercurynews.com/2007/05/30/conservatives-favor-freedom-while-liberals-favor-equality/.

"Wizard's Top 200 Comic Book Characters." *Comic Vine*. https://comicvine.gamespot.com/wizard/4010-2081/forums/wizards-top-200-comic-book-characters-644479/.

Wolf, Mark J. P. "World-Building in Watchmen." *Cinema Journal*, vol. 56, no. 2, Winter 2017, 119–125. EBSCOhost, doi:10.1353/cj.2017.0006.

Wolf, Naomi. *Give Me Liberty: A Handbook for American Revolutionaries*. New York: Simon & Schuster, 2008.

Wondygirl. "Captain America's Birth Date?" *Wondygirl*, 29 May 2012, wondygirl.tumblr.com/post/23991657686/captain-americas-birth-date.

Worcester, Kent. "The Punisher and the Politics of Retributive Justice." *Law Text Culture University of Wollongong Australia*, 2012. https://ro.uow.edu.au/cgi/viewcontent.cgi?referer=https://www.google.com/&httpsredir=1&article=1299&context=ltc.

"World War I Casualties." *Census.gov*, 2009–2011. https://www.census.gov/history/pdf/reperes112018.pdf.

"World War Two Casualties by Country 2019." *World Population Review*, 2019. http://worldpopulationreview.com/countries/world-war-two-casualties-by-country/.

Wright, Bradford. *Comic Book Nation: The Transformation of Youth Culture in America*. The Johns Hopkins University Press, 2001.

Zinn, Howard. *The Indispensable Zinn: The Essential Writings of the "People's Historian,"* edited by Timothy Patrick McCarthy. New York: The New Press, 2012. ProQuest Ebook Central. https://ebookcentral-proquest-com.dist.lib.usu.edu/lib/usu/detail.action?docID=903087.

Index